Global Challenges in Public Finance and International Relations

Deniz Şahin Duran
Tokat Gaziosmanapaşa University, Turkey

Yusuf Temür
Tokat Gaziosmanapaşa University, Turkey

Doğan Bozdoğan
Tokat Gaziosmanapaşa University, Turkey

A volume in the Advances in Finance, Accounting, and Economics (AFAE) Book Series

IGI Global
DISSEMINATOR OF KNOWLEDGE

Published in the United States of America by
IGI Global
Business Science Reference (an imprint of IGI Global)
701 E. Chocolate Avenue
Hershey PA, USA 17033
Tel: 717-533-8845
Fax: 717-533-8661
E-mail: cust@igi-global.com
Web site: http://www.igi-global.com

Library of Congress Cataloging-in-Publication Data

Names: Duran, Deniz Sahin, 1979- editor. | Temur, Yusuf, 1967- editor. | Bozdogan, Dogan, 1983- editor.
Title: Global challenges in public finance and international relations / Deniz Sahin Duran, Yusuf Temur, and Dogan Bozdogan, editors.
Description: Hershey : Business Science Reference, [2018]
Identifiers: LCCN 2018030425| ISBN 9781522575641 (hardcover) | ISBN 9781522575658 (ebook)
Subjects: LCSH: International finance. | International finance--Law and legislation. | Fiscal policy. | International economic relations.
Classification: LCC HG3881 .G57267 2018 | DDC 332/.042--dc23 LC record available at https://lccn.loc.gov/2018030425

This book is published in the IGI Global book series Advances in Finance, Accounting, and Economics (AFAE) (ISSN: 2327-5677; eISSN: 2327-5685)

British Cataloguing in Publication Data
A Cataloguing in Publication record for this book is available from the British Library.

All work contributed to this book is new, previously-unpublished material. The views expressed in this book are those of the authors, but not necessarily of the publisher.

For electronic access to this publication, please contact: eresources@igi-global.com.

Advances in Finance, Accounting, and Economics (AFAE) Book Series

Ahmed Driouchi
Al Akhawayn University, Morocco

ISSN:2327-5677
EISSN:2327-5685

Mission

In our changing economic and business environment, it is important to consider the financial changes occurring internationally as well as within individual organizations and business environments. Understanding these changes as well as the factors that influence them is crucial in preparing for our financial future and ensuring economic sustainability and growth.

The **Advances in Finance, Accounting, and Economics (AFAE)** book series aims to publish comprehensive and informative titles in all areas of economics and economic theory, finance, and accounting to assist in advancing the available knowledge and providing for further research development in these dynamic fields.

Coverage

- Accounting information systems
- Economic Policy
- Applied economics
- Entrepreneurship in Accounting and Finance
- Field Research
- Economics of Agriculture and Biotechnology
- Microeconomics
- Risk Analysis and Management
- Macroeconomics
- Statistical Analysis

IGI Global is currently accepting manuscripts for publication within this series. To submit a proposal for a volume in this series, please contact our Acquisition Editors at Acquisitions@igi-global.com or visit: http://www.igi-global.com/publish/.

The Advances in Finance, Accounting, and Economics (AFAE) Book Series (ISSN 2327-5677) is published by IGI Global, 701 E. Chocolate Avenue, Hershey, PA 17033-1240, USA, www.igi-global.com. This series is composed of titles available for purchase individually; each title is edited to be contextually exclusive from any other title within the series. For pricing and ordering information please visit http://www.igi-global.com/book-series/advances-finance-accounting-economics/73685. Postmaster: Send all address changes to above address.

Titles in this Series

For a list of additional titles in this series, please visit: www.igi-global.com/book-series

Organizational Auditing and Assurance in the Digital Age
Rui Pedro Marques (University of Aveiro, Portugal) Carlos Santos (University of Aveiro, Portugal) and Helena Inácio (University of Aveiro, Portugal)
Business Science Reference • copyright 2019 • 404pp • H/C (ISBN: 9781522573562) • US $225.00 (our price)

International Firms' Economic Nationalism and Trade Policies in the Globalization Era
Harish C. Chandan (Argosy University, USA) and Bryan Christiansen (Global Research Society, LLC, USA)
Business Science Reference • copyright 2019 • 299pp • H/C (ISBN: 9781522575610) • US $215.00 (our price)

FinTech as a Disruptive Technology for Financial Institutions
Abdul Rafay (University of Management and Technology, Pakistan)
Business Science Reference • copyright 2019 • 302pp • H/C (ISBN: 9781522578055) • US $195.00 (our price)

The Circular Economy and Its Implications on Sustainability and the Green Supply Chain
Ulas Akkucuk (Bogazici University, Turkey)
Business Science Reference • copyright 2019 • 327pp • H/C (ISBN: 9781522581093) • US $215.00 (our price)

Planning and Analyzing Foreign Direct Investment Projects Emerging Research and Opportunities
Halil Sarıaslan (Başkent University, Turkey)
Business Science Reference • copyright 2019 • 338pp • H/C (ISBN: 9781522576969) • US $215.00 (our price)

Maintaining Financial Stability in Times of Risk and Uncertainty
Abhishek Behl (Indian Institute of Technology Bombay, India) and Sushma Nayak (Symbiosis International University (Deemed), India)
Business Science Reference • copyright 2019 • 377pp • H/C (ISBN: 9781522572084) • US $265.00 (our price)

Global Trends of Modernization in Budgeting and Finance
Denis Ushakov (Suan Sunandha Rajabhat University, Thailand)
Business Science Reference • copyright 2019 • 354pp • H/C (ISBN: 9781522577607) • US $215.00 (our price)

Corporate Insolvency Law and Bankruptcy Reforms in the Global Economy
Amit Kashyap (Nirma University, India)
Business Science Reference • copyright 2019 • 261pp • H/C (ISBN: 9781522555414) • US $185.00 (our price)

IGI Global
DISSEMINATOR OF KNOWLEDGE

701 East Chocolate Avenue, Hershey, PA 17033, USA
Tel: 717-533-8845 x100 • Fax: 717-533-8661
E-Mail: cust@igi-global.com • www.igi-global.com

Editorial Advisory Board

Table of Contents

Detailed Table of Contents

Section 3
International Taxes and Taxation Policies

Taxes cannot be denied in order to prevent financial crises and economic crises. In times of crisis, it is sometimes possible to intervene in these periods by decreasing the existing tax rates and sometimes by applying new taxes. The Robin Hood tax is based on the idea of giving it to the poor. According to this idea, the financial sector will be taxed in times of crisis and the tax burden that countries have to bear will be reduced. Moreover, the important point here is related to the usage area of the income derived from taxation of the financial sector. These taxes will be transferred directly to the public (i.e., to the people who suffer from the crisis). Thus, the idea of transferring from the rich to the poor will take place. In this chapter, the applicability of Robin Hood tax will be determined by considering the main features of the tax, and the tax will be examined before the social state principle. In this direction, the superior aspects of the said tax will be determined, and some suggestions will be made.

The BEPS Action Plan, which was prepared by OECD upon the call of G20 countries in order to overcome this problem, was announced on 19 July 2013, and it was approved in the G20 Leader's Summit that was held in Saint Petersburg in September 2013. This chapter discusses the mentioned action plan and the probable effects of this plan to Turkey. In this respect, evaluation of the mentioned action plan will be made from the Turkey perspective by focusing on the most important actions of the OECD Action Plan that it put forward for ensuring the international tax equity.

The aim of this chapter is to investigate the potential impacts of globalization on tax revenues with reference to theoretical explanations within the context of tax and globalization. In the study, G10 country group and the data belonging to these countries between the years of 1990 and 2015 are used. In order to determine the relationships between tax revenues and globalization, cross-sectional dependency test, slope heterogeneous tests, and bootstrap panel Granger causality tests were used to understand the direction of causality between long-term coefficient estimations and variables. While the results of the long-run coefficient obtained from the study show differences according to the countries, a bi-directional causality relationship is determined between tax revenues and foreign trade. The diminishing effect of globalization found on the tax revenues of nation states considered within the scope of the study. It can be thought that these outcomes may provide some preliminary information to policymakers.

Along with the global financial crisis that took place in 2008, the ineffectiveness of other policies used for exiting from the crisis has brought back the feasibility of fiscal policy as an alternative. It is accepted that the only way to overcome the severe shrinking of the total demand during the 2008 global financial crisis is expansionary fiscal policy applied globally. However, differences in the subjective conditions of the EU member countries in particular have not made it possible to implement an expansionary fiscal policy for all of the member countries. More developed EU countries have begun to carry out from expansionary fiscal policies, while the less developed ones have begun to conduct contractionary fiscal policies. With the awareness that the financial stability is a public good, the obstacles, challenges on the global fiscal policy implementation by the EU member states are discussed by examining fiscal policies performed during and after the 2008 global financial crisis.

The Maastricht Treaty brought many innovations in the process of harmonization of the EU. This treaty, which was realized in 1993, aims to harmonize the economic, financial, legal, and political aspects of the EU members. Two basic financial criteria were identified in the financial stability and harmonization process. The first is the ratio of member countries' budget deficits to GDP. The second is the ratio of the member country's public debt to the GDP. In this chapter, it will be revealed how EU member countries are adapting to financial criteria. For this purpose, reports and statistics published by international organizations such as OECD and EU will be examined. It will be seen in many of the EU member countries can not adapt to these criteria. Especially after the 2008 Global Financial Crisis, there were difficulties in adapting to these criteria. The EU Council put into effect several legal regulations in the harmonization process. Although many legal sanctions were put into effect for this purpose, success in complying with the financial criteria were not achieved.

In the context of globalization, there is a dire need for understanding various governance practices abroad. Good corporate governance needs to address the principles of government and public enterprise relationship and create the fundamental pillars based on which the governing board can become effective. This chapter focuses on understanding the standard practices in global corporate governance issues and

Nations (UN) classification through panel data analysis method. According to the results of the Pedroni cointegration test, the null hypothesis suggesting no cointegration among the series at 1% significance level is rejected in all seven tests. According to pooled mean group estimator estimation results, the coefficients of foreign direct investment and trade which have long-term impacts on economic growth are also identified. Accordingly, the coefficients of both variables are statistically significant. A 1% increase in foreign direct investment and trade increase economic growth by 0.24% and 0.02%, respectively.

Foreword

Public finance is an emerging science that deals with the provision of resources necessary for the production of public goods and services undertaken by states, making public expenditures, establishing a reasonable balance between public revenues and expenditures, and examining a number of policy instruments used in state intervention in the economy.

Economic problems at a global scale, both in the past and in the future; The phenomenon of international economic relations and the new functions undertaken by the states in the face of these developments increase the importance of public finances.

In this book, *Global Challenges of Public Finance and International Relations*, is included the reviews prepared by academicians from different universities. The studies in the book mainly focus on issues arising from international economic relations and public finance issues related to globalization.

I believe that this work which edited by Tokat Gaziosmanpaşa University Faculty of Economics and Administrative Sciences Department of Finance faculty members Assoc. Dr. Prof. Deniz Şahin Duran, Dr. Doğan Bozdoğan and Dr. Yusuf Temür will make significant contributions to the public finance literature, and I hope it will be useful to readers.

Yusuf Ziya Taşkan
Ankara Yildirim Beyazit University, Turkey

Preface

The main purpose of this edited book is to systematically examine the present international financial events and institutions, international financial relations, fiscal difficulties and dilemmas, discussions and solutions for potential problems. In other words, this study aim to identify, categorize and rank the latest international financial needs arising from increasing globalization and the solutions and organizations for meeting these needs. The key focuses will be the following:

- What are the latest international public needs (public goods and/ services), the financing forms of these needs, the possible problems and proposed solutions?
- What are the latest issues, problems and proposed solutions in international taxation?
- What are the effects of the recent developments in the scope and nature of international fiscal relations on countries' systems of income and expenditure and on international fiscal policies?
- What are the current aims, policies, functions and effects of international financial institutions?

International public finance whose importance and study issues are rising is an important subdicipline of public finance. International finance is a very controversial and dynamic field. First of all, international financial events and institutions are constantly changing, developing and expanding in a dynamic process. This too require the conduction of studies that will discuss the new agenda and propose solutions for dilemmas and problems. The dynamism of international public finance necessitates that the studies that have been conducted in this field be revised and refreshed with new ones. Thus, scientists of public finance are expected to make researches on international finance and provide solution and innovation. With a multinational focus, the proposed book has the potential to broaden the study area of international public finance and offer solution and innovation, providing new study areas for scientists of finance. On the other hand, there are many topics and debates in international financial issues that have not been resolved, although there are some definitions and concepts that have been accepted to date. For instance, although the concept of international public goods has been established, new international public needs arise day by day. The issue of financing of international public goods is still a serious matter of debate because a healthy financing mechanism has *not* yet been established. Again, for example, while there are many taxation problems and debates that have not yet been resolved internationally, many new tax-related problems like international transfer pricing, taxation of virtual profits, taxation of electronic commerce are beeing added to existing ones. These are increasing the need for studies in this direction. It is possible to increase the number of examples which reveal why this editorial book is important. Undoubtedly, by presenting many important information to related literatures along with the valuable academic studies of participants, the book will provide significant contributions to the topics beeing discussed.

This book has total of 14 chapters and is divided in to five sections: "Overview of Globalization," "The Effects of Globalization on Public Finance System," "International Taxes and Taxation Policies," "International Economic Relations in the European Union," "International Finance."

Chapter 1 points out that globalization refers to the integration of economic, social, political, cultural and technological connections between countries. In this context, the concept of globalization includes every country and every social structure in the world with all its aspects. For this reason, the global influence of globalization can be said. Today, the irrefutable reality of the changing and transforming characteristics of the globalization process is accepted by the states, and determinations are made in this sense and measures are taken in the sense of negative effects. This change also affects international public finance. The common problems of the global world that arise in changing public finances are desired to be solved. In this study, different perceptions and dimensions of the phenomenon of globalization are examined. In this context, perceptions of globalization have been confused and the dimensions of globalization and the problems brought about by these dimensions have been tried to be revealed.

Chapter 2 focuses on the answer to the question that has been researched theoretically and empirically. KOF Globalization Index has been used as the measure of globalization unlike the empirical literature that explores the relationship between globalization and external debt. In the study where panel data analysis method has been used, the findings show that there is a positive relationship between KOF Globalization Index and external debt in developing countries. When it is examined from the perspective of the sub-indexes of globalization, it is seen that the economic globalization index is positively related to external debt. Social and political globalization has no effect on external debts. Impact of the control variables used in the analysis on external debts is significant and negative. From this, it can be said that general globalization and economic globalization have increased external debt of the nations.

Chapter 3 is about that the relationship between public debt and economic growth is examined for OECD countries. In order to determine this relationship, the data between 2002 and 2016 is analyzed using panel threshold regression methods. The findings of the study suggest that the relationship between public debt and economic growth is linear. The public debt threshold is estimated at 99.75% for OECD countries but it is statistically insignificant. While the public debt to GDPratio is both below and above this threshold, the effect of public debt on economic growth is negative and statistically significant. There is no evidence of the existence of a non-linear relationship between public debt and economic growth. These findings are expected to guide policymakers in the implementation of fiscal policies.

Chapter 4 examines the effects of structural adjustment programs designed under the supervision of IMF and World Bank on labor markets. This leading financial institutions are part of global financial system and they finance countries. In return, the countries satisfy the requirements imposed by IMF and World Bank.. The requirements imposed by IMF and World Bank includes devastating measures for Labor Market, including privatization, deregulation of labor market and flexibilization. There is convincing evidence that structural adjustment programs slowdown economic growth so hurts employment. Besides, the labor markets started to be constituted by unsafe work places without rules as a result of deregulations and flexibilizations. Most of the workers lost social security and work place security. Feminization, child labor, increasing work incidents are the main severe results of the policies designed under pressure of IMF and World Bank on labor Market.

Chapter 5 shows that the global economic and social actors are restructuring both private production and public production patterns. This change process is called as globalization. The globalization process brings new opportunities with it. One of these opportunities is to increase the efficiency of the local government economics in public finance. The processes of globalization and localization are twin processes and are progressing simultaneously. With the globalization, international capital wants to minimize the nation state and to communicate with local governments themselves. In this context, becoming a member of a local government gets ahead of being a nation-state citizen. In the globalization process, existing public goods productions are trying to simulate the market. Such efforts require the public economy to adapt to the market and such adaptation is characteristic of the local government economics itself. International capital, on the other hand, sees central government as a force to be overcome and wants to establish first-hand commercial relations with the local units.

Chapter 6 points out that taxes cannot be denied in order to prevent financial crises and economic crises. In times of crisis, it is sometimes possible to intervene in these periods by decreasing the existing tax rates and sometimes by applying new taxes. The basis of the Robin Hood tax is based on the idea of giving it to the poor. According to this idea, the financial sector will be taxed in times of crisis and the tax burden that countries have to bear will be reduced. Moreover, the important point here is related to the usage area of the income derived from taxation of the financial sector. These taxes will be transferred directly to the public, ie to the people who suffer from the crisis. Thus, the idea of transferring from the rich to the poor will take place. In this chapter, the applicability of Robin Hood tax will be determined by considering the main features of tax and the tax will be examined before the social state principle. In this direction, the superior aspects of the said tax will be determined and some suggestions will be made.

Chapter 7 underlines the BEPS Action Plan, which is prepared by OECD upon the call of G20 countries in order to overcome this problem, was announced on 19 July 2013, and it was approved in the G20 Leader's Summit that was held in Saint Petersburg in September 2013. "The measures package, which is developed within the scope of G20/OECD Base Erosion and Profit Shifting (BEPS) project in order to create a fairer and more modern international tax system globally," was approved in the G20 Leader's Summit Final Declaration that was held under the presidency of Turkey in Antalya between the dates of 15-16 November 2015. In this study, it is aimed to discuss the mentioned Action Plan and the probable effects of this Plan to Turkey. In this respect, evaluation of the mentioned Action Plan will be made from the Turkey perspective by focusing on the most important actions of the OECD Action Plan that it put forward for ensuring the international tax equity.

Chapter 8 investigates the potential impacts of globalization on tax revenues with reference to theoretical explanations within the context of tax and globalization. In the study, G10 country group and the data belonging to these countries between the years of 1990 - 2015 are used. In order to determine the relationships between tax revenues and globalization, cross-sectional dependency test, slope heterogeneous tests are, and moreover bootstrap panel Granger causality tests were used to understand the direction of causality between long-term coefficient estimations and variables. While the results of the long-run coefficient obtained from the study show differences according to the countries, a bi-directional causality relationship is determined between tax revenues and foreign trade. Besides the diminishing effect of globalization found on the tax revenues of nation states considered within the scope of the study. It can be thought that these outcomes may provide some preliminary information to policymakers.

Chapter 9 underlines along with the global financial crisis that took place in 2008, the ineffectiveness of other policies used for exiting from the crisis has brought back the feasibility of fiscal policy as an alternative. It is accepted that the only way to overcome the severe shrinking of the total demand during 2008 global financial crisis is expansionary fiscal policy applied globally. However, differences in the subjective conditions of the EU member countries in particular have not made it possible to implement an expansionary fiscal policy for all of the member countries. More developed EU countries have begun to carry out from expansionary fiscal policies, while the less developed ones have begun to conduct contractionary fiscal policies. With the awareness that the financial stability is a public good, the obstacles, challenges on the global fiscal policy implementation by the EU member states are discussed by examining fiscal policies performed during and after 2008 global financial crisis.

Chapter 10 discourses the Maastricht Treaty brought many innovations in the process of harmonization of the EU. This treaty, which was realized in 1993, aims to harmonize the economic, financial, legal and political aspects of the EU members. Two basic financial criteria were identified in the financial stability and harmonization process. The first is the ratio of member countries' budget deficits to GDP. The second is the ratio of the member country's public debt to the GDP. In this study, it will be revealed how EU member countries are adapting to financial criteria. For this purpose, reports and statistics published by international organizations such as OECD, EU will be examined. It will be seen in many of the EU member countries can not adapt to these criteria. Especially after the 2008 Global Financial Crisis, there were difficulties in adapting to these criteria. The EU Council put into effect several legal regulations in the harmonization process. Although many legal sanctions were put into effect for this purpose, success in complying with the financial criteria were not achieved.

Chapter 11 shows that in the context of globalization, there is a dire need for understanding various governance practices at abroad. Good corporate governance needs to address the principles of government and public enterprise relationship and create the fundamental pillars based on which the governing board can become effective. This paper focuses on understanding the standard practices in global corporate governance issues and problems, policy implications by considering a select country wise analysis like Australia, Canada, Scotland, New Zealand, Iceland, India and UAE etc. Hence, the paper makes a comparative study of present corporate governance practices in selected countries.

Chapter 12 explains that foreign aids are important for the development of poor countries. Therefore, in the literature, special attention is given to the analysis of foreign aids. This chapter investigates the factors affecting flow of foreign aids to developing and less developed countries and also welfare impacts of foreign aids. For this purpose, panel data on 71 countries receiving aids from Development Assistance Committee member countries are employed for the period between 1996 and 2013. The results show statistically significant impacts of real income per capita, trade openness, migration flows as a share of total population and governance measures. Moreover, although foreign aids are found to improve the welfare of receipt countries; for donor countries, results do not indicate any evidence of welfare effects. As a conclusion, the poverty, donor's interest represented by decline in migration flows and governance quality are found to be significant determinants of foreign aid allocation.

Chapter 13 points out that the importance of global public goods (GPGs) is increasing every day. As a result, the concept become an important part of international policy making. There is a huge literature on the definition and classification of GPGs, as well as the financing problems of them. GPGs are generally financed through the development aids given by international organisations and some developed countries. Literature is generally concentrated on the determination of the amount of aids devoted to different categories of GPGs, such as environment, health, peace-keeping and knowledge. Differently from the literature, a new and more general classification is also used in this study. The main sectors included in the analysis are: social infrastructure and services, economic infrastructure and services, production sectors, Multi-sector/Gross Cutting, and Humanitarian Aid. For the first time in the literature, principal components and cluster analysis methodologies were used to determine the performance of the countries providing official development aids in this study.

Chapter 14 detects the impacts of FDI and foreign trade on the economic growth of middle income countries. Therefore, this study aims to examine the relationship among economic growth, foreign direct investments, and trade in 27 middle-income countries according to the United Nations (UN) classification through panel data analysis method. According to the results of the Pedroni cointegration test, the null hypothesis suggesting no cointegration among the series at 1% significance level is rejected in all seven tests. According to pooled mean group estimator estimation results, the coefficients of foreign direct investment and trade which have long-term impacts on economic growth are also identified. Accordingly, the coefficients of both variables are statistically significant. A 1% increase in foreign direct investment and trade increase economic growth by 0.24% and 0.02%, respectively.

The proposed book will be a reference book and gain a place in the public finance collections of academic libraries. The book will be usable for all executors/bureaucrats, academicians andresearchers of public finance and forall undergraduate and postgraduate students that receive online, distance or face to face education at public finance.

International public finance lesson which has just begun to take place in undergraduate and graduate education programs in the field of public finance at many university and are becoming increasingly important. Because it will include all contents of international finance lessons and recent developments in international public finance, this editorial book will be a complementary source for undergraduate and graduate students. Furthermore, the book will probably be used as a course book or contribute to the development of better course books since the present international finance course books are unsatisfactory. Furthermore, the book will help academicians that intend to compose a book of international finance and look for new research topics. Lastly, this book has a feature of guide book for practitioners/ bureaucrats in public finance field and it will be reference for the development of the necessary work towards implementation.

Deniz Şahin Duran
Tokat Gaziosmanpaşa University, Turkey

Yusuf Temür
Tokat Gaziosmanpaşa University, Turkey

Doğan Bozdoğan
Tokat Gaziosmanpaşa University, Turkey

Acknowledgment

We have many individuals to thank for their impressive efforts, help and encouragement on our book. First, we would like to praise people at the IGI Global. Their invaluable suggestions are very important for us to give the final shape of our book. Not only did they us to make critical decisions about carefully structuring our book, but also they provided useful and informative feedback to increase our commitment and effort to complete our book.

We would like to express appreciation to the Editorial Advisory Board members. We would like to thank each our authors for their excellent contributions. The final words of thanks belong to Yusuf Ziya Taşkan who is Professor in finance law.

Deniz Şahin Duran
Tokat Gaziosmanpaşa University, Turkey

Yusuf Temür
Tokat Gaziosmanpaşa University, Turkey

Doğan Bozdoğan
Tokat Gaziosmanpaşa University, Turkey

Section 1
Overview of Globalization

Chapter 1
The Globalized World With Different Perceptions, Dimensions, and Problems

Aysun Yilmaztürk
Balikesir University, Turkey

ABSTRACT

Globalization refers to the integration of economic, social, political, cultural, and technological connections between countries. In this context, the concept of globalization includes every country and every social structure in the world with all its aspects. For this reason, the global influence of globalization can be said. Today, the irrefutable reality of the changing and transforming characteristics of the globalization process is accepted by the states, and determinations are made in this sense and measures are taken in the sense of negative effects. This change also affects international public finance. The common problems of the global world that arise in changing public finances are desired to be solved. In this chapter, different perceptions and dimensions of the phenomenon of globalization are examined. In this context, perceptions of globalization have been confused, and the dimensions of globalization and the problems brought about by these dimensions have been revealed.

INTRODUCTION

Globalization, a process which has a long history, is considered as a new phenomenon since its effects have been felt recently. In this new case, various elements such as people, societies, cultures, economies, states, institutions, rules, production systems, communication styles and models etc. are affected and change. Economic aspect of this transformation is especially prevalent in today's world. With globalization, which is a process difficult to resist, states, societies and economic systems have to go through this transformation.

The first section of this study examines the concept of globalization from a historical perspective. Section two has been focused on various perspectives towards the concept, while section three deals with the major dimensions and problems of globalization.

DOI: 10.4018/978-1-5225-7564-1.ch001

GLOBALIZATION

Various theories and concepts have been developed to explain certain periods in the historical process of societies. The history of globalization, which is one of the popular concepts of today's world where international relations are becoming more and more intense, goes back a long way. Social, economic, political and cultural structures have been constantly changing since the Industrial Revolution of 1776. The Roman Empire and the Ottoman Empire constituted the examples of globalization before the 19th century. In the 19th century, there were colonial peripheries linked to colonial metropoles such as England during the period where colonial empires were established. The development of the automation network with the industrial revolution has accelerated the globalization process.

Although it goes long way back, globalization has become a key concept that emerged in the 1960s, frequently used in the 1980s and considered important by scientists after the 1990s. The increase in the use of the concept after the 1980s depended on the integration process that happened in almost all areas due to technological developments and the influence of some factors. The concept of globalization, which has become popular since the 1990s, has begun to be questioned by the world thinkers, especially in America, since these years. As a matter of fact, Malcolm Waters, one of the important early writers on globalization, wrote that in 1994, the entire "globalization" books in the American Library of Congress were published and numbered 34 after 1987 and this number was raised to 284 in February 2000 (Waters, 2001, p.25).

According to Malcolm Waters, who states that the term "global" has been used as an adjective that describes the whole world for over 400 years, globalization should be dealt with using a multidimensional approach as an integrated economic, political and cultural process. In this multidimensional theory, globalization has been developing throughout a historical process and it has shown its real character suddenly and very rapidly since 1990s. Since the modernization process that started in the 16th century, economic integrations, international relations, cultural relations and cognitive processes have developed rapidly over time. Now is the moment when these developments are felt most severely.

All authors, except two, agree that Marshall McLuhan is the first person to develop the concept (Yusufoğlu, 2005, p.13) In the books he wrote in 1960 and 1963, M. McLuhan assessed the developments in the field of communication and indicated that the world was turning into an electronic global village (McLuhan, 2014). McLuhan did not include concepts such as globalization and globality in his work, but he used the concept of "global" as "global embrace", "global village" and "global armistice" (Bülbül, 2004, p.26). After a long period of infusion or incubation in the field of communication, the term globalization has become the term most frequently used by popular media and all social sciences, especially by international relations (Çiftçi, 2015, p.28).

Although globalization is defined similarly by different authors, there are some arguments on its content (Hablemitoğlu, 2005, p.40). It is beneficial to take a look at the arguments of some authors considered to be theorists or actor thinkers of globalization, especially those of Anthony Giddens, Immanuel Wallerstein, Zygmunt Bauman, Ronald Robertson, Malcolm Waters and David Harvey.

Anthony Giddens defines globalization is as the intensification of worldwide social relations which link distant localities in such a way that local happenings are shaped by events. According to Giddens, who sees globalization as the highest point throughout the human history, the process the world goes through is the globalization of modernism or a natural extension of the ongoing modernization process. To him, the intensification of social relations "is a consequence of the time-space distinction that comes with high modernism, and through such intensification, relations of people and societies on a global scale become real for the first time in the history of mankind" (Giddens, 2000, p.54). Giddens thinks that globalization is the result of modernization. As a historicist philosopher, Ronald Robertson focuses on historicism and states that globalization has been under development for several centuries, and contrary to Giddens, he argues that it is a process that has allowed modernization to spread for centuries.

Not denying the importance of modernization in the character of globalization today, he emphasizes that the origins of globalization go back to the time when religions and metaphysical thought arouse (Robertson, 1999, p.26). According to Robertson, class, social and national values progress from simple to complex. We can talk about global values and a global culture, just like national and universal values. Globalization involves comparative interactions. This interaction between cultures and values is more like an interaction between equals.

David Harvey, on the other hand, refers to globalization as a "time-space compression," underlining that this compression brings about radical changes in our view of the world. The term "compression" refers to the "speeding up of the pace of life" and "the overcoming spatial barriers". For example, travel time was reduced by 70 times from 1500 to 1960. Between 1500 and 1840, average speed was 16 km per hour. This speed reached 100 km per hour between 1850 and 1930. It is seen that the number of all telephone calls made in 1971 is equal to the number of calls made in only 1 day in 2003.

Multinational corporations have spread their production in various countries across the globe. The variety of examples can be increased. According to Harvey, time in the rhythm of human life disciplines human life and production activities at a dizzying digital speed. This situation has begun to shrink the world conceived by humans. The increase that has been observed in the speed of human perception and communication skills since the 15th is called "time-space compression". Globalization is considered to be a consequence of this compression. According to Harvey, "global economies and cultures come into intense and instant contact with each other" (Harvey, 2014, p.160).

Zygmunt Bauman considers nation-state structure as an important actor of globalization. He argues that the continuation and preservation of this structure will ensure global development. The weakening of the sovereignty of a nation state is not a positive development; because the presence of many ethnic groups brings with it geographical and social disintegration. In this context, Bauman is concerned with establishing a balance between globalization and localization.

Zygmunt Bauman is interested in the current outcomes of globalization without touching upon its historical development. He emphasizes that globalization is a new phenomenon in terms of its consequences and that it creates uncertainty in all areas of life, which in turn creates an inconceivable pressure on human beings (Bauman, 2018, p.58). The collapse of the Eastern Bloc did not bring a new world order where capitalism began to dominate the economies, but a world in disarray. The bipolar world during the Cold War period also allowed the weak states between these blocks to sustain their economic, cultural and military sovereignty. Though knowing who was on which side caused the world to have a divided structure, it meant integrity even if paradoxical in some sense (Bauman, 2016, p.68).

Immanuel Wallerstein also uses the concept of the "world system", and just like Bauman, he underlines that the nation state structure has been dominant in some places. This concept, including the state-policy parameter, is based on a dependency relation between the developed capitalist states in the center and the weak countries in the periphery in proportion to their power. The success of capitalism depends on the creation and maintenance of a meaningful division of labor between the central and peripheral countries (Wallerstein, 1993, pp.19-25). According to Wallerstein, globalization refers to the expansion of these mutual dependencies in a way to go beyond economic and political dimensions and to cover social and cultural values.

Finally, Malcolm Waters, one of the most important thinkers on globalization, pays attention to Robertson's, Wallerstein's and Giddens's comments, and agrees with Bauman that globalization is a historical process. At the same time, he addresses these ideas from a critical and analytical perspective and suggests that globalization should be addressed as an economic, political, and cultural process by adopting a multidimensional approach. Globalization involves a system of all individual and social relations established in the world. Therefore, it covers and encompasses humanity in one way or another. With the use of technology, distances have been reduced and lost meaning. This reduction has brought both the expansion of the fields of human rights and women's rights and the opportunity for social reactions to combine. Economic and social crises reveal the transformational power of globalization. Just as the emergence of capitalism broke up the traditional feudal relations of the Middle Ages, the crisis of capitalism created new opportunities by leading to international initiatives. In addition, globalization has had an accelerating effect on relieving the local pressures on people's lifestyles.

DIFFERENT PERCEPTIONS OF GLOBALIZATION

Globalization is defined as the expansion and development of worldwide economic, social, political and cultural relations. This definition includes all elements such as different geographies, cultural formation, economic-social and political structure, state government, goods and services, capital accumulation, technological infrastructure and lifestyles, regardless of physical distance. Globalization is a structural transformation process which is based on the principle of mutual dependence and which increases the level of communication, interaction and relationships among all these elements.

The main determinants of the global system are nation states, multinational corporations, international institutions and non-governmental organizations (Saraç, 2006, p.18). Based on these determinants and the definition given above, globalization refers to the integration of economic, social, political, cultural and technological connections between countries. Accordingly, the integration is expected to make a positive contribution to all the countries in the world, especially to the developing countries. At this point, however, it is not possible to mention about a consensus on the consequences of globalization.

Although global interdependence is generally accepted, there is some disagreement on how to best conceptualize globalization and what its structural consequences are. While some economists claim that globalization will increase world welfare and reduce the development gap between countries, some point out that globalization is a new form of colonialism (Bayramoğlu & Başar, 2016, p.4). The approaches that evaluate scientific thinking and actual state may be listed as follows: Hyperglobalist Approach, Skeptical Approach and Transformationalist Approach.

Hyperglobalist Approach

Discourses of hyperglobalists or radicals such as Robertson, Ohmae, Greider, Pelmulter, Drucker, Appadurai, Fukuyama, Hardt and Hobsbawn often coincide with neoliberal discourses. According to this approach, the nation state which became effective after the industrial revolution, lost its importance with the emergence of globalization and was replaced by the universal market. Through transnational production, trade and financial networks, globalization eliminates the national nature of economies. The unlimited world economy becomes a "Single Market". The market mechanism works more efficiently and effectively than the governments.

The basis of the hyperglobalist approach was laid by Ohmae's (1990) explanations of national borders. According to him, national borders and the economic logic that made them useful lines of demarcation in the first place have effectively disappeared (Ohmae, as cited in: Ceglowski, 1998, p.17). It is stated that integration of money and commodity markets at the global scale lies behind the neutralization of nation states especially in economic terms with globalization (Kaya, 2009, p.5). The national economic policies have become less influential both due to commitments made to international organizations such as the IMF, WB and WTO and the budgeting and investment decisions of foreign economic institutions, such as multinational corporations.

According to the advocates of this view, there will be those who will benefit from this development in the globalization process as well as those who will suffer from it. The winners and losers are formed together; it is possible that all countries will have comparative advantage in producing certain goods, although the situation of some groups in the economy will get worse due to global competition.

Another issue is that regional authorities will become widespread, replacing central authorities. A new global division of labor is replacing the traditional center-periphery structure. The global society is taking the place of nation states.

Skeptical Approach

Those in this group, who are opposed to radicals/hyperglobalists, are called counter globalists. The skeptical approach is the system of thinking that is against the globalization process. Thinkers like Samir Amin, Chomsky, Gerbier, Huntington, Martin, Schuman, and Wallerstein, who represent this approach, point out that globalization is not a new process and large movements of money and goods took place in the past, too.

Sceptics are opposed to the idea that globalization is a new process and they present evidence that it has been an ongoing process for centuries (Bryane, 2003, p.8). Advocates of this view make statistical conclusions from the trade flows of the world and the investment and labor of the 19th century and do not accept that globalization is a new process. For example, they claim that removal of all barriers such as customs etc. in the world economy is nothing but reversion to how the world was 100 years ago. Whatever the benefits of the global economy, its trials and tribulations, it is no different from the economies that existed during the previous periods. As Giddens says, sceptics are suspicious of globalization.

According to sceptics, globalization is not something unexpected or extraordinary; this process has been exaggerated by the hyperglobalists and turned into a legend. The reason is that, contrary to the claims, the world economy has been less integrated than it was in the past during the process called globalization (Çiftçi, 2015, p.28). Regionalism emerges in the face of the globalization process and is expressed as an alternative to globalization. The world is not heading towards a global civilization but towards a division in line with new understandings; because globalization will lead to new conflicts between different cultures, different civilizations or different regions rather than integration (Bozkurt, 2000, p.22). Regionalism stands for the opposite of globalization. It is not a way station to globalization; it is just the opposite, an alternative. The economic, political and social elements that define globalization policies are characterized mostly by being regional rather than global. Examples may include the OECD member countries or a few regional trading blocs across the world (NAFTA, MERCOSUR, EU and ASEAN). The world is being divided by new understandings, thus paving the way for new conflicts based on socio-economic differences.

Transformationalist Approach

According to transformationalists, including Giddens, Friedman, Habermas, Hirst and Thompson, Bauman and Waters, globalization is a process that rapidly reshapes modern societies and world order. It is also the main political power behind the economic, cultural, social and political changes. Globalization is a period of reconstituting the authority, functions and power of nation states. There is no clear-cut distinction between external and internal affairs of countries. This approach asserts a new sovereignty regime shaped less by geographical areas and more by intense supranational relations. Despite the hyperglobalists who agree that the nation states have come to an end and the counter-globalists who argue that nothing has changed, transformationalists disagree with both groups, arguing that a new sovereignty regime has emerged. For this reason, sovereignty is today defined by more complex and less geographical boundaries. A new global market that is much more integrated than the previous market has been formed. All relations are developing incrementally at a dizzying speed. The volume of goods exchanged is incommensurably greater than that in the 19th century. The economy is becoming increasingly dependent on the tertiary sector.

Although transformationalists admit that national governments have restructured their authorities and powers, they reject the hyperglobalist view that sovereign nation states have come to an end and the skeptical view that nothing has changed compared to the past.

Transformationalists, contrary to hyperglobalists, do not see the world as a single society. Rather, they suggest that some countries or societies have become more similar to each other, while others have become increasingly marginal. The existing power relations around the world are not fully integrated or completely separated, as claimed by the other two approaches. Globalization both divides and integrates.

Transformationalists, who are in between these two extremes, seem to be closer to radicals than sceptics regarding the course of globalization. The transformationalist approach argues that globalization is an actual process and that it is necessary to assess the situation, get position and make an effort to minimize the negative consequences rather than being a party to or taking a stand against.

DIMENSIONS OF GLOBALIZATION

Globalization is not a new phenomenon in human history. It is now entering its third period. With the influence of mercantilism toward the end of the 1400s, the first wave of globalization began to take place, eventually leading to the emergence of colonialism. The second wave was experienced as a result of industrialization and its effects in the 1890s, and colonialism transformed into imperialism. The third wave began with the formation of multinational corporations in 1970s, the great changes in communication in the 1980s, and the dissolution of the Soviet Union in 1990 and, consequently, the end of a rival to Western dominance in the East-West Bloc. The third wave which refers to the recently experienced globalization is related to the developments in information technologies and communication and the great change in the reorganization of production (TASAM, 2018). "In this last phase, which is called the New World Order, the world went through a period when traditional political blocs disappeared, liberals gained power in all areas and the developments in communication and transport technologies led to important changes. The process is still going on and the world is heading towards an economic, political and cultural globalization. All these political, economic, cultural and social developments constitute the components of globalization. In this context, increased economic and political influence of the USA and the West with the collapse of the USSR, increased impact of multinational corporations on the world economy, the internationalization of financial markets and the development and expansion of transportation and communication technologies complete the components of globalization (TASAM, 2018).

In general, the definitions of globalization emphasize the economic dimension, and globalization is perceived as the integration and interdependence of economic activities around the world. According to such definitions, globalization is an economic and political construct in which capital, management, employment, knowledge, natural resources and organizations are fully internationalized. With this new construct, economic competition goes beyond national economies, extending to the whole planet (Kaya et al., 2017, p.2041). Besides, the view that globalization covers the entire political, economic and social dimensions of social life is generally accepted. According to this view, globalization is perceived as a process that eliminates the differences between social and cultural structures resulting from spatial distances through developments in transportation, information and communication technologies (Gökdere, 2001, p.85).

As you can see, globalization is expressed as a phenomenon that concerns various disciplines and market including economics, social studies, political studies, communication and technology and the real and tertiary sector as well as affecting all areas and enabling the establishment of interactive relations between these areas. In this sense, globalization has some major areas of impact. Globalization is said to have various dimensions based on its impact areas and form of expansion. According to Taylor and Flint, who offers the broadest coverage, there are eight dimensions of globalization, i.e. economic, financial, technological, cultural, political, ecological, geographical and sociological (Taylor & Flint, 2000, p.4). In this study, we will address the economic, technological, political, environmental and socio-cultural dimensions which are the basic impact areas of globalization.

Economic Dimension and Its Problems

The economic dimension is the most prominent dimension of globalization whose history dates back to the oldest times. Economic globalization is the integration of economies with the world economy. As a result of the developments in information and communication technologies, goods, services, capital and labor mobility increases among countries, and consequently, economic relations intensify and countries get closer to each other (Çelik, 2012, p.68).

Malcom Waters describes economic globalization as the center of capitalism and defines the current economic situation as "global capitalism". To Waters, the globalization of the economy has evolved through five stages to this date. This classification corresponds to the classifications proposed by many economists and economic historians at different times, and does not contradict the views of commentators in other fields. The economic developments that prepared globalization are summarized as follows:

- **The Period of Mercantilist Capitalism and Colonialism (1500-1800):** The first multinational corporations emerged as pioneering models. These companies were essentially state sponsored privileged companies that transferred natural resources in colonized regions to colonial countries.
- **Entrepreneurial and Financial Capitalism (1800-1875):** It is the time when transportation and construction services were improved and capital made investments to take control of the markets. It is the initial phase of control of consumer markets.
- **International Capitalism (1875-1945):** It is the period when investments rapidly increased in order to have economic resources and to get a market share around the world and the US-based cartels gained power by making international investments.

- **Multinational Capitalism (1945-1960):** It is the period when US-based cartels become dominant in the marketplace through investment and marketing. In this period which coincided with the bipolar "Cold War" period, giant state companies started to make joint investments in the Warsaw Pact and a regional integration took place within the block.
- **Today's Global Capitalism (1960-1990):** In this period, the number and power of multinational corporations based in Europe and Japan increased rapidly, and an understanding of risk partnership became widespread through inter-firm alliances. Europe and Japan-based multinational corporations competed with the US and experienced increased productivity in their search for international investments and markets. During this period, multinational corporations began merging in order to create monopolies or increase productivity at the local level, which was one of the major characteristics of this period.

Mass production and consumption can be said to have emerged with the industrialization of production in the 20th century and the formation of the consumer society. Increased demand in all countries due to population growth and use of resources also brings continuous investments and demand for capital. The movement of labor, products, goods and services was speeded up. This increased the number of international agreements that companies made to maximize profits, thus uniting the world markets. Economic borders of nation states like customs walls began to disappear, and investment and trade areas for multinational corporations increased. The economic borders and the areas of sovereignty determined by nation states began to be questioned and forced to become more concessive. Developments and growth in world trade increased economic interdependence between countries. Therefore, countries had to take account of other countries and international economic movements when developing their macro and microeconomic policies. The transformation of countries' economic policies, the reasons for this transformation and the new economic order will be discussed in more detail in the next section.

The components of global economy consist of functions such as global division of labor, global production, global trade and global consumption. Thus, three dimensions of economic globalization stand out: Commercial globalization, financial globalization and globalization of production (Seyidoğlu, 2017, p.142).

In economic terms, commercial globalization is the oldest form of globalization. The history of mankind shows that commercial enterprises at the international level go back to the oldest ages when the mankind existed. Commercial life even with written rules existed in Mesopotamia around 5000 BC. In Europe, important trade routes and the port cities reached through these routes were the main trade centers. The coastal cities reached by the Silk Road, which connected India and China to the West, developed commercially. After the 1500s, the ports of Netherlands, Spain and Britain became the new centers of colonial trade, and the companies founded there started to dominate the world trade. In the early 1900s, the process mass production started with the introduction of factories. Since three-fourths of the world was colonized by the Western countries, the markets with markets with depth and breadth came to the fore. Thus, traders started to search for new markets outside of Europe to sell industrial products.

The spread of commerce which started after the Second World War was the first step of globalization. Commercial globalization was initiated in 1947 with the liberalization of international trade around the world by removing barriers to foreign trade (quotas and tariffs) within the framework of the GATT (General Agreement on Tariffs and Trade). This was the period when the US passed through the customs barriers and broke into secure markets by means of investments made through multinational corporations. Indeed, the United States played the leading role in the formation of the GATT. The currency used and the common symbol was the USD dollar. Starting with investments in the common market area, the USA also supported all regionalization efforts such as EEC, EU, WTO, NAFTA, ASEAN. The promotion of regional integrations over the world and the integration of weaker countries was the policy for holding and growing the markets.

After 1970s, the protectionist approach has been adopted in the world trade due to the increase in money supply and inflation, and the slowdown in economic growth, and the increase in the debt stock of developed countries, which are the locomotives of the global economic system. In the following period, an economic approach based on foreign trade, adopting the reduction of the public's role in the economy and envisaging the implementation of structural reforms aimed at the market economy, influenced many countries (Yılmaztürk & Buhur, 2017,p.87).

After 1980, the pressure of neoliberal policies on national economies was prevalent throughout the world. During these years, significant increases were observed in foreign direct investment in the countries close to the Western Bloc, all barriers to the flow of goods and services were removed and efforts were made for free movement of capital.

Today, the World Trade Organization replaced the GATT and took over its functions. Indeed, the most important step taken towards globalization was the signing of the GATT and the establishment of the WTO. The WTO is responsible for ensuring economic liberalization required by the new world order. However, it is not possible to say that the free trade principle has been fully accepted. The reason is because the ongoing agreements and the quotas imposed by the WTO on international trade mostly served to increase the needs, profit aspirations and market shares of developed countries rather than ensuring economic development of developing countries.

Globalization has not removed, but on the contrary, increased the absolute inequality between rich and poor countries. This is one of the negative consequences of globalization. The same also holds true for competitive advantage which is in favor of the wealthy countries.

The improved access to domestic and foreign markets as a result globalization increased foreign trade and economic growth, thus leading to an increase in productivity and average income. However, due to the lack of the means for income generation, the poor cannot take advantage of this increase as much as others, and globalization causes greater income inequality both within and between countries. As a matter of fact, the income gap between the richest and the poorest 20 percent of the world population in 1960 was 1/30, 1/60 in 1990 and 1/75 in 2000. There are various indicators of such income inequalities in the world created by the process of globalization. One of these indicators is the Gini coefficient. According to the data from the IMF, the Gini coefficient is 0.70 around the world and is very close to 1 which indicates absolute level of inequality. This coefficient is 0.25 - 0.35 in countries such as Sweden and Canada; 0.40 in the US, Russia and China and greater than 0.50 in most of the African and South American countries (Savaş, 2012, p.164).

During the early years of the Industrial Revolution, the gap between the richest and poorest parts of the world economy stood at a ratio of roughly 2:1, while this ratio is 20:1 today. According to the report published by the United Nations Development Program (UNDP), the richest 8% of the world's population get half of the world's total income, while the remaining 92% are left with the other half (Ar, 2016, p.190). For example, the US and Western constitute 25% of the world's population, but consume 75% of the earth's resources. Today, 3 billion people around the world live on an income of less than 2 dollars per day. At the same time, 1.3 billion people earn less than 1 dollar a day. The richest 1% of the world population receives as much as the poorest 57%. (Kurtoğlu, 2017, p.278).

On the other hand, as the number of tax havens increased as a result of economic globalization, big companies began to pay lower amounts of tax, which led to the tax burden on capital being shifted to the labor. According to the United States Government Accountability Office's 2007 Report, Citigroup had 427 tax haven subsidiaries, Morgan Stanley had 273, Bank of America had. 115, the collapsed Lehman Brothers had 57, JP Morgan Chase had 50, Goldman Sachs had 29. For example, Goldman Sachs reported profits of over $2 billion and paid federal taxes of $14 million. Out of 100 largest U.S. corporations, 83 have subsidiaries in offshore tax havens (Kitapçı, 2017, p.244).

Although the globalization process has some negative impacts on income distribution, it is wrong to consider that the effect of globalization is homogeneous and standard. For example, the welfare state is withering away with the effect of globalization in some countries, while new welfare states emerge in some others. Examples may include China, India and Mexico. These developing countries with a total population of more than 3 billion doubled their foreign trade volume in national income in the 1990s and their GDP per capita grew at an annual average rate of 5%. The situation is different for the other 2 billion people who constitute the underdeveloped part of the world. In the underdeveloped countries, the trading volume declined and per capita income either decreased or increased slightly. Besides, poverty increased in these countries (Özdemir, 2007, p.224).

At this point, the issue of poverty, just like income equality, emerges as one of the important effects of economic globalization. Poverty rates declined in some regions of the world during the globalization process, but this decline did not spread evenly across the world. According to the World Bank, poverty around the world decreased from 30% in 1990 to 23% in 2011, and the absolute number of the poor decreased by 141 million. Similarly, in China, the incidence of poverty falls from 33% to 17%, and the number of the poor decreased by 163 million. However, both the incidence of poverty and the number of the poor increased in Sub-Saharan Africa, Latin America and the Caribbean (Ghose et al., 2010, p.127). The table below shows the proportion of people living on an income of $ 1.25 a day worldwide. The World Bank has updated the extreme poverty line to $ 1.25 in 2008, based on the purchasing power parity.

Despite recent progress in poverty reduction, more than 2.2 billion people are living in poverty (United Nations Human Development Report, 2015:4). In conclusion, it is clear that a progress has been achieved in poverty reduction around the world with the globalization process. But this progress seems to be uneven.

Table 1. Proportion of people living on an income of $ 1.25 a Day worldwide

	1990	2010	2015
Developing Countries in the World (Except China)	41	26	20,5
Developing Countries in the World	47	22	23,5
World	36	18	18
Sub-Saharan Africa	56	48	28
South Asia	51	30	25,5
Southeast Asia	45	14	22,5

Source: Kitapçı, İ. (2017). An Assessment of Today's Major Global Problems, *PESA International Journal of Social Studies*, 3(14), 241-257.

One of the inevitable facts of economic globalization is global crisis. Today, the balances of power within the global economy are changing, and financial crises emerge as a result of different parameters of today's globalized world. It is stated that the global economy has become increasingly multipolar, especially with the rise of the newly emerging economies. For example, with globalization, different parts of a product have begun to be manufactured in different countries. Parts of a car manufactured in Mexico may come from four different countries including the US. Therefore, if the demand for cars decreases in the United States, manufacturing will begin to decline not only in Mexico but also in at least four countries, including the United States. Vertical specialization increases dependence on the global economy (Özgür & Yetkiner, 2011, p.28). These mutual commercial dependencies emerging as a result of globalization are also increasing the likelihood of crises spreading across more regions (domino effect).

For this reason, these years we are in now will be called the Age of Crisis, as Krugman says. 1992-1993 European Monetary System crisis, the Tequila Crisis (1995), the Asian Financial Crisis (1997-1998), the Russian crisis (2000), the financial crisis of Latin America crisis (2000) and the financial crisis of Turkey (2001) followed each other. With the effects of these crises were still present, the world was shaken by the Mortgage crisis in the United States (2008) and the crisis affected the developed countries in a short span of time due to financial globalization, leading to unemployment and stagnation in almost every country (Savaş, 2012: 140). This global financial crisis caused the global economy's center of gravity to shift from the West to the East. This crisis not only caused the US banking model to be questioned but also caused China and India to consider themselves in a different position from the US economy (Heywood, 2013, p.81).

In conclusion, financially realistic approaches are needed to prevent crises. Particularly the low-income countries are unable to use tax policy instruments sufficiently due to their low levels of GDP per capita, urbanization and technological development, and they face economic shocks and crises due to high indebtedness. For this reason, in this world where liberalization activities are on the rise, financially realistic development strategies need to be developed (Aktan et al, 2006, p.54).

After having discussed the basic economic problems caused by globalization, we would like to once again touch upon the issue of commercial globalization, one of the dimensions of economic globalization. In this sense, it is certain that trade has played the most historically important role in integrating the relations between countries and people (Çiftçi, 2015, p.28). Since the very beginning of the history of mankind, trade has had an essential function of human life in the development of human relations and exchange between civilizations, has played crucial role than states in communication between societies and cultures and sometimes has shaped the roles of states (Waters, 2001).

With the globalization of economy, trade stopped being seen as an "external function" of countries in the international area. Besides, the supply-demand balances changed and new commercial channels emerged. As a matter of fact, the rise of electronic trading over the Internet disrupts the markets. Online shopping has become a serious source of illicit money.

Other dimensions of economic globalization are financial globalization and globalization of production. Financial globalization refers to the removal of barriers and restrictions on short and long term capital flows and the integration of domestic markets with the world markets. In this framework, the world has become a single financial market with increased international capital flows. The globalization of production means the spread of offshore production. In today's world, a significant part of production around the world is carried out by multinational corporations which conduct business outside the borders of their countries.

The world is globalized on one hand and regionalized on the other. Increased cooperation among countries has led to the emergence of global organizations such as the World Trade Organization, the International Monetary Fund, the United Nations, the Organization for Economic Cooperation and Development, the North Atlantic Pact and the World Bank. There are also regional organizations such as the European Union, the North American Free Trade Agreement, the Asia-Pacific Economic Cooperation and the African Union.

Apart from these organizations, there are groups such as the G-7, G-10 and G-20, which are made up of powerful states that steer the world economy. Among them, the most important is the G-7, which is composed of the US, Japan, Germany, the UK, France, Canada and Italy. The share of these countries in world trade is 52%. They produce 65% of the global GDP. The G-7 countries are further developing while steering the world economy. Globalization makes the developed countries more prosperous and the gap between the rich and the poor keeps widening.

Technological Dimension and Its Problems

Every historical period has some prominent symbols: Just as we can say that the symbols of the age of enlightenment are printing press and books and of the industrial revolution are lightbulb and factories, we can say that the symbols of the globalization process are the internet and media. Popular culture products produced by the giant culture industry through radio, television, internet and all written and visual means of mass communication are circulating around the world. As a global language, the English language is now the dominant language of the digital media. The globalization of technology removed physical limits in areas such as communication, transportation and security, increased mutual interaction and altered the interaction of time, space and power.

The acceleration of mechanization through economic globalization, which is another dimension of technological globalization, has led to unemployment, on the one hand, while reducing costs and increasing profits on the other. Production and marketing of goods by the developed countries almost anywhere around the world and the transfer of technology to these countries is the result of globalization in technology. At this point, the reality is that the developed countries have a technology-based economy, while the developing countries are obliged to transfer this technology.

The developments in transportation, communication and information technologies have shortened distances. As a result, the time and space concepts have lost their meaning and the world has become a global village. Knowledge has become one of the most important factors of production. Access to information has become easier which reduced costs. The society has been designated as "Information Society". The economic structure has become a structure where the tertiary sector is dominant.

Although technological developments have still an important role in globalization, they are not the only determinants in this process. Economic and political conditions also constitute the conditions of the time and place where technological developments are experienced.

Political Dimension and Its Problems

Political globalization refers to the absence of the absolute sovereignty of a state's political borders over a certain area as well as increased interaction between the systems of government and increased external intervention and interaction on the basis of democracy, non-governmental organizations, human rights and freedoms. In addition, it is a process where the functions of nation states, which have a monolithic structure at the levels of political and cultural symbols such as religion, language, ethnicity etc., change and where international organizations come to the fore (Celik, 2012, p.69).

In international relations, it is assumed that the rise of the national states and traditional diplomacy began with the Treaty of Westphalia. This agreement, dated 1648, is also regarded as the beginning of modern state and international relations. During the formation of nation states, nationalism, national culture and national sensitivities, which were the products of the nation states, were in the forefront. Yet the paradigm of nation is now questioned in the postmodern period. Especially the emergence of civil society and the demands for multiculturalism, which were speeded up by the developments in the field of communication and culture, affected the weakening of sovereign states.

In the 1970s, industrialized countries experienced an economic crisis in which stagnation and inflation coexisted, and the number of debates about the quality of the state increased in this period. The debates mostly focused on the power, position, form and function of states. The concept of welfare state, which was the dominant concept during that period, lost prestige, and the social attitudes and the political mechanisms that regulate themselves according to these attitudes began to change. The state's dominant position in the economy was associated with the crisis and the gap arising from Keynesian politics was filled by neoliberal approaches. The origins of the current political globalization process may be closely linked to the rise of neoliberalism in the late 1970s.

With the collapse of the Eastern Bloc at the beginning of 1990 and the disintegration of the Soviet Union, the concept of state became more controversial in the search for a new world order. The transition from a bipolar to a unipolar world has been one of the major political developments in the process of the spread of globalization. The world has transformed into a capitalist economic structure that includes the former communist countries.

With the globalization of capital in the world economy, the state has weakened and state sovereignty has begun to wane. Moreover, the developments between the independent and sovereign states and the hegemonic powers and the power blocs were also effective in the gradual weakening of the sovereign state. The fact that international law accepts individuals and non-state organizations as subjects in addition to nation-states is another factor that limits state sovereignty.

Within the scope of the political dimension of globalization, political power and regimes are structurally transformed, "global politics (global governance)" emanating from the interaction between the main actors of globalization gains strength and the traditional distinction between domestic and foreign policy ceases to exist (Bayar, 2008, p.27).

As a result, just as the distinction between "domestic and foreign" capital, production and marketing is gradually disappearing, so the internal and external political parameters are often intertwined with each other. The welfare state, national development, international relations, national or international politics or civil actors and global social movements are no longer assessed to be nation-specific by using the national criteria, which are the benchmarks. The concept "think locally act globally" is an inevitable reality in the global process (Çiftçi, 2015, p.30).

Environmental Dimension and Its Problems

The rapid increase in production and consumption with the spread of industrialization has begun to cause harm to the environment and natural resources. Growing levels of externalities due to environmental factors are affecting countries adversely. Environmental externalities affect more than one country, which means this is a global issue and even a problem of transgenerational nature. Major environmental problems including droughts, desertification, climate change, flood disasters, greenhouse effect, endangered rainforests, unplanned urbanization, air pollution, acid rain, marine pollution and nuclear wastes cause irreversible damage to the ecosystem and these environmental problems are becoming globalized. Especially the famines that have emerged recently due to climate changes and droughts have regional effects and bring about the problem of hunger, and they may become an issue that trigger social conflicts and even threaten the world peace in the near future. At this point, the world population is estimated to be over 9 billion in 2050. The vast majority of this population growth is expected to happen in the developing countries. This situation is likely to further trigger off the important problems such as hunger, poverty, environmental pollution and migration (Lawton, 2011, p.3).

Particularly with the rapid increase of production and consumption as a result of the industrialization and rapid advancements of technology in the 20th century, natural resources started to deteriorate and become depleted and the power of nature to recover itself was damaged. The developed and developing countries have been engaged in a race to develop, produce and consume at the cost of environmental degradation. The former aimed to maintain power, while the latter aimed to be able to keep up with the developed countries (Mutlu, 2006, pp.61-62).

Various global problems we face today, especially climate change, originate from the events of the 20th century whose effects are still present today. In the 20th century, world population grew by a factor of four to more than 6 billion. Besides, industrial output increased by a factor of 40 and energy consumption increased by a factor of 16 (Dasgupta, 2011, p.171).

Among all environmental problems, climate change and global warming due their environmental impacts have reached a level that will prevent sustainable living. Serious problems in water resources have been experienced due to global warming and these problems are expected to cause a decrease in the number of agricultural and forest products as well as energy shortages and population movements from coastal areas to inner areas. The warming caused by the effect of increasing temperature at the global level leads to changes in other climate elements it is related to. Global warming caused by increased temperatures results in other problems such as drought, reduction in the volume and quality of water resources, freshwater-seawater mixing, sea level rise, melting of snow and ice, extreme evaporation, increase in meteorological disasters, changes in precipitation amount and regime and fires. In addition to its physical effects, global warming also has some economic, sociological and psychological effects (Karaman & Gökalp, 2010, p.60).

The effect of greenhouse gases emerges as another important environmental problem. It is scientifically acknowledged that emissions of greenhouse gases, especially carbon dioxide, which result from the use of conventional fossil fuels such as coal and oil, have increased and caused climate change. Climate change is now an integral part of the world's energy equation. The vast majority of carbon dioxide emissions are generated from coal and liquid petroleum, i.e. energy production and transportation. Especially the rise in energy prices after 2003 led to a considerable reduction in prices of coal compared to gas, thus leading to the increased use of coal by the developing countries. China and India consumed more coal than oil in 2005. In 2007, the world's biggest producer of greenhouse gases, China surpassed the United States. In 2008, China and India surpassed all developed countries in terms of coal consumption. At the same time, these countries are advancing in a way to double the carbon emissions of the OECD's other countries by 2020 and of the richest 26 countries by 2030. It is almost certain that these countries will be responsible for most of the excess carbon emissions in the atmosphere after 2050 (Montgomery, 2014, p.217).

On the other hand, coal, oil and conventional biomass constituted 95% of global energy consumption in 1930; however, in 1990, natural gas, nuclear energy, hydro-electric power, wind power, solar power and biofuels were included in this percentage. The use of low-carbon sources and technologies and renewable energy sources such as solar, wind, geothermal and biomass in the upcoming years seems to be a more rational solution (Montgomery, 2014, pp.416-428).

If the superpowers (the US, China, India, Japan and the EU) do not take serious steps to solve global warming and climate change resulting from greenhouse gas effect, the world will not be able to effectively cope with this problem. There is no authority on the world which is able to request the US to reduce it demand for petroleum, China to reduce its coal use and Indonesia to end its role in deforestation (Montgomery, 2014, pp.414-415).

Solving global environmental problems transcends the capacity of nation states, requiring the involvement of international organizations in this process more effectively. At the same time, state-civil society relations need to be strengthened to help individuals gain awareness and the act of energy saving must be turned into a habit. Another important point is that countries should focus on long-term benefits, not on short-term costs when cooperating to solve environmental problems.

Today, the United Nations is the principal international organization that initiates and implements comprehensive environmental protection activities around the world. In addition to the UN, the World Bank, the OECD, the Organization of the Black Sea Economic Cooperation and many other international and regional organizations carry out activities to protect and improve the environment.

Social-Cultural Dimension and Its Problems

Another dimension of globalization is socio-cultural globalization. During the process of globalization, societies must adapt to the rapid changes in technology, communication and transportation. Advances in technology and communication increase the interaction between individuals and societies living in different geographies. Social dimension of globalization refers to the movement and spread of ideas, knowledge and individuals at a global scale. Such movement brings about global culture and background as well as carrying the risk of alienation in terms of different cultures. Changing economic structures and universal values put pressure on the local identities of societies. Socio-cultural globalization requires belonging to a single culture. For example, it leads the world toward a culture in which people eat the same foods and uses products of the same brand. Companies like McDonald's, Coca Cola, Benetton, Adidas, etc., which allow for the generation of the same consumption patterns became a world brand and the products they produce began to be widely used around the world. It is important for societies to protect cultural differences when considering the changes in the world and taking advantage of innovations.

In addition to the threat to preservation of cultural diversity posed by the single and dominant Western culture, other problems caused by social globalization may include population density, rapid population growth, increased elderly population, difficulties in accessing resources, migration and refugee problem, global terrorism, increased health problems due to reasons such as pollution and epidemics.

Demographic issues, especially the growth of the older population and the decline in the youth population, constitute one of the important social problems. The world population of 7.3 billion in 2015 is expected to reach 8.5 billion by 2030 and 9.7 billion in 2050. According to the data issued by the United Nations in 2015, 62% of world population are aged 15-59 years, and 12% are 60 or over. The median age is estimated to increase. In OECD countries, the median age of 37.9 years in 2010 will rise to 42.8 years by 2030. The median age of 45 in Germany and Japan will rise up to 65 in the next decades. The most important reason for this increase is because the average life expectancy is increasing day by day and the fertility rates are decreasing. The life expectancy at birth was 67 years between 2000-2005, while it was 70 years between 2010-2015. As of 2015, 12% of the world's population was aged over 60 years. It is estimated that this ratio will increase to 25% by the year 2050. Again, according to the statistics issued by the United Nations in 2015, the number of persons aged 60 or above is expected to be 1.4 billion in 2030, 2.1 billion in 2050 and 3.2 billion in 2100.

Population ageing reveals the need to review public health, elderly care services, labor market, social security and pension systems. The ageing population poses an economic threat: Sales of expensive commodities such as houses, cars etc. will fall and the number of people taking entrepreneurial risks will decrease. The decline in the youth population, together with the increase in the ageing population, will lead to a decline in economic efficiency.

Migration is a major problem brought by social globalization. Factors such as income inequality among the regions, differences in the population structure of the rich and poor countries, labor requirement, the existence of migration networks and climate change are among the factors that cause cross-border migration. For example, some reports predict that there will be hundreds of millions of climate refugees worldwide by 2050.

The global migration statistics show that the major areas of Europe, Northern America and Oceania were net receivers of migrants between 1950 and 2015. On the other hand, Africa, Asia and Latin and the Caribbean were net senders. Between 2000 and 2015, the annual net migration to Europe, Northern America and Oceania averaged 2.8 million persons, revealing that these places hosted the largest number of migrants. High-income countries received an average of 4.1 million net migrants annually from lower- and middle-income countries between 2000 and 2015 (United Nations, 2015, p.28).

Global cooperation plays the most important role in solving global migration problems. But nowadays migration and refugee policies are shaped around the national interests of the countries. Migration is a phenomenon not covered by international legal regimes. Therefore, countries are seeking solutions to migration-related problems through platforms established at global and regional level. However, these efforts need to be made in a more global and consistent framework (Nakhoul, 2014, p.131).

Another problem brought by the social dimension of globalization is global terrorism. Today terrorism threatens the whole world. It is seen that terrorist groups commit random acts of terror and unlimited violence. The nature of terrorism has also changed in today's global world. Global terrorism is transforming into terrorist networks in which citizens of different countries can commit acts of terrorism around the globe by using modern means of communication such as the internet and satellite-telephone and weapons of mass destruction (chemical, biological, nuclear, airliners etc.). Besides, the cause of global terrorism is increasingly evolving from national independence to religious and ethnic nationalism (Aktan &Vural, 2004, p.1).

On the other hand, the joint initiatives of the United States and the EU within the framework of combating global terrorism have their own contradictions. Technological elements that can be used in the production of chemical and nuclear weapons are being transferred mainly by the European countries such as England, Germany and France to the countries such as Iraq, Iran and Syria, which the USA blames for terrorist activities. After all, the highest level of technology required for high-impact actions is in the hands of the West, and the groups that commit acts of terror somehow get this technology from the West (Gençtürk, 2012, p.8).

In conclusion, it should not be forgotten that terrorism is aimed at destroying freedoms and instilling fear, anxiety and chaos and it is not clear where, when and how terrorism strikes and who will be its victims.

CONCLUSION

Globalization, a phenomenon that began in the 1970s, is a stage of the capitalist system, which has been in effect since the industrial revolution. This stage followed the general crisis that emerged as a result of the economic, social and political problems that existed before itself and was shaped by the dynamics of this crisis. Capital played the most important role in this shaping. The dynamics of the change include the free market economy, global production systems, neoliberal understanding of state and the values of the Western culture. The IMF, the World Bank and the World Trade Organization are the main institutions that rebuilt the "new world order".

On the one hand, it is argued that globalization has some advantages such as economic growth, technological experience and technological development, competition, increased employment, the shortening of the distances between countries and regions and the disintegration of oligopolies. On the other hand, globalization is said to have some negative consequences such as the problem of income inequality and sharing, national and international development deficits and imbalances, erosion and environmental problems.

In conclusion, if globalization policies are implemented correctly in line with the institutionalized policies, they may accelerate economic growth. Knowledge has become as important as capital with the rapid development of science and technology, which is a factor that will promote social welfare and economic recovery. However, although this positive picture shows that economic policies in both developed and developing countries are becoming increasing similar, it is also seen that income inequality between countries is increasing as a result of globalization. Per capita income levels of developed countries came close to each other after 1980. However, the per capita income gap between developing and developed countries is widening significantly today. With increasing inequality, the number of people around the world who live on less than $1 a day has increased up to 1.3 billion in the last 10 years.

In this century, when even the developed capitalist countries are not able to solve the problem of inequality, taking more constructive steps to solve the problems of international terrorism, proliferation of weapons of mass destruction, global warming, migration and the environmental-social-cultural problems is of great importance for leaving a better world for our children.

REFERENCES

Aktan, C. C., Dileyici, D., & Istiklal, Y. V. (2006). Contemporary Approaches in Public Finance. In C. C. Aktan & İ. Y. Vural (Eds.), *Change in Globalization and Fiscal Policy*. Ankara: Seçkin Publishing.

Aktan, C. C., & Vural, İ. Y. (2004). *Global Terror Problem*. Retrieved June 8, 2018, from http://canaktan.org/yeni-trendler/global-sorunlar/global-teror.htm

Ar, K. N. (2016). Example of Turkey Income Inequality in the 21st Century. *Entrepreneurship and Development Journal*, *10*(2), 187–202.

Bauman, Z. (2016). *Social Results of Globalization* (6th ed.; A. Yılmaz, Trans.). İstanbul: Ayrıntı Publication.

Bauman, Z. (2018). *The Search for Politics* (4th ed.; T. Birkan, Trans.). İstanbul: Metis Publishing.

Bayar, F. (2008). The concept of Globalization and the Globalization Process in Turkey. *International Economic Issues Journal*, *32*, 25–34.

Bayramoğlu, T., & Başar, E. E. (2016). *Globalization: Economic and Social Trends*. Ankara: Savaş Publication.

Bozkurt, V. (2000). Globalization: Concept - Development and Approaches. *The Journal of Business Power Industry Relations and Human Resources*, *2*(1), 17–26.

Bryane, M. (2003). Theorising the Politics of Globalisation: A Critique of Transformationalism. *Journal of Economic and Social Research*, *4*(2), 3–17.

Bülbül, K. (2004). *Globalization, Culture and Politics: Globalization Approaches in Turkish Intellectual and Political Life* (Unpublished Doctoral Dissertation). Ankara University Institue of Social Sciences, Ankara, Turkey.

Ceglowski, J. (1998, March). Has Globalization Created a Borderless World? *Business Review (Federal Reserve Bank of Philadelphia)*, 17–27.

Çelik, M. Y. (2012). Globalization with Different Perceptions and Dimensions, *Dumlupınar Üniversity. The Social Science Journal*, *32*(2), 57–73.

Çiftçi, İ. (2015). *Shaking Earth in Our Hands: Globalization*. İstanbul: Vadi Publishing.

Dasgupta, P. (2011). *Economy*. Ankara: Dost Publishing.

Gençtürk, T. (2012). The Concept of Terror and Different Approaches to International Terrorism. *Başkent University Center for Strategic Studies*, 1-11. Retrieved June 8, 2018, from http://sam.baskent.edu.tr/makaleler/tgencturk/TerorUluslararasi.pdf

Ghose, A. K., Majid, N., & Ernst, C. (2010). *Global Employment Problem*. Ankara: Efil Publication.

Giddens, A. (2000). *The World Fleeing from Our Hand* (O. Akınhay, Trans.). İstanbul: Alfa Publishing.

Gökdere, A. (2001). An Overview of Globalization, *Ankara. Journal of European Studies*, *1*(1), 71–101.

Hablemitoğlu, Ş. (2005). *Globalization, From Dreams to Truths* (2nd ed.). İstanbul: Social Transformation Publications.

Harvey, D. (2014). *The Status of Postmodernism* (7th ed.; S. Savran, Trans.). İstanbul: Metis Publishing.

Heywood, A. (2013). *Global Politics* (N. Uslu & H. Özdemir, Trans.). Ankara: Adres Publication.

Karaman, S., & Gökalp, Z. (2010). Impacts of Global Warming and Climate Change Over Water Resources. *Journal of Agriculture and Social Research*, *3*(1), 59–66.

Kaya, M. (2009). Globalization Approaches. *Journal of Dicle University. Ziya Gökalp Faculty of Education, 13*, 1–16.

Kaya, M., Doğan, B. B., & Kaya, S. B. (2017). An Assessment upon the Factors Providing a Basis for the Generation of Globalism. *Social Sciences Studies Journal, 3*(12), 2041–2060. doi:10.26449ssj.276

Kitapçı, İ. (2017). An Assessment of Today's Major Global Problems, *PESA Internatıonal. The Journal of Social Studies, 3*(14), 241–257.

Kurtoğlu, R. (2017). *Global Economic Crisis and the New World Order*. İstanbul: Destek Publication.

Kurtulmuş, N. (2001). *Trans-Industrial Transformation, Globalization and Human Resources Dimension*. İstanbul: İz Publishing.

Lawton, S. J. (2011). *Demographic Change and the Environment Twenty-ninth Report*. Retrieved June 8, 2018, from https://assets.publishing.service.gov.uk/government/ uploads/system/uploads/attachment_data/file/228980/8001.pdf

McLuhan, M. (2014). *The Gutenberg Galaxy; Formation of Typographic Man* (G. Ç. Güven, Trans.). İstanbul: Yapı Kredi Publishing.

Montgomery, S.L. (2014). *Global Energy Powers, 21st Century and After* (E. G. Şenol, Trans.). Ankara: Salmat Printing and Publishing.

Mutlu, A. (2006). Health Services and Environmental Pollution in the Context Global Public Goods: Production, Finance and Management Problems. *The Journal of Finance, 150*, 53–78.

Nakhoul, T. E. (2014). *International Labor Migration and Turkey*. Ankara: T.C. Ministry of Labor and Social Security, General Directorate of Foreign Relations and Overseas Worker Services.

Özdemir, S. (2007). *Welfare State in the Process of Globalization*. İstanbul: Istanbul Chamber of Commerce Publication.

Özgür, G., & Yetkiner, H. (2011). Economics in Difficult Times. In E. Aslanoglu (Ed.), *Global Economic Crisis and Economic Policy*. Ankara: Efil Publishing.

Robertson, R. (1999). *Globalization - Social Theory and Global Culture* (Ü. H. Yolsal, Trans.). Ankara: Science and Art Publications.

Saraç, Ö. (2006). *Global Tax Competition and National Tax Policies*. Ankara: Finance and Law Publications.

Savaş, V. F. (2012). *Global Finance and Macroeconomics*. Ankara: Efil Publication.

Seyidoğlu, H. (2017). *International Economics, Theory and Practice*. İstanbul: Güzem Can Publishing.

TASAM. (2018). *Dimensions and Effects of Globalization*. Retrieved June 8, 2018, from http://tasam.org/tr-TR/Icerik/211/kuresellesmenin_boyutlari_ve_etkileri

Taylor, P., & Flınt, C. (2000). *Political Geography World Economy, Nation-State and Locality* (4th ed.). New York: Routledge.

United Nations Development Programme (UNDP). (2015). *World Population Prospect the 2015 Revisions, Volume II: Demographic Profiles*. Department of Economic and Social Affairs Population Division. Retrieved June 8, 2018, from http://esa.un.org/unpd/wpp/publications/Files/WPP2015_Volume-II-Demographic-Profiles.pdf

Wallerstein, I. (1993). *Geopolitics and Geoculture* (M. Özel, Trans.). İstanbul: İz Publishing.

Waters, M. (2001). *Globalization* (2nd ed.). London: Routledge.

Yılmaztürk, A., & Buhur, S. (2017). Fıscal Consolidation Practices In Turkey After 1980. *Journal of Tax Issues*, *350*, 85–100.

Yusufoğlu, Y. (2005). *Global Imperialism*. İstanbul: Belge Publishing.

KEY TERMS AND DEFINITIONS

Financial Globalization: Financial globalization refers to the removal of barriers and restrictions on short- and long-term capital flows and the integration of domestic markets with the world markets.

Global Economic Problems: As an important global economic problem in the world, income inequality, poverty, economic crises, quotas for international trade, tax havens are examples.

Global Environmental Problems: Major environmental problems including droughts, desertification, climate change, flood disasters, greenhouse effect, endangered rainforests, unplanned urbanization, air pollution, acid rain, marine pollution and nuclear wastes cause irreversible damage to the ecosystem and these environmental problems are becoming globalized.

Global Social Problems: Other problems caused by social globalization may include population density, rapid population growth, increased elderly population, difficulties in accessing resources, migration and refugee problem, global terrorism, increased health problems due to reasons such as pollution and epidemics.

Global System: Global system is an economic and political construct in which capital, management, employment, knowledge, natural resources and organizations are fully internationalized. The main determinants of the global system are nation states, multinational corporations, international institutions, and non-governmental organizations.

Globalization: Globalization is defined as the expansion and development of worldwide economic, social, political, and cultural relations. This definition includes all elements such as different geographies, cultural formation, economic-social and political structure, state government, goods and services, capital accumulation, technological infrastructure, and lifestyles, regardless of physical distance. Globalization is a structural transformation process which is based on the principle of mutual dependence and which increases the level of communication, interaction, and relationships among all these elements.

International Institutions: It refers to all kinds of mergers that operate at international level, which do not have commercial purpose, concern more than one state, but do not have any state characteristics. Such as the World Trade Organization, the International Monetary Fund, the United Nations, the Organization for Economic Cooperation and Development, the North Atlantic Pact and the World Bank.

Political Globalization: The globalization of political refers to the absence of the absolute sovereignty of a state's political borders over a certain area as well as increased interaction between the systems of government and increased external intervention and interaction on the basis of democracy, non-governmental organizations, human rights, and freedoms.

Social-Cultural Globalization: Advances in technology and communication increase the interaction between individuals and societies living in different geographies. Social-cultural dimension of globalization refers to the movement and spread of ideas, knowledge and individuals at a global scale.

Technology Globalization: The globalization of technology removed physical limits in areas such as communication, transportation and security, increased mutual interaction and altered the interaction of time, space, and power.

Section 2

The Effects of Globalization on the Public Finance System

Chapter 2
The Impact of Globalization on External Debts:
Evidence From Developing Countries

Serap Barış
Gaziosmanpasa University, Turkey

ABSTRACT

In this chapter, the answer to this question has been researched theoretically and empirically. KOF Globalization Index has been used as the measure of globalization unlike the empirical literature that explores the relationship between globalization and external debt. In the study where panel data analysis method has been used, the findings show that there is a positive relationship between KOF Globalization Index and external debt in developing countries. When it is examined from the perspective of the sub-indexes of globalization, it is seen that the economic globalization index is positively related to external debt. Social and political globalization has no effect on external debts. Impact of the control variables used in the analysis on external debts is significant and negative. From this, it can be said that general globalization and economic globalization have increased the external debt of the nations.

INTRODUCTION

One of the main macroeconomic problems of underdeveloped and developed countries in the world is increasing external debt. In these countries, the failure of supplying the investments required for the acceleration of economic growth from domestic sources (insufficient domestic savings and foreign exchange shortfall) have increased the need for external debt. This need has emerged after World War II and the Developing countries turned to external sources and external borrowing especially after 1970. External borrowing, which is regarded in classical theory as a form of financing to be resorted to under extraordinary circumstances, has evolved into a standard practice because of the changing economic conditions of the day. Liberalization of capital movements starting from the second half of the 1980s as well as the acceleration of globalization starting from the middle of the 1990s increased the dependence of the countries on each other and the need for loans; and, in this regard, credit facilities were expanded

DOI: 10.4018/978-1-5225-7564-1.ch002

while low cost and affordable borrowing options were created as well. In the past thirty years, there has been an increase in public debt stock in most developed countries. For example, public debt stock in OECD countries were about 30% of GDP in the early 1980s but then rose to 50% in 2005. Is globalization really an important factor in increasing external debt of the nations - limiting their economic growth- as suggested by some authors and mentioned here as well?

Globalization, one of the key concepts of the twenty-first century, is one of the most debated concepts. While the analyses of world capitalism proceeded on an international basis until the 1980s, this internationally based process was substituted by the globalization as a result of an intense paradigm change (Heywood, 2014, p. 27). Globalization can be expressed as a process in which common values in economic, political, social and cultural spheres spread across the world beyond the national borders. So; globalization is a multidimensional concept and the definitions vary depending on from which discipline it is handled.

Globalization is different from such similar concepts as internationalization, liberalization, universalization or westernization. However; these concepts are close to each other and sometimes used interchangeably (Gygli, 2018). Globalization is a phenomenon that includes liberalization, internationalization and universalization but also exists everywhere with its economic, social, political, cultural and ideological impacts. As McGrew (2010) also put it simply, globalization means the expansion, deepening and acceleration of mutual links around the world. According to Dreher (2006), who introduced KOF globalization index, "it is a process of creating networks of connections among intra- and multi-continental distances, mediated through a variety of flows including people, information and ideas, capital, and goods. Globalization is a process that erodes national boundaries, integrates national economies, cultures, technologies and governance, and produces complex relations of mutual interdependence." According to another definition, globalization refers to the spreading of some common values in economic, political, social and cultural spheres beyond the local and national borders across the world (DPT, 2000, p.3). This new process led to liberal economic order in the economic arena and liberal political order in the political arena. According to the definition of the World Bank (2000), globalization is "the freedom and ability of individuals and businesses to initiate voluntary economic transactions with the individuals and institutions of other countries." According to Stiglitz (2015), globalization means the reduction of transportation and communication costs and the integration of national economies by removing the obstacles against the flow of goods, services, capital, labor and information. The most researched dimension of globalization, as defined by the World Bank, is *economic globalization*.

As suggested by Stiglitz (2004), globalization is a process that must be well managed and its impacts are not the same in all countries regardless of which dimension is mentioned, particularly the economic-political sphere. While some countries benefit from globalization at the maximum level by minimizing the risks and uncertainties, some other countries that cannot manage the process well suffer from globalization. In this context; globalization is particularly effective in strengthening the positive impact on economic variables, particularly economic growth, for developed countries with a strong institutional structure, a well developed financial sector and robust macroeconomic policies. Therefore, it is important to know from which perspective the globalization is addressed.

However, regardless of which dimension is mentioned, it can be said that globalization leads to significant changes in many parameters (social, cultural, political, etc.), especially economic parameters (growth, employment, foreign trade, indebtedness, unemployment, inequality, poverty etc.) of the nation states. One of these economic parameters is external debt. In recent years, an increasing number of studies - with the emergence of new indicators - have focused on the impacts of globalization on economic variables, particularly economic growth. Few studies have examined the relationship between globalization and external debt.

In this study, it is aimed to examine the relationship between globalization and external debt in developing countries. While the impacts of globalization on external debts are analyzed in the existing literature, it is seen that such variables as trade and finance gaps, foreign direct investment, tariff rates are widely used as the indicators of globalization. KOF Globalization Index, which is the most widely used globalization index according to Pofratke (2015), has been used instead of the existing literature in this study. Since the index has a long time series and various sub-indexes other than general indexes (economic, social and political), globalization - external debt relation could be examined in detail by creating more than one model.

Following the theoretical and empirical background, the impression of external debts and globalization in the world will be evaluated in the study. After that, globalization - external debt relation will be examined by using panel data analysis methods for the countries having different income levels. The last part is is comprised of the outcome of the study and the proposal of the policy.

BACKGROUND

External borrowing, which is defined as the acquisition of external sources by the domestic institution (state or public) and individuals, has become a policy instrument which is frequently resorted to by developing countries, in particular, in order to maintain economic development processes. Such that countries resort to external borrowing because of many reasons such as the fact that they cannot borrow from their own capital markets or pay the financing of the importation of raw materials, intermediary and investment goods for the investments required for industrialization and development as well as the balances and budget deficits that have become chronic and also economic reforms in addition to extraordinary expenditures, defense spending and their debts due (Ulusoy, 2016, p.60). As a result, External borrowing has turned into an important public income over time. Some economists such as Keynes and Harrod-Domar who focus on the impacts of external debt on economic growth point out that external borrowing provides an additional source of domestic investment, and thus economic growth, while some economists beginning with Griffin and Enos (1970) state that external borrowing decrease the productivity of economy. An important approach in this regard is largely concerned with the level of these debts, rather than whether external borrowing is made or not. It points out that reasonable borrowing levels in developing countries will support growth in these countries; because investment yields are higher in these countries compared to developed countries. This is the case, however, if the external debts received are used for productive projects to repay these debts. Ward et al. (2002) and Pattillo et al. (2004) show empirical evidence that external debt in low levels affects the economic growth positively while additional debts over certain thresholds or turning points have a negative effect on the growth. Thus, it has been found in many empirical studies that there is a negative relationship between external debt and economic growth in the countries having a high level of external borrowing (Farzin, 1988; Were, 2001; Bilginoglu & Aysu, 2008; Malik et al., 2010).

There are mainly two important reasons why the government is resorting to external borrowing instead of domestic borrowing. The first is to provide additional income to existing resources in the economy and to create new payment opportunities in the second foreign currency. The first reason is especially important for countries that have insufficient domestic savings to support investment projects. These resources provided by external borrowing can be used for investment and consumption. External sources increase the investment capacity of the country. However, if these debts are directed to consumption instead of investment, external borrowing does not contribute to the increase of investments. Countries having foreign exchange troubles can also resort to external borrowing to solve this problem. Especially developing countries meet their necessary investment and intermediate goods through imports in order to realize their economic growth. These countries having a low level of export revenues face such a foreign exchange bottleneck that the best way for them is to resort to external borrowing.

Unlike domestic borrowing, external borrowing is a real resource for the economy. However; when interest and capital payments are made, there is a source of funds from the country. In other words; the debtor country has to reduce its investments, consumption or both at the level of debt service during the payment of debts. Moreover; since this service is normally done with foreign currency, only the decrease in total expenditures will not be enough and the required exchange rate will also have to be provided. External debt service becomes important as the external debt and principal payments of the country increase. This rate, which shows how much of the foreign exchange earned by the export of goods and services goes to the debt repayment, especially shows the external debt pressures that the relevant country faces in the short term (Karluk, 2009, p.158).

Given the course of borrowing of developing countries, it is seen that they borrow from international financial institutions that emerged after World War II. Small-scale debt problems emerged in several countries starting from these periods, but a large-scale debt crisis started to emerge in many developing countries, especially in Latin America, in the 1970s. Increase in the number of countries following an outward-oriented policy was also seen as an important factor in the spread of this debt crisis. For this reason, it can be said that outward openness level of the countries determines the degree of being influenced by global events (Kazgan, 1985, p.181). With the beginning of the liberalization of capital movements (financial globalization) towards the end of the 1980s, external borrowing increased among the countries. Acceleration of globalization since the mid 1990s increased the dependence of countries on each other and the need for loans; credit facilities expanded and low-cost and affordable external resource utilization opportunities were created in this respect (Öztürk & Özyakışır, 2005, p.1). All these developments bring such questions to mind: (i) is there a relationship between globalization and external debt? (ii) if there is a relationship between these two variables that are experiencing a simultaneous development, through what mechanisms, how and in which direction does this relationship come about?

Theoretical explanations on the relationship between globalization and external debts differ from each other. According to an opinion, countries which have trade openness can improve their debt position by increasing their foreign trade (both imports and exports). In particular, the monitoring of the growth strategy based on exports will increase the foreign exchange income of the developing countries. In addition; if a rapid industrialization process can be achieved in the domestic market through imported capital goods, it can increase the economic prosperity of the country. High production growth and development in the country will reduce dependence on external borrowing (Zafar & Butt, 2008, p.3). As a result, outward-oriented economies are expected to have a tendency to have a lower level of debt (Woo, 2003). This view which suggests that there is a negative relationship between globalization and external debt has not found much support empirically. Chiminia and Nicolaidou (2015) examined the determinants of external debt in 36 sub-Saharan African countries in the period 1975 to 2012. This study in which a large number of economic and political explanatory variables, including outward openness, have been used indicates that external debt burden decreases in outward-oriented economies with a high level of economic activity. Bittencourt (2015) who focuses on the determinants of external debt in South America's young and democratic countries (9 countries) has also found that outward openness negatively affects external debt.

Contrary to this argument, there are also some suggestions that there is a positive relationship between external debt and globalization. Considering that balance of payments always have deficit because of the fact that imports are more than exports in developing countries, it was inevitable to eliminate this deficit and the foreign exchange bottleneck. For these reasons, these countries have had to borrow from IMF, World Bank and international commercial banks since 1970s. Aside from the fact that these loans / debts maintain the outward openness of the economy, the commitments made by the countries in order to receive this credit enable the country to maintain its outward openness through economic policies (Kazgan, 1985, p.175). Furthermore; since these countries removed government restrictions on financial markets without providing the necessary conditions in the 1980s, banks and other institutions resorted to borrow from foreign markets without exercising due diligence. These debts could not be repaid due to the financial crises that occurred later (Seyidoglu, 2015, p.601). With regard to these debts that could not be paid at due date, attempts were made to settle the external debts of developing countries through debt-deferral agreements made in the second half of the 1980s and early 1990s.

Another relationship between external debt and globalization takes place through taxation. Customs taxes are an important source of income for developing countries - especially the poor ones - (WTO, 2003, p.2). Trade liberalization requires the gradual removal of customs tariffs. Budget deficits resulting from the diminution of budgetary resources in these countries will be compensated by external borrowing due to insufficient domestic resources. Even in the 2000s, many developing and emerging market economies are still heavily dependent on customs duties in public finance (Caliari, 2005, Baunsgaard & Keen, 2005).

High dependence on export of primary goods (agricultural and land based products and raw materials) is also a major reason for high level of external borrowing in developing countries. Firstly, the prices of these goods have been falling steadily for the last 40-50 years. Between 1977 and 2001, prices for 41 of the 46 leading goods were reduced. Secondly, the prices of these goods are exposed to sharp fluctuations. The decline and volatility in prices have made the income flow of these countries unpredictable (Caliari, 2005). In addition; since many developing countries producing similar goods simultaneously carry out trade liberalization, the prices of the goods exported by these countries have fallen due to the excessive supply of similar goods (Khattry & Rao, 2002). As a result, these countries whose export revenues decreased had to resort to external borrowing.

The limited empirical literature on the relationship between globalization and external debt reveals that the trade openness in developing countries worsens their external debt position. As we have already mentioned, almost all of the studies except for one or two studies agree that there is a positive relationship between globalization - or openness / trade openness as used in many studies - and external debts. Examples from these studies are presented in Table 1. While a small number of studies are focused directly on globalization - external debt relation, a substantial part of the studies are focused on the determinants of external debt stock in which the outward openness variable is included in the equations. Import / GDP, export / GDP and foreign trade volume / GDP variables were used in these studies as the indicators of globalization or outward openness. When Table 1 is examined, it is seen that almost all studies except for Azzimonti et al. (2012) have selected the developing countries as the sample.

Table 1. Summary of literature

Studies	Sample	Method	Result
Osuji & Surajudeen (1998)	7 Sub-Saharan Africa countries, 1972-1992	Regression analysis	An increase in the import / GDP ratio leads to an increase in external debt.
Lane (2000)	87 developing countries, 1970-1995	Cross-section and panel data analysis	There is a positive relationship between trade openness and external debt.
Zafar & Butt (2008)	Pakistan, 1972-2007	ARDL model	In the long run there is a positive relationship between external debt and trade liberalization.
Colombo & Longoni (2009)	61 developing countries, 1970-2001	Pooled OLS, GMM	There is a strong and positive relationship between foreign debt and trade openness.
Azzimonti et al. (2012)	22 OECD countries, 1973-2005	Panel data analysis (FE)	As financial markets are more integrated with international markets, public debt is increasing.
Zakaria (2012)	Pakistan, 1972-2010	Generalized Methofs of Moments (GMM)	Trade openness has a significant positive effect on foreign debts.
Kizilgol & Ipek (2014)	Turkey, 1990-2012	ARDL model	Trade openness has a positive effect on short and long term external debt.
Imimole et al. (2014)	Nigeria, 1986-2010	Cointegration test, Parsimonious Error-Correction Model	Trade openness has no effect on external debt.
Chiminya & Nicolaidou (2015)	36 Sub-Saharan Africa countries, 1970-2012	Pooled OLS, Panel data analysis (FE)	In open economies, external debt burden is decreasing.
Awan, et al (2015)	Pakistan, 1976-2010	ARDL model	Trade openness ratio has a positive effect on external debt stock.
Bittencourt (2015)	9 South American countries, 1970-2005	Dynamic panel data analysis	Trade openness negatively affects foreign debt.
Bölükbaş (2016)	Turkey, 1998-2011	VEC model	There is a positive relationship between trade openness and external debt.
Al-Fawwaz (2016)	Jordan, 1990-2004	ARDL model	External openness ratio and foreign trade volume variables have positive effects on external debt stock.
Bölükbaş & Peker (2017)	Turkey, 1998-2011	VAR model	External debt is positively influenced by trade openness.
Akduğan (2017)	Turkey, 1970-2015	ARDL model	Trade openness variable has a positive effect on foreign debt stock.

Source: It was created by the author using related studies

Only a few studies have found evidence that trade openness do not have any effect on the external debts of countries. For example, Imimole et al. (2014) investigated the determinants of external debt in Nigerian economy and showed that the outward openness of the economy had no effect on external debts. Again, a small number of studies (Chiminia and Nicolaidou, 2015 & Bittencourt, 2015) found that outward openness decreases external debt.

Development of External Debts in the World

When historically examined, the reasons and impacts of external borrowing as well as the solutions of emerging problems in underdeveloped and developing countries are different from the ones in developed countries. Especially after World War II, the main objective of these countries is to get rid of underdevelopment, to industrialize and to remove developmental differences between developed countries and themselves. It is thought that the savings required to achieve this aim and other national resources are generally inadequate and therefore it is compulsory to resort to external resources / debts. External debts essentially entered into the agenda of the world economy through the shocks of energy and oil crises in the 1970s and increased its significance after the declaration of Mexico in 1982 that it will not be able to pay its external debts. Latin American countries such as Brazil, Argentina and Chile, which followed Mexico, also played a major role in spreading the problem.

Since the early 1980s, not only Latin America, but also nearly half of the developing Third World countries have faced significant international payment problems. There are many factors which are effective in the emergence of these problems and they can vary depending on the countries. Though it is difficult to generalize, the increases in oil prices, the stagnation in developed countries, the increase in real interest rates, the decrease in prices of basic agricultural products, the policies for domestic consumption in underdeveloped countries and the early financial liberalization movements in the 1970s are important reasons for external borrowing (Ulusoy, 2016, pp. 317-325). Structural weakness of the economies of these countries and the unsuccessful domestic economy policies have been effective in the continuation of international payment problems for many years.

The course of external debts in the world will be examined in terms of developing countries within the data provided by the World Bank's "International Debt Statistic Database". World Bank categorizes the countries on the basis of GNP per capita within the analytical framework (calculated by the *World Bank Atlas* method). Countries are classified as low, medium and high income economies accordingly. The first two groups are generally categorized as developing countries, including underdeveloped countries. Here, the developments in the external debt stocks and ratios of these countries are explained and evaluated. The most important external debt indicators are regarded as the share of external debt stock in GNP and the share of external debt in exported goods and services. Figure 1 indicates the share of external debt stocks of low and middle income country / country groups in GNP for the period 1980-2016. In this regard; it is seen that the external debts of these countries are more than 100% with a constant tendency of increase in the 1980s and 1990s, and it is seen that they have a tendency to decrease after 2005 especially compared to the previous years. The highest external debt among these country groups belongs to low income countries. Such that, external debts / GNP ratio has increased to over 500% in these countries from the second half of the 1980s until 2000s. The most important reason lying behind the decline in External borrowing in these countries since 2000s is that these countries' external debts to IMF, World Bank and African Development Bank have been written off. IMF decided to write off the external debts of 19 poor countries in December 2005; then the World Bank decided to erase the external debts of the poorest 18 countries. The vast majority of these countries whose debts were written off are from Africa, except for the four Latin American countries (Honduras, Nicaragua, Guyana, Bolivia). Regarding these debts written off, Paul Wolfowitz, World Bank President of that period, said that "leaders of 38 countries in Africa and the other regions of the world will no longer have to make a

Figure 1. External debt stocks (% of GNI)
Source: WB (2018), International Debt Statistics 2018, The World Bank

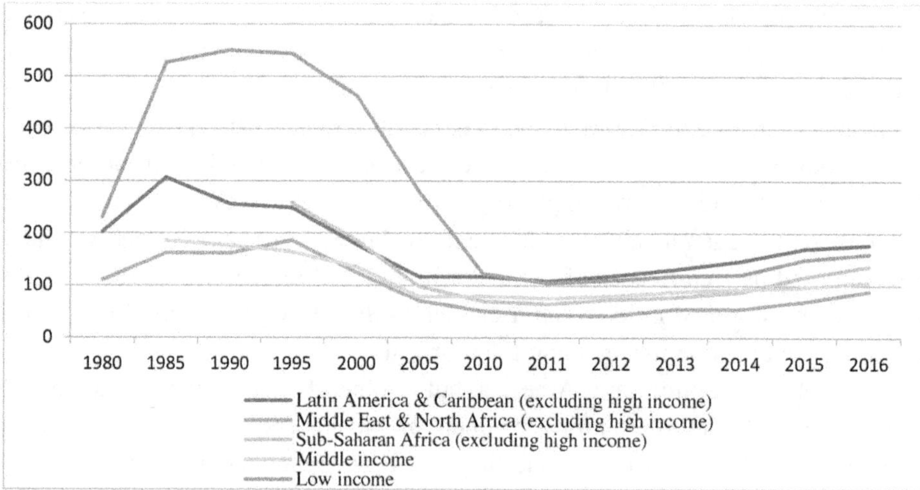

choice between using their budget to repay their unbearable debts and spending their budget for the sake of their people" (IMF, 2005). The country group relatively having the lowest external debt / GNP ratio within this group is the Middle East and North Africa. While the share of external debts in the GNP was 110% at the beginning of this period, it had a trend of decline in the 2000s as in other countries. The situation in developing (middle income) countries is similar to that of the Middle East and North Africa.

Another indicator of external debt, the external debt / export ratio, is a measure used to obtain information about the long-term impacts of export revenues on total debt stock, which shows the indebtedness of a country as well as its external debt payment capacity (Evgin, 2000). Table 2 shows the share of external debt stock of low and middle income country groups in the export of goods and services for the period 1975-2016. The external debt / export ratio of middle income countries rose from around 12% in 1975 to 36% in 2000. In low income countries, the situation is even worse. While the rate of external debt to the exports of goods and services was 20% in low-income countries in 1975 which was the onset of the period, it reached up to around 115% in 1995. The first reason of the increase is the increase in external debt stock and the second reason is the decrease in exports due to external and internal economic crises. The rate which started to fall as of 2000 decreased to 27% in 2012 and was realized as 33% by the end of 2016. Realization of these improvements despite the Global Financial Crisis in 2008 should be viewed as a significant achievement. In accordance with the most basic debt ratios (external debt / GNP, external debt / export), it can be said that the burden of external debt in developing countries followed a moderate course in the 2000s.

Figure 2 indicates the situation of external debt stock in dollar in developing countries. It is seen that external debt stock has continuously increased since the second half of 1970s. A remarkable issue in the period under review is the increase in short-term debt since 2006.

When the debt indicators of low and middle income countries were examined in 2016, which is the latest year whose data was published by International Debt Statistics (2018), it is seen that external debt stocks increased moderately compared to the previous year (4.1%). However; external debt ratios continue to deteriorate. Deterioration in debt indicators partially depends on the growth and decline in

Table 2. Total external debt stocks (% of exports of goods, services and primary income)

	1975	1980	1985	1990	1995	2000	2005	2010	2011	2012	2013	2014	2015	2016
Latin America & Caribbean (excluding high income)	21,4	34,3	57,1	41,4	35,1	36,6	28,6	23,1	23,2	25,4	27,5	30,2	36,2	38,1
Middle East & North Africa (excluding high income)	..	..	..	..	56,1	38,2	25	14,9	12,4	12,4	14,2	14,8	16,3	18,4
Sub-Saharan Africa (excluding high income)	14,8	23,2	51,1	61,9	74,5	62,7	37,5	22,4	22	23,6	24,6	24,4	27,8	31,9
Middle income	12,2	20,3	29,2	31,8	37,2	35,9	26,3	22,5	22,3	23,2	24,8	25,4	24,9	25,9
Low income	20,1	34,6	75,7	81,2	114,4	78,7	61	29,4	27,7	27,3	29,6	29	31,6	33

Source: IDS (2018), International Debt Statistics 2018, The World Bank

Figure 2. External debt stocks in low & middle income countries
Source: IDS (2018), International Debt Statistics 2018, The World Bank

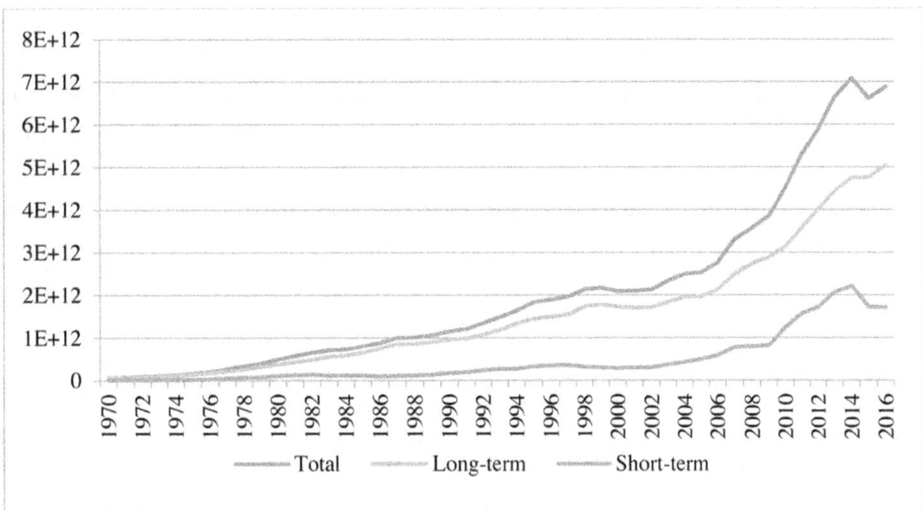

international commodity prices according to the World Bank (2018). 25% of low and middle income countries kept their external debt-GNP ratio above 60% at the end of 2016; and their debt-export ratio exceeded 150% in 44% of these countries (IDS, 2018). Total external debt of low and middle income countries increased by 4.1% in 2016 to about 6.9 trillion dollars (Table 3).

Table 3. External debt indicators (2016)

	Total debt**(millions dolar)	Total debt to GNI (%)	Total debt to export (%)	Reserves to total debt (%)	Debt services to export (%)	Short term debt (millions dolar)	Long term debt (millions dolar)
Low & middle income	6.786.978	26,0	106,7	81,4	14,2	1.709.557	5.052.221
East Asia & Pasific*	2.308.374	17,2	67,6	153,0	7,2	1.013.538	1.277.174
Europe & Central Asia	1.552.544	53,3	168,0	35,7	25,9	216.201	1.276.445
Latin America &Caribbean*	1.740.663	38,1	177,6	42,7	29,5	268.697	1.451.996
Middle East & North Africa*	224.687	18,4	89,1	99,4	8,6	47.374	164.189
South Asia	626.729	21,6	116,8	66,1	16,2	107	504.053
Sub-Saharan Africa*	453.980	31,9	137,1	30,8	11,6	56.752	378.365
Low income	121.291	33,0	160,4	-	8,7	9.948	103.391
Middle income	6.755.687	25,9	106,0	82,4	14,3	1.699.608	4.948.830
Lower middle income	1.774.683	28,6	124,6	46,8	16,9	267.732	1.451.941
Upper middle income	4.981.004	25,0	100,6	95,1	13,5	1.431.877	3.496.890

Source: IDS (2018), International Debt Statistics 2018, The World Bank
*Excluding high income ** Total debt stock is the sum of short and long-term debt plus IMF credit.

The short-term external debt stock, which constitutes about one-fourth of total external debt, remained almost stationary compared to the previous year. Only 9.948 million dollars belong to low income countries while the rest belongs to middle income countries. According to the World Bank's International Debt Statistics, the share of short-term debts in the total debts was 13-14% in 2000 while it reached to 25% with almost a double increase by 2016 (IDS, 2018). This increase in short-term debts actually indicates a risky situation, but it has sometimes been tried to compensated with the increase in reserves.

The View of Globalization in the World

Globalization must be measured - with the help of an indicator - in order to be able to determine its effects on economies analytically. But there is also no standard measure of globalization which is a very complex and multidimensional process without a universally accepted definition. Because it is quite difficult to find an indicator / index that catches all its aspects (Caselli & Gemelli, 2008). Single indicators such as foreign trade openness or financial openness as a percentage of GDP are often used as a proxy for globalization. However, globalization encompasses much more than outward openness and capital movements. It is a process that has social and political aspects as well as economic. For that reason, many composite indicators or indexes have been used to measure globalization in recent years. KOF Globalization Index which is frequently used in literature while examining the state of globalization in the world (see. Pofratke, 2015) and which is also included in the analyses in this study as an indicator of the globalization variable will be used here.

Size of globalization with regard to the regions and the world average is indicated in Figure 3 in accordance with KOF Globalization Index data. Figures 3 and 4 have been prepared by the authors by using data from KOF Globalization Index (KOF, 2018a). Globalization level increased rapidly between 1990 and 2007 across the world; and has been slower since the 2008 Global Financial Crisis. Globalization level indicated a slight decline in 2015 and the global level of globalization declined for the first time since 1975. This decline was due to the decrease in economic globalization; and social globalization remained stable while political globalization slightly rose (KOF, 2018b). As will be noted, the North American countries have had the highest level of globalization from 1970 onwards while the South Asian countries have had the lowest level of globalization. North America, Europe and Central Asia regions are above the world average while Sub-Saharan Africa and South Asia regions are below the world average. In addition, globalization level is almost world average in the Middle East, North Africa, East Asia and Pacific regions (Figure 3). It is clear that globalization has increased by an average of 15-20 points across the world since the 1970s, which was faster in the 1990s than previous years.

Figure 4 indicates the status of globalization level in the countries with different income levels. The chart reveals an interesting situation. Globalization level is the highest in high income countries while it is the lowest in low income groups. This situation also points out the existence of a direct relationship between globalization and income level. Thus, a significant part of the studies in the literature prove that there is a positive relationship between globalization and income level / economic growth (Dreher, 2006; Dreher et al., 2008; Chang & Lee, 2010; Villaverde & Maza, 2011; Chang et al., 2013; Gurgul & Lach, 2014; Hayaloğlu et al., 2015; Türedi, 2016) .

KOF 2018 version of the latest published KOF Globalization Index was calculated for 209 countries as of 2015. Table 4 indicates the situation of several countries taken from the world ranking of globalization. It is seen in Table 4, which only includes the general globalization index of the countries, that European countries rank in the top 10. While USA ranks as the 24th, Turkey ranks as the 47th and Russia ranks as the 56th, such underdeveloped countries as Sudan and Afghanistan take place at the last.

Figure 3. The level of globalization in terms of regions in the World
Source: IDS (2018), International Debt Statistics 2018, The World Bank

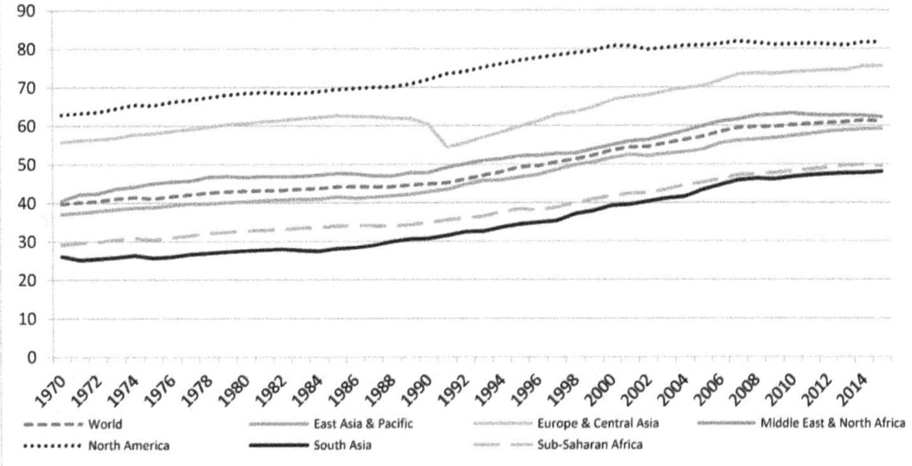

Figure 4. Level of Globalization by Different Income Groups
Source: IDS (2018), International Debt Statistics 2018, The World Bank

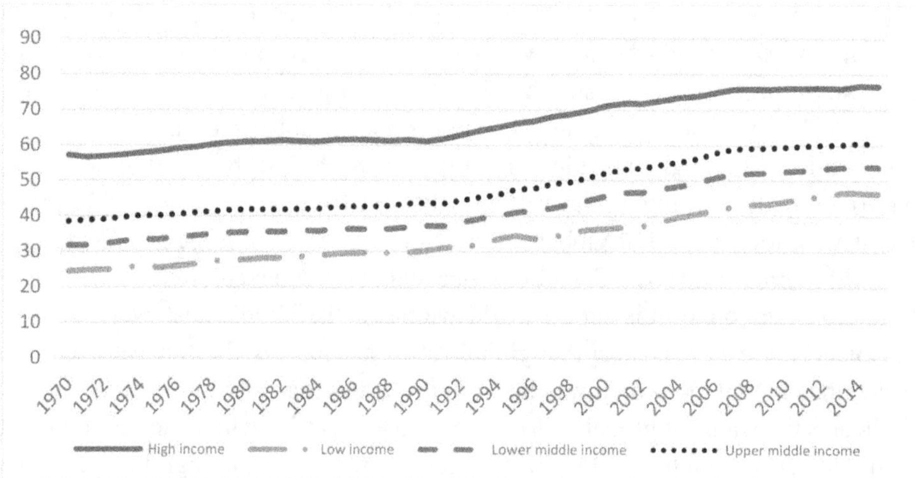

Table 4. KOF globalization ındex country ranking (2015)

Rank	Country	Index	Rank	Country	Indexs
1	Belgium	90,47	23	Singapore	80,01
2	Netherlands	90,24	24	United States	79,95
3	Switzerland	89,70	35	Japan	77,30
4	Sweden	88,05	47	Turkey	70,87
5	Austria	87,91	50	Mexico	70,46
6	Denmark	87,85	56	Russian Federation	69,06
7	France	87,34	87	China	61,23
8	United Kingdom	87,23	83	Indonesia	62,04
9	Germany	86,89	96	Brazil	59,64
10	Finland	85,98	130	Pakistan	51,70
14	Canada	83,45	172	Sudan	41,82

Source: https://www.kof.ethz.ch/en/forecasts-and-indicators/indicators/kof-globalization-index.html (12.04.2018)

MAIN FOCUS OF THE CHAPTER

Date Set and Model

The impact of globalization on foreign debts has been tested for 55 developing countries (indicated in Annex 1) in the period covering 1992-2015. The countries and the data period were determined by the availability of data.

GNP ratio to external debt stock was used as a dependent variable in the study. External debt stock is the amount of debt that can be paid as money, goods or services to non-residents. This amount of debt consists of the sum of public debt, publicly guaranteed debt and non-guaranteed long-term debt of private sector, IMF credits and short-term debt.

In empirical studies examining the relation between globalization and foreign debt, it is seen that such variables as trade and financial openness, direct foreign investments, tariff rates are frequently used to represent globalization. KOF globalization index which has a long time series and various sub-indexes (economic, social and political) was used in this study to represent globalization. We also did not find a study directly analyzing the relationship between KOF Globalization Index, and external debt. KOF Globalization Index was developed by Dreher (2006) and updated by Dreher et al. (2008). The KOF globalization index is published annually by KOF Swiss Economic Institute. The index has measured the globalization level of almost every country in the world on economic, social and political scales since 1970. This is the most widely used globalization index in the literature (Potrafke, 2015). *KOF 2018 version* the most recent KOF Globalization Index published, was calculated for 209 countries covers the period from 1970 to 2015. KOF index has three sub-indexes as economic, social and political as well as one general index. In accordance with KOF 2018 version - unlike previous versions - the weight of each sub-index within the general index is equal to each other and determined as 33.3%. Again unlike previous versions; the economic globalization index is composed of two sub-indexes as trade and financial globalization while social globalization is composed of three sub-indexes as interpersonel globalization, information globalization and cultural globalization. There are 42 variables in total included in KOF general globalization index which is the sum of these sub-indexes. Each of the variables in the index has values between 1 and 100. The lowest level of globalization is indicated by 1 while the highest level of globalization is indicated by 100. The weights used for the calculation of the sub-index are obtained by using the principal components analysis (KOF, 2018a).

Four control variables as economic growth, inflation, domestic savings and population were also used in the study. These variables, which are thought to affect the external debt stock, were decided by considering the literature. Economic growth was included in the model with GDP per capita in dollars, inflation variable was included in the model as GDP deflator, domestic saving variable was included in the model as the ratio of domestic savings to GDP and population was included in the model as the sum of population of the countries in million people. All of these variables are annual and have been obtained from World Development Indicators (WDI).

The variables used in the study and their summary information are indicated in Table 5.

Panel data analysis method was used in this study which analyzes the relationship between globalization and external debt. Panel data analysis is a method of estimating economic relations by using cross-sectional (horizontal or vertical) data having a time dimension (Pazarlioglu & Gurler, 2007, p.37). Therefore; both time series and horizontal cross section data are jointly used in this method as well as creating a data set which contains both dimensions (Gujarati & Porter, 2009, p.59). Stata 14 package program was used in order to perform the analyses. Descriptive statistics related to the data used in the analysis are indicated in Table 6.

Four different models have been estimated to examine the relationship between globalization and external debt in the study. So that, the relationship between the four dimensions of globalization and foreign debts has been examined separately. These dimensions consist of the general KOF Index, which includes all of the sub-indexes, and economic, social and political index. Therefore, we consider the following models:

Table 5. Variables used in model

Variable name	Symbol of the variable	*	Definition		Source
External Debt	Debt	+	Ratio of external debt stock to GNP	%	World Bank (2018)
Per capita income	GDP	-	GDP per capita	$	
Domestic saving	Sav	-	Gross domestic savings to GDP ratio	%	
Inflation	Inf	-	GDP deflator	%	
Population	Pop	-/+	Total population of the country	person	
Overall globalization	Kof	+	Overall globalization index score	Index	KOF (2018c)
Economic globalization	Kofec	+	Economic globalization index score	Index	
Social globalization	Kofsoc	+	Social globalization index score	Index	
Political globalization	Kofpol	+	Political globalization index score	Index	

*Estimate of relationship between external debt and variables.

Table 6. Descriptive statistics

Variables	Mean	Std. Dev.	Min	Max	Obs
Debt	60.29184	63.46053	0	897.9592	1320
Gdp	3051.091	2829.228	138.7168	16007.09	1320
Sav	19.6518	13.53941	-71.82182	60.49045	1320
Inf	45.29965	486.263	-29.69107	15544.38	1320
Pop	7.99e+07	2.25e+08	141925	1.37e+09	1320
Kof	54.85935	10.01822	26.30192	79.61491	1320
Kfec	49.44392	12.04116	16.71884	82.38122	1320
Kfsoc	48.34523	14.07634	13.23182	81.38122	1320
Kfpol	66.01134	18.67257	10.96053	95.31072	1320

$$Debt_{it} = \beta_0 + \beta_1 Gdp_{it} + \beta_2 Sav_{it} + \beta_3 Inf_{it} + \beta_4 Pop_{it} + \beta_5 Kof_{it} + u_{it} \quad (1)$$

$$Debt_{it} = \beta_0 + \beta_1 Gdp_{it} + \beta_2 Sav_{it} + \beta_3 Inf_{it} + \beta_4 Pop_{it} + \beta_5 Kofec_{it} + u_{it} \quad (2)$$

$$Debt_{it} = \beta_0 + \beta_1 Gdp_{it} + \beta_2 Sav_{it} + \beta_3 Inf_{it} + \beta_4 Pop_{it} + \beta_5 Kofsoc_{it} + u_{it} \quad (3)$$

$$Debt_{it} = \beta_0 + \beta_1 Gdp_{it} + \beta_2 Sav_{it} + \beta_3 Inf_{it} + \beta_4 Pop_{it} + \beta_5 Kofpol_{it} + u_{it} \quad (4)$$

$Debt_{it}$, the dependent variable used to represent external debt in all models, shows the ratio of "i" country's external debt stock in year "t" to GNP. Kof_{it}, the independent variable whose relationship with external debts is examined, is the KOF index score indicating the overall level of globalization of "i" country in year "t". Furthermore; economic, social and political globalization levels are also measured as sub-dimensions of globalization in the annual KOF globalization index. In the analysis, the relationship between each sub-index and external debt were examined separately. For this reason, three different models have also been created in which each sub-globalization component is used. $Kofec_{it}$, $Kofsoc_{it}$ and $Kofpol_{it}$, the independent variables in other models (2, 3, and 4), are the KOF index scores indicating, respectively, the level of economic, social and political globalization of country "i" in year "t".

In addition to these variables, the control variables which are mentioned to have an effect on external debt in the theoretical and empirical literature have been included in the analysis for each model.

Among the control variables; Gdp_{it} indicates GDP per capita of "i" country in year "t", Sav_{it} indicates total domestic savings rate of "i" country in year "t", Inf_{it} indicates the inflation rate of "i" country in year "t" and Pop_{it} indicates the total population of "i" country in year "t".

Analysis and Results

The method used in the study is panel data regression analysis. Pooled ordinary least squares (POLS), fixed effects model (FE) and random effects model (RE) which show the combination of data are generally used in panel data. In the POLS model, it is assumed that all parameters are common. In FE and RE models, one-way (OWFE) or two-way (TWFE) effects are modeled. When one-way effects are considered, it is assumed that the parameters of the model change either through horizontal cross-sectional units or over time. In two-way model, it is assumed that the model parameters change both through unit and over time. For this reason, it is necessary to determine the existence of unit and time effect in order to be able to make an estimator selection.

ANOVA F test which tests the existence of the individual effect by comparing POLS and FE models, was performed in the first step. It has been observed that both the unit and time effects are available in the test result. Secondly, Breusch-Pagan Lagrange Multiplier (LM) test was applied to compare POLS and RE models. According to the test results, there is a unique effect of the units but there is no time effect. These two test results indicate that POLS model is inconsistent. Hausman test was performed to determine the consistent model between FE and RE models. According to Hausman test results, H_0 hypothesis suggesting that "difference between the parameters is not systematic" was rejected. Therefore, FE model was identified as a consistent model. The results of these tests are indicated in Table 7.

It is assumed that there is no varying variance, autocorrelation and horizontal cross-sectional dependence in panel data models. Model is consistent and effective under these assumptions. The existence of these assumptions is required to be tested in order to be able to say that we will use a consistent FE model in our study work though it is effective. Modified Wald Test (Greene, 2000) was applied to test the assumption of homoscedasticity in FE model. Since H_0 hypothesis suggesting that "variances are homoscedastic for the units" was rejected as a result of the test, it is accepted that there is a problem of heteroscedasticity. Durbin-Watson and Baltagi-Wu Locally Best Invariant (LBI) tests were applied to test the correctness of the assumption of non-autocorrelation. If the test results are close to 2, it is interpreted as there is no autocorrelation; if it is far from 2, it is interpreted as there is an autocorrelation problem.

Table 7. Tests determining unit and time effect

	Cross section	Time	Both
ANOVA F	13.81 (0.0000)	1.96 (0.0045)	14.87 (0.0000)
LM	1406.20 (0.0000)	0.00 (1.0000)	1510.22 (0.0000)
Hausman	89.11 (0.0000)		

It is seen that there is an autocorrelation in accordance with the test results. Pesaran (2004) CD Test was applied to determine whether there is a correlation between the units. The reason for preferring this test is that it gives more accurate results in case it is N> T (Tatoglu, 2016, p.229). Test results show that there is a correlation between the units. Test results for the econometric assumptions are given in Table 8.

Data for both units and time ara analyzed by using Panel data. The path which is followed by data over time is important because time dimension of data is included in the analysis. For this, the stability of the series needs to be determined. Panel unit root tests can be considered as the first and second generation. First generation unit root tests are used where there is no correlation between horizontal cross-sectional units. Second generation panel unit root tests were developed to solve the problems that might arise due to horizontal cross-section dependency. Since horizontal cross sectional dependency was determined as a result of the tests on econometric assumptions, Pesaran (2003) Unit Root Test which is a second generation unit root test was applied. All series, except for economic globalization, are stable at the level in this regard. It is seen that economic globalization series is not stable at the level but stable at the first difference. Therefore, the first difference of economic globalization was used in the analysis.

As a result of testing the econometric assumptions, it was determined that there is heteroscedasticity, autocorrelation and correlation between the units. Validity of variances and thus standard errors, t and F statistics, R^2 and confidence intervals are affected due to the existence of these problems. For this reason, standard errors were estimated through Prais-Winsten regression to make the necessary correction and resistance. In accordance with panel regression analysis findings in Table 10, all models are significant and R^2 values are between 21% and 26%. In accordance with the results of the analysis, there is a positive significant relationship between the general globalization index (Kof) and the economic globalization index (Kofec) and the external debts at the 1 percent significance level. In this regard, the increase in general globalization level, especially economic globalization level, in developing countries is regarded

Table 8. Diagnostic Test Results

Wald Test	52046.78 (0.0000)
D.W. – Baltagi Wu	0.252522 - 0.55967457
Pesaran (2004) CD	17.753 (0.0000)

Table 9. Panel unit root test (Pesaran 2003)

Variables	Level Values	First Differences
Debt	-3.756 (0.000)	
Gdp	-3.544 (0.000)	
Inf	-11.386 (0.000)	
Sav	-4.310 (0.000)	
Pop	-14.591 (0.000)	
Kof	-3.854 (0.000)	
Kfec	-0.397 (0.346)	-12.437 (0.000)
Kfsoc	-4.079 (0.000)	
Kfpol	-7.506 (0.000)	

as an important reason for increasing foreign debt. Many studies in the sample of developing country in empirical literature (Osuji & Olowolayemo, 1998; Lane, 2000; Zafar & Butt, 2008; Colombo & Longoni, 2009; Zakaria, 2012; Kizilgol & Ipek, 2014; Awan et al., 2015; Bölükbaş, 2016; Al-Fawwaz, 2016; Bölükbaş & Peker, 2017; Akduğan, 2017) have concluded that there is a positive relationship between trade openness and external debts. No relationship could be determined between social (Kofsoc) and political (Kofpol) globalization and external debts.

Table 10. Panel regression estimations (dependent variable: External Debt Stock)

Independent Variables	Model 1	Model 2	Model 3	Model 4
Gdp	-3.15* (0.002)	-1.88*** (0.061)	-2.19** (0.029)	-2.59** (0.010)
Inf	-2.56** (0.010)	-3.83* (0.000)	-2.40** (0.016)	-2.56** (0.011)
Sav	-2.90* (0.004)	-2.99* (0.003)	-3.09* (0.000)	-2.97* (0.003)
Pop	-4.59* (0.000)	-4.45* (0.000)	-3.92* (0.000)	-5.79* (0.000)
Kof	4.92* (0.000)	-	-	-
Kofec D1.	-	2.97* (0.003)	-	-
Kofsoc	-	-	-1.63 (0.104)	-
Kofpol		-	-	0.85 (0.393)
C (fixed term)				
R^2	0.2268	0.2689	0.2163	0.2111
chi2 (28)	411.84 (0.000)	280.26 (0.000)	391.48 (0.000)	368.65 (0.000)
Observations	1540			

(Prais-Winsten regression, correlated panels corrected standard errors: PCSEs)

Note: *, **, ***, The estimated coefficients are statistically significant at 1%, 5% and 10% significance levels, respectively.

A negative and significant relationship has been determined between the control variables used in the analysis and external debt in all models. Accordingly, the increase in per capita income leads to a decrease in external debt. Theoretically, if an economy has more income, it may not require outsourcing and it may reduce borrowing. Barro (1979) theoretically and empirically argued that the temporary increase in the income play a cyclical role on the external debt of the USA. Waheed (2017) concluded that the increase in GDP in the countries which export and import oil reduces external borrowing and this effect is strong. Hajivassiliou (1987), Tiruneh (2004) and Bittencourt (2013) similarly concluded that income per capita or income growth negatively affects foreign debts. On the other hand, a higher income is an indicator of credit rating and may lead to a further increase in the debt stocks of the country after a while as well as leading to much more borrowing. According to Akduğan (2017), GDP per capita has a significant and positive effect on external debt.

The impact of the inflation variable on external debts is negative and significant in all models. There is no theoretical or empirical consensus on the inflation-external debt relationship. Colombo and Longoni (2009) and Waheed (2017) found that inflation positively affects external debt while Assibey-Yeboah and Mohsin (2014) determined that there is a negative relationship.

The impact of savings on external debts is significant and negative in all models in conformity with the theoretical and empirical expectations (Waheed, 2017; Koyuncu & Tekeli, 2010). Moreover, the relationship is very strong (at 1% significance level). The increase in the level of domestic savings will reduce the need for the country's external savings.

Population variable which is available in all models also show a significant and strong negative relationship. The results of theoretical and empirical studies in the literature suggest that population growth prevents economic growth and development (pessimists), increases the growth depending on the circumstances of the countries (optimists) and even that there is no significant and important impact on economic growth (Tekeli & Gunsoy, 2015). Therefore, the impact of population growth on economic growth may be positive, negative or even insignificant (unimportant).

FUTURE RESEARCH DIRECTIONS

In this study, the impacts of globalization on foreign debts have been examined both theoretically and empirically in the sample of developing countries. In this study where KOF globalization index was used to represent globalization in empirical analysis, unlike the previous literature, it has been concluded that general and economic globalization index have a positive impact on external debts in developing countries. It is also clear that much more studies are needed to generalize the results obtained in this study. It is also surprising that there are quite a few studies on globalization-external debt relation although there are numerous studies which analyze globalization and the impacts of globalization on economic growth. For this reason, further studies can be carried out by considering the issues mentioned below:

- Different analysis techniques can be used,
- Separate analyses can be made for short and long term debts,
- Analyses can be made in a single country sample.
- Besides these control variables, other macroeconomic variables which are considered to be effective on external debt can also be analyzed.

- KOF general globalization index and economic, social and political globalization indexes that are its sub-indexes have been used in the study to represent globalization. These sub-indexes also have their own sub-indexes. For example, the sub-indexes of economic globalization are trade and financial globalization. Impacts of economic globalization on external debts can be analyzed in more detail by using these sub-indexes.

CONCLUSION

External borrowing, which is of great importance for both developed and developing countries, is an important tool for countries to achieve their socio-economic goals. Development of financial and economic relations between countries bring out the issue of borrowing as an ordinary method today. Inadequate capital accumulation, oil crisis in 1970s and the heavy outcomes of this crisis led to an increase in foreign borrowing levels of developing countries in their development efforts. In fact, the external financing network established after the Second World War increased the exports of developed industrial countries while expanding the imports of developing countries and also served to increase the level of openness of both sides. Following the 1974 crisis, international banks (mainly US based), IMF and World Bank, in which new functions were constantly imposed, provided loans to these countries which were frequently in a financial bottleneck under a variety of credit terms. These loans enable the country to maintain its openness and also the commitments made by countries in the interest of these loans enable them to remain open through economic policies. In short, when developing countries tried to develop by being opened to foreign countries through foreign trade, capital and foreign exchange deficits led to external borrowing, and external borrowing led to further openness in the economy. The concept previously named as foreign trade, or openness turned into internationalization and finally globalization in the following years. All these developments bring such questions to mind: (i) is there a relationship between globalization and foreign debt? (ii) if there is a relationship between these two variables that are experiencing a simultaneous development, through what mechanisms, how and in which direction does this relationship come about?

In this study, the relationship between external debt and globalization has been examined theoretically and empirically in the sample of developing countries. GNP ratio to external debt stock was used as a dependent variable in the study. Having preferred KOF globalization index as a measure of globalization, the study tests globalization-external debt relationship for 56 developing countries (indicated in Annex 1) during the period 1995-2015. KOF Globalization Index was developed by Dreher (2006) and updated by Dreher et al. (2008). *KOF 2018 version* of the latest published KOF Globalization Index was calculated for 209 countries as of 2015. KOF index has three sub-indexes as economic, social and political as well as one general index.

Four control variables as economic growth, inflation, domestic savings and population were also used in the study. In accordance with the results of the analysis, there is a positive significant relationship between the general globalization index (Kof) and the economic globalization index (Kofec) and the external debts at the 1 percent significance level. In this regard, the increase in general globalization level, especially economic globalization level, in developing countries is regarded as an important reason for increasing foreign debt. Many studies in the empirical literature on developing country sampleOsuji & Surajudeen, 1998; Lane, 2000; Zafar & Butt, 2008; Colombo & Longoni, 2009; Zakaria, 2012;Kizilgol

& Ipek, 2014; Awan, Anjum & Rahim, 2015; Bölükbaş, 2016; Al-Fawwaz, 2016; Bölükbaş & Peker, 2017; Akduğan, 2017) support the results here. The increasingly open economic policies, globalization (with the present discourse) of nation states have led to an increase in their foreign borrowing. It can be said that the magic concept called globalization has made developing countries dependent on external sources rather than helping them to develope.

No relationship has been determined between social and political globalization and external debts. A negative and significant relationship has been determined between the control variables used in the analysis and external debt in all models.

REFERENCES

Akduğan, U. (2017). Türkiye'de dış borç stokunun belirleyicileri. *Business and Economics Research Journal, 8*(2), 183–202.

Al-Fawwaz, T. M. (2016). Determinants of External Debt in Jordan: An Empirical Study (1990–2014). *International Business Research, 9*(7), 116–123.

Assibey-Yeboah, M., & Mohsin, M. (2014). The real effects of inflation in a developing economy with external debt and sovereign risk. *The North American Journal of Economics and Finance, 30*, 40–55. doi:10.1016/j.najef.2014.07.004

Awan, R. U., Anjum, A., & Rahim, S. (2015). An Econometric Analysis of Determinants of External Debt in Pakistan. *British Journal of Economics, Management & Trade, 5*(4), 382–391.

Azzimonti, M., de Francisco, E., & Quadrini, V. (2012). *Financial Globalization and the Rising of Public Debt*. Retrieved March 26, 2018, from http://www-bcf.usc.edu/~quadrini/papers/PDpap.pdf

Barro, R. (1979). On the determination of public debt. *Journal of Political Economy, 87*(5, Part 1), 240–270. doi:10.1086/260807

Baunsgaard, T., & Keen, M. (2005). *Tax revenue and (or?) trade liberalization*. IMF Working Paper No. 2005(112). Washington, DC: IMF.

Bilginoğlu, M. A., & Aysu, A. (2008). Dış Borçların Ekonomik Büyüme Üzerindeki Etkisi: Türkiye Örneği. *Erciyes Üniversitesi İİBF Dergisi, 31*, 1–23.

Bittencourt, M. (2015). Determinants of Government and External Debt: Evidence from the Young Democracies of South America. *Emerging Markets Finance & Trade, 51*(3), 463–472. doi:10.1080/1540496X.2015.1025667

Bölükbaş, M. (2016). The Relationship Between Trade Openness and External Debt in Turkey: A Cointegration Analysis. *Balkan and Near Eastern Journal of Social Sciences, 2*(4).

Bölükbaş, M., & Peker, O. (2017). Ticari Dışa Açıklık ve Dış Ticaret Hadleri Dış Borçlanma Üzerinde Etkili mi? Türkiye İçin Bir Analiz. *Sosyoekonomi, 25*(34), 213–225.

Caliari, A. (2005). The debt-trade connection in debt management initiatives: need for paradigm change. In Debt and Trade: Time to Make the Connections. Dublin, Ireland: Veritas Publication.

Caselli, M., & Gemelli. (2008). Measuring… What? Notes on Some Globalization Indices. In *Regionalisation and the Taming of Globalization*. West Midlands, UK: Academic Press.

Chang, C.P., Berdiev, A.N. & Lee, C.C. (2013), Energy Exports, Globalization and Economic Growth: The Case of South Caucasus, *Economic Modelling*, 33, 333¬ 346.

Chang, C. P., & Lee, C. C. (2010). Globalization and Growth: A Political Economy Analysis for OECD Countries. *Global Economic Review*, *39*(2), 151–173.

Chiminya, A., & Nicolaidou, E. (2015). *An empirical ınvestigation into the determinants of external debt in Sub Saharan Africa*. Biennial Conference of The Economic Society of South Africa, University of Cape Town. Retrieved March 28, 2018, from http://2015.essa.org.za/fullpaper/essa_3098. pdf

Colombo, E., & Longoni, E. (2009). *The Politics of External Debt in Developing Countries*. Working paper series no.176. Retrieved March 13, 2018 http://dems.unimib.it/repec/pdf/mibwpaper176.pdf

DPT. (2000). *Küreselleşme Özel İhtisas Komisyon Raporu. 8. Beş Yıllık Kalkınma Planı*. Ankara: DPT Yayını.

Dreher, A. (2006). Does Globalization Affect Growth? Evidence from a new Index of Globalization. *Applied Economics*, *38*(10), 1091–1110. doi:10.1080/00036840500392078

Dreher, A., Gaston, N., & Martens, P. (2008). *Measuring Globalization-Gauging its Consequences*. New York: Springer.

Evgin, T. (2000). *Dünden Bugüne Dış Borçlarımız*. Ankara: Hazine Müsteşarlığı Matbaası.

Farzin, Y. H. (1988). *The Relationship of External Debt and Growth: Sudan's Experience, 1975-1984*. World Bank Discussion Paper. Retrieved April 16, 2018, from http://documents.worldbank.org/curated/en/534071468776091039/pdf/multi-page.pdf

Griffin, K. B., & Enos, J. L. (1970). Foreign assistance: Objectives and consequences. *Economic Development and Cultural Change*, *18*(3), 313–327. doi:10.1086/450435

Gurgul, H., & Lach, Ł. (2014). Globalization and economic growth: Evidence from two decades of transition in CEE. *Economic Modelling*, *36*, 99–107.

Gygli, S., Haelg, F., & Sturm, J. E. (2018). *The KOF Globalization Index–Revisited*. KOF Working Paper 439. Retrieved March 11, 2018, from https://www.ethz.ch/content/dam/ethz/special-interest/dual/kofdam/documents/Globalization/2018/KOF_Globalization%20Index _Revisited.pdf

Hajivassiliou, V. A. (1987). The external debt repayments problems of LDC's: An econometric model based on panel data. *Journal of Econometrics*, *36*(1-2), 205–230. doi:10.1016/0304-4076(87)90050-9

Hayaloğlu, P., Kalaycı, C., & Artan, S. (2015). Küreselleşme Farklı Gelir Grubundaki Ülkelerde Ekonomik Büyümeyi Nasıl Etkilemektedir? *Eskişehir Osmangazi Üniversitesi İİBF Dergisi*, *10*(1), 119–152.

Heywood, A. (2014). *Küresel Siyaset. (Üçüncü Baskı). (Çev. N. Uslu, H. Özdemir)*. Ankara: Adres Yayınları.

IDS. (2018). *International Debt Statistics 2018*. The World Bank.

IMF. (2005). *IMF Survey, 34*(18).

IMF. (2008). *Globalization: A Brief Overview*. Retrieved February 02, 2018, from https://www.imf.org/external/np/exr/ib/2008/pdf/053008.pdf

Imimole, B., Imoughele, L. E., & Okhuese, M. A. (2014). Determinants and sustainability of external debt in a deregulated economy: A cointegration analysis form Nigeria (1986-2010). *American International Journal of Contemporary Research, 4*(6), 201–214.

Karluk, R. (2009). *Cumhuriyetin İlanından Günümüze Türkiye Ekonomisinde Yapısal Dönüşüm, Tıpkı 12. Baskı*. İstanbul: Beta Yayınları.

Kazgan, G. (1985). *Ekonomide Dışa Açık Büyüme*. İstanbul: Altın Kitaplar Yayınevi.

Khattry, B., & Rao, J. M. (2002). Fiscal Faux Pas? An Analysis of the Revenue Implications of Trade Liberalization. *World Development, 30*, 1431–1444.

Kizilgol, O. A., & Ipek, E. (2014). An Empirical Evaluation of the Relationship between Trade Openness and External Debt: Turkish Case. *International Econometric Review (IER)*, 42-58.

KOF. (2018a). *KOF Globalization Index*. Retrieved May 19, 2018, from https://www.kof.ethz.ch/en/forecasts-and-indicators/indicators/kof-globalization-index.html

KOF. (2018b). *KOF Globalization Index: Globalization Down Worldwide in 2015*. Retrieved May 17, 2018, from https://www.kof.ethz.ch/en/news-and-events/media/press-releases/2018/01/kof-globalization-index-globalization-down-worldwide-in-2015.html

KOF. (2018c). *KOF Globalization Index*. Retrieved May 16, 2018, from https://www.kof.ethz.ch/en/forecasts-and-indicators/indicators/kof-globalization-index.html

Koyuncu, F. T. & Tekeli, S. (2010). 1990 Sonrası Dönemde Türkiye'de Dış Borç Stoku Üzerinde Etkili Olan Ekonomik Faktörlerin Analizi. *Ekonomi Bilimleri Dergisi, 2*(1).

Lane, P. R. (2000). *Empirical perspectives on long-term external debt*. Retrieved March 19, 2018, from http://qed.econ.queensu.ca/pub/students/dunbar/826/4/lane.pdf

Malik, S., Hayat, M. K., & Hayat, M. U. (2010). External debt and economic growth: Empirical evidence from Pakistan. *International Research Journal of Finance and Economics, 44*(44), 1450–2887.

Mcgrew, A. (2010). Globalization and global politics. In J. Baylis, S. Smith, & P. Owens (Eds.), *The Globalization of World Politics: An Introduction to International Relations* (5th ed.; pp. 14-31). Oxford. Retrieved May 13, 2018, from http://www.good-governance-debates.de/wp-content/uploads/2015/03/Globalization-and-global-politics-by-Anthony-McGrew_2010.pdf

Milanovic, B. (2002). *Can We Discern the Effect of Globalization on Income Distribution? Evidence from Household Budget Surveys*. Policy Research Working Paper; No. 2876. World Bank. Retrieved May 17, 2018, from https://openknowledge.worldbank.org/handle/10986/19276

Osuji, L. O., & Olowolayemo, S. O. (1998). The impact of trade liberalization policy on Sub-Saharan African countries' debt burden. *African Economic and Business Review, 1*(2), 59–73.

Öztürk, S., & Özyakışır, D. (2005). Türkiye Ekonomisinde 1980 Sonrası Yaşanan Yapısal Dönüşümlerin GSMH, Dış Ticaret ve Dış Borçlar Bağlamında Teorik Bir Değerlendirmesi. *Mevzuat Dergisi, 94*, 1–20.

Pattillo, C., Poirson, H., & Ricci, L. (2004). External debt and growth: Implications for HIPCs. In *Debt relief for poor countries* (pp. 123–133). London: Palgrave Macmillan. doi:10.1057/9780230522329_6

Pesaran, H. (2004). General Diagnostic Tests for Cross Section Dependence in Panels, University of Cambridge, *Working Paper*, 0435.

Potrafke, N. (2015). The Evidence on Globalization. *World Economy, 38*(3), 509–552.

Seyidoğlu, H. (2015). Uluslararası İktisat Teori, Politika ve Uygulama. İstanbul: Güzem Can Yayınları.

Stiglitz, J. E. (2004). Globalization and Growth in Emerging Countries. *Journal of Policy Modeling, 26*(4), 465–484. doi:10.1016/j.jpolmod.2004.04.010

Stiglitz, J. E. (2015). *Globalization and Its Discontents*. Penguin.

Tatoğlu, F. (2016). *Panel Veri Ekonometrisi Stata Uygulamalı*. İstanbul: Beta Yayınevi.

Tiruneh, M. W. (2004). An empirical investigation into the determinants of external indebtedness. *Prague Economic Papers, 3*(3), 261–277. doi:10.18267/j.pep.242

Türedi, S. (2016). *Küreselleşmenin Ekonomik Büyüme Üzerindeki Etkisi: Gelişmekte Olan Ülkeler İçin Panel Veri Analizi. International Osmaneli Social Sciences Congress, Korkuteli.*

Ulusoy, V. (2016). *Devlet Borçlanması, 9. Baskı*. Trabzon: Umuttepe Yayınları.

Villaverde, J., & Maza, A. (2011). Globalization, Growth and Convergence. *World Economy, 34*(6), 952–997.

Waheed, A. (2017). Determinants of External Debt: A Panel Data Analysis for Oil and Gas Exporting and Importing Countries. *International Journal of Economics and Financial Issues, 7*(1), 234–240.

Ward, H. P., Ricci, L., & Pattillo, C. A. (2002). *External Debt and Growth*. IMF Working Papers 02/69. International Monetary Fund. Retrieved May 11, 2018, from http://www.imf.org/en/Publications/WP/Issues/2016/12/30/External-Debt-and-Growth-15714

Were, M. (2001). The Impact of External Debt on Economic Growth and Private Investment in Kenya: An Emprical Assessment. *Wider Development Conference on Debt Relief*, Helsinki, Finland.

Woo, J. (2003). Economic, Political, and Institutional Determinants of Public Deficits. *Journal of Public Economics, 87*(3-4), 387–426. doi:10.1016/S0047-2727(01)00143-8

World Bank. (2018). *World Development Indicators*. Retrieved from http://databank.worldbank.org/data/source/world-development-indicators

World Bank. (2000). *Beyond Economic Growth: Meeting the Challenges of Global Development*. Author.

WTO. (2003). *Liberalizing Trade and Safeguarding Public Revenues*. Communication from the International Monetary Fund, WT/TF/COH/16.

Zafar, S., & Butt, M. S. (2008). *Impact of Trade Liberalization on External Debt Burden: Econometric Evidence from Pakistan.* MPRA Papers No. 9548, 1-17.

Zakaria, M. (2012). Interlinkages Between Openness and Foreign Debt in Pakistan. *Doğuş Üniversitesi Dergisi, 13*(1), 161–170. doi:10.31671/dogus.2018.122

ADDITIONAL READING

Bremmer, I. (2014). The new rules of globalization. *Harvard Business Review, 92*(1), 103–107.

Crafts, M. N. (2000). Globalization and growth in the twentieth century (No. 0-44). International Monetary Fund.

Hudson, M. (1991). *Trade, development and foreign debt.* Pluto.

Irani, F. N. H. A., & Noruzi, M. R. (2011). Globalization and Challenges; What are the globalization's contemporary issues? *International Journal of Humanities and Social Science, 1*(6).

Kraay, A., & Nehru, V. (2004). *When is External Debt Sustainable?* Washington, DC: World Bank. Retrieved October 26, 2017, from http://siteresources.worldbank.org/INTDEBTDEPT/DataAndStatistics/20263265/When-is-Debt-Sust.pdf

O'rourke, K. H., & Williamson, J. G. (2002). When did globalization begin? *European Review of Economic History, 6*(1), 23–50. doi:10.1017/S1361491602000023

Pattillo, C., & Ricci, L. A. (2011). External debt and growth. *Review of Economics and Institutions, 2*(3), 30. doi:10.5202/rei.v2i3.45

Rodrik, D. (1998). Globalization, social conflict and economic growth. *World Economy, 21*(2), 143–158. doi:10.1111/1467-9701.00124

Rodrik, D. (1998). Has globalization gone too far? *Challenge, 41*(2), 81–94. doi:10.1080/05775132.1998.11472025

Rodrik, D. (2011). *The globalization paradox: democracy and the future of the world economy.* WW Norton & Company.

Rosenberg, J. (2005). Globalization theory: A post mortem. *International Politics, 42*(1), 2–74. doi:10.1057/palgrave.ip.8800098

Sachs, J. D. (1989). Developing Country Debt and Economic Performance. The International Financial System. In Developing Country Debt and Economic Performance, Volume 1: The International Financial System (pp. 12-0). University of Chicago Press.

Scholte, J. A. (2005). *Globalization: A critical introduction.* Macmillan International Higher Education. doi:10.1007/978-0-230-21207-7

United Nations. (2008). Development and Globalization: Facts and Figures, *United Nations Conference on Trade and Development*-2008.

KEY TERMS AND DEFINITIONS

Economic Globalization: Economic globalization refers to the intensification and expansion of mutual economic interactions on the world scale. Economically, three dimensions of globalization—trade, financial, or financial and globalization of production—draw attention.

External Debt: Total external debt is debt owed to nonresidents repayable in currency, goods, or services. It is the sum of public, publicly guaranteed, and private nonguaranteed long-term debt, short-term debt, and use of IMF credit.

External Debt Burden: Total external debt stocks to gross national income. Total external debt is debt owed to nonresidents repayable in currency, goods, or services.

External Debt Service: The external debt to be paid in a certain period is composed of the sum of principal installments and interest.

Globalization: Globalization can be expressed in economic, political, social and cultural spheres as a process in which common values spread across national borders and spread worldwide. However, globalization is a multidimensional concept, and the definitions vary according to which discipline it is.

Trade Openness: Trade openness is an expression of how free or how strictly it is in countries' trade relations with the outside world.

APPENDIX

Table 11. Countries used in the analysis

Albania	Costa Rica	Kazakhstan	Peru
Algeria	Cote d'Ivoire	Kenya	Philippines
Argentina	Dominican Republic	Kyrgyz Republic	Romania
Bangladesh	Ecuador	Lebanon	Russian Federation
Belize	Egypt, Arab Rep.	Malaysia	St. Lucia
Bhutan	El Salvador	Mauritania	Sudan
Bolivia	Gabon	Mauritius	Swaziland
Botswana	Georgia	Mexico	Thailand
Brazil	Ghana	Mongolia	Tunisia
Bulgaria	Guatemala	Morocco	Turkey
Cameroon	Guyana	Nicaragua	Ukraine
China	Honduras	Nigeria	Vietnam
Colombia	India	Pakistan	Yemen, Rep.
Congo, Rep.	Indonesia	Panama	

Chapter 3
Is There a Threshold Effect of Public Debt on Economic Growth?

Seher Gulsah Topuz
Eskisehir Osmangazi University, Turkey

Taner Sekmen
Eskisehir Osmangazi University, Turkey

ABSTRACT

In this chapter, the relationship between public debt and economic growth is examined for OECD countries. In order to determine this relationship, the data between 2002 and 2016 is analyzed using panel threshold regression methods. The findings of the study suggest that the relationship between public debt and economic growth is linear. The public debt threshold is estimated at 99.75% for OECD countries but it is statistically insignificant. While the public debt to GDP ratio is both below and above this threshold, the effect of public debt on economic growth is negative and statistically significant. There is no evidence of the existence of a non-linear relationship between public debt and economic growth. These findings are expected to guide policymakers in the implementation of fiscal policies.

INTRODUCTION

The financial crisis in the United States spread to other countries and turned into a global financial crisis. Following the bailout and financial stimulus packages implemented during the crisis, these developments led to an increase in public debt in the several developed countries. This rapid increase in public debt, called also as debt trap, can have negative reflections on the macroeconomic performance of countries with some factors such as inflation, interest rates and increasing uncertainty. The incorrect policies applied to eliminate this negative economic situation can bring about permanent financial problems. Even though most policy makers have strong belief that high public debt reduces economic growth, the existence and direction of such relationship has been discussed both theoretically and empirically by several economists for a long time.

DOI: 10.4018/978-1-5225-7564-1.ch003

According to the traditional view between debt and growth, while debt increases total demand and output in the short term; it is possible to reduce output in the long-term due to the crowding out effect of debt on capital (Kumar & Woo, 2010, p. 5). Thus, the negative relation between the two variables is explained in the literature by the crowding out effect of debt on investments (Friedman, 1978). On the other hand, this effect is also presented as quite small back-of-the envelope calculations (Panizza & Presbitero, 2013, p. 175). Increase in productive expenditures in countries with high debt-to-GDP ratios causes an increase in the marginal product of the capital and hence interest rates which can have a crowding out effect (Teles & Mussolini, 2014, p. 8). The crowding out effect arises from government's increasing interest rate on debt used by state to finance its expenditures, which makes private sector access to credit difficult. Under these circumstances, it can be said that the increase in public debt will harm economic growth (Diamond, 1965, Gale & Orszag, 2003; Baldacci & Kumar, 2010). There are other alternative channels in the literature that show the negative impact of the debt on economic growth as well as the crowding out effect. The increase in public debt may lead to the formation of an inflationary environment in high-debt countries (Sargent & Wallace, 1981). It can be considered that the negative effect of higher public debt, which increases uncertainty or causes inflation and financial pressure, may be higher (Cochrane, 2011). For this reason, it can be said that debt have a negative effect on the economy in the short-term (Panizza & Presbitero, 2013, p. 177). On the other hand, uncertainty over macroeconomic variables such as high and volatile inflation and interest rates, depending on the level of external borrowing, may give rise to divergent imlications on economic activity. An unstable economic environment reduces the efficiency and productivity of the capital by distorting the effective resource allocation and leads to adverse effects of economic growth (Presbitero, 2006, p. 8). When economic growth and the public-debt relationship are evaluated in the short-term, especially if households assume non-Ricardian behavior and the economic output is far from potential output, fiscal policies can have a temporary positive impact on economic growth through demand-side incentives (Preima et al., 2015, p. 2).

Two different opinions about the effect of public debt on economic growth actually lead to the idea that it may be non-linear as opposed to the generally accepted negative linear relationship between the two variables, and this idea continues to be questioned with increasing interest. Reinhart and Rogoff (2010) study is the main work that increases the interest of economists in questioning the validity of the non-linear relationship with the influence of the economic conditions created financial crisis. The Reinhart and Rogoff's (2010) study, which focuses on determining the long-term macroeconomic effects of high-level public debt and external borrowing, is one of the pioneer work examining the non-linear relationship between public debt and economic growth by calculating the threshold value of public debt. These authors who use comprehensive data set of 44 developed and developing countries prove that the high level of public debt affects negatively economic growth. These findings of the authors indicate that the debt threshold is 90%, and that the public debt stock over this level has a negative impact on economic growth. On the other hand, in the "normal" debt levels, the linkage between public debt and economic growth is founded as not stronger. Reinhart and Rogoff's (2010) study increases curiosity, which is the nonlinear relationship between variables, and researches continue with different samples and methods on the accuracy of the threshold value obtained after this study. The results supporting non-linear relationship between public debt end economic growth are obtained in some studies (Kumar & Woo, 2010; Cecchetti et al.,2011; Chudik et al., 2017; Dreger & Reimers, 2013; Kontbay, 2013; Baum et al., 2013; Gómez-Puig & Rivero, 2015; Checherita-Westphal & Rother, 2012), while it is argued that the linear relationship between public debt end economic growth is valid in other the studies (Eberhardt

& Presbitero, 2015; Calderón & Fuentes, 2013; Teles & Mussolini, 2014; Schclarek, 2004). In addition to these results, there are also studies which suggest that there is no significant relationship between public debt and economic growth (Baglan & Yoldas, 2013) or that the non-linearity may change according to different examples and specifications (Égert, 2015a, 2015b). When we consider all these different results, it is not surprising that economists would continue to investigate the accuracy of the relationship between these variables with great interest.

In this study, the relationship between public debt and economic growth is examined by using 30 OECD countries data of 2002-2016 and Hansen (1999) panel threshold method. This paper attempts to make some modest contribution on ongoing discussion by presenting new evidence in determination of whether the threshold value proposed by Reinhart and Rogoff (2010) is valid and which level of the public debt level affects economic growth. The findings indicate that the public debt threshold is 99,750% in relation to public debt and economic growth, but this estimated threshold is not statistically significant. In other words, there is no regime change in relation to public debt and economic growth. Moreover, above and below this threshold, the impact of public debt on economic growth is statistically significant and negative. Hence, the results of the study do not support the view that the relationship between public debt and economic growth is not linear.

The rest of this paper is organized as follows: The second part is a comprehensive literature review that includes studies focusing on the non-linear relationship between public debt and economic growth. In the third part, methods and data set used in the study are introduced. In the fourth part, findings based on econometric model estimates are presented and the results of the study are discussed in the last part.

LITERATURE REVIEW

After the global financial crisis, the increase in the ratio of public debt in GDP in many countries has attracted attention again to public debt and economic growth relationship. Economists question the existence and direction of the relationship in both short and long terms, and they test the empirical validity of the negative, positive, or non-linear effects of public debt on economic growth on different periods, samples and methods. When the literature is examined, it is possible to evaluate the results obtained from the related studies in three different categories. According to these results, studies can be classified as having a negative relationship, the existence of a non-linear relationship and insignificant relationship between public debt and economic growth or that the direction of the relationship may vary according to the method and data set used.

The Findings on Non-Linear Relationship

The reason why the relationship between public debt and economic growth is frequently questioned in the last period is mainly the interesting when considering the results obtained by Reinhart and Rogoff (2010). The authors analyzed the data from 20 developed and 24 developing countries for 1790-2009 period by using descriptive statistics. Evidence suggests that the relationship between public debt and real GDP growth is not linear and that the public debt threshold is 90%. Economic growth is adversely affected when the share of public debt in GDP exceeds 90%. However, when the public debt is at "normal" levels, it is stated that the relation with economic growth is weak.

There are many studies in the literature that investigate the threshold effect between public debt and growth and argue that there is a non-linear relationship. Kumar and Woo (2010) investigate whether high public debt have any effect on long-term economic growth by using 38 developed and developing country data for the period 1970-2007. Authors who analyze the dynamic growth model by using a set of panel data estimators point out that there is an inverse relationship between initial public debt and economic growth. The negative effect is lower in developed economies than in emerging economies. In addition, evidence supporting non-linear relations is obtained. It is claimed that there is a significant negative relationship especially over 90% of the public debt to GDP ratio. The inverse relationship between the two variables reflects a slowdown in the increase in labor productivity resulting from the decline in investments and the slow growth in capital stock per worker. Caner et al. (2010) estimate a public debt threshold of 77% with a total of 101 developed and developing countries' data for period 1980-2008. The authors use the Hansen (1996, 2000) threshold regression model to determine the public debt threshold value. When the sample is reduced in subsamples with developing countries, the threshold value is estimated at 64%. It is also emphasized that the moderate public debt accelerates the economic growth by encouraging investments and the public debt to GDP ratio above the threshold reduces the economic growth. Pattillo et al. (2011) examine the non-linearity relationship between external debt and economic growth by using a large panel data set covering the period 1969-1998 of 93 developing countries, including Sub-Saharan, Africa, Asia, Latin America and the Middle East. The results show that there is a non-linear relationship between debt and economic growth. After the debt to GDP ratio has risen above 35-40%, the average effect on economic growth is also negative. Although the marginal effect of debt is estimated to be positive at very low debt levels and negative at high levels, it is stressed that it is difficult to determine the threshold level. Cecchetti et al. (2011) examine which debt level have negative effects on economic growth for 18 OECD countries, with the belief that higher levels of debt may damage the economy. Authors who study 1980-2010 period indicate that both private and public debt are obstacles to economic growth, but the threshold values they obtained vary according to different debt indicators. The threshold is about 85% of GDP for public debt, while it is 90% for corporate debt and 85% for household debt.

Another study suggesting that the relationship between public debt and economic growth is not linear are carried out by Checherita-Westphal and Rother (2012) who use data from 12 euro-area countries for the 1970-2008 period. It is revealed that the current public debt level has a detrimental effect on economic growth for many countries. Economic growth reaches its maximum when public debt-to-GDP rises to about 90-100%. The inverted-U relationship between the two variables arises through channels of public investments, private savings and total factor productivity, and public debt can also affect simultaneously economic growth through multiple channels. The relationship between public debt and economic growth are analyzed by Minea and Parent (2012) using the PSTR model for 20 developed economy data for 1980-2009 period. The relationship between public debt and economic growth is negative when public debt-to-GDP ratio is between 90 and 115 percent. The public debt threshold value is estimated at 115% and the increase in public debt below the threshold has a negative effect on economic growth. Unlike other studies, when the public debt to GDP ratio exceeds this threshold, the direction of the relationship turns into positive. Kourtellos et al. (2013) analyze the effect of public debt on economic growth by using the structural threshold regression (STR) model that allows to endogeneity of regressors and threshold variable. The difference of this study lies in the fact that the qualifications of countries' democratic institutions are taken into consideration and democracy is included as a threshold variable. In the study which public debt are included in the Solow growth model, high public debt leads to low economic growth in Low-Democracy regime countries while there is no significant effect of public debt on economic growth in the High-Democracy regime countries. Berke (2016) investigates the impact of public debt on economic growth in EU-13 countries for the period 1970-2011. When dummies are used for 30% and 90%, the effect of public debt on economic growth at public debt levels above 90% is negative but still insignificant.

Another study performed by Chudik et al. (2017) analyzes data for 40 countries and 1965-2010 period by using dynamic panel data models considering cross-sectional dependency error. The results obtained for the entire sample indicate that there is no universally applicable threshold effect. However, when the debt trajectory is considered, a statistically significant threshold effect is obtained in countries with public debt exceeding 50%-60% and it is also stated that the debt trajectory is more important than the public debt-to-GDP ratio for economic growth. In addition, there is a negative relationship between long-term economic growth and rising public debt-to-GDP ratio regardless of the threshold level. Unlike other studies, the effect of public debt on the short run economic growth are examined by Baum et al. (2013). The impact of the debt-to-GDP ratio on the economic growth is positive up to 67% the debt-to-GDP ratio in 12 Euro-Zone countries for the period of 1990-2010. However, it starts to decrease over the this threshold value and gradually loses its statistical significance. If public debt to GDP ratio exceeds 95%, the public debt affects negatively economic activity. Kontbay (2013) uses data from 1970 to 2009 to determine the threshold level of public debt-to-GDP and total external debt-to-GDP ratios in 128 developed and developing countries. it is stated that the public debt to GDP ratio starts to have serious problems if it is over the level of 69% for the high income OECD countries, 47% for middle income countries and 30% for low income countries. The thresholds for total external debt-to-GDP ratios are 80%, 50% and 70%, respectively, in the same group of countries. Total external debt-to-GDP ratios has negative effects on economic growth over these threshold values, but it is statistically insignificant.

As a different study from others, Dreger and Reimers (2013) divide the public debt period into two types, sustainable and unsustainable. Dreger and Reimers (2013) determine that the relationship between economic growth and the public debt to GDP ratio is not linear for 12 Eurozone countries. They also note that sustainable public debt has a positive impact on economic growth and that the negative effect is limited to the Euro zone and nonsustainable public debt.

The Findings on Negative Linear Relationship

On the other hand, there are some studies that suggest a linear relationship between public debt and economic growth. Schclarek (2004) defines the relationship between external debt and economic growth as linear rather than inverted-U. Analyzes based on data from 54 developing countries and 24 industrial countries for the period 1970-2002 suggest that the relationship between public external debt and economic growth is always negative and significant for developing countries. This negative relationship is not robust for industrial countries, and it is also shown that there is no evidence for inverted-U relationship in industrial countries. Afonso and Jalles (2013) who evaluate the relationship between economic growth, productivity and the public debt, use data from 155 countries for period 1970 and 2008. The authors suggest that the debt-to-GDP ratio has a negative relationship with the per capita GDP growth rate for all countries. This result is also valid for the OECD country sub-sample, but a statistically significant relationship can not be reached when the non-linearity relation is tested by adding quadratic-debt-term to the same model. In the analysis using the dummy for the public debt threshold value, countries with a debt to GDP ratio below 30% the grow faster than countries with a debt to GDP ratio over 90%. It is also suggested that the public debt threshold level to is 59% for the whole sample.

Calderón and Fuentes (2013) research the existence of negative relationship between public debt and economic growth by examining Latin America and Caribbean countries for the period 1970-2010.It is indicated that there is a robust negative relationship between the public debt to GDP ratio and economic growth. The study provides evidence for the existence of a non-linear relationship according to the level of development of countries. The authors also state that the negative effect of public debt on economic growth can be reduced by strong institutions, internal policies and outward-oriented policies. Bökemeier and Greiner (2013) examine the relationship between public debt and economic growth with 7 developed countries' dataset covering the period from 1790 to 2012. The authors obtain evidence of the existence of a strong negative relationship in empirical analyzes based on 5, 3, and 1-year time intervals. There is no evidence of nonlinear relationship especially for annual and 5-year growth rates. Pescatori et al. (2014) who can not identify a specific debt threshold assume that the relationship between public debt and economic growth has become rather weak at high debt levels in developed countries. In addition, the debt trajectory affects the relationship between public debt and economic growth, and if a country has a high but declining public debt to GDP ratio, it can achieve similar growth faster as its counterparts.

Teles and Mussolini (2014) using 72 OECD and non-OECD country data for period 1972-2004 argue that the public debt-to-GDP ratio has a nagative affect on economic growth if the model is isolated from productive public expenditures. The reason for this result is seen as the reduction of future generation savings for debt repayment. Eberhardt and Presbitero (2015) analyze 118 countries' data between 1961 and 2012 and mainly focus on the long-term relationship between total public debt and economic growth. It is underscored that countries with high public debt-to-GDP ratios are more likely to have a negative impact on long-term growth performance. While there is evidence of the existence of a negative relationship between countries in the study, no evidence is found for the public debt threshold within countries. It is also shown that there is a complex relationship between public debt and economic growth which is significantly different across the countries. The study of Gómez-Puig and Rivero (2015) focuses on the two-way causality relationship between public debt and economic growth by using the 1980-2013 period data in 11 EMU countries. The study takes into account heterogeneity as well as time-varying nature among the countries. According to Granger causality and endogenous break test results, there are some evidence of negative Granger causality in some countries. In the study where different results are obtained Belgium, Greece, Italy and Netherlands have a negative effect of public debt on economic growth after the endogeneously determined break point and over the public debt threshold ranging from 56% to 103% according to the countries.

The Findings on Different Results

Baglan and Yoldas (2013) who focus on the relationship between public debt and macroeconomic activities, use 20 developed economy data for the period 1954-2008. In the study, it is firstly tested whether the relationship between the public debt and economic growth is linear, but a statistically significant relationship is not found. On the other hand, the public debt threshold value is determined as 18% for 3 and 5 year horizons and 58% for 10 years in the threshold analysis. When the authors classify countries into two groups according to their average public debt to GDP ratio, they find that negative threshold effect emerges for countries with relatively low average public debt to GDP ratios as the public debt to GDP ratios increase towards moderate levels. The GDP growth rate slows in countries with high public debt to GDP ratios as the relative public debt to GDP ratio increases, but no significant threshold effect is observed.

Finally, there are also some papers that the direction of the relationship may vary according to the method and data set used. Égert (2015a) questioned the validity of the relative 90% threshold between public debt and economic growth by using the data set of Reinhart and Rogoff (2010). In the study, it is claimed that the non-linear relationship between two variables is not robust. They also argue that the public debt threshold level could even fall to 20% of GDP and that non-linearity could change with different examples and specifications. Égert (2015b) analyzes the relationship between public debt and economic growth using data from 29 OECD countries for 1960-2010 period in a similar way to other work. When the results obtained are interpreted, they emphasize the difficulty of saying that there is a non-linear relationship between the two variables. It is also suggested that the direction of the relationship is sensitive to factors such as data set and model selection, thus this threshold level may change and the popular result of Reinhart and Rogoff (2010) is not a specific number.

METHOD

The static panel data model developed by Hansen (1999) is used to find the threshold level of government debt. Hansen (1999, p. 347) suggests a prediction for a balanced panel data set $\left\{y_{it}, q_{it}, x_{it} : 1 \le i \le n, 1 \le t \le T\right\}$ i and t represent individual and time respectively. The model with only one possible threshold value is as follows:

$$y_{it} = \mu_i + \beta_1' x_{it} I\left(q_{it} \le \gamma\right) + \beta_2' x_{it} I\left(q_{it} > \gamma\right) + e_{it} \tag{1}$$

where y_{it} is dependent variable, q_{it} is threshold variable and, regressor x_{it} is a *k*-dimensional vector. $I(.)$ is the indicator function and $e_{it} \sim \left(0, \sigma^2\right)$ represents independent and identically distributed *(iid)* error terms. γ is the threshold parameter in the model and the observations are divided into two "regimes" depending on whether q_{it} is larger or smaller than γ. β values are the slope coefficients of the two different regimes. Equation (1) can be rewritten as:

$$y_{it} = \begin{matrix} \mu_i + \beta_1 x_{it} + e_{it},\ q_{it} \le \gamma \\ \mu_i + \beta_2 x_{it} + e_{it},\ q_{it} > \gamma \end{matrix} \tag{2}$$

Furthermore, when $x_{it}\left(\gamma\right) = \begin{pmatrix} x_{it} I\left(q_{it} \le \gamma\right) \\ x_{it} I(q_{it} > \gamma) \end{pmatrix}$ and $\beta = \left(\beta_1' \beta_2'\right)'$, Equation (1) can be written in a different form:

$$y_{it} = \mu_i + \beta' x_{it}\left(\gamma\right) + e_{it} \tag{3}$$

Table 1. Debt and economic growth: summary of the empirical literature

Authors	Period and Method	Country Sample	Direction of Relationships
Reinhart and Rogoff (2010)	1790-2009 Descriptive analysis	20 developed and 24 developing countries	Non-linear Relationship
Kumar and Woo (2010)	1970-2007 Dynamic panel regression	38 advanced and emerging economies	Non-linear Relationship
Caner et al. (2010)	1980-2008 Hansen (1996,2000)	26 developed and 75 developing countries	Non-linear Relationship
Pattillo et al. (2011)	1969-1998 Panel regression	93 developing countries	Non-linear Relationship
Cecchetti et al. (2011)	1980-2010 Hansen (1999)	18 OECD countries	Non-linear Relationship
Checherita-Westphal and Rother (2012)	1970-2008	12 Euro-area countries	Non-linear Relationship
Minea and Parent (2012)	PSTR model 1980-2009	20 advanced economies	Non-linear Relationship
Kourtellos et al. (2013)	1980-1989 1990-1999 2000-2009 Hansen (2000)- Caner and Hansen (2004)	82 countries	Non-linear Relationship
Berke (2016)	1970-2011 Panel regression	EU-13	Non-linear Relationship
Chudik et al. (2017)	1965-2010 ARDL (DL)-Cross-section ARDL (DL)	40 countries	Non-linear Relationship
Baum et al. (2013)	1990-2010 Dynamic- Non-dynamic threshold panel method	12 Euro Area	Non-linear Relationship
Kontbay (2013)	1970-2009 Dynamic panel threshold regressions	128 developed and developing countries	Non-linear Relationship
Dreger and Reimers (2013)	1991-2011 Panel regression	12 Euro area countries	Non-linear Relationship
Schclarek (2004)	1970-2002 Panel regression with System-GMM and Nonlinear effects	59 developing & 24 industrial countries	Negative Linear Relationship
Afonso and Jalles (2013)	1970-2008 Panel regression	155 countries	Negative Linear Relationship
Calderón and Fuentes (2013)	1970-2010 Panel regression	Latin America and Caribbean Countries	Negative Linear Relationship
Bökemeier and Greiner (2013)	1790-2012 Panel regression	7 developed countries	Negative Linear Relationship
Pescatori et al. (2014)	1875-2012 Descriptive analysis	19 advanced Economies	Negative Linear Relationship
Teles and Mussolini (2014)	1972-2004 OLS and 2step GMM process	74 OECD-Non OECD countries	Negative Linear Relationship
Eberhardt and Presbitero (2015)	1961-2012 Dynamic panel regression	118 countries	Negative Linear Relationship
Gómez-Puig and Rivero (2015)	1980-2013 Granger Causality	11 EMU	Negative Linear Relationship
Baglan and Yoldas (2013)	1954-2008 Hansen(1996)	20 advanced economies	Non-linear Relationship Insignificant
Égert (2015a)	1790-2009 Non-linear bivariate threshold models	20 advanced countries	Different Results
Égert (2015b)	1960-2010 Bivariate Linear threshold model	29 OECD countries	Different Results

To eliminate individual effects (μ_i), Hansen (1999, pp. 348-349) suggests to remove individual-specific means. For this, when the average of the equation (1) over the time index *t*, the following expression is obtained:

$$\overline{y}_i = \mu_i + \beta' \overline{x}_i(\gamma) + \overline{e}_i \tag{4}$$

In this equation, $\overline{y}_i = T^{-1}\sum_{t=1}^{T} y_{it}$, $\overline{e}_i = T^{-1}\sum_{t=1}^{T} e_{it}$ and $\overline{x}_i(\gamma) = T^{-1}\sum_{t=1}^{T} x_{it}(\gamma) = \begin{pmatrix} T^{-1}\sum_{t=1}^{T} x_{it} I(q_{it} \le \gamma) \\ T^{-1}\sum_{t=1}^{T} x_{it} I(q_{it} > \gamma) \end{pmatrix}$.

By taking the difference between Equations (3) and (4):

$$y_{it}^{*} = \beta' x_{it}^{*}(\gamma) + e_{it}^{*} \tag{5}$$

where $y_{it}^{*} = y_{it} - \overline{y}_i$, $x_{it}^{*}(\gamma) = x_{it}(\gamma) - \overline{x}_i(\gamma)$ and $e_{it}^{*} = e_{it} - e_{it}$. For any given γ, β can be estimated by ordinary least squares:

$$\hat{\beta}(\gamma) = \left(X^{*}(\gamma)' X^{*}(\gamma)\right)^{-1} X^{*}(\gamma)' Y^{*} \tag{6}$$

The vector of residuals is $\hat{e}^{*}(\gamma) = Y^{*} - X^{*}(\gamma)\hat{\beta}(\gamma)$ and the sum of squared errors is $S_1(\gamma) = \hat{e}^{*}(\gamma)' \hat{e}^{*}(\gamma) = Y^{*\prime}\left(I - X^{*}(\gamma)\left(X^{*}(\gamma)' X^{*}(\gamma)\right)^{-1} X^{*}(\gamma)'\right)Y^{*}$. The least squares estimators of γ is as follows:

$$\hat{\gamma} = arg \min_{\gamma} S_1(\gamma) \tag{7}$$

Finally, the slope coefficient estimate is $\hat{\beta} = \hat{\beta}(\hat{\gamma})$ for $\hat{\gamma}$.) and residual variance is:

$$\hat{\sigma}^2 = \frac{1}{n(T-1)} \hat{e}^{*\prime}\hat{e}^{*} = \frac{1}{n(T-1)} S_1(\hat{\gamma}) \tag{8}$$

The null hypothesis $H_0 : \beta_1 = \beta_2$ shows that there is no threshold effect.

METHODOLOGY AND DATA

The empirical model used to investigate the relationship between government debt and economic growth is as follows:

$$y_{it} = u_i + \beta_1 \hat{D}_{it} I\left(\hat{D}_{it} \le \gamma\right) + \beta_2 \hat{D}_{it} I\left(\gamma < \hat{D}_{it}\right) + \delta X_{it} + \varepsilon_{it} \tag{9}$$

This model is a single threshold model. y_{it} is the dependent variable and it shows *i* country's growth rate of GDP per person at period *t*. ε_{it} is the error term and u_i indicates country-specific fixed effects. $\tilde{D}_{it}$ is the threshold variable and represents government debt. γ represents the threshold parameters for government debt in the single threshold model. Lasty, X_{it} is the vector of control variables and I is the indicator function.

The information and descriptive statistics of all variables used in the study are given in Table 2. According to this information, the highest ratio of government debt to GDP in the OECD countries is 237.95% and the average ratio of government debt to GDP is 71.68%. It can be said that OECD countries have a relatively high public debt-to-GDP ratio. Table 3 demonstrates the correlation coefficients of the variables. The correlation coefficient between public debt and per capita GDP growth rate is statistically significant and negative.

Table 2. Variables and descriptive statistics

Variables	Data Definitions and Sources	Obs.	Mean	Std. Dev.	Min.	Max.
Per capita GDP Growth Rate (y)	Annual percentage growth rate of GDP per capita based on constant 2010 U.S. dollars, OECD Data	210	1.477	3.094	-9.862	16.342
Initial Income *(linpercap)*	The logarithm of the previous period of GDP based on constant 2010 U.S. dollars, OECD Data	210	10.425	0.600	9.043	11.593
Inflation Rate $\left(\pi\right)$	Annual percentage change of consumer price index, OECD Data	210	2.114	1.540	-1.524	9.450
Population Growth *(popg)*	Annual population growth rate, OECD Data	210	0.520	0.718	-1.951	2.793
Investment *(inv)*	Net investment in nonfinancial assets (% of GDP), OECD Data	210	1.633	0.973	0.106	5.400
Trade Openness *(topen)*	Exports of goods and services (constant 2010 US$) plus imports of goods and services (constant 2010 US$) (% of GDP), OECD Data	210	0.964	0.581	0.227	3.751
Government Debt (debt)	General government debt (% of GDP), OECD Data	210	71.682	41.825	7.6	237.95

Note: Data used in the study cover the period between 2002 and 2016 and all data are used with a two-year average. Hansen (1999) model requires balanced panel data. Mexico, New Zealand, Turkey and Iceland do not have enough data for the relevant period. Therefore, after these countries are excluded from the sample, $T = 7$ and $N = 30$ and the number of observations is 210.

Table 3. Correlation matrix

	Y	*linpercap*	*輓fl*	*Popg*	*輓v*	*topen*	*debt*
Y	1.000						
Linpercap	-0.290***	1.000					
輓fl	0.106	-0.404***	1.000				
Popg	-0.166**	0.569***	-0.104	1.000			
輓v	0.103	-0.189**	0.203***	-0.231***	1.000		
Topen	0.111	0.110	0.038	0.122*	0.103	1.000	
Debt	-0.252***	0.146**	-0.389***	-0.153**	-0.067	-0.356***	1.000

Note: ***, ** and * denote significant level of correlation coefficients at %1, %5 ve %10 respectively.

EMPIRICAL RESULTS

In order to determine whether government debt to GDP ratio have a threshold value in relation to public debt and economic growth, model (9) is estimated using least squares estimators. The findings of the single threshold model are shown in Table 4. In Table 4, $\hat{\gamma}$ denotes the threshold value and is estimated as 99.750. Table 4 also shows the F-statistics of the estimated threshold parameters and the boostrapted p-values of these statistics. The F-statistic of the threshold parameter is smaller than the critical values of 1%, 5% and 10%. These findings show that the threshold parameter is statistically insignificant. Therefore, the findings show that there is no threshold relation between public debt and economic growth in the estimated model.

Estimates of the panel threshold regression model of the relationship between public debt and economic growth are given in Table 5. As mentioned earlier, the results in Table 5 are derived from the single threshold model estimates. Table 5 also shows the effects of public debt on economic growth, depending on the public debt threshold value. $\hat{\beta}_1$ and $\hat{\beta}_2$ are coefficients indicating the regime-dependent effect of public debt on economic growth. Estimates of the threshold parameter showed no regime change in relation to public debt and economic growth. This result is also supported by findings on regime coefficients. When we look at the $\hat{\beta}_1$ and $\hat{\beta}_2$ coefficients, it is seen that both have statistically significant and negative sign. Therefore, these findings suggest that public debt negatively and linearly effects economic growth. In other words, this relationship does not change depending on the level of public debt in the model predicted. When we look at the magnitudes of the coefficients that show mar-

Table 4. Threshold estimates

Test for Single Threshold	
$\hat{\gamma}$	99.750
F-Statistic	7.65
p-value	0,420
(%10, %5 ve %1 critical values)	(12.2675), (14.9305), (19.7277)

Note: 1000 bootstrap replications were used for test.

ginal effects, it appears that the negative effect of public debt on economic growth is greater when public debt is below 99,750%. Finally, the effects of the variables that are frequently used in empirical growth literature are controlled in the model. All variables except population growth rate and inflation rate are statistically significant in regression model. The effects of population growth rate and the the inflation rate on the per capita GDP growth rate are negative as expected. On the other hand, the initial income level coefficient is statistically significant and negative. This finding supports the conditional convergence hypothesis, which states that rich countries are growing slowly while poor countries are growing rapidly. Finally, the coefficients of investment and trade openness are positive and statistically significant as expected.

It can be concluded that the results obtained in the study are in line with the traditional view that there is a negative relationship between the public debt and economic growth. However, the results show similarities and differences when compared to previous empirical studies examining the sample of OECD countries. Afonso and Jalles (2013) point out that the relationship between public debt and economic growth for the OECD sub-sample is negative similar to our results, and they do not find a significant relationship when they test non-linear relationships. In addition, Égert (2015b) emphasizes that it is difficult to say that there is a non-linear relationship between two variables according to the results of 29 OECD countries. From this point of view, especially when we examine the studies carried out with

Table 5. Panel regression estimates

Threshold Point Estimate $\left(\hat{\gamma}_1\right)$	99.750
p-value	(0.420)
$\hat{\beta}_1$	-0.066*** (-3.08)
$\hat{\beta}_2$	-0.044*** (-2.63)
Linpercap	-26.013*** (-9.00)
輓fl	-0.283
	(-1.60)
Popg	-1.112 (-1.41)
輓v	1.822*** (3.31)
Topen	7.459*** (3.32)
R^2	0.4505
Number of observations	210

Note: t-statistics of coefficients are in brackets. ***, ** and * denote significant level of regression coefficients at %1, %5 ve %10 respectively.

OECD data, it can be seen that these results, which economists can not find non-linear relations, also support our analysis results. On the other hand, if we assume that OECD countries are mostly developed countries, we can conclude that our results are consistent with Bökemeier and Greiner (2013), which indicate that there is a negative relationship between public debt and growth in developed countries and that there is no mention on the existence of a non-linear relationship. Finally, our results are also consistent with those of Eberhardt and Presbitero (2015), Calderón and Fuentes (2013), and Schclarek (2004), who work with different samples but support a negative relationship.

When the results of the study are evaluated in terms of the threshold level, some of the studies find a threshold value of about 90-100% for the relationship between public debt and economic growth similar to the 99.750% threshold value we have estimated (Reinhart and Rogoff (2010), Cecchetti et al. (2011), Checherita-Westphal and Rother (2012), Kumar and Woo (2010) and Baum at al. (2013)). However, the threshold value that is determined significantly in these studies is separated from our results in this respect.

CONCLUSION

The inspiration of this study is the rapidly rising public debt to GDP ratios in many countries following the 2008 financial crisis. The rapid rise in public debt to GDP ratios has created serious concerns for the future macroeconomic conditions of the countries and it has been emphasized that it may cause negative effects on capital growth and economic growth due to rising inflation, interest rates and instability. The validity of these theoretically discussed effects by economists has been questioned empirically for years. The study of Reinhart and Rogoff (2010) based on a large historical database has led to reexamination of the public debt and economic growth relationship in the years after the crisis. However, the emergence of many studies supporting or criticizing this study suggests that there is no consensus on the direction of relationship and threshold level.

In this study, it is aimed to examine whether the public debt have a threshold effect on the economic growth with Hansen (1999) panel threshold method. Data from 30 OECD countries covering the years 2002-2016 are used for this purpose. The public debt threshold level is determined as 99.75% for public debt and economic growth relationship. However, this threshold value is statistically insignificant, and public debt has a negative effect on economic growth above and below this threshold level. Thus, the findings show that there is a linear negative relationship between public debt and economic growth, and that there is no evidence of non-linear relationship. The results of this study are similar to the results of the Afonso and Jalles (2013) study, which fails to determine a public debt threshold for the relevant sample in relation to public debt and economic growth, and therefore suggests that the relationship is linearly negative. Moreover, our results are parallel to the views that Bökemeier and Greiner (2013) advocate a strong negative relationship in developed countries and Égert (2015b) stated that it is very difficult to prove that it is a non-linear relationship.

Many studies in the literature investigate the validity of the threshold value at the level of 90% determined by Reinhart and Rogoff (2010). The threshold value of 99.75% determined in our study can be said that it is at similar level in Cecchetti et al. (2011), Checherita-Westphal and Rother (2012), Kumar and Woo (2010) and Baum et al. (2013), but it is not statistically significant. When evaluated in this respect, our findings are different from studies pointing the existence of non-linear relations in the literature.

As a result, the findings of the research do not support the results of Reinhart and Rogoff (2010) for OECD countries. On the contrary, it shows that there is a negative relationship between public debt and economic growth. The views on the crowding out effect in the theoretical literature may explain why the negative relationship may have emerged in our study. The increase in interest rates crowd out private investments and affect the economy negatively. On the other hand, it can be said that effective resource allocation can not be achieved and economic growth is negatively affected due to the inflationary environment, low level of market confidence and uncertainty conditions in the high debt levels.

Kumar and Woo (2010) emphasize that the negative relationship between these two variables reflects a slowdown in the increase in labor productivity resulting from a slowdown in investment and slow growth in capital stock per worker. Therefore, governments should implement appropriate fiscal policies that will not increase the public debt to GDP ratio regardless of the level of debt in the context of negative relationship. When all these results are evaluated together, it can be said that the 90% threshold value which is commonly referred to in the literature is not a magic and generally accepted number. Similarly, Panzer and Presbitero (2014) highlight that the threshold effect is not as strong as thought. It can therefore be concluded that it is still difficult to make clear interpretations for this relationship in which different results are obtained when examined with different samples and methods.

REFERENCES

Afonso, A., & Jalles, J. T. (2013). Growth and productivity: The role of government debt. *International Review of Economics & Finance*, *25*, 384–407. doi:10.1016/j.iref.2012.07.004

Baglan, D., & Yoldas, E. (2013). *Government debt and macroeconomic activity: a predictive analysis for advanced economies.* Board of Governors of the Federal Reserve System.

Baum, A., Checherita-Westphal, C., & Rother, P. (2013). Debt and growth: New evidence for the euro area. *Journal of International Money and Finance*, *32*, 809–821. doi:10.1016/j.jimonfin.2012.07.004

Berke, B. (2016). Avrupa Birligi'nde Kamu Borç Stokunun Ekonomik Büyümeye Etkisi: Panel Veri Analizi. *Sosyoekonomi*, *24*(27), 121. doi:10.17233e.12580

Bökemeier, B., & Greiner, A. (2015). On the relation between public debt and economic growth: An empirical investigation. *Economics and Business Letters*, *4*(4), 137–150.

Calderón, C., & Fuentes, J. R. (2013). *Government debt and economic growth.* Inter-American Development Bank, IDB-WP-424.

Caner, M., Grennes, T. J., & Köhler-Geib, F. F. N. (2010). Finding the tipping point-when sovereign debt turns bad. The World Bank.

Caner, M., & Hansen, B. E. (2004). Instrumental variable estimation of a threshold model. *Econometric Theory*, *20*(5), 813–843. doi:10.1017/S0266466604205011

Cecchetti, S. G., Mohanty, M. S., & Zampolli, F. (2011). The real effects of debt. Bank for International Settlements, 352.

Chalk, N., & Tanzi, V. (2002). *Impact of large public debt on growth in the EU. The Behaviour of Fiscal Authorities*. Basingstoke, UK: Palgrave.

Checherita-Westphal, C., & Rother, P. (2012). The Impact of High Government Debt on Economic Growth and Its Channels: An Empirical Investigation for the Euro Area. *European Economic Review*, *56*(7), 1392–1405. doi:10.1016/j.euroecorev.2012.06.007

Chudik, A., Mohaddes, K., Pesaran, M. H., & Raissi, M. (2017). Is there a debt-threshold effect on output growth? *The Review of Economics and Statistics*, *99*(1), 135–150. doi:10.1162/REST_a_00593

Cochrane, J. H. (2011). Understanding Policy in the Great Recession: Some Unpleasant Fiscal Arithmetic. *European Economic Review*, *55*(1), 2–30. doi:10.1016/j.euroecorev.2010.11.002

Diamond, P. A. (1965). National debt in a neoclassical growth model. *The American Economic Review*, 1126–1150.

Dreger, C., & Reimers, H. E. (2013). Does euro area membership affect the relation between GDP growth and public debt? *Journal of Macroeconomics*, *38*, 481–486. doi:10.1016/j.jmacro.2013.07.012

Eberhardt, M., & Presbitero, A. F. (2015). Public debt and growth: Heterogeneity and non-linearity. *Journal of International Economics*, *97*(1), 45–58. doi:10.1016/j.jinteco.2015.04.005

Égert, B. (2015a). The 90% public debt threshold: The rise and fall of a stylized fact. *Applied Economics*, *47*(34-35), 3756–3770. doi:10.1080/00036846.2015.1021463

Égert, B. (2015b). Public debt, economic growth and nonlinear effects: Myth or reality? *Journal of Macroeconomics*, *43*, 226–238. doi:10.1016/j.jmacro.2014.11.006

Friedman, B. M. (1978). Crowding Out or Crowding in? The Economic Consequences of Financing Government Deficits. *NBER Working Paper*, w0284.

Gómez-Puig, M., & Sosvilla-Rivero, S. (2015). The causal relationship between debt and growth in EMU countries. *Journal of Policy Modeling*, *37*(6), 974–989. doi:10.1016/j.jpolmod.2015.09.004

Hansen, B. E. (1996). Inference when a nuisance parameter is not identified under the null hypothesis. *Econometrica*, *64*(2), 413–430. doi:10.2307/2171789

Hansen, B. E. (1999). Threshold Effects in Non-Dynamic Panels: Estimating, Testing and Inference. *Journal of Econometrics*, *93*(2), 345–368. doi:10.1016/S0304-4076(99)00025-1

Hansen, B. E. (2000). Sample splitting and threshold estimation. *Econometrica*, *68*(3), 575–603. doi:10.1111/1468-0262.00124

Kontbay, S. (2013). *Growth beyond the debt threshold* (Doctoral dissertation). Clemson University.

Kourtellos, A., Stengos, T., & Tan, C. M. (2013). The effect of public debt on growth in multiple regimes. *Journal of Macroeconomics*, *38*, 35–43. doi:10.1016/j.jmacro.2013.08.023

Kumar, M., & Woo, J. (2010). Public debt and growth. *IMF Working Paper*, 10/174.

Minea, A., & Parent, A. (2012). Is high public debt always harmful to economic growth? Reinhart and Rogoff and some complex nonlinearities. *CERDI, Etudes et Documents*, E 2012.18.

Panizza, U., & Presbitero, A. F. (2013). Public debt and economic growth in advanced economies: A survey. *Schweizerische Zeitschrift für Volkswirtschaft und Statistik, 149*(2), 175–204.

Pattillo, C., & Ricci, L. A. (2011). External debt and growth. *Review of Economics and Institutions, 2*(3), 30. doi:10.5202/rei.v2i3.45

Pereima, J. B., Merki, M., & Correia, F. M. (2015). *Economic growth and public debt: Addressing unobserved heterogeneity*. Retrieved from https://www.anpec.org.br/encontro/2015/submissao/files_I/i6-4a0181c0d6c126116a0d2a88269dca48.pdf

Pescatori, A., Sandri, D., & Simon, J. (2014). Debt and growth: Is there a magic threshold? *IMF Working Paper*, 14/34.

Presbitero, A. F. (2006). The debt-growth nexus: A dynamic panel data estimation. *Rivista İtaliana Degli Economisti, 11*(3), 417–462.

Reinhart, C. M., & Rogoff, K. S. (2010). Growth in a Time of Debt. *The American Economic Review, 100*(2), 573–578. doi:10.1257/aer.100.2.573

Schclarek, A. (2004). Debt and economic growth in developing and industrial countries. *Lund University Department of Economics Working Paper, 2005*, 34.

Teles, V. K., & Mussolini, C. C. (2014). Public debt and the limits of fiscal policy to increase economic growth. *European Economic Review, 66*, 1–15. doi:10.1016/j.euroecorev.2013.11.003

Chapter 4
New Labor Dynamics of Global Public Finance System

Hakan Ulucan
Independent Researcher, Turkey

ABSTRACT

This chapter examines the effects of structural adjustment programs designed under the supervision of IMF and World Bank on labor markets. These leading financial institutions are part of global financial system and they finance countries. In return, the countries satisfy the requirements imposed by IMF and World Bank. The requirements imposed by IMF and World Bank includes devastating measures for labor market, including privatization, deregulation of labor market, and flexibilization. There is convincing evidence that structural adjustment programs slowdown economic growth so hurts employment. Besides, the labor markets started to be constituted by unsafe work places without rules as a result of deregulations and flexibilizations. Most of the workers lost social security and workplace security. Feminization, child labor, increasing work incidents are the main severe results of the policies designed under pressure of IMF and World Bank on labor market.

INTRODUCTION

The leading global financial institutions, International Monetary Fund and World Bank, have so much power on the public finance system on the countries. The effect of the institutions has increased since 1980s with the new globalization era. The effects of these institutions came into process via structural adjustment programs designed by these institutions. IMF and World Bank lend to countries having economic difficulties. IMF and World Bank lending includes a conditionality. This conditionality imposes some specific measures and budget cuts to countries in return of the IMF or World Bank loans opened for them. Countries borrow from IMF and pay back not only with the amount they borrowed. They also implement the specific measures in agenda given by IMF. This process and its details have made capital gains more than labor. In other words, labor is the loser of this process.

DOI: 10.4018/978-1-5225-7564-1.ch004

The labor is marginalized ideologically in this process. The labor has been started to be analyzed as the total of individuals whose function is only to carry out their tasks in their workplaces (Ulucan, 2017). This means that the term labor has been isolated and separated from its human characteristic. Besides, labor has been announced as harmful for the other pieces of the economic system. The benefits of the labor have been implied as harmful for the interests of society in the literature and in the media. This belief manipulated the public as if the satisfaction of the needs of labor can harm the economic growth and development. The terms such as minimum wage, labor union, and social security have been regarded as negative factors for economy. Minimum wages and unions have been announced as the main causes of low level of investment. Low growth rates are declared to be the results of non-flexible labor markets. Unemployment has only been evaluated by reading numbers and rates, losing humanitarian perspective on the issue (see Stiglitz, 2002.)

On the other hand, flexibilization of labor, de-unionization, and deregulations of the labor market have been used as tools to marginalize the labor in the economies. The main results of this new trend are reduced security of the labor, increase in informal employment, feminization, the use of child labor, increasing work accidents. The new trend open ways for exploiting the labor. Deregulation process has abolished the rules and legislations on relations between employers and workers. The flexibilization has made the market so flexible that even child labor is easily employed with ignorable wages.

IMF and World Bank services policies serves to abolish the obstacles against the process summarized above. They accelerated this process by forcing their structural adjustment programs including harmful measures for workers. The countries passed these reforms without operating democratic process. The consequences of these policies are deindustrialization, unemployment, feminization, child labor, increasing number of work accidents.

STRUCTURAL ADJUSTMENT PROGRAMS AND LABOR

The Effect of Structural Adjustment Programs on Growth and Employment

There are direct and indirect effects of structural adjustment programs on labor. Structural adjustment programs influence macroeconomic variables and so employment. This effect can be regarded as indirect because it works via the channel of main macroeconomic variables. The growth rates is one of the most important variables related with employment.

There is convincing evidence that IMF programs hurt economic growth and labor. Vreeland (2000) present one of the studies indicating a negative relationship between growth rates and structural adjustment programs. According to this study, the slowdown of economic growth is accompanied by reduction of labor share in manufacturing industry in the countries under IMF program. This fact also explains why IMF programs are chosen by countries at the expense of reduction of economic growth. Capital gains more than labor under these policies. This means that poorer groups loses but richer groups are getting richer under such policies.

The methodology of Vreeland (2000) corrects the selection problem by using Heckman's selection correction approach for the data set of countries. The selection problem occurs because the countries choosing to enter into an IMF program are different from those that didn't apply an IMF program. An estimation ignoring these differences provides biased results. Vreeland's correct this problem and finds out that IMF programs deteriorate the income of workers. The share of capital is increased by the programs however growth rates become also lower. This means that even capital can lose in the long run due to lower growth rates under structural adjustment programs.

The Effect of Structural Adjustment Programs on Labor Rights

What is the source of the deterioration of economic power of labor in the countries applying IMF programs? This question is tried to be answered at this point. Blanton et al. (2015) suggest that IMF and World Bank programs harms labor rights in the countries under their effects. The policy reforms recommended by these institutions deteriorate labor institutions in the countries. One other effect is that the labor protective laws or regulations are taken out of agenda step by step in the countries exposed to the programs. Blanton et al. (2015) show this effect by using a panel data set consisting of 123 countries and the years from 1985 to 2002. These econometric findings show that the impact of these institution on the labor rights are significantly negative.

The negative effects on the labor rights are normally expected to be more negative for the countries with low democratic standards. In the countries with lower development level of democracy, the worker parts of the society have difficulties to announce their claims. Caraway et al. (2002) show that IMF and World Bank take into account the democracy level of the countries in their policy design and recommendation for the countries. They design more harmful policies for the labor in the countries with lower democracy level while they recommend more relaxed policies for labor for the countries with higher democratic standards.

Abouharb and Cincgarelly (2007) suggest that structural adjustment policies generally produce a negative impact on poorer parts of the society. One of the reason is privatization of public services imposed by structural adjustment policies. The government implementing these policies privatized health care, education, and water. This drastic privatization results in significant layoffs. The programs impose the governments to cut or even eliminate subsidies for farming, education, health care, and water.

These programs also impose flexible labor policies. These policies cause deterioration off worker rights and working conditions. Abouharb and Cingarelly (2007) suggest that The World Bank's public position on the importance of protecting worker rights has essential contradictions. To illustrate, Abouharb and Cingarelly (2007) show that the Bank's World Development research in 2006 accepts the importance of worker rights for more equal economic development. The report also accepts the importance of labor unions in ensuring sustainable economic development. World Bank in this report even accepts that labor unions promotes productivity increases by reducing labor turnover. Nevertheless, at the same time, the Bank announce the opposite position in important annual reports named. These reports provide the details of the policies. The World Bank presents ranking to each country in the reports. Countries without minimum wage and rules about the number of hours a worker can work are ranked as top countries. This view also contradicts with ILO rules encouraging countries to implement a minimum wage. This also contradicts with suggestion of ILO of regulation of hours of work and to enforcement of laws protecting freedom of association and collective bargaining by promoting labor unions. Abouharb and Cingarelly (2007) also show that the structural adjustment programs reduce the respect for worker rights, especially the rights of public sector workers, female workers, and low wage workers, in developing countries applying these programs. These workers faced the real wage reductions under the environment of increases in costs of living.

Evaluations of Structural Adjustment Programs and Their Consequences

One other issue relating with the results of structural adjustment programs is "deindustrialization". Stein (1992) shows that IMF and World Bank models deindustrialize the countries under their programs. The programs reduced the share of manufacturing sector in favor of service sectors. This produces another harmful impact on the labor. This is because of the nature of the production of the manufacturing and the service sectors. The production process in the manufacturing sector takes longer time and are discriminated into sub-processes. Each process needs a specialization of the worker increasing the importance of the labor in the sector. On the other hand the process in the service sector is simpler. The production of the service is instantaneous. This results in short term contracts with workers in the service sector. In some services, daily contracts are observed. Labor is deprived of security under this process.

IMF and World Bank cannot be separated from new globalization era started in 1980s. Trade liberalization is one of the first phenomena of the era. The economic models of IMF and World Bank also support trade liberalization. The important question at this point is "What was the effect of trade liberalization on deindustrialization?" Shafaeddin (2005) shows that the effect of trade liberalization has adverse effects on manufacturing sector especially for the low and middle income countries in Africa and Latin America. Only in minority of the countries in East Asia, the performance of manufacturing sector was improved. Majority of the developing countries were deindustrialized. There was a shift from the developing industries to the sectors with static comparative advantage. These sectors were generally resource based and labor intensive sectors with low added value. As a result, these countries were stuck in the vicious cycle of underdevelopment and middle income trap. The globalization and institutions plays similar roles within a country and the world. In a country, these policies make poor parts of the society poorer. In the world, the make poor countries poorer, at least put poor countries in middle income trap.

Figure 1. Manufacturing employment in the world
Source: Statistics and Databases of ILO

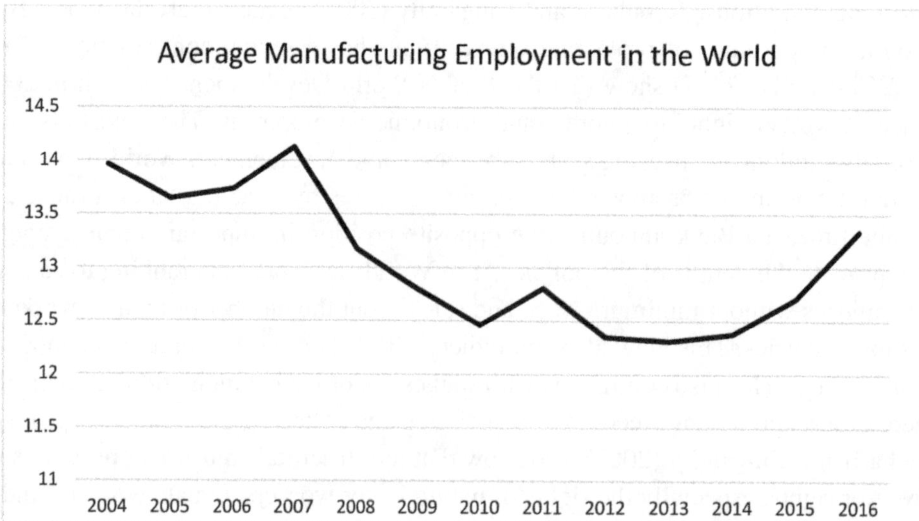

One another factor causing the reduction of manufacturing sector is financilization (see Yeldan, 2002). Financialization process initiated and stimulated by the IMF and World Bank policies. Figure 1 presents manufacturing employment share in total employment in the World. The world experienced a reduction in manufacturing employment while manufacturing employment was also decreasing in the developing countries.

The adverse effect on labor is also clear when the poverty and income distribution indicators of the countries applying structural adjustment programs of the IMF and World Bank. Oberdabernig (2010) analyzes the effects of IMF structural adjustment programs on poverty and income distribution indicators of 94 countries from the years from 1982 to 2009. In the countries under structural adjustment programs, the poverty gaps get widened. Gini coefficients show that income distribution gets worsened. Oberdabernig also shows that the adverse effects are also permanent in the long run.

One other feature of the IMF programs is that they ignore the employment in their programs. Stiglitz (2002) suggestsCha that, In East Asia crisis of 1998, IMF insisted on monetary and fiscal tightening. The result was the increase of the adverse effects of the crisis. Stiglitz also suggests that IMF programs are not successful in job creation. The main result of the programs is unemployment. Unemployment triggers social chaos. Social chaos scares foreign and domestic investors. The country fails to attract investment. The low investment levels result in high unemployment levels. This story is a vicious cycle faced by the countries applying IMF programs. Indonesia was one of the countries which can be seen as example to this story according to Stiglitz.

Stiglitz (2002) shows that the measures in capital the market in this trend were aimed at ensuring the capital mobility. They argues that the taxation of capital harms capital mobility. This policy can be regarded as two faced because in this trend no one from these institutions insisted on taking measures for labor market mobility. The advocates of capitalism always talk about free movement of production factors but they generally mean capital by production factor when they talk about mobility. The mobility of labor is left behind capital as shown by data about migration.

Vaidya (2006) demonstrates the amount of migration in closer time period. 75 million people, 2,3 percent of the World's population, migrated in 1965. 84 million people migrated in 1975. This is 2,1% percent of the World's population. 2,2 percent of the World's population, 105 million people migrated ten years later. In 2000, the number reached to 175 million and the share in World population was 2,9 percent. The number will be 230 million according to the forecasts, 2,6 percent of the World population in 2050 (Vaidya, 2006). Well known rhetoric of supporters of globalism is that it allows free movement of the factors between countries. This rhetoric is true for financial capital and intermediary goods. However the free mobility of the labor is limited as can also be seen from the numbers of migration (see Ulucan, 2017).

Clauwaert and Schömann (2012) suggest that drastic measures are imposed by structural adjustment programs was about working time and atypical employment. The working time was increased. The limit of overtime was increased by from 25% to 50% in Hungary, and the measures was based on argument that these measures would be permanent and they are designed only as measure against crisis. In design of laws, the democratic procedures were bypassed. Another example is Lithuania, overtime was not previously allowed by labor laws in Lithuania. In this process, firstly the regulation about overtime is liberalized and overtime is introduced. In Portugal, overtime payments were decreased by the reforms. The increase in working time decreased health of the workers. These changes made work places riskier.

The other measures were for atypical employment. These measures allowed labor contract with lower social security contribution. The reforms decreased the social security of the workers under these type of contracts according to Clauwaert and Schömann (2012).

Deregulations, flexibilizations of the labor market was cost sided measures favoring capitalists. IMF and World Bank models impose these measures to the countries. The deregulations created labor markets without rules. The cost reduction became most important motivation in the markets. As a result, in some labor intensive sectors, women are started to be preferred over men, to make further cost reductions. This phenomenon is mostly observed in informal sectors. The women employed in these sectors are those who wanted to add extra income to her household. Therefore, these women can be convinced for very low wage levels. Makoba (2010) uses feminization in a negative meaning for women to define this trend. Makoba explains that female labor is exploited to reduce costs of labor. Feminization is a practice in which women's are more chosen mainly in low skilled jobs since they can be made consent to wage levels under minimum standards more easily than male workers since they see their work as not primary one but as a modest support to income of their families. Feminization is mostly used in export-led sectors in which the reduction of costs possesses significant importance in competition. The share of females in textile sector in developing countries confirms the argument of Makoba.

Feminization is not only one tool as a result of the global policies promoted by IMF and World Bank to reduce costs of production. Besides, child labor started to be used more often in the production to diminish the cost of labor in an environment of deregulations. Child labor has become a permanent and severe problem in developing and underdeveloped countries. There are about 170 million child workers in the World according to the study of International Labor Organization (ILO) (2013). ILO states that almost half of them works in unsafe jobs in unsafe work places. Asia and pacific are the leading areas with highest number of child workers. There are about 80 million child workers in this region. This region is followed by Sub-Saharan Africa follows Asia and pacific with about 60 million child workers. Latin America and Caribbean regions with 13 million and 9,2 million child workers are the other regions respectively. Agriculture sector is the sector with highest share of child workers in sectoral composition of child workers. The problem in Services and Industry should also be taken into account. About 100 million child workers are employed in the agriculture while 54 million and 12 million child workers are employed in service sectors and in industry respectively (ILO, 2013).

As clear, the destructive cost of globalization process accelerated by IMF and World Bank doesn't only include the exploitation of the females in the production but also the use of children in the production process. Another indicator that should be demonstrated to assess the consequences of the structural adjustment programs on the labor market is the vulnerable employment data. ILO (2013) evaluates vulnerable employment as total individuals who are self-employed, unpaid family workers, and the workers without social security. Vulnerable employment also related with informal sector employment because it includes informal sector workers. ILO (2013) reports that the increase in the vulnerable employment was drastic in 2000s. The number of people who have vulnerable employment was about 1,5 billion at the beginning of 2000s. The number has increased to level above 1.5 billion since then. Although the share of vulnerable employment decreased in 2010s due to the increase in population, the absolute number is so high that the World's socio-economic system can be regarded as fragile.

Solutions and Recommendations on the Effects on Labor

The adverse consequences caused by the IMF structural adjustment programs and World Bank Policies calls for reevaluation of policies for labor market. The consequences show that the policies stimulated by IMF and World Bank causes unsustainable results. A new demand sided perspective should be developed in redesign of labor markets. The policies of the global institutions are also harmful for economic growth. Although the policies increased relative share of capital income, these policies can even be harmful for capital in the long run by reducing the growth rates of the economy. The new demand sided perspective should be designed in a perspective that both labor and capital works in a cohesion. The increase in wages would increase the aggregate demands for the goods by increasing the profit levels. The labor friendly policies can also increase the productivity in the long run. The laws against labor can push capital to laziness since it makes it easier to make profit by extorting the surplus produced by labor. On the other hand capitalists search for the ways to increase the productivity in a labor protective environment. Therefore labor friendly policies make the economy gains in the long run.

COMMENTS ON FUTURE DEVELOPMENTS

The future prospects should deal with the consequences of Industry 4.0. Globalism initiated with the first industrial revolution. So far, there have been 4 industrial revolutions. The first industrial revolution is started by exploration of the machines with steam power in production and transportation. The second industrial revolution is shaped by transition into Fordism as a new production method. The third industrial revolution is the digital revolution of computers and software. The fourth industrial revolution (industry 4.0) is the shift to substitute robots for humans in production.

Globalism cannot be separated from these revolutions. World experienced two great globalism eras and one globalism explosion in the past two centuries, as Williamson (2005) argues. The first era ended as a result of First World War and the second one started with the end of Second World War according to his study. His study also suggests that the period between these two is a period which can be regarded as opposite of globalization. Studies analyzing the winners and losers of the globalization eras, the studies generally emphasize on the income equalities between countries and income inequalities within countries. The studies in the literature reported a drastic divergence among income levels of countries. This inequality among countries are so dramatic that the most of the overall income inequality can mostly be explained by income inequality between countries (Williamson, 2005).

In a very close future, the globalism process will be determined by fourth industrial revolution. The revolution which just started currently in developed countries will also affect the developing countries in a close future. The future developments will base on the industry 4.0. The new industrial revolution will make human share some jobs with machines. In this environment policies should be aimed at increasing employment. Tightening policies on labor cannot be solution in the environment of industry 4.0. Therefore existing IMF and World Bank programs may even produce more severe labor market outcomes in the future, unless a reform will be handled in their programs taking into account the labor friendly policies.

CONCLUSION

This chapter shows that IMF and World Bank policies have destructive effects on labor market by imposing deregulations of labor market, privatizations, and flexibilization. These destructive effects are deindustrialization, lost of worker rights, the reduction in the real wages, feminization, child labor, and work accidents. The chapter also demonstrated that have reduced social security and safety of jobs. The argument of this study is that the overall impact of IMF and World Bank Policies on labor market is negative. Public sector workers, disadvantaged groups suffered from negative effects. The negative effects are not only the result of direct policies on the labor market. Labor is also harmed by IMF and World Bank Policies via the negative effect of the structural adjustment programs on growth rate and labor market. Therefore, a reevaluation of the IMF and World Bank policies is a requirement. Devastating effects on the labor market make it impossible to continue with the existing view on labor market.

REFERENCES

Abouharb, M. R., & Cingranelli, D. (2007). *Human rights and structural adjustment*. Cambridge University Press.

Blanton, R. G., Blanton, S. L., & Peksen, D. (2015). The impact of IMF and World Bank programs on labor rights. *Political Research Quarterly*, *68*(2), 324–336. doi:10.1177/1065912915578462

Caraway, T. L., Rickard, S. J., & Anner, M. S.. (2012). International negotiations and domestic politics: The case of IMF labor market conditionality. *International Organization*, *66*(1), 27–61. doi:10.1017/S0020818311000348

Clauwaert, S., & Schömann, I. (2012). The crisis and national labour law reforms: A mapping exercise. *European Labour Law Journal*, *3*(1), 54–69. doi:10.1177/201395251200300105

ILO. (2013). *Informal economy and decent work, A policy guide supporting transitions to formality*. International Labor Organization.

Makoba, J. W. (2010). Globalization and Marginalization of Labor: Focus on Sub-Saharan Africa. In Globalization in the 21st Century (pp. 87-112). Palgrave Macmillan US.

Oberdabernig, D. A. (2013). Revisiting the effects of IMF programs on poverty and inequality. *World Development*, *46*, 113–142. doi:10.1016/j.worlddev.2013.01.033

Shafaeddin, M. S. (2005). Trade liberalization and economic reform in developing countries. *The IMF. World Bank and Policy Reform*, *155*, 2–20.

Stein, H. (1992). Deindustrialization, adjustment, the World Bank and the IMF in Africa. *World Development*, *20*(1), 83–95. doi:10.1016/0305-750X(92)90138-L

Stiglitz, J. E. (2002). Employment, social justice and societal well-being. *International Labour Review*, *141*(1-2), 9–29. doi:10.1111/j.1564-913X.2002.tb00229.x

Ulucan, H. (2017). Destructive Effects of the Globalism on the Labor Market: Some Observations on the World and Turkey. Lambert Academic Publishing.

Vaidya, A. K. (2006). *Globalization: encyclopedia of trade, labor, and politics* (Vol. 1). Abc-clio.

Vreeland, J. R. (2002). The effect of IMF programs on labor. *World Development*, *30*(1), 121–139. doi:10.1016/S0305-750X(01)00101-2

Williamson, J. G. (2005). Winners and losers over two centuries of globalization. In *Wider perspectives on global development. Palgrave Macmillan UK.*

Yeldan, E. (2002). *Neoliberal Küreselleşme İdeolojisinin Kalkınma Söylemi Üzerine Değerlendirmeler*. Praksis.

Chapter 5
The Local Government Economics in Globalization Process

Berkan Karagöz
Bozok University, Turkey

ABSTRACT

The global economic and social actors are restructuring both private production and public production patterns. This change process is called globalization. The globalization process brings new opportunities with it. One of these opportunities is to increase the efficiency of the local government economics in public finance. The processes of globalization and localization are twin processes and are progressing simultaneously. With globalization, international capital wants to minimize the nation state and to communicate with local governments themselves. In this context, becoming a member of a local government gets ahead of being a nation-state citizen. In the globalization process, existing public goods productions are trying to simulate the market. Such efforts require the public economy to adapt to the market and such adaptation is characteristic of the local government economics itself. International capital, on the other hand, sees central government as a force to be overcome and wants to establish first-hand commercial relations with the local units.

INTRODUCTION

In the study, the globalization and decentralization relations and the increasing prevalence of The Local Government Economics in this process are examined. The Local Government Economics have new roles and new functions to be introduced in the globalization process. The Globalization of production and capital causes redefinition of competition, changes competition conditions and the most important, foresees the establishment of competition in the public economy. This structure, which means the establishment of relations between the spatial units, leads to a growing tendency of the Local Government Economics within the Public Economics. The globalization and decentralization redefine the way it perceives the place, processes and relationships in the place. The boundary concept, the key concept of

DOI: 10.4018/978-1-5225-7564-1.ch005

the spatial paradigm is dimmed and the local units rise to the primary level in the form of perception of the place because the concept of border has ceased to exist. One of the most important factors shaping local governments is, of course, gaining global dimensions of economic and technological conditions.

The attitude towards the phenomenon of globalization varies from person to person and even from time to time. There are those who perceive globalization as a positive and inevitable process, at any cost. In the second group tend not to see this phenomenon alone as inevitable, but at the same time tend to see the encouragement as a process that needs to take place. In the last group argue that the harmful consequences of globalization are outweighing their benefits. In the context of Turkey, as a result of the intense influence of the mass media in general it seems to be in the majority in the first set.

THE GLOBALIZATION AND DECENTRALIZATION PROCESS

The Globalization and Decentralization are complementary concepts. In this context, *the Globalization* can be defined as the integration of national markets. Especially, the capital flows are the main determinant in the definition of the globalization process. On the other hand, the concept of space is redefined by the new conditions that arise. In the process of globalization, where the concept of border and the limitations have lost importance, the local government structures have easy mobility instead of cumbersome nation-state structures is a more effective and useful unit in terms of the capital flows. The capital must provide its fluidity within the national borders. This brings the process called as *the Decentralization* to the agenda. There is a new mechanism that the entire system defines with the units (Harvey, 1999). The units foresee a new social structure advocating the local identity.

Along with the globalization, the main economic actor is the local units. New production and capital patterns are based on the character of flexible production organization (Hirst and Zeitlin, 1991) and the flexible production organization characterization brings together decentralization. The flexible manufacturing is organized to be able to respond to fluctuations in demand around the world and variable needs for products (Lipietz, 1986). The aim is to sustain profitability. In addition, international production should be able to keep the production process open to change and to adapt local labor to this process. International capital, on the other hand, is seeking more income by increasing its fluidity.

Decentralization refers to the formation of units that effectively utilize their own capacities and facilities and which can be incorporated into the international trade system and the world trade system (Eraydın, 2001, pp. 369).

While the globalization has accelerated with the aim of overcoming the borders of the nation state and increasing trade and capital flows, the flexibility in production and new division of labor has led to the emergence of local features and localized new production structures. For this reason, the globalization and decentralization are not two opposing tendencies, but complementary processes.

Decentralization implies the rediscovery of local identities and the use of local potential (Cooke, 1989). The regions and cities competitions in the platform of the country and the world, these qualities and identities are invaluable as an advantage. For this reason, the local units, which are defined as part of the nation and the whole nation within the national identity promoted during the development periods of the nation states, rediscover their local identities in order to participate in the process of globalization and to be advantageous in this process (Stöhr, 1990). The local culture and local characteristics are now an important element of competitive advantage. Thus, localization, the autonomization of local units and the identification of local identities gain importance as a driving element of the globalization process, and these two processes do not evolve counter to each other but complement each other in the dialectical framework (Eraydın, 2001, pp. 370).

With the globalization, central administration's administrative tutelage on local governments is minimized and public authorities are regulated in favor of local governments taking into account the priority. The arrangement of public authorities in favor of local governments is accompanied by a greater share of local government units in intergovernmental revenue distribution and it brings the flexibility of movement in terms of local units in a certain frame. In other words, the globalization means reducing the qualifications of central government, giving priority to local units in administrative and financial direction.

There are also unfavorable opinions about the combination of globalization and decentralization. Because, There are a lot of scientific studies on the events of globalization and decentralization and it is not possible for the problems brought by the globalization, which is strongly emphasized in these studies, to come from its superior at the local level. Therefore, an accurate argument for the link between globalization and fiscal decentralization based on uncertainty and risk understanding is required (Kovancılar, Miynat and Bursalıoğlu, 2007, pp. 109).

Local governments, which are competent in financial terms with the localization, have to cooperate with the central government and international organizations in resolving the economic and environmental problems brought by the globalization. Despite the local autonomy of struggling with global problems, local elements are inadequate to fight alone (Kovancılar, Miynat and Bursalıoğlu, 2007, pp. 110).

When the issue is approached in terms of public expenditures, which are the main determinant of decentralization and centralization, data shows that in terms of public expenditures, decentralization and centralization differ from country to country. While countries with strong federal structures such as Australia and Canada are centralizing expenditures, some countries have shifted a significant share of public expenditure to local governments. This is especially the case in Latin American countries. (Kovancılar, Miynat and Bursalıoğlu, 2007, pp. 111). In the post-1980 period, with the wave of globalization, decentralization has increased in some countries, while some countries have become more centralized despite globalization. The countries whose administrative structure is largely centralized are becoming more localized with globalization, while countries based on the local, regional or state system are more centralized in the globalization process. This development has resulted in greater growth of the public, especially in the developing countries, with fiscal decentralization.

THE LOCAL UNITS AND GLOBALIZATION

Joints of the Local Units to the Global System

It is not a natural outcome that local units take part in globalization, but local units must show special efforts (Eraydın, 2001, pp. 371-373):

1. The structural characteristics of local units that are important in the world system are production and communication potentials, identities and competitiveness.
2. External conditions are also important for local units to participate in the global system. It is necessary to be in the right structure at the right time and to apply the right strategy. The characteristics of other competitors, the contest rules, the regulation mechanisms, the politics, the technological

structure, the human and changing value judgments, the changing expectations of human as a consumer are external conditions.

3. It is important to establish a governance system that should be formed with the participation of the right actors.
4. It must be the best in a branch by specializing in a different branch from the others (the strategy of differentiation)
5. It is necessary to achieve superiority by providing the cheapest conditions for different uses (the low-price strategy)
6. It is necessary to have inventiveness and creativity capacity and to develop solidarity networks.
7. It is important to be a knowledge city.
8. It is necessary to provide easy adaptation to changing conditions and technological structure.

The centers where global capital accumulation is concentrated and the global system is controlled are global local units. These local centers are units where specialized services are financed, production is carried out in the predecessor industrial sectors, and innovation movements are found. Apart from that, there are national local units trying to join the global system. These local units try to join the global system either with information capacities, creative capacities, or by building up technological know-how. Apart from that, there are local units trying to adapt to the global system by experiencing structural transformation, specializing in specific areas, gaining the characteristic of cheap labor area. The local units, which do not have a certain competitive power and become increasingly isolated in the way of new competition, can not be integrated into the global system.

The competition between cities means that cities compete with other cities by using their skills they possess and develop with their economic and social accumulation. According to the World Bank (1999), trends in the 21st century are the tendencies of competition and decentralization between cities. The competition between cities refers to a process in which differences are transformed into flourishes, where superiority and inadequacies are taken into consideration. In the process, the local resources should be mobilized by developing local specialization, entrepreneurship, innovation policies.

In order to be able to take place in the top row among cities, it is necessary to focus on high-skilled and high-income jobs, ecofriendly services and goods production, products and services with the desired characteristics in production, economic growth rate to reach full employment, the areas where the city is specialized will be determined according to the potential of the city and the city should be found to have a potential to rise to the top in the existing urban hierarchy (Kara, 2008, pp. 17). On the other hand, the main factors affecting the success in competitiveness are the existence of forward-looking civilian leadership, the flexibility of the workforce, a public sector that can respond quickly to developments, an effective public-private partnership and an environment suitable for entrepreneurship (Kara, 2008, pp. 17). The cities attracting mobile investments in wealth-generating sectors; attracting public resources; attracting big events, organizations and investments; attracting European Union funds; strengthen local brands and attracting quality population that are superior to each other (Lever, 1999, pp. 1029).

Opponents of the neoliberal policy approach, however, argue that different policies are at the basis of these proposed policies. According to them, the strengthening of local governments is aimed to establish a direct relationship between these units and the global market. It is argued that local governments will be transformed into easy-to-manage units for reasons such as the low competitiveness of local governments in the global arena and the lack of opportunities to resist demands and pressures of international capital. Local governments that are so weak and powerless but seemingly equipped with authority will not be able to go beyond being a market for global capital. Moreover, local governments will be used as tools to overcome the congestion in certain sectors, especially in finance and construction (Güler, 1996, pp. 156).

Effects of International Capital on the Nation State

The new strategy of production and capital finds itself in a more minimal state definition (Ohmae, 1990). The state is a form of technology paradigm that prioritizes economies of scale, accumulation regime supported by mass production, and regulatory mechanisms guaranteeing demand (Jessop, 1990). This definition of the state has moved away from seeing the state as the main unit with tendencies emerging as the new accumulation regime, the globalization of production and the prominence of the individual. The concept of nation-state is losing its meaning as changed the meaning of social order, production system, and also sources of accumulation. The power of government institutions, political elites and bureaucrats is weakened with the change.

The capital movements are the subject of which the state is in the most conflict with new conditions. One of the main functions of the nation state is to control capital movements and to prevent the capital from escaping from the country, while new production and accumulation process makes flexibility in this respect compulsory (Eraydın, 2001, pp. 368). In this context, the legitimacy of the nation-state has become questionable. The new production organization and international capital wants the dissolution of nation-states. The rules of the economic units under the nation-state instead of the rules set on a higher scale, in other words, the rules set by the nation-state, is desired to be raised to the primary position. For benefiting from the state's subsidy mechanisms, it is difficult to absorb this situation. Again, especially for local production units with international competition, national regulations are unfavorable for their development. It is also clear that the development strategies of the local units themselves will conflict with regulation such as high-level economic targets, decisions and sometimes resource transfer obligations.

According to Keleş (2001), the argument that the internationalization of capital movements, which have acquired new qualities negatively affects the nation-state is correct, but in some ways it is exaggerated. Because decentralization is not a secret vehicle or weapon that distorts the national integrity of the countries. Second, it is unlikely to see anybody of the state objecting to foreign capital, the investment of multinational partnerships in the country and the receipt of foreign loans. However, the reduction of the public sector has come to the agenda with the globalization. The assignment or sale of public services by private companies is the direct result of the globalization. According to Keleş (2001), the real impact of globalization has seen on the identities of cities, the quality of urban services, environmental values and urban infrastructure. Since the globalization, at any cost, means that the fluidity of the capital and ensuring free movement, that all obstacles which prevent to overcome to this aim has been on the agenda of globalization.

The sum of the interests of individuals, private entrepreneurs, capital owners has emerged a new public interest. In terms of the presentation of public goods, there is no longer a possibility to provide co-ordination from the center, but instead local mechanisms where co-ordination can be provided spontaneously are needed. In addition, it is also clear that central governments will no longer be able to take their decisions according to their own preferences and according to their specific criteria. Indeed, the dimensions of nation-states have remained largely inadequate for the solution of small problems and for the resolution of large problems. For this reason, when economic logic necessitates the globalization and the regional integration, political and administrative logic necessitates governments to be governed in smaller pieces (Keleş, 2001, pp. 573).

According to Proud'homme (1994), the granting of some powers to local governments will neutralize functions such as ensuring fair distribution of income, eliminating regional inequalities, and ensuring macroeconomic stability which are in the hands of central governments. An also according to Ohmae (1990), economies no longer have a notable nationality and the task of national managerial agents at the global level is to fulfill the tasks that global economies demand from them at the local level. In other words, only global corporations and global market forces have a say in the world economy and they show tendency in favor of decentralization. According to Kazgan (2005) the transformation of local governments into powerless units in the face of international capital and institutions also implies the innerly erosion of the nation-state aristocracy.

According to Stiglitz (2002), the IMF, the World Bank and the WTO, three global organizations governing globalization dominate the global scene. These organizations' programs do not respect centrality in administration but they recommend policies and steps for decentralization as the contraction of the state, that the public withdraw from certain, that the public transfer their functions to the private sector and the privatization of public economic organizations (Güler, 1996, pp. 143).

The dominant discourses of these organizations have been democratization, privatization and decentralization. To develop local governments as the closest organizations to the public and making it more autonomous is at the head of the values that the industrialized western countries share and strive to excellently. The suggestions of these organizations on localization are considered as the main reason for accelerating the decentralization tendencies of the globalization process (Cenikli, 2010, pp. 11).

According to Cenikli (2010), the decentralization phenomenon needs to be evaluated differently in terms of developing and developed countries. In some countries, the management mantra has changed as a natural process because some basic values such as local democracy, participation, and productivity mentalities have spontaneously evolved. But in some countries, this change is seen as a necessity for adaptation to developed countries. These two separate approaches lead to a different assessment of the cause of the decentralization movements coming with the new structuring. So some writers view decentralization as an extension of the development process of local democracy and globalization, while some authors describe it as an imposition of western hegemony.

The globalization refers to a process formed by the combination of complex structures. This process involves the transfer of sovereignty from the hands of local communities to the global arena and worries that the nations will lose some of the strength that they had in the past (Cenikli, 2010, pp. 16). International capital movements have brought the model of the local state based on the individual rather than the big, gigantic, harsh, interventionist, traditional state model.

Adaptation of the Public Economy to the Market

The concept of the local unit, which compete with all the cities and regions in the world and try to gain competitive power, is in a state of confrontation. It is indicated that in the traditional competitiveness discussions, the situation of the production factors, the conditions of the demand, the status of the related and supporting units, the strategies and structural features of the units (firm) and the human resource, capital and technology provide relative advantages. The elements that define the competitiveness of local units are local values, culture, economic structures and institutions. In fact, local units do not compete; competitiveness is realized by the companies and individuals involved in these. For this reason, there is a need for regulatory mechanisms to create an environment in which locational units can create a common strategy and synergistic effects.

The adaptation of the public economy to the market involves the inclusion of the competition system in the public economy and is based on creating a market-like mechanism based on competition in the public economy. The competition in the public economy refers to a race mechanism between the local public goods producer units in the public goods and services market. The competition system in the public economy is a market-like structure established between the public goods producer units at the same level to provide efficiency in resource allocation. The existence of a competitive environment depends on the ability of local producers of public goods to freely make financial and economic decisions. Only local units in the public economy can make public production under competitive conditions and the competition can force individuals to clarify demand (Stiglitz, 2000, pp. 736).

The aim of competition in the public economy is to maximize the welfare of individuals. The competition in the public sector brings together the whole of the taxpayer, consumer and voter roles. The competition allows public goods production to be produced with less cost. The establishment of a competitive environment in the public economy necessitates adapting the market model to the public economy. The adaptation depends on the establishment of regulations called "fiscal decentralization" that recognize the freedom of movement for local governments. It is insistently argued that the prices of the public goods are determined according to the market rules and all of the cost is beared by the local users (Keleş, 2001, pp. 565).

The adaptation of the public economy to the market is based on the state model of fiscal change. It is argued that the model of fiscal change offers a narrow view of the local units as a mere public producer unit rather than a necessary and integral part of the democratic system. The model of fiscal change is the construction of a market-based public economy. However, it is criticized as a socially weak model as it assumes no public roots and items. Because it provides a mechanical analysis of the public economy (Bailey, 1999, pp. 15). A public economic plane, completely isolated from institutional factors, may not be consistent with reality. For this reason, the model of the fiscal change and the state model of the Public Choice Theory should be synthesized. According to second generation theories, thanks to competitive territories the incentives for lower transaction costs and reliable promises are emerging and there is a state model that protects the market (Weingast, 1995, pp. 25). The state model that protects the market is the state model in which the political systems of the countries are at a minimum level of damage to the private and public markets (Karabacak, 2012, pp. 390).

In the Public Economics, the competition founded between local public goods producers is called as the horizontal competition. The horizontal competition; describes the competition between public units with equal financial and administrative power (Dileyici and Vural, 2006, pp. 160). The greater the number of local units in a given geographic area, the possibility of choosing between alternative local units' increases. The horizontal competition can be realized more easily in smaller countries than in countries with larger geographical areas. The optimal average population measure required to live in an administrative region is also important for the horizontal competition (Triesman, 2002, pp. 12).

The level of competition between local public goods producer units depends on the structure of local units, local autonomy and the size of transfers from the center (Boyne, 1996). First, the local units must be quite large and small. Policies that should be made in favor of median voting in very large local units may be exchanged for the economic rent expectation of the monopoly public entity, which sees rents. Second, the level of the local autonomy affects the mobility of local units and the quality and quality of public production. Third, transfer size affects the level of competition between local units. The over-transfer can cause financial illusion and it is difficult to make comparisons with other local units since the actual cost of local public production is not clear and the over-transfer ceases to function of tax-price mechanism. The over-transfer, on the other hand, will negatively affect the immigration mechanism, which is the most important element of competition between local public goods producers.

The free market mechanism under perfect competition is an optimal mechanism in terms of economic efficiency (Durmuş, 2008, pp. 33). The Pareto efficiency will also be provided since profit maximization is assumed to be the most cost-effective method of production for consumers who move with motivation, and consumers who act with the goal of maximizing utility are considered to optimally divide their budgets. When all assumptions of the perfect competition model are valid and income distribution data is taken, Pareto optimality will be provided through the invisible hand of the market without the need of any planner (Durmuş, 2008, pp. 43).

There is a similarity between the decentralization model and a competitive market (Oates, 1985: 749; Oates, 2006: 23). The construction of competitive governments in the public economy can be done by borrowing some institutions of the private market by the public economy and internalizing them in accordance with their own structure. The most important of the institutions that need to be borrowed from the private market here is the atomic which is one of the basic conditions of the perfect competition market envisaged in neoclassical microeconomic theory. This is because the atomistic producer units correspond to local public goods producers in the public economics. Unlike private markets, it is easier to realize the atomic rule in the public economy, and for some reasons it may not happen in practice as it is in special markets. This may be due to the existence of only a limited number of competent local authorities in a given geographical area, due to the presence of local units of different sizes for reasons like the economic development or excessive migration.

Tiebout's work on local public goods in 1956 has an important place in the analysis of competition in the local government economics. In his work, Tiebout claimed that under certain assumptions, the person who is identified as consumer-voter would be carried by the administrative units that best fit his preferences for public goods and taxation (Tiebout, 1956). The local units will be able to create a mechanism similar to the special market shopping mechanism in the public economy, producing local public goods / tax packages and moving the local mass to produce the local public goods / tax package appropriate for the consumer-voter. In the private market, the person who shows preference by purchasing the private good will increasingly prefer to be the one where public goods are produced in the public economy.

Through the Tiebout hypothesis, which is described in the literature as "voting by feet", individuals can effectively demonstrate their preferences for the local public goods. Therefore, Tiebout's theory can overcome the ambiguity of the demand for public goods with local presentation. Tiebout has developed this hypothesis as a solution to the problem that individuals will not reveal their own preferences in the consumption of public goods put forward by Samuelson (Oates, 2006, pp. 22). This theory constitutes a supporting argument for the production of local public goods and services rather than the production of central public goods and services (Cullis & Jones, 1998, pp. 303). The Tiebout effect further increases the welfare gain from fiscal decentralization (Cullis & Jones, 1998, pp. 297; Oates, 1999, pp. 1124). The Tiebout hypothesis is based on voter-consumer behavior. Because, at the basis of the thesis of fiscal federalism, the area of interest between voters and managers is getting closer.

The Tiebout model is a hypothesis that maximizes consumer-electoral prosperity by means of moving within the available resources. On the other hand, it is a more comprehensive hypothesis than Oates' decentralization theorem. The Tiebout hypothesis helps developing policies that promote migration and residential movements to increase resource efficiency and policies that enable voters-consumers to become more informed about the level of local public goods production. The Tiebout hypothesis poses many challenges to be tested, and testing some is very difficult (Bailey, 1999, pp. 64):

1. A large number of competing local units further increase consumer-voter welfare.
2. Numerous local units within the same metropolitan area cause racing at a high level.
3. Many competing local units cause to form more homogenous communities.
4. Local taxes and expenditures affect settlement mobility.
5. The migration motif is explained by the fact that the local units have different tax-public service packages.
6. The level of tax and public service is reflected on property values.

The Tiebout hypothesis is a hypothesis that can only allow you to choose between options. The taxpayer-voter must be supported by decentralization theorem in order to be able to be included in the description of the preference, and the incomplete side of the hypothesis must be restored (Bailey, 1999, pp. 68).

The Privatization of Local Public Goods

The supporters of globalization advocate the privatization of local public goods production without distinction between domestic and foreign firms. The local government economics is shaping itself in this direction. In this direction, the dependency on the international financial markets affects the quality and price of local public goods. While new public administration focuses on privatization, performance measurement and customer service, public actors in the new concept of public goods production regard the private sector as an actor in service provision but it takes into account the demands and expectations of citizens as well as the implementation and management of market mechanisms by public services in private sector contracts (Perry, 2006, pp. 3).

The privatization is the transfer of all or part of the property of public assets to private enterprises. On the other hand, the privatization is implemented in the form of participation in the local services, which are described as public services, by the private sector with some methods. Along with privatization practices, the deregulation policies that require the state to withdraw from positions that affect market actors' decision-making processes and the liberalization policies that allow new firms to enter the market have begun to be implemented by most countries.

In theoretical framework, it is argued that private sector firms work more effectively because they work with hard budget constraints, unlike public enterprises that work with soft budget constraints. Especially in most developing economies, local services have been provided by the public sector for some time; evaluating supply conditions and demand structure; there is no multi-country empirical evidence comparing the performance advantage of public and private sectors in the presentation of these services.

However, when compared to public enterprises, there are studies that mainly support the efficiency of private sector operation (Stiglitz, 1999).

Stiglitz (1999) points out that there is a lack of institutional infrastructure to implement the privatization and competition policies of developing countries; developing countries need to take the necessary measures to overcome these institutional infrastructural deficiencies if they want to repeat the successes of developed countries' privatization and competition policies. Stiglitz (1999) states that emerging countries must have bankruptcy law that operates effectively through competition and regulatory policies as well as legal infrastructure that performs fair and effective contracts in order to achieve success in privatization.

The underlying reason for the increase in the tendency of local units to benefit from the private sector in service provision is related to economic reasons. Increasing productivity and efficiency in service delivery is the main factor. In this context, it is suggested that the competition to be formed within the framework of the transfer of the services with the private sector contract and tender will have a cost-reducing effect and thus increase the productivity-effectiveness in the service presentation (Boyne, 1988). However, the researches have very controversial results in terms of the effect of competition between firms in terms of productivity about production with lower cost in the presentation of local quality services. With privatization, there are many studies that have found that the cost per unit in service delivery is decreasing. When everything is considered equal, it is expected that the firm that gives the best price in the procurement process will make the cheapest production of the company and therefore the company will minimize the production costs (Hodge, 1998, pp. 381).

There are many studies that have found that the privatization of local services is a cost-reducing factor, and there are also data that prevent them from being accepted without a doubt. Some economists suggest that there is no cost variation when services are transferred to a private sector. On the other hand, some economists have found that production costs are higher when services are offered by private firms instead of local units. Aside from the debate on the increase or decrease of costs, perhaps what is more important in these studies is the reduction in costs in research that finds a reduction in costs. According to the results of the researches, as theoretically suggested, competition among firms does not play a significant role in reducing the costs, and it is observed that certain firms offering services are on monopoly (Hodge, 1998, pp. 99).

The privatization of local public goods and services does not involve a uniform method (Vural, 2015, pp. 18). Nowadays, as privatization spreads, local governments have been using various methods in the supply of some services, such services are prevented from being delayed by bureaucracy, productivity increase is seen in production. Reasons such as resource inadequacy, bureaucratic evacuation, lack of technical personnel and out of tutelage supervision encourage local governments to use alternative service delivery methods.

There are four important methods of privatizing municipal services and introducing them to foreign capital:

1. The contracting out method (Acarturk, 2001, pp. 47-48): This method, often seen in the presentation of local services, is a form of privatization that local governments frequently resort to. According to this method local services are offered by the private sector, within the framework of a contract. The municipalities responsible for providing services provide the service to the private sector by providing financing and supervision. In the tender management, the municipality, the contracting private company and the public can be mentioned in a triple relation. The municipality, setting the general standards for the service, must check the quality of the service, its price and other effects on the environment and take the necessary precautions. While the municipality is responsible for the execution of the service, it is more organizer. With the tender method, services such as garbage collection, sweeping of streets, maintenance of parks, etc., which do not require the employment of qualified personnel and which can be effectively offered by the private sector, are offered. In the case of such services, it is not possible for the private sector to reduce the public interest or increase the public interest in submitting it to the municipality. However, it can be argued that

the cost of providing private sector will decrease and that the citizens will receive more and better quality services. The success of the tender method depends on the realistic calculation of the estimated cost, the better determination of the terms of the contract and the degree of intensity of competition on the market. With increasing competition, significant reductions in costs can be seen. Besides, the increase in the quality of the service and the activity are expected in the presentation. It also contributes to the resolution of workers' problems. However, applications of bribery and incitement type damage the healthy operation of the system. The bribery between the private sector representatives and the municipal authorities can completely eliminate the positive effects of competition.

2. The concession method (Acarturk, 2001, pp. 48-49): It is a form in which the local government transfers the financing and administration of a public service to a private enterprise in whole or in part. On the other hand, there is a guarantee monopoly that the private entrepreneur can take the counterpart of their investments. This guarantee is usually limited to a certain geographical area. The concession shall be regulated by a contract between the concessionary administration and the person or company entitled to the concession. The concession is usually granted to make a service that is a natural monopoly. It is the responsibility of the municipal authorities to provide the service at a certain quality, quantity and reasonable price, and must be stated in this contract. Some economists anticipate that a natural monopoly firm will tend to reduce production of goods and services it produces because it is unrivaled in the market and will raise prices. These economists argue that in order to produce services with natural monopoly quality at an optimal level, the emerging harm of the private operator should be subsidized or the service must be provided by establishing an organization, taking into account the public interest of the public entity. Generally, one or more persons or companies are awarded for the realization of municipal services such as water, gas, electricity, metro, sewage, which are privileged, natural monopoly. In this method, beneficiaries pay the service directly to the server company in the form of fees or user prices. Concession is granted by auction. Thus, in the process of granting a concession, competition in a manner similar to that of the tender may be effected, but if there is no competition after the concession is granted, it may create unfair profits for the concessionaire or firm. The most important problem in this system is to determine the price. In these service areas, monopolistic profits need to be removed from the community by considering community benefit. If the monopolist is released in price determination, it may require a high price by cutting down production. For this reason, the municipality must subsidize the production of natural monopolies or subsidize the cost of the firm in order to reach the optimal production level.
3. The build-operate-transfer method (Acarturk, 2001, pp. 50-51): The build-operate-transfer model shall be carried out by a company which has the right to operate an investment or service falling within the scope of the commission, the costs to be incurred during the investment and operation period. For the purpose of submitting a public service or public works that requires high funding, the capital of the system is transferred to the relevant public institution unconditionally and free of charge after the capital has been established and operated by the private sector (domestic, foreign or joint ventures). Generally, it is aimed to make public investments such as highways, metro construction, big bridges, airports, power plants and similar public buildings that demand big capital and advanced technology without bringing burden to the state. The main objective of the municipalities is to make projects such as metro, tourism facilities and shopping complexes, which are long-term financial resources, without bringing direct financial or technical burden to

the municipality. Projects that are to be realized with this model usually result in cooperation with private sector foreign capital. The related companies, after carrying out the project, operating for a certain period and covering the cost and making profits, make the transfer of the facility to the relevant municipality. The joint venture company designs and finances the project and the municipalities do not have any repayment commitments. The model can also cause foreign capital to play a role in the delivery of local services. Besides providing the most advanced technologies, it also provides quality in foreign capital, materials and workmanship.

4. Method of selling stock (Acarturk, 2001, pp. 52): It is directly related to the privatization public offering, the block sale to domestic and foreign capital, the sales method such as institutional supply in international markets, the position within the sector to be privatized, the technology it has, the need for investment, competition and integration opportunities at international level, market share and competition situation. Land, buildings, municipal enterprises and all kinds of property owned by municipalities can be subject to sale by "direct sale" or "sale through stock" models. In the direct sales model, the assets of the public enterprise are subject to sales in whole or in part. In the other model, all or some of the shares of the public entity are transferred to private persons or entities through stocks. In order to be able to implement such an application, the capital of the public enterprise to be privatized must be divided into shares and must be found in the capital company status.

The increase in the level of fiscal decentralization with globalization brings the subnational units to reach new global sources of income. The liberalization of international commercial and financial flows allows local units to obtain financial deficits from alternative sources of finance. Non-inflationary and non-inflationary resources can be provided by local units by local entities. In new economic order international capital and local governments act together. International capital tends to seize municipal areas in the use, acquisition and profitability of the rents within the jurisdictions of local governments.

Solutions and Recommendations

Downsizing the state with economic globalization has foreseen a shift from the Leviathan state to the liberal state. A small and effective government prospect in economic terms is the basis of post-1980 reforms. Growth of the state in terms of economic influence is seen as a factor reducing its effectiveness. Reducing public spending, that is, narrowing the scope of the state's economic impact, will be possible with local public service provision, ie fiscal decentralization.

FUTURE RESEARCH DIRECTIONS

Often the idea that fiscal spending will be limited by fiscal decentralization in the process of globalization has been brought to the agenda very often. However, the reforms in this area over the years have not revealed that there is a continuous positive relationship between decentralization and efficiency in public expenditure. On the contrary, with fiscal decentralization, a new type of inefficiency and inefficiencies have emerged in the field of public expenditures. This situation, which can be defined as the new Leviathanism, provides strong evidence that the fiscal inertia can not be achieved with public activity and that the source of inactivity is shifted from the center. The multiplicity of economic conditions can severely hamper the achievement of fiscal discipline by having more than one authoritative expenditure unit.

CONCLUSION

Some important results can be listed as follows:

1. The Globalization and Decentralization are twin concepts. But for the local units take part in globalization, local units must show special efforts.
2. The new strategy of production and capital finds itself in a more minimal state definition.
3. The concept of the local unit, which compete with all the cities and regions in the world and try to gain competitive power, is in a state of confrontation.
4. The adaptation of the public economy to the market involves the inclusion of the competition system in the public economy and is based on creating a market-like mechanism based on competition in the public economy. The competition in the public economy refers to a race mechanism between the local public goods producer units in the public goods and services market.
5. The supporters of globalization advocate the privatization of local public goods production without distinction between domestic and foreign firms. The local government economics is shaping itself in this direction. In this direction, the dependency on the international financial markets affects the quality and price of local public goods.

REFERENCES

Acartürk, E. (2001). Yerel yönetimlerin hizmet sunumunda alternatif yöntemler. *Balıkesir Üniversitesi Sosyal Bilimler Dergisi, 6*, 46–59.

Bailey, J. S. (1999). *Local government economics*. London: Macmillan Press Ltd. doi:10.1007/978-1-349-27415-4

Boyne, G. A. (1996). Competition and Local Government: A Public Choise Perspective. *Urban Studies, 33*(4-5), 703-721.

Boyne, G. A. (1998). The determinants of variations in local service contracting: Garbage in, gabage out. *Urban Affairs Review, 34*(1), 150–164. doi:10.1177/107808749803400107

Cenikli, E. (2010). *Türkiye'de yerel yönetimlerin vergilendirme yetkisi, küreselleşme ve yerelleşme bağlamında bir inceleme* (Unpublished doctoral dissertation). University of Anadolu, Eskişehir.

Cooke, P. (1989). Locality, economic restructuring and world development. In P. Cooke (Ed.), The changing face of urban Britain: Localities. London: Unwin Hyman.

Cullis, J., & Jones, P. (1998). *Public finance and public choice*. Oxford, UK: Oxford University Press.

Dileyici, D., & Vural, T. (2006). *İdarelerarası rekabet ve mali yerinden yönetim, Kamu ekonomisi ve kamu politikası*. Ankara: Seçkin Yayıncılık.

Durmuş, M. (2008). *Kamu ekonomisi*. Ankara: Gazi Yayınevi.

Eraydın, A. (2001). Küreselleşme-yerelleşme ve işlevleri farklılaşan kentler. Ankara: Mülkiyeliler Birliği Yayınları.

Güler, B. A. (1996). *Yeni sağ ve devletin değişimi, yapısal uyarlama politikaları 1980-1995*. Ankara: Todaie Yayını.

Harvey, D. (1989). *The condition of postmodernity: An enquiry into the origins of cultural change*. Cambridge, UK: Basil Blackwell.

Hirst, P., & Zeitlin, J. (1991). Flexible specialization versus post - fordism: Theory, evidence and policy implications. *Economy and Society*, *20*, 1–51.

Hodge, G. (1998). Contracting public sector services: A meta-analytic perspective of the international evidence. *Australian Journal of Public Administration, Vol*, *57*(4), 98–111. doi:10.1111/j.1467-8500.1998.tb01565.x

Jessop, B. (1990). *State theory: putting the capitalist state in its place*. University Park, PA: Pennsylvania University.

Kara, M. (2008). *Bölgesel rekabet edebilirlik kavramı ve bölgesel kalkınma politikalarına yansıması*. DPT Uzmanlık Tezi.

Karabacak, B. N. (2012). *Mali yerelleşme alanında ortaya çıkan yeni yaklaşımlar: kuşaklar arası çatışma mı? Maliye dergisi, 163*. Temmuz-Aralık.

Kazgan, G. (2005). *Küreselleşme ve ulus devlet: yeni ekonomik düzen*. İstanbul: İstanbul Bilgi Üniversitesi Yayınları.

Keleş, R. (2001). Küreselleşme ve yerel yönetimler. Ankara: Mülkiyeliler Birliği Yayınları.

Kovancılar, B., Miynat, M., & Bursalıoğlu, S. (2007). *Kamu maliyesinde küresel değişmeler*. Ankara: Gazi Kitabevi.

Lever, W. F. (1999). Competitive cities in Europe. *Urban Studies (Edinburgh, Scotland)*, *36*(5-6), 1029–1044. doi:10.1080/0042098993349

Lipietz, A. (1986). New tendencies in international division of labour: Regimes of accumulation and nodes of regulation. In A. J. Scott & M. Storper (Eds.), Production, work and territory. London: Allen Unwin.

Oates, W. E. (1985). Searching for leviathan: An ampirical study. *The American Economic Review*, *75*, 4.

Oates, W. E. (1999). An essay on fiscal federalism. *Journal of Economic Literature*, *37*(3), 1120–1149. doi:10.1257/jel.37.3.1120

Oates, W. E. (2006). The many faces of tiebout model, The tiebout model at fifty: essays in public economics in honor of Wallace Oates. Cambridge, MA: Lincoln Institute of Land Policy.

Ohmae, K. (1990). *The borderless world.* New York: Harper Business.

Perry, J. L. (2006). *Democracy and the new public service.* Retrieved May 13, 2018 from https://soc.kuleuven.be/io/egpa/HRM/milan/Perry2006.PDF

Proud'homme, R. (1994). *On the dangers of decentralization. Transportation, water and urban development department.* Policy research working paper, 1252.

Stiglitz, J. E. (1999). Promoting competition and regulatory policy: with examples from network industries. Speech. The World Bank, Beijing, China.

Stiglitz, J. E. (2000). *Economics of the public sector.* New York: W.W. Norton Company.

Stiglitz, J. E. (2002). *Küreselleşme büyük hayal kırıklığı.* İstanbul: Plan B Yayınları.

Stöhr, W. B. (1990). *Global challenge and local response: ınitiative for economic regeneration in contemporary europe.* London: Mansell.

The World Bank. (1999). *World Development Report 1999/2000 Overview.* Author.

Tiebout, C. M. (1956). A pure theory of local expenditures. *Journal of Political Economy, 64*(5), 416–424. doi:10.1086/257839

Treisman, D. (2002). *Decentralization and the quality of government. Department of Political Science,* University of California.

Vural, T. (2015). Özelleştirme kavramının yerel yönetimler açısından değerlendirilmesi. *Maliye Araştırmaları Dergisi, 1,* 17–28.

Weingast, B. R. (1995). The economic role of political ınstitutions: Market-preserving federalism and economic development. *Journal of Law Economics and Organization, 15*(1).

ADDITIONAL READING

Ahmad, E., & Brosio, G. (2006). *Handbook of fiscal federalism.* Cheltenham: Edward Elgar Publishing. doi:10.4337/9781847201515

Aktel, M., & Memişoğlu, D. (2005). *Yerel yönetim reformlarının başarısızlık nedenleri, Yerel yönetimler üzerine güncel yazılar-I: reform.* Ankara: Nobel Yayın Dağıtım.

Bardhan, P. (2006). Decentralization and development, Handbook of fiscal federalism. In A. Ehtisham & G. Brosio (Eds.), *Edward Elgar Publishing.*

Bird, M. R. (2005). Fiscal Federalism, The encyclopedia of taxation and tax policy. In G. Gravelle (Ed.), *J.J., Cordes, R.D., Ebel & J.* Washington: The Urban Institute Press.

Blankart, C. B., & Borck, R. (2004). *Local public finance, Handbook of public finance.* Massachusetts: Kluwer Academic Publishers.

Brennan, G., & Buchanan, J. M. (1980). *The power to tax: analytical foundations of a fiscal constituon.* Cambridge: Cambridge University Press.

Breton, A. (1996). *Competitive governments: an economic theory of politics and public finance.* New York: Cambridge University Press.

Buchanan, J. M. (1996). Federalism and individual sovereignty, Cato journal, Vol. 15, Nos. 2-3 (Fall/ Winter 1995/96).

Burki, J., Perry, G., & Dillinger, W. (1999). *Beyond the center: decentralizing the state, Prepublication* (conference edition). The World Bank. doi:10.1596/0-8213-4521-4

Dilger, R. J., Moffett, R. R., & Struyk, L. (1997). Privatization of municipal services in America's largest cities. Public administration review. January-February, Vol. 57, No. 1.

Dowding, K., John, P., & Biggs, S. (1994). Tiebout: A survey of the empirical literature. *Urban Studies (Edinburgh, Scotland), 31*(4-5), 767–797. doi:10.1080/00420989420080671

Emrealp, S., & Horgan, D. (1993). *Belediyelerde alternatif hizmet sunma yöntemleri.* İstanbul: Başbakanlık TOKİ-IULA/EMME.

Falay, N. (2006). *Yerel yönetimlerin hizmet ve harcama sorumlulukları, Mali yerelleşme: teori ve uygulama üzerine yazılar* (pp. 9–29). İstanbul: Güncel Yayıncılık.

Falay, N. (2010). Yerel yönetimler ve özelleştirme süreci, Mahalli idareler maliyesi üzerine yazılar. In F. Altuğ, Ö. Çetinkaya, & S. İpek (Eds.), Bursa: Ekin Basım Yayın Dağıtım.

Fisman, R., & Gatti, R. (2002). Decentralization and corruption: Evidence across countries. *Journal of Public Economics, 83*(3), 325–545. doi:10.1016/S0047-2727(00)00158-4

Göktürk, A. (2006). Bölgesel dengesizliğe küreselleşme-yerelleşme penceresinden bir bakış. Bölgesel kalkınma politikalar ve yeni dinamikler. In A. Arı (Ed.), İstanbul: Derin Yayınları.

Güler, B. A. (2000). Yerel yönetimleri güçlendirmek mi? ademi merkeziyetçilik mi?. *Çağdaş yerel yönetimler dergisi,* Cilt 9, Sayı 2, Nisan, 14-29.

Güler, B. A. (2005). *Yeni yönetim anlayışında kökler,* Okumalar Notu, 30 Aralık 2005.

Güner, A., & Yılmaz, S. (2006). *Mali yerelleşme: teori ve uygulama üzerine yazılar* (pp. 1–6). İstanbul: Güncel Yayıncılık.

Hassett, K. A., Hubbard, R. G., & Jensen, M. H. (2011). *Rethinking competitiveness. American enterprise institute for public policy research.* AEI.

Kenyon, D. A. (1997). Theories of interjurisdictional competition. *New England Economic Review,* (March-April): 13–35.

Kloos, P. (2000). The Dialectics of globalization and localization, The Ends of globalization: bringing society back in. In D. Kalb & ... (Eds.), New York: Rowman and Little-Field.

Kösecik, M., & Özgür, H. (2005). *Yerel yönetimlerde reform: geleneksel modelin değişim süreci, Yerel yönetimler üzerine güncel yazılar-I: reform.* Ankara: Nobel Yayın Dağıtım.

Litvack, J., & Seddon, J. (2004). *Desantralization briefing notes.* World Bank Institute.

OECD, (1999), *Fiscal decentralisation in emerging economies.*

Poggi, G. (2007). *Devlet doğası, gelişimi ve geleceği.* İstanbul: İstanbul Bilgi Üniversitesi Yayınları.

Savas, E. S. (1987). *Privatization the key to better government.* New Jersey: Chatham House Publishers.

Yılmaz, H. H., Emil, M. F., & Kerimoğlu, B. (2012). *Yerel yönetimler maliyesi.* Ankara: MHD Yayınları.

KEY TERMS AND DEFINITIONS

Competition Between Cities: The cities compete with other cities by using their skills they possess and develop with their economic and social accumulation.

Competition in the Public Economy: It refers to a race mechanism between the local public goods producer units in the public goods and service market.

Decentralization: The autonomization of local units and the identification of local identities gain importance as a driving element of the globalization process.

Globalization: The integration of national markets to the world.

Privatization: The transfer of all or part of the property of public assets to private enterprises.

Reduction of the Public Sector: The assignment or sale of public services by private companies.

Tiebout Hypothesis: Under certain assumptions, the person who is identified as consumer-voter would be carried by the administrative units that best fit his preferences for public goods and taxation.

Section 3

International Taxes and Taxation Policies

Chapter 6
Investigation of Robin Hood Tax in Financial Crisis Periods and Analysis of Social State Policy in Taxation

Doğan Bozdoğan
Tokat Gaziosmanpaşa, Turkey

ABSTRACT

Taxes cannot be denied in order to prevent financial crises and economic crises. In times of crisis, it is sometimes possible to intervene in these periods by decreasing the existing tax rates and sometimes by applying new taxes. The Robin Hood tax is based on the idea of giving it to the poor. According to this idea, the financial sector will be taxed in times of crisis and the tax burden that countries have to bear will be reduced. Moreover, the important point here is related to the usage area of the income derived from taxation of the financial sector. These taxes will be transferred directly to the public (i.e., to the people who suffer from the crisis). Thus, the idea of transferring from the rich to the poor will take place. In this chapter, the applicability of Robin Hood tax will be determined by considering the main features of the tax, and the tax will be examined before the social state principle. In this direction, the superior aspects of the said tax will be determined, and some suggestions will be made.

INTRODUCTION

It can be said that the flexible exchange rate regime, which has been shifting from Bretton Woods' fixed parity system since the early 1970s, has increased the price volatility of exchange rates. Parallel to this, the maintenance of fixed exchange rates in a situation where capital movements are free is considered as a reason for the speculative attacks on exchange rates in the 1990s. The number and depth of crises have increased after the European Currency Exchange Mechanism Crisis, which lived at the beginning of the 1990s. The Asian Crisis following this crisis, the Latin American Crisis and finally the 2008 global crisis are considered as the consequences of the liberation of capital movements.

DOI: 10.4018/978-1-5225-7564-1.ch006

The necessity of taking short or long term measures against the crisis can not be ignored. At this point, in the year of 1972, following the idea of taxation of capital movements by James Tobin for financial crises, the two-tiered tax practice developed by Paul Bernd Spahn in the 1990s came to light. Finally, the financial transaction tax, which is discussed in the European Union countries after the 2008 crisis, is another important precautionary tax.

Taxes cannot be denied in order to prevent financial crises and economic crises. In times of crisis, it is sometimes possible to intervene in these periods by decreasing the existing tax rates and sometimes by applying new taxes. Taxes that come up frequently in times of crisis are the Tobin tax, the Spahn tax, and the new tax, the Robin Hood tax.

The basis of the Robin Hood tax is based on the idea of giving it to the poor. According to this idea, the financial sector will be taxed in times of crisis and the tax burden that countries have to bear will be reduced. Moreover, the important point here is related to the usage area of the income derived from taxation of the financial sector. These taxes will be transferred directly to the public, ie to the people who suffer from the crisis. Thus, the idea of transferring from the rich to the poor will take place. Therefore, the applicability of this tax in times of crisis should be examined not only in terms of the economic benefits but also in the theoretical frameworks such as being fair or not and its suitability should be demonstrated.

Robin Hood Tax, which is planned to be collected over financial transactions and to collect about € 57 billion a year, is considered to be collected at 0.1% in the purchase and sale of bonds and stocks and 0.01% in derivative transactions. According to calculations by campaigners, 1333 new wind power plants can be built with a $ 2 billion source, and even when 30 billion dollars is spent, all people around the world can get access to clean water. On the other hand, Robin Hood Tax is also an issue in the European Union. The Financial Transactions Tax, previously proposed by the European Commission, together with the pressures intensifying especially after the crisis, was discussed in the meeting of the EU Finance Ministers on 9 October 2012 and was held in Germany, France, Spain, Italy, Austria, Belgium, Portugal, Greece, Slovenia, Slovakia and Estonia. They expressed a positive opinion on taking tax on financial transactions.

As it is known, the power of taxation is the power of the states. Laws and taxation principles are the first to come to mind as the limiters of this power. The principles of taxation include the principles of legality, equity, certainty, solvency, justice and social state.

In this chapter, the applicability of Robin Hood tax will be determined by considering the main features of tax and the tax will be examined before the social state principle. In this direction, the superior aspects of the said tax will be determined and some suggestions will be made.

Global Financial Crises

No major economic or financial crisis has been found until the end of the 1960s in the 1929 World Depression, the most important economic crisis in the development of capitalism. Only the crisis that the Suez Canal Company brought to England in 1956 is exceptional. In this respect, England experienced risks in international trade despite the surplus of payments in 1956-1957. The Bank of England had to use almost all of the dollar reserves to preserve the value of the pound (Boughton, 2001:21).

The period after 1970, when international capital mobility increased, was the period of crises that began with the collapse of the Bretton Woodets system. Financial capital mobility, which has increased internationally, has revealed the financial crisis phenomenon for both developed and developing countries. Considering the recent periods, it should be noted that crises have an impact on developing countries.

The impact of globalization cannot be ignored in the fact that the financial crises experienced have such a wide spread and spread rate.

Globalization in the financial sectors has affected the national economies in a short time. As a result of the globalization in the financial sectors, there has been an artificial expansion in the economy called macroeconomic warming or balloon effect. Eventually, as a result of globalization, hot money flows arising from the imbalances between the interest rates and the exchange rate in the markets have occurred. Therefore, it is generally accepted that short-term international capital flows are the most important factor in the emergence of financial crises.

In this context, financial crises in the world should be mentioned. The reasons for these crises are important in determining the policies to be applied to these crises. Major financial crises;

- European exchange rate crisis,
- East Asian crisis,
- Russian crisis,
- 1994-1999-2001 crisis in Turkey,
- 2008 crisis,
- The 2011 crisis.

European Exchange Rate Mechanism Crisis

After the Bretton Woods system in 1979, the European Monetary System was established as a reaction to the large fluctuations in the dollar and with the idea that the current exchange rate uncertainty within the European Community harmed investment and hence trade. The aim of the European Monetary System is to ensure stability in exchange rates. The general idea of this system is that it will facilitate a possible rapprochement in the economies of the countries of the European Community (De Grauwe & Verfaille, 1988: 77). Finally, Germany was the pioneer of this system established in the Community.

In Germany, which is an important part of the European Monetary System, the increasing public debt and the contractionary monetary policy followed by inflationary pressure have forced the contractionary monetary policy without financial expansion due to the fact that the currencies of the other countries' economies have been fixed in their economies. countries have been pushed into recession. However, the fact that the European Monetary System countries did not agree on a common economic policy despite problems in their economies led to the emergence of the European exchange rate mechanism crisis in September 1992 (Buitter et al., 1998: 3; cited in: Bayar, 2014: 217). The first major crisis of financial character is important. In the emergence of the crisis, the interest rates of European countries, which are particularly high compared to the US interest rates, attract foreign capital to the stable region, the overvaluation of the national currencies and the increase in the current account deficit are important factors (Fratzscher, 2002: 15). The weak fiscal policy implemented in European countries before the crisis and the inability to yield from the results of the tight monetary policy are among the causes of the crisis.

In order to attract the foreign capital required to finance current account deficits, interest rates were kept high and hampered investments. Finally, a recession has emerged. The European exchange rate crisis has in fact revealed the importance of fiscal policy in the European Union countries. It is understood that the tight fiscal policy and the sustainability of fiscal discipline can hinder financial crises.

East Asian Crisis

The Asian countries that entered the literature as the "Tig Miracle of East Asia" added to the economic development of Japan in the last quarter of the twentieth century. Kong, South Korea, Singapore and Taiwan) are known for their peninsula. During 1994-1996, they achieved rapid economic growth with low inflation, balanced budget, controlled public debt, high investment and savings, and increased foreign exchange reserves. increased. It is the speculative capital movements with the banking and financial sector that can be seen as the source of the Asian crisis.

The causes of this crisis in Thailand in 1997 are quite complicated. When the general evaluation is made, it is seen that this crisis which started in Thailand has spread to South Korea and Indonesia in a short time and negatively affected Hong-Kong, Malaysia and the Philippines.

Asian countries have a successful appearance in the economic field. Hence, for many countries, this success has been hope. At this point, determining the causes of the crisis in these countries has gained importance. The causes of the crisis (Bozdoğan, 2018: 13);

- Fixed exchange rate regimes for a long time,
- Current and non-repayable debts caused by the trade and non-commercial goods from commercial goods which cause rapid deterioration of the structure of debt portfolios of banks,
- Relaxation of the corporate review and audit mechanism,
- Large external deficits in many countries, particularly Thailand.
- Increasing the competitiveness of the People's Republic of China and putting it in a difficult position by the Asian countries that adopt an export-based growth model.

In this crisis, notable use of fiscal policies. In other words, the effective use of taxes, which have an important role as a fiscal policy tool, increased the impact of the crisis.

Russian Crisis

After the dissolution of the Soviet Union in 1991, democratic policies were introduced in Russia and liberal policies were introduced in the economy. During the transition period, Russia provided large amounts of hot money from international organizations. This money was used to finance public deficits rather than investing. In other words, this resource could not be used efficiently. In addition, Russia's foreign exchange revenues fell sharply due to the decline in world oil prices. As a result, Russia has started to have difficulties in paying its short-term debts and hence the uneasiness in the Russian market has begun.

In this process, the rumors that the ruble will be devalued in a short period of time necessitated the intervention of the Central Bank of Russia in the market. Accordingly, the market was sold in dollars. However, the very low level of central bank reserves required the devaluation of the Ruble. As a result, Russia declared moratorium in 1998 and declared that it could not pay its debts (Black et al., 2000: 1803).

It can be said that the destruction of this crisis in Russia is quite high. The table below shows the economic indicators of Russia during the crisis period.

According to Table 1, in 1998, the crisis year in Russia, there was a decline of 4,9. Inflation rate increased by 75% in 1998 compared to 1997 and was realized as 84.4%. In the end, the unemployment rate in Russia increased and became 11.89%.

Table 1. Russian economic data in the crisis period

Variables (%)	1996	1997	1998
Growth	-3.4	0.9	-4.9
Inflation rate	21.8	11	84.4
Unemployment rate	9.6	10.81	11.89
Current account deficit / GDP	2.7	-0.02	0.08

Source: IMF Reports

1994-1999-2001 TURKEY CRISIS

24th January 1980 Decisions in Turkey can be said that the cause of the crises in the 90s. Turkey exported in 1980 with the decision open, export-oriented, has adopted a liberal economy. However, it was not possible to control inflation after 1980. In the end, macro balances could not be improved and the competitiveness of foreign markets could not be achieved. Moreover, the public sector and the current account deficit grew and domestic and foreign debt increased. As a result, the balance of exports and imports has deteriorated.

The causes of the 1994 crisis are the political and economic mistakes made in the first period of 1994 in addition to the above mentioned issues. In the 1999 crisis, the crisis in Russia played an effective role in 1998. With the global crisis, Russia has ceased its declared moratorium on capital inflows, while on the other hand lead to capital flight from Turkey.

When looking at the 2001 crisis, it is possible to list the reasons (Parasız, 2001: 851);

- Strategic errors due to the inability to predict the possible effects of the devaluation of the East Asian countries on the Turkish economy in 1997,
- Wrong way in domestic debt policy,
- State banks have to pump 20 quadrillion Turkish liras to the economy and write this to their balance sheets as bank losses,
- The private sector is responding to the increase in demand by price increase instead of production increase.

2008 Crisis

Increasing speculative capital movements as a result of financial freedom has been a major problem especially for developing countries. It is also possible to say that speculative capital movements are at the core of the 2008 crisis. This crisis II. It is the biggest economic destruction after World War II.

The 2008 crisis began in the USA and spread all over the world. It should be noted that globalization has a significant impact on the width and speed of this spread. The source of this crisis that started in 2007-2008 is the mortgage crisis that started in August 2007 in the USA. Market structure, supervisory problems and policies followed throughout the process have caused many negativities (Tong and Wei, 2008). In the early 2000s, the US Central Bank decided to lower interest rates in order to overcome the stagnation of the US economy. Interest rates decreased from 6.5% to 1%. The aim is to increase consumption and therefore to stimulate the economy. This situation has also been reflected in real estate prices and the prices in question have increased extremely. Real estate owners, who saw that their houses were valued, tried to take their second and third houses this time and they used a high amount of loans from the banks.

In the past, a large portion of housing loans were given to high-quality customers (prime mortgage), while over time, loans were introduced to lower-quality customers (subprime mortgage). In the middle of 2008, in the US, low-income groups using subprime mortgage loans preferred largely variable-rate loans (Kanberoğlu and Kara, 2013: 38). The recent increase in the interest rates and the decrease in house prices in the FED have caused people not to repay their loans. This situation made the crisis inevitable.

2011 Crisis

The measures taken for the 2008 crisis can be considered as the beginning of a new crisis. In this period, expansionary policies created new crisis dynamics (Sezgin, 2012: 141). Among the measures taken during the 2008 crisis, it was ensured that fiscal policies were loosened, taxes were reduced, expenditures were increased and the resulting budget deficit was tried to be closed by borrowing. The following table shows the gross public debt of the European Union between 2009-2011.

Tax Measures for the Prevention of Financial Crises

Taxes are an important fiscal policy tool in crisis periods. Therefore, it cannot be denied that there is an interaction between tax policies and crises. While the tax policy has an impact on the crisis before the crisis, the crisis and after the crisis, it is also affected by the crisis.

Tax measures, which are frequently brought to the agenda during the financial crisis, can be either reduced or increased existing taxes, but are also applied as new taxes. Taxes which are frequently mentioned as new tax are the Tobin tax and Spahn tax.

Tobin Tax

Following the collapse of Bretton Woods' fixed parity system in the early 1970s, neo-liberal economic understanding based on liberalization and disorder became increasingly dominant on a global level (Erdoğdu, 2007:259, Bozdoğan et al., 2013:198). The ultimate consequence of this is the liberation of capital movements.

It has emerged, in particular, of the idea of imposing taxation on money transfers to prevent capital movements, which are a danger for developing countries. This idea was put forward by James Tobin in 1972 and is known as the Tobin tax.

Table 2. Gross public debt (billion euro)

	2009-3	2009-4	2010-1	2010-2	2010-3	2010-4	2011-1
EU	8.595	8.758	9.029	9.374	9.466	9.772	10.320

Source: Eurostat

The Tobin taxation represents a mechanism that focuses on the conversion of certain currencies into another currency. accordingly, it is considered to apply a low rate of taxation on semantic movements, which is the area covered by the veggie (Bozdoğan et al., 2013:99).

The Tobin tax is an easy mechanism. What needs to be done is to apply a low-rate Advalorem tax on this transaction during the conversion of any currency to another (Şen et al., 2004:95).

The Tobin tax has been applied by certain countries and has not found a common application area due to the negative effects of international transaction and liquidity volume, contrary to financial liberalization, inefficiency in international markets and insufficient speculation.

Spahn Tax

This tax is an alternative application that develops the idea of taxing capital movements from the Tobin tax. Developed by German economist Paul Bernd Spahn. According to Sphan, the Tobin taxation is an application that can disrupt financial transactions and cause a liquidity problem (Spahn, 1995: 1). In addition, Spahn thinks the Tobin tax has a deterrent effect on speculation.

The Spahn tax basically depends on these principles (Bozdogan et al., 2013:101);

- A generic low Tobin tax that is always applied,
- 2% tax on spot currency transactions,
- 0,1% tax on derivative transactions,
- Additional prohibitive tax at periods of intensive speculative processing.

From here, Spahn actually offers a two-step tax proposal. This two-tier tax is only an additional tax to be applied during times of crisis, when the exchange rate is experiencing great turbulence. Minimum rate tax will apply continuously. With this tax, the goal is to generate a significant amount of income. The second level of tax will be the automatic braking function against the speculative attack.

A Tax Applicable in Financial Crisis Periods: Robin Hood Tax and Robin Hood Taxes in Terms of Social State Policy in Taxation

Following the 2008-2009 global financial crisis, many suggestions were made for the "Robin Hood Tax in or the financial transaction tax on banks. The 2008 financial crisis revealed Tobin-like taxes, particularly in the euro area. Robin Hood tax has provided public support. The idea of 2011 taking the rich from the rich to the poor bul has found considerable support (Baldwin, 2011: 5).

A wide range of non-governmental organizations and social movements, including trade unions, environmental organizations, religious organizations and humanitarian organizations in the United States, Europe and Australia, supported the Robin Hood tax through a campaign launched in February 2010 on the basis of the idea that global problems would be resolved through global efforts.

The Robin Hood tax is based on the Tobin tax. Tobin tax is applied only on foreign exchange transactions. Such a tax can significantly reduce the volume of foreign exchange transactions. Speculative foreign exchange transactions are more dangerous than other financial transactions. These transactions have a large share in economic crises and economic downturn. The problem of the lack of international coordination of the Tobin tax is obvious. This problem is taken into account by the defenders of the

Robin Hood tax and it is stated that each country should be in a structure to be implemented with the currency (Daniels, 2010: 4).

Nowadays, the importance of short-term speculation in the markets cannot be denied. In other words, short-term speculation has a large trade volume. Therefore, a single type of tax per transaction will make short-term speculative movements more costly. Considering that transaction taxes have a balancing element on asset values, Robin Hood tax will be an important application in developing macroeconomic performance and preventing other crises (Esener and Binis, 2012: 132). Finally, the Robin Hood tax can have a very limited impact on individual or retail banking. This is due to the fact that Robin Hood tax is targeted at high-frequency large-volume trading undertaken not by banking activities but by financial institutions (Seely, 2010: 12; cited by: Esener and Biniş, 2012: 132).

It is expected that Robin Hood Tax, which is planned to be collected on financial transactions and which is expected to be around 57 billion Euro annually, will be collected as 0.1% in bond and stocks purchase and 0.01% in derivative product transactions. According to the calculations made by the campaigners, 1333 new wind power plants can be installed with $ 2 billion and even 30 billion dollars of all people around the world can gain access to clean water. On the other hand, the Robin Hood Tax in the European Union is an issue that is heavily debated. Financial Transactions Tax, previously proposed by the European Commission, was discussed at the meeting of EU Finance Ministers on October 9, 2012 and Germany, France, Spain, Italy, Austria, Belgium, Portugal, Greece, Slovenia, Slovakia and Estonia. reported positive views on taxation on financial transactions. Robin Hood is a tax rate of 0.01% to 0.05% on all financial transactions, stocks, bonds, foreign exchange and derivative assets. Therefore, this tax will provide an increase in revenue through the financial sector. Robin Hood tax is limited to the transactions between the actors in the financial markets. Simple consumer transactions (such as salary checks and cross-border revenues) are outside the scope of this tax.

The income to be obtained through this tax can be used to help people who are adversely affected by the financial crisis and to combat poverty at national and global level (Esener and Biniş, 2012: 131).

In the survey conducted by OXFAM, it is stated that the poorest countries face a deficit of 65 billion dollars due to financial crises, even in 2009. Therefore, a tax to be taken over the banks will contribute to the fight against the financial crisis of poor countries and poor people. Some of the revenue from banks can be used for the cost of achieving the Millennium development goals (Robin Hood Tax, 2011b: 13). The impact of this tax is exemplified as follows: applying this tax for just a minute can provide enough income for the meningitis vaccine of 1.5 million African children or to apply this tax for only five days to establish a Global Climate Risk Management Mechanism in insuring the countries against the damages of natural disasters and micro-crop insurance in developing countries can be used to provide capacity (OXFAM, 2011: 2; cited by: Esener and Binis, 2012: 132).

The success of the Robin Hood tax depends on international co-ordination. In fact, there are also opinions that coordination is not necessary at this point. However, when the coordination is not provided, the capital will choose the countries that do not apply this tax as an escape route. Thus, this tax will lose its effectiveness. Therefore, international coordination is very important.

Views of World Countries on Robin Hood Tax

It is very important that the countries of the world look at this tax when determining the applicability of the Robin Hood tax. Because, as mentioned above, the international coordination is essential in ensuring the effectiveness of the Robin Hood tax. It should be noted that most countries support the Robin Hood tax.

Between December 1998 and March 1999, the Canadian Commons had the public pressure to isi impose a government tax on financial transactions in accordance with the international community Aralık. As a result of the increasing support of the public, a resolution (law proposal) No 164-83 was issued on 23 March 1999. Canada is the first country to declare a tax imposed to control international currency speculation (Robin Hood Tax, 2011a: 3-4).

As it is known, finance capital is an important destructive force on the economies of the country. France, Germany, Britain, Japan, Austria and Belgium support the Robin Hood tax against this destructive force. In addition, this tax is supported in the United States and Brazil (Esener and Binis, 2012: 133). It is known that the European Parliament and the European Commission have positive views on this tax. Robin Hood tax is included in the Liberal Democrats as a resource to fund global poverty in party programs (Esener & Binis, 2012: 133).

A 0.5% stamp duty is levied on stock purchases of joint stock companies in the UK. The income from this tax is about £ 3 billion a year. Thus, the UK is the country that applies the most comprehensive range of the Robin Hood tax.

Investigation of Robin Hood Tax in Terms of Social State Policy in Taxation

The countries have unlimited taxation authority has various limitations. These are the tax regulations and the principles of taxation in the current Constitution of the countries. In fact, the regulations contained in the constitutions of some countries are directly related to the principles of taxation.

There are many taxation principles. Thus, a taxation policy that protects the fair and the taxpayer can be followed. The principles of taxation;

- Principle of legality,
- Principle of Justice
- Principle of equality
- Principle of generality
- Principle of reciprocity
- Financial power principle,
- Dimension principle,
- Equality principle,
- The rule of law,
- Legal security principle,
- Social state principle,

is possible to sort. Since these principles are related to the study, the "social state principle" will be announced and will be considered in the case of Robin Hood tax.

The concept of Social State, which emerged in Western democracies in the 20th century, states that the state's interventions in social and economic life that exist in society to provide social peace and justice are legitimate and necessary (Koyuncu, 2016: 188). Therefore, the task of the Social State is to create a living standard that is livable and suitable for human dignity.

The principle of social state is a means by which the state is obliged to take into account or take into account its basic objectives and duties. The foundation of the constitutional objectives of the state constitutes the goals and duties of a state. In this context, the tools to be used to reach the targets within the scope of the social state principle can be classified as follows (Tanör &Yüzbaşıoğlu, 2013: 103-104; Submitted by: Koyuncu, 2016: 190);

- Social rights,
- To take measures to limit the right to property and private enterprise to the public interest.
- Observing social justice principles in the field of taxation,
- Determining the means of development and social balance through planning mechanisms.

Therefore, the principle of social state will reach its basic goals as it provides social justice. At this point, it can be said that the Robin Hood tax detailed above has a structure which is very suitable for the social state principle. The idea of "give the rich to the poor unsur in the main logic of the tax is already a target of the social state. The fact that the tax does not constitute a very serious tax burden while doing so also has a vision that maintains both low and high income. The proportional value of the tax also proves this. Because the ratio is between 0.01% and 0.05% of the financial transaction made in low amounts.

Robin hood tax aims at high-volume large volume trading undertaken by financial institutions. The taxes collected and the income obtained through these transactions in crisis periods will be used to help people who are adversely affected by the financial crisis and to overcome stagnation and to combat poverty both nationally and globally. This is an indication of how powerful the social aspect of the Robin Hood tax is.

CONCLUSION

Especially in the 1990s, short-term finance movements played a role in increasing investments. This situation has indirectly increased investments and contributed to growth. However, the withdrawal of resources from the economy caused financial instability. These instabilities are particularly negative for developing countries.

Countries show a number of reflexes in the local sense against emerging financial crises. Especially in the 2000s, it is seen that states use their regulatory powers more. However, the search for a solution at the global, not local level, will yield better results.

In order to prevent financial escalation in financial crises, tax regulations are frequently applied recently. Tobin tax, Spahn tax and Robin Hood tax are important tax practices. International tax awareness can be ensured with a small tax rate on financial transactions.

The final version of financial transaction taxes is the Robin Hood tax. This tax, which is based on the logic of taking the rich from the rich to the poor, only tax the financial sector. The income to be obtained from this is used to provide support to people affected by the crisis. This social aspect makes Robin Hood tax more powerful than other financial transaction taxes. Therefore, it can be said that this tax can be used as an effective fiscal policy tool during financial crisis periods. what is important is the international recognition and implementation of this tax.

This tax, which directly corresponds to a very important concept such as the principle of social state in taxation, needs to be developed and well explained to the country administrations. It is also important that the support given to this tax by the various integrations is expressed louder.

REFERENCES

Bayar, Y. (2014). Comparatıve Analysıs Of Eurozone Sovereıgn Debt Crısıs And European Exchange-Rate Mechanısm Crısıs. *Management and Economics Research Journal*, (22), 211-231.

Boughton, J. M. (2001, September). Was Suez in 1956 the First Financial Crisis of the TwentyFirst Century. *Finance & Development*, 20–23.

Bozdoğan, D., Buyrukoğlu, S., & Bozdoğan, K. (2013). Spahn Tax as a Derivative of Tobin Tax in the Prevention of Financial Crisis. *The Journal of Customs and Trade*, (1), 90-105.

Buiter, W. H., Corsetti, G. M., & Pesenti, P. A. (1998). Princeton Studies in International Finance: Vol. 84. *Interpreting the ERM Crisis: Country Specific and Systemic Issue*.

Daniels, B. (2010). The Robin Hood Tax: A Rejection. *The Wilberforce Society Policy Paper*, 1-4. Retrieved from http://thewilberforcesociety.co.uk/wp-content/uploads/2011/10/The-Robin-Hood-tax-A-rejection-Ben-Daniels.pdf

De Grauwe, P., & Verfaille, G. (1988. Exchange Rate Variability, Misalignment, and the European Monetary System. In R. C. Marston (Ed.), Misalignment of Exchange Rates. Chicago: University of Chicago Press.

Erdoğdu, M. (2007). Tax Policies That May Reduce Turkey's Financial Crisis Risks. *Marmara University Journal of Social Sciences Institute*, *7*(27), 259–279.

Esener, Ç. S., & Biniş, B. (2012). New Solutions to Old Debates: A new Transaction Tax Proposal. *Business and Economics Research Journal*, *3*(4), 123–142.

Fratzcher, M. (2002). On Currency Crises and Contagion. *European Central Bank Working Papers*, (139), 10-16.

Kanberoğlu, Z., & Kara, O. (2013). The Impact of the Global Crisis on Social Life: The Case of Van. Mugla Sıtkı Kocman University Institute of Social Sciences Journal, (31), 35-48.

Koyuncu, C. (2016). *Principles of Constitutional Taxation*. Bursa: Ekin Publishing.

Robin Hood Tax. (2011a). *Robin Hood Tax Campaigner Kit*. Retrieved from www.robinhoodtax.ca

Robin Hood Tax. (2011b). *There Is an Alternative (Time For a Robin Hood Tax)*. Policy Brief. Retrieved from http://robinhoodtax.org/sites/default/files/There_is_an_Alternative.pdf

Seely, A. (2010). The Tobin Tax. *Business & Transport Section*. Retrieved from http://www.parliament.uk/documents/commons/lib/research/briefings/snbt-01346.pdf

Şen, H., Keskin, A., & Öz, E. (2004). Can Tobin Tax Be a Solution to Prevent Speculative Foreign Exchange Movements? *Journal of Tax Problems*, (190), 92-108.

Sezgin, Z. (2012). Second Episode of the Global Crisis: 2011European Debt Crisis. *Journal of Business Research*, *4*(2), 141–150.

Spahn, P. B. (1995). *International Financial Flows and Transactions Taxes: Survey and Options*. University of Frankfurt/International Monetary Fund (IMF). Working Paper WP/95/60.

Tanör, B., & Yüzbaşıoğlu, N. (2013). *Turkish Constitutional Law According to the 1982 Constitution*. İstanbul: Beta Publications.

KEY TERMS AND DEFINITIONS

Financial Crisis: The financial crisis shows a deterioration in financial markets where the adverse selection and moral hazard problems worsen, and financial markets do not allow the transition of funds to the most productive investment areas.

Robin Hood Tax: The revenue received from the financial sector is public the tax that comes from the idea that it will be transferred to the affected people and received from the rich and given to the poor.

Spahn Tax: The basic idea on which the Spahn tax is based and it is impossible to distinguish speculative trading transactions. Therefore, Spahn's tax is designed as two-tier. First of all, quite small a financial transaction tax is always envisaged. On the other hand, in the foreign exchange market, only volatility in the foreign exchange market there is a tax to be taken and in a painful rate.

Tax: Tax is the money that the state receives from the individuals and organizations in a difficult and unrequited manner in order to meet the financing of public expenditures. In this definition, em being unrequited alan means that the person or institutions cannot claim any special or direct goods and services from the state as a response to the taxes they have paid.

Taxation Authority: İt is defined as the legal and actual power of the state on taxation based on its domination over the country.

Tobin Tax: It has emerged, in particular, of the idea of imposing taxation on money transfers to prevent capital movements, which are a danger for developing countries. This idea was put forward by James Tobin in 1972 and is known as the Tobin tax.

Chapter 7
OECD Action Plan in Base Erosion and Profit Shifting in Taxation and the Situation of Turkey

Elvan Cenikli
T. C. Muğla Sıtkı Koçman Üniversitesi, Turkey

ABSTRACT

The BEPS Action Plan, which was prepared by OECD upon the call of G20 countries in order to overcome this problem, was announced on 19 July 2013, and it was approved in the G20 Leader's Summit that was held in Saint Petersburg in September 2013. This chapter discusses the mentioned action plan and the probable effects of this plan to Turkey. In this respect, evaluation of the mentioned action plan will be made from the Turkey perspective by focusing on the most important actions of the OECD Action Plan that it put forward for ensuring the international tax equity.

INTRODUCTION

Tax avoidance refers to the fact that the action which cause the taxation is not caused, except for the tax burden. Because the tax laws refer to the birth of a tax debt as a result of the occurrence of a tax-causing event. When the taxpayers avoid this action, tax debt also disappears, which in the end allows them to avoid the tax payment without acting contrary to the law (Akdoğan, 2002: 160). Tax avoidance is a fact that has legal grounds as different from tax evasion. Taxpayers try to minimize their tax burdens through tax planning without acting in contravention of laws. Minimization of financial liabilities within a legal framework requires a systematic tax planning. The taxpayer can choose to reduce tax burdens by taking advantage of the gaps in national and international law and tax laws through good tax planning. We see that especially today, transnational corporations display the behavior of tax avoidance by eroding their bases through tax planning. In the international tax literature, this phenomenon is called Base Erosion and Profit Shifting-BEPS).

DOI: 10.4018/978-1-5225-7564-1.ch007

As a tax avoidance strategy, BEPS is an important tax problem for both international companies and countries. BEPS is defined as a tax planning strategy by the OECD countries, which stipulates countries to reduce their profits using deficiencies in taxation rules and disputes by shifting profits to the places of which economic activity or the tax burden is low (OECD, 2016: 1). BEPS causes states to lose corporate tax revenues considerably, largely due to the fact that their profits are being shifted by transnational corporations from the countries in which they operate to the countries that provide more tax advantages. The struggle against BEPS as an international tax problem has caused the countries to seek common global rules of tax laws instead of seeking solutions on its own. For this purpose, a 15-item "Action Plan" has been prepared by the OECD with the request of the G20 countries (Erdem, 2018: 73). The "Action Plan on Base Erosion and Profit Shifting", announced by the OECD in July 2013, summarizes 15 actions in three main chapters (Bicer and Erginay, 2015: 55). Compliance of corporate tax at international level; within the framework of this plan that consists of coordination of the taxation and the principle of substance over from, and administration of transparency supported by predictability and certainty in taxation, a strategy has been developed that includes 15 actions to reduce and neutralize BEPS opportunities.

MAJOR PROBLEMS IN BEPS ACTION PLAN, SOLUTION SUGGESTIONS AND THE SITUATION OF TURKEY

The 15-point BEPS Action Plan, which is an important example of global tax policy, focuses on certain global tax issues. The taxation of the digital economy, harmonization of hybrid financial instruments, strengthening of the rules of foreign controlled corporations' profits, prevention of base erosion through interest discount, making the transparency and the principle of substance over form a taxation principle, the prevention of abuse of double taxation agreements, prevention of avoiding from status of being a permanent establishment through artificial ways, ensuring compliance with transfer pricing rules and providing international coordination in fighting with BEPS and to develop joint mechanisms are the major issues that BEPS Action Plan has focused on.

Taxation of Digital Economy in Struggle With BEPS

To tax digital companies, an international standard and the cooperation of countries are required to tax the digital companies. The most important organization in this regard is the OECD and its initiatives are supported by the G20. The difficulties caused by the digital economy in implementing the existing international rules have been addressed in the action plan titled "Taxation of the Digital Economy", Action Plan No. 1. First of all, there are some proposals for the determination of these difficulties with a comprehensive approach and by taking into consideration both direct and indirect taxation and the development of proposals for important solutions (Birinci and Eser, 2017: 453). In the BEPS Action Plan, the following three important issues are discussed in the taxation of electronic commerce and digital economy (Bicer, 2018; Ferhatoğlu, 2018: 223).

Solution of Physical Link Problem

One of the elements that is accepted as a basis on the share of traditional taxation authority is the concept of workplace as a physical asset. The term 'workplace' stated in Article 5 of the OECD Model Tax Treaty sets out the state in which the acquired commercial income is to be taxed and 1. paragraph of the Article 5 of the Model Treaty provides a general definition of the workplace. The term 'permanent establishment' in the OECD Model Treaty is defined as a fixed place of work in which the works of an undertaking are carried out completely or partly through that establishment (Alganer and Yilmaz, 2016: 47). Changing business models in the digital economy make it difficult for digital corporations to follow their revenue administrations. The most important reason for this is that it allows new business models to operate without a physical entity (such as a building or factory). In the new economy, the tax rules connected to the physical existence (nexus)-the workplace loses their validity. (Kahraman, 2018). One of the important issues of recent studies in this regard is the concept of permanent establishment. Works done about this subject is aimed at changing the definition of permanent establishment in the OECD Model Tax Treaty (Alganer and Yılmaz, 2016: 60) in order to be able to prevent more profit shifting and base erosion. If the revenue generating activities provided by this new approach exceeds certain digital element thresholds, a state may have the authority to tax the enterprise in the source country (Erdem, 2017: 26). Thus, even if the place that exceeds certain boundaries is not permanent, it can be defined as a virtual workplace.

In addition to this, companies can get rid of a significant portion of their tax burden by showing the fixed places of activities as the organizer or supporters of the main activity as the main activity place. In this respect, Article 5 (4) of the OECD Model Tax Treaty suggests that exceptions regarding the organisation of the permanent establishment should be restricted to the extent that such exclusions apply only to preparatory and supervisory activities (Ferhatoglu, 2018: 224). Given the international developments, a solution agreed by all countries among the three proposals has not yet been reached. That is why the countries have begun to unilaterally give place for their own regulations in their domestic legislation.

Taxation of Certain Digital Transactions Through Withholding

Another proposal for taxation problems in the digital economy is to tax the goods and transactions through their online sales at source in other words to collect a withholding tax. Thus, solving the problem of physical link is anticipated to be subject to a withholding tax on non-resident online goods and service providers to be supported. However, in considering this option, it is also argued that there are some drawbacks in terms of EU law and commercial obligations (Erdem, 2017: 26).

Taxation by Way of Equalization Tax

The implementation of an "equalization" fee that aims to eliminate tax inequality between countries in the taxation of the digital economy is another option which is recommended in the report. This tax has been proposed to prevent non-resident foreign companies from selling goods and services without paying the income tax in a way that disproportionate the equality with the resident domestic companies, such as in insurance companies. An equalization tax to be paid as a consumption tax on these payments made to a foreign company would be beneficial in terms of ensuring clarity, certainty and equality for all stakeholders in case a non-resident company has a significant economic presence in the same country, and to prevent the overloading on small and medium sized enterprises (Ferhatoğlu, 2018: 226; Erdem, 2017: 26).

Situation in Turkey

Fundamental issues relating to the taxation of digital economy in Turkey are dealt with in a holistic approach in taxation system. In this context, the subject is evaluated as a whole in terms of "permanent establishment", "controlled profit of the company" and "transfer pricing" issues and practices besides corporate taxes and VAT (Biçer ve Erginay, 2018: 58).

In Turkey, a regulation on the taxation of digital economy through cuts in resources was also made. Article 9 of Law No. 6745 dated 20/8/2016 authorizes the Council of Ministers by adding a paragraph to Article 11 of the Tax Procedure Law. With this regulation, the Council of Ministers is authorized to determine whether or not the persons paying the tax are obliged to pay tax, whether the persons who pay or mediate the payments are subject to tax cuts according to the laws of taxation, whether the subject of payment is the purchase of goods and services or not, and the payment is made in electronic medium or not, irrespective of that the payee makes this price a subject of discount in determination of the tax assessment, to have tax cuts done to those who are a party or mediator to the taxable transactions, to determine different amounts of tax cut provided that it is between the lower and upper limits set forth in the tax laws related to taxable transactions subject to job classes, job categories, sectors, and commodity groups. On the other hand, according to the clauses added on the regulations referring to this paragraph added to the Tax Procedural Code are also dated to Article 94 titled "Tax Cut" of the Income Tax Law no. 193 with Article 7 of Law No. 6745 and Article 65 of Law No. 6745 In accordance with the 15th article entitled "Tax Cut" and the 30th article titled "Tax cut in limited liability", The Council of Ministers has made it possible to apply for withholding on all kinds of payments made by those who have the responsibility for withholding within the scope of the said authorization. With these arrangements, the Council of Ministers is authorized to have tax cuts done on those who are party or intermediary to taxable transactions and to determine different cut rates under certain conditions. With this authorization regulation, all commercial transactions are aimed to be recorded, especially the commercial transactions carried out over the internet. The aforementioned regulations entered into force on 09.07.2016 (Tunç and Akgül, 2017: 7; Erdem, 2017:33).

Eliminating the Negative Effects of Hybrid / Mixed Instruments / Institutions in Fighting Against BEPS and the Situation in Turkey

Differences in tax legislation between countries tend to create disadvantages for some countries and advantages for some others. Hybrid incompatibilities also carry negative effects that lead to injustice among taxpayers by reducing the tax incomes of countries, creating inequality of competition against small and medium sized enterprises in favor of multinational corporations, creating financing imbalance and transparency problems in terms of countries, leading to economic inefficiency and lower taxation of capital incomes compared to labor incomes. Recommendations for the elimination of hybrid institutions or instruments that make up the second article of the BEPS Action Plan have been expressed in many OECD reports. Major proposals in this regard include regulations in the internal legal rules governing a number of amendments, exemptions and reductions in the OECD Model Agreement to ensure coordination between countries (OECD, 2015a: 16).

The OECD's BEPS Project did not include a specific recommendation for the resolution of the problem of taxation of hybrid financial instruments in the tax treaty law. In this regard, the BEPS Project did not contribute to the solution of the problem. However, the proposals for the measures to be taken in the domestic laws of the countries for the elimination of hybrid incompatibilities in the BEPS Project could not be implemented due to contradictory provisions of tax treaties (Ferhatoğlu, 2015: 29). In this regard, Turkey should make regulations in the national law (income and corporate taxes) to neutralize the hybrid incompatibility instruments and arrange the discount limitations besides the effects of the multilateral instrument that was developed within the framework of 15. Action on the agreements to prevent the double taxation (Erdem, 2018: 88).

Strengthening the Controlled Foreign Corporation Rules and Situation in Turkey in Struggle Against BEPS

The concept of controlled foreign institution is one of the tax security institutions in fighting harmful tax competition. In this practice, even though taxpayers investing abroad in certain conditions are not physically distributed profit share from these subsidiaries, they are considered to have been distributed profit share in terms of tax applications, and after that, the revenues of these subsidiaries are made subject to corporate taxation in that country after the necessary offsets are completed. Thus, through the revenue of the controlled foreign corporation, it is assumed and taxed that the profits of the entities controlled by individuals and institutions outside the country are distributed in the country where the partners are residents, even though the profit is not actually distributed (Öner, 2017: 178). Through the establishment of the revenue of controlled foreign institution,it is aimed to eliminate the tax inequality between the taxpayers who direct their non-commercial and non-industrial investments to the countries which implement low tax rates abroad and the taxpayers who make domestic investments. The third Article of the Action Plan is concerned with the dissemination and development of this concept on the country basis. Within this scope, domestic legislation regulations are proposed on the definition, exceptions, thresholds, determination, calculation, income attribution and prevention of double taxation of controlled foreign institutional income (Erdem, 2018: 88).

Regulation on the strengthening of foreign institutional rules controlled in Turkey is regulated by corporate tax law. Even if some taxpayers who invested on the foreign subsidiaries under certain circumstances specified in Article 7 of the Corporate Tax Law are not physically distributed profit share by their subsidiaries, it is accepted as if they are distributed profit share in terms of taxation practices and by this means, the revenues of these subsidiaries are subjected to corporate tax in Turkey.

The concept of controlled foreign entity refers to the foreign affiliates controlled by fully accountable real persons and entities by means of having at least 50% direct or indirect ownership of their collective or separate capitals, profit share and the right to vote. With the expressions "direct or indirect" and "separately or collective" mentioned in the article, it is prevented that the share of the partnership of the foreign affiliate is divided between the group companies or real persons and is kept out of the coverage by being below the control ratio stated in the article (GİB, 2018).

Restricting the Base Erosion Through Reduction of Interest and Other Financial Payments and Situation in Turkey

One of the most used methods to reduce the tax base for international taxation is interest and financial expenditures. Interest payments lead to the erosion of the base in different ways. Examples include the use of high net worth foreign resources, borrowing among group companies through profit adjustment, transfer of the resources obtained from partners by way of borrowing rather than adding capital, borrowing with high/low interest rates from partners or related persons according to their peers (Öz, 2018 253). The 4th Article of the Action Plan in Fighting with BEPS is to take measures to limit the deterioration of the tax base through interest reduction and other financial payments. The common approach in this regard is that an operator's net interest rate cuts should be directly linked to the taxable income resulting from their economic activities and that the national legislation in this area should be coordinated with international rules (OECD, 2015b: 14). In this context; 4. Action Plan has suggested certain practices of interest rate cuts. The first of these is the "fixed rate rule" which is considered because it is easier to implement and more controllable. In this rule, interest rates are allowed to be reduced at a certain rate of interest, depreciation and pre-tax profit of the enterprises (between 10% and 30%). Other methods such as "group rate rule", "de minimis threshold", "forwarding of nondeductible / unavailable interest rate", "special rules for the banking and insurance sector according to risk situations" were also counted as interest rate reductions (Küçükkaya, 2016: 19).

When we look at the OECD's package of measures regarding the situation of Turkey, different and effective recommendations are brought to limit the interest expenses and to make the practices in the borrowing transaction more transparent in BEPS 4. Action Plan based on the risks that the countries carry. In the BEPS 4th Action Plan, "Fixed Rate Rule" is the foreground as the recommended practice for restricting interest rate cuts. Fixed rate rule is a method which can be used by all companies operating in the local or international arena. The fixed rate is foreseen to be determined by tax authorities. It is recommended to limit the deduction of expenses from the tax base related to the interest transactions carried out by the companies with the related and unbound persons in relation to the determined rate. It is observed that there are restrictions in Turkey on the deduction of interest expenses from the tax base. However, unlike the features described in the BEPS 4th Action Plan, it does not meet the fixed rate rule, but it is regulated with another practice under the name of financing expense reduction. (Öz, 2018:259). According to the article 41/9 of the Income Tax Law, in a way not to exceed the 10% of the sum of interest, commission, late charge, profit share, exchange rate difference on the foreign resources used in the enterprise, except those added to the cost of the investment in accordance with the exceeded part in the establishments which their foreign assets used exceed their own resources, similar expenses and cost elements and the part that is determined by the Council of Ministers cannot be subject to deduction. The same practice applies also in terms of the Corporate Tax Act. Accordingly, in accordance with Article 11 / i of the Corporation Tax, it is resolved and decreed that except the credit institutions, financial institutions, financial leasing, factoring and financing companies, in a way not to exceed the 10% of the sum of interest, commission, late charge, profit share, exchange rate difference on the foreign resources used in the enterprise, except those added to the cost of the investment in accordance with the exceeded part in the establishments which their foreign assets used exceed their own resources, and similar expenses and cost elements and the part that is determined by the Council of Ministers cannot be subject to deduction. In this application called "Financing Expense Constraint", the Council of Ministers is authorized to diversification of the ratio in respect of the sectorsand the Ministry of Finance is entitled to determine the procedures and principles regarding the implementation of the paragraph. However, the Council of Ministers has not yet determined the rate of financing expense limitation. In this context, in terms of ensuring compliance with the BEPS 4. Action Plan, certain regulations are deemed necessary on Income and Corporate Tax Laws in Turkey.

Implementation of Transparency and the Principle of Substance Over Form in Fighting Against BEPS and Turkey

Transparency in taxation is an important element in the fight against tax avoidance and tax evasion. Taking account of the principles of transparency and substance over form, fighting against corruptive tax practices more effectively is one of the issues that the OECD places emphasis. The concept of substance over form is complementary to the principle of transparency as a concept that prioritize the essence of legal forms rather than its appearance in the reflection of financial transactions to accounting and in making the evaluation regarding them. With the BEPS Action Plan No. 5, the OECD recommends that taxpayer-specific taxation practices shall be subject to "spontaneous" and "compulsory" information exchange between Member States as a means of transparency in fighting corruptive taxation practices (Çamurcu, 2017: 233). This approach has the potential to pioneer information exchange agreements between countries. 5. Action Plan mainly focuses on preferential tax regimes for the taxation of intellectual property rights such as "patent box" (property box regime, innovation box or IP box). The plan adopts the "connection point-nexus" approach against these regimes used for profit-shifting in OECD countries (OECD, 2015c: 14), with a framework for automatic exchange of advance ruling to ensure transparency as in the case of the European Union

Within the scope of the OECD 5th Action Plan, the OECD has some expectations from the countries with which it cooperates to ensure transparency and substance over form principles for fighting against corruptive taxation. The most important of these is that the countries make domestic legislation regulations in a way to support their own information exchange obligations in order to ensure the exchange of mandatory and spontaneous information (Çamurcu, 2017: 241).

Another plan that emphasizes transparency is the 12th Action Plan, which envisions taxpayers' aggressive tax planning strategies to be publicly announced. One of the most important problems that tax authorities confronted worldwide is the inability to reach comprehensive information on aggressive tax planning strategies in a timely manner. Early access to such information will be operational for risks, legislative changes and audits (OECD, 2015c: 16). 12. The Action Plan provides a framework for countries seeking to establish rules for taxpayers' aggressive tax planning obligations, while not imposing a requirement on the part of the countries. The objective of the mandatory disclosure regime is to increase the awareness of tax administrators about new techniques for tax planning, to increase transparency in tax planning, and to deter the taxpayers and those who encourage them in aggressive tax planning (Brauner, 2018: 27).

From the perspective of Turkey,standards have been determined or a several countries which also includes Turkey on the subject of international exchange of information even before the 5. Action Plan. The application which takes its basis from the US Treasury Department under the Foreign Accounts Tax Compliance Act in 2010 constituted the background of the International Automated Information Exchange ("CRS"). On July 21, 2014, "Standards on Automated Exchange of Financial Information in Tax Matters" was published, and Turkey, at a meeting held in Berlin in 2014, has committed to comply with these standards (Konca, and Taşkın, 2017: 38).

The Law No. 7018 on Confirmation of Mutual Administrative Assistance in the Tax Matters, the "The Compliance Law of the Approval of Mutual Administrative Assistance Agreement on Tax Issues" signed in Cannes on November 2011 was published in the Official Gazette dated 20.05.2017 and numbered 30071. The "Mutual Administrative Assistance Agreement on Tax Issues", which was published upon the compliance approval in the official gazette on 20 May 2017, constitutes the legal basis for the reporting under CRS. (Konca and Taşkın,2017:38).

Among the comprehensive co-operation methods envisaged between the Contracting Parties and the "Agreement on Mutual Administrative Assistance in Tax Matters", which have been drafted by the Organization for Economic Co-operation and Development (OECD) and the Council of Europe in order to combat tax losses and tax evasion and signed by many countries, there are information exchange, simultaneous tax inspections, tax inspections abroad, mutualization in cash proceeds and notification issues. Furthermore, administrative assistance is not limited to the residents and citizens of the state parties, third-country residents and citizens have also been taken on the scope of the contract. Our country has limited the taxes that the agreement will cover in terms of Turkey with the income, corporate and VATs with the reservations while being a party to the "Administrative Assistance in Tax Matters Agreement". In addition, such contracts shall not apply to tax claims arising before the date of entry into force for Turkey. According to Article 27 of the Convention, the cooperation facilities provided by the contract shall not restrict and be restricted by the possibility of assistance provided in the existing international agreements between related parties or international agreements and other arrangements that are going to be made in the future on tax matters. Turkey is expected to start automatic information exchange from 2019 within the framework of aforesaid agreement.

In Fighting Against BEPS, Preventing the Abuse of Preventive Agreements of Double Taxation and Turkey

International agreements can be abused by legal or illegal means. The reason for this is that there are many forms that aim to use the agreement contrary to the principle of honesty without actually understanding it. Different forms of abuse, such as treaty shopping, transfer pricing, triangular applications, changing income characteristics are also described as barriers to international trade, countries' agreement effort and financial equality in the OECD Tax Treaty Model (Özgenç, 2018: 287). 6. Action Plan identifies the strategies of and proposes a set of measures against the abuse of the contractual agreements that led to BEPS, primarily agreement exchange. PPT "Principle Purpose Test" has been introduced as a means of "Limitation on benefits" (LOB) or a more general anti-abuse instrument. The PPT method gives tax authorities the power to reject the tax advantages that are agreed upon, while the rule LOB allows to unilaterally determine the domicile of the corporations in an effective way. Both methods are highly recommended for countries, and countries are expected to use one or all of the rules in their tax treaties (Brauner, 2018: 17-18).

When addressing the issue for Turkey, it is necessary to evaluate it together with the 15th Action Plan. The Multilateral Agreement on the Implementation of Measures for the Prevention of Base Erosion and Profit Shifting was opened for signature on 31 December, 2016 by OECD andsigned with the participation of 68 countries' representatives at a signing ceremony on 7 June 2017. Turkey has also signed the agreement as one of the 68 countries. Regarding the Agreement, when we look at the Turkey's position document, it is seen that the signed multilateral international tax agreement will be valid for 90 tax treaties in force it is going to be co-administered with the existing agreements. However, there are also articles which Turkey did not find necessary to accept because there are sufficient provisions in existing agreements and upon which it has made reservations. When the agreement is evaluated in general, the most important article for Turkish companies is the 7th Article titled as the "Prevention of Treaty Abuse". With this Article, Limitation of Benefit will be required to meet the requirements of the newly signed multilateral tax treaty in order to benefit from the advantageous articles of the agreements. For this, the condition of succeeding the "Benefit Test" is sought. Where the aforementioned test cannot be succeeded, for example, the withholding tax rate, which is valid and higher in domestic legislation, may be applied instead of the discounted withholding rate provided by agreement in terms of dividend distribution. This would naturally lead to a significant increase in tax burden for companies. Another important issue for Turkish companies operating abroad is related to the articles of the Agreement related to permanent establishments. With these Articles, the scope of the definition of permanent establishment is restricted. In addition, the status of commercial activities in other countries, which are considered to be non-permanent establishments at present, due to being preparative and supportive, are directly affected by the relevant provisions of the Agreement. In this respect, it is beneficial for Turkish companies operating abroad to check their activities in countries where they do not have any permanent establishment but make trade. In this context, risk-based permanent establishment analysis can be performed to test the situation.(Gözlüklü ve Biçer, 2018:2).

Preventing the Avoidance From the Status of Permanent Establishment With Artificial Ways in Fighting Against BEPS and in the Situation in Terms of Turkey

Article 5, which defines the "workplace" of the OECD Model Agreement, attributes the taxation authority of an entity for an enterprise in another country to the conduct of a business activity through a workplace. Although there is no workplace, if operating on behalf of a representative (agency, middleman, etc.), in case that it meets the criteria in the OECD model, then a hypothetical workplace is accepted and taxation is made accordingly (Akçaoğlu, 2018: 331-332). Action Plan No. 7 is intended to change the definition of permanent establishment in the OECD Model Tax Treaty in order to transfer more profits and to prevent base erosion. In this context, countries are expected to revise their domestic legislation by expanding the definition of workplace.

As a country that is a party to the tax agreements which takes the OECD Model Agreement as a model, Turkey is obliged to comply with the elements of the definition of the workplace in the OECD Model Agreement. 7. Action Plan seeks to cut in some of the prevalent tax evasion strategies. As mentioned earlier, two issues are emphasized in particular, and domestic law regulations on their prevention are proposed. The first of these is that the OECD definition of workplace does not include commercial activities carried out through middlemen, and the second is the manipulation of "preparatory or auxiliary activities" (Akçaoğlu, 2015: 11-14), which is an exception to the definition of workplace.

View on separation of Tax Law Procedures Article 156 of Tax Procedures Law in Turkey defines the "permanent establishment" as the place that is allocated to or used in the commercial, industrial, agricultural or professional activities, such as stores, offices, editorial rooms, clinic, factory, branch, salesroom, workshop, warehouse, laboratories, exhibition hall and show rooms, education and training places, home office, auction hall, hotels, cafes, entertainment and sports places, fields, vineyards, gardens, farms, animal husbandry facilities, fishery and catching quarters, salt works, stone and mine quarries, construction site, cargo and passenger transport vehicles, ferry boats, mobile vehicles, electronic media or areas.

The amendment of the domestic law, as stipulated by the BEPS Action Plan, is included in the Draft Bill on Tax Procedures. 130 introduces a new definition of "**workplace in electronic environment** " to broaden the concept of workplace. Accordingly, the business will be considered to be established in the electronic environment when an internet, extranet, intranet or similar telecommunication medium or vehicle is allocated to, or used in, commercial, industrial or professional activities. The Ministry of Finance shall be authorized to determine the scope of the electronic workplace and issues regarding the fulfilling of responsibilities of the taxpayers, to make middlemen working in provision of goods and services or in payment of the prices of these through the electronic workplace, or the receiver of the goods and services jointly and severally liable for the payment of taxes and to determine the procedures and principles regarding the implementation.

Transfer Pricing in Fighting With BEPS and the Situation in Turkey

The most important issue that international taxation and BEPS focus on is transfer pricing and the Arm's Length Principle. The fact that 4 of the BEPS' 15 Action Plans (8-9-10-13) are involved in direct transfer pricing is indicative of this. International transfer pricing is based on pricing rules and practices used in the sale of physical goods, intangible rights and services between group companies among different countries or different tax jurisdictions. OECD predicates the Arm's Length Principle on transfer pricing, of which the conceptual explanation is given in Article 9 of the OECD Model Tax Treaty. The Principle of Arm's Length expresses that the price or the cost applied in the purchase or sale of goods or services made with related parties is in accordance with the price or cost that will arise if there is no such relationship (Tokay, 2010, 16; 49). In order to guide multinational corporations and tax authorities, within the scope of the 8-9-10. Action Plans, a number of regulations have been made to finalize and strengthen the principle of Arm's Length. This study concentrated on 3 parts. The first of these is related to intangible assets included in the 8. Action plan, the second is related to the risks and capital stated in the 9th Action plan and the third is related to the other transactions with high risks (OECD, 2015c: 15). With these three action plans, some rules are being developed to prevent the use of intangible rights, risk and capital, and other high-risk transactions within the group of companies for the purposes of base erosion and profit shifting. In this context, it is proposed to update the relevant sections of the OECD Transfer Pricing Guide and the relevant sections of the OECD Model Agreement, and it is recommended that the transfer pricing rules should give results that are in line with the value created (Erdem, 2018: 92, Biçer and Erginay, 2015: 56).

Another Action Plan supporting the 8-9-10. Action Plans is the 13th publicly announced. Within the scope of the 13th Plan, which requires the transfer pricing documentation to be re-audited, to remove the difficulties and provide uncertainties in practice and to provide transparency for tax administrations, and aimed to provide reasonable accommodation costs for taxpayers. 13. Action Plan requires three standardized documentation, namely Country by Country reporting, Master File and Local File to provide information exchange and transparency between countries and to standardize the information and documents that are demanded from taxpayers (Köprü, 2015: 53). Country-based reporting includes the countries in which there is information on the distribution of income, taxes, and indicators of economic activity (physical assets, number of employees, expenses of employees) among all countries in which the multinational operator operates, as well as the countries where all constituent entities are located.

The Master File requires information on the organizational structure of multinational business groups, the definition of commercial activities, the intangible assets they own, the financial transactions between in-group enterprises and the financial and the information regarding the financial and tax status of the group. In the Country by Country reporting, contrary to the Master File, detailed information on the transactions within the group is requested (Ateş, 2018: 377-378).

The main international guideline on Transfer Pricing arrangements is the "OECD Transfer Pricing Guide for Multinational Enterprises and Tax Administrations" published by the OECD in 2010 and*revised in 2017. Regarding Turkish Tax Legislation, legislation in compliance with the OECD standards on transfer pricing has been regulated by the Law on Corporate Taxes No 5520. With the relevant article, if the* institutions purchase or sell goods or services at costs or prices that are determined by the related parties in contradiction with the principle of conformity with the precedents, their revenues shall be deemed to be distributed in whole or in part through implicit transfer pricing. The law describes the purchase and sale of goods and services, who are the related parties, and the principle of Arm's Length. The law requires taxpayers to fill in an additional form with the related persons to the Corporate Tax Statement regarding the purchase or sale of goods or services they perform during an accounting period. In addition, the taxpayers registered in the Large Taxpayers Office of the Republic of Turkey with respect to the transactions carried out by the taxpayers in the domestic and foreign transactions with the related persons and taxpayers of other institutions with the related persons within an accounting period, are held responsible to prepare the "Annual Transfer Pricing Report" (Gücüyener, 2015: 74) until the end of the period of the declaration of corporate tax and to submit them to the Administration or those authorized to conduct the tax examination, if requested.

Innovations in the "Transfer Pricing Guide" revised by the OECD in 2017 are not just specific arrangements, they also contain a number of rules and recommendations for reporting within the scope of the 13. Action Plan. When we evaluate the aforementioned three record keeping obligations regarding the transfer pricing between economically or personally interrelated constitutions in terms of Turkey, the only "Country Specific Certification 'is used in Turkey and the other two certification types are totally new for Turkey.Köprü, 2015; Ateş, 2018: 331).

Coordination, Joint Resolution Mechanisms, Multilateral Instrument Development Strategies in Fighting With BEPS and Turkey

Coordination is another important issue which countries emphasize in struggling with BEPS. One of the top priorities for this purpose is real and timely information sources. The 11th Action Plan on the measurement and monitoring of BEPS emphasizes data collection and analysis methods by measuring and monitoring the tax loss caused by BEPS. The plan periodically requests information from member countries under the scope of OECD BEPS and expects to use new sources of information with analyses including spillover effects across countries. OECD's Tax Policy Analysis and Tax Statistics are carried out by (WP2) (Kara and Öz, 2016: 177).

Another base of the coordination, which isthe plan designed to make conflict resolution mechanisms more effective, isthe 14. Action Plan. With the current arrangement, Article 25 of the OECD Model Agreement states that the "KAU MAP Mutual Agreement Procedures" is a coordination process that serves to ensure that the contracting states implement the provisions of the treaty in the most correct manner, eliminate existing conflicts and prevent new conflicts The inadequacy of the mutual agreement procedure (KAU) for resolving the increasing international tax disputes *led to a concentration of work on the arbitrage method*, which is seen as an alternative method in this field but is partly criticized in terms of the partial delegation of taxation authority (Ferhatoğlu, 2008,197; 193). 14. the Action Plan, for this purpose, is planned to encourage these mechanisms to be more effective within the scope of the Double Taxation Prevention Agreements and to make them more efficient to use taxing mechanisms in order to make it easier for taxpayers to solve their problems related to economic double taxation resulting from transfer pricing in general (Bicer and Erginay, 2015:67).

The most important action plan coordinating the BEPS Action Plan, which is the first example of a global tax policy, focuses on developing a multilateral instrument, is the 14. Action Plan. Action 15 presents an analysis of legal issues related to the development of a multilateral instrument-agreement to ensure that countries are accelerating the implementation of the BEPS treaty measures. In this context, signingthe OECD multilateral agreement is considered to be an important step towards the updating of international tax rules through the rapid implementation of the BEPS package. In addition,it leads to an international tax system that works better for contracts, businesses to be more precise and predictable and to be for the benefit of citizens, and as well as freeing the signatories from the burden of renegotiating the thousands of tax treaties bilaterally.

For this purpose, in accordance with Action Plan 15, Multilateral Agreement ("Multilateral Convention to Implement Tax Treaties Related Measures to Prevent Base Erosion and Profit Shifting" or "Multilateral Instrument - MLI ") of which the text was drafted on 24.11.2016 by the Organization for Economic Development and Cooperation (OECD) was signed by 68 countries that also includes Turkey on 06/07/2017 in the signing ceremony held in Paris.

CONCLUSION

Meeting in July 2013, the G20 Finance Ministers called the OECD to develop a comprehensive action plan that would lead to co-operation on BEPS. Action Plan on "Base Erosion and Profit Shifting" (briefly "BEPS") prepared by the OECD upon the call of G20 countries was announced on July 19, 2013 and found appropriate at the G20 Leaders Summit that has met in Saint Petersburg in September 2013. In this direction, with the action plan, which consists of 15 actions and is expected to be completed within 2 years, the G20 countries that are not OECD members, have taken the first steps in the tax affairs simultaneously with the OECD. In the G20 Leaders Summit Final Declaration which was held in Antalya on 15-16 November, 2015 in Presidency of Turkey, the package of measures developed "in order to achieve a globally fairer and more modern international tax system, the G20 / OECD Tax Base Erosion and Profit Transfer (BEPS) Project" are approved, G20 countries in the summit held in Antalya, the G20 countries, also repeated their commitment to the progress towards the development of the transparency of the tax system and the commitment to the implementation of the "automatic exchange of information" and "exchange of information based on the demand" by the end of 2017 and 2018. In care of the OECD, thanks to the OECD BEPS Action Plan that is regarded as "the most radical reforms in international taxation system", it is expected that they can increase the tax revenues of the developing countries such as Turkey, which anticipates the positive contribution to both developing countries and the world economy. Within the framework of the application of the regulations, following the application effectively will be extremely important in terms of ensuring tax equity both in national and international level (Yilmaz, 2015:4). Although BEPS action plans are not legally binding, the minimum standards in the package are the standards to which each participating country is committed to comply in fighting with BEPS Project. Since even the presence of an entity that does not participate in the minimum standards can be regarded as an open door by companies, it may weaken the fight with BEPS and lead to the failure of the standards to achieve its purpose. There are sub-working groups still continue to work, and the progress of the countries in this process will be determined with the countries' supervision which will be carried out by the OECD in 2020 (Diclehan, 2018: 152).

In 2015, as the host country in the G20 Leaders Summit, Turkey has been one of the countries agreed on minimum standards. The standards, which Turkey has emphasized and undertaken to apply at minimum level, are the actions plans aimed at fighting against corruptive tax regimes, developing the mutual agreement procedures, re-evaluating the transfer pricing documentation and country by country reporting and preventing the use of double taxation agreements for tax avoidance. The government therefore needs to develop regulations related to Action Plans to fight with BEPS. For the implementation of Action Plans for fighting with the BEPS, there will be need for new laws and in this respect changes in the secondary regulations such as the decision of the Council of Ministers and notifications. Even the OECD has a property of being an important reference in our global tax policy, it is crucial and necessary for Turkey to make domestic law regulations in order to follow the dynamic and innovative structure of the OECD.

REFERENCES

Akçaoğlu, E. (2015). *Beps action 7: preventing artificial avoidance of parmanent establishment status.* Text of Speech, International Tax Law Conferences Series 5, Preventing Base Erosion and Profit Shifting in Taxation, Politcs, Law, Action, ANAMED, İstanbul, Turkey.

Akçaoğlu, E. (2018). Beps action 7: preventing artificial avoidance of parmanent establishment status. In *Base Erosion and Profit Shifting in Taxation, International Tax Law Conferences Series-5* (pp. 327-349). Beta Press.

Akdoğan, A. (2002). *Public Finance*. Ankara: Gazi Press.

Alganer, Y., & Yılmaz, Ö. (2016). OECD model tax agreement and relation between permanent establishment and transfer pricing. *Marmara University, Journal of Economics and Administrative Sciences, 38*(2), 45–61. doi:10.14780/muiibd.281307

Ateş, L. (2018). Beps action 13: Documantation in transfer pricing. In *Base Erosion and Profit Shifting in Taxation, International Tax Law Conferences Series-5* (pp. 369-397). Beta Press.

Biçer, R. (2018). *Taxation problems continue in the digital economy*. Retrieved from https://www.dunya.com/kose-yazisi/dijital-ekonomide-vergilendirme-sorunlari-devam-ediyor/407639

Biçer & Erginay. (2015, December). BEPS action plan and the effects of turkey. *Journal of Tax Issues*, 54-68.

Birinci, N., & Eser, L. Y. (2017, September). BEPS action plan and evaluation in preventing tax losses and leaks. *International Journal of Economic Studies, 3*(3), 447–459.

Brauner, Y. (2018). International approaches to BEPS: what is BEPS? In *Base Erosion and Profit Shifting in Taxation, International Tax Law Conferences Series-5* (pp. 1-37). Beta Press.

Çamurcu, Z. N. (2017). Transparency as a tool for combating tax paradise: a study based on the OECD-BEPS action plan no. 5 (2015 Final Report). *International Journal of Public Finance,* (2), 226-244.

Diclehan, B. (2016). *Base erosion and profit shifting and Turkey experiences.* Retrieved from https://home.kpmg.com/content/dam/kpmg/pdf/2016/06/tr-sorumlu-vergicilikbasak-diclehan.pdf

Diclehan, B. (n.d.). *Part II: responsible taxation at the ınternational level.* Retrieved from https://home.kpmg.com/tr/tr/home/gorusler/2016/06/sorumlu-vergicilik.html

Erdem, T. (2017). New World Order, Electronic Commerce and Tax. *Financial Solution*, (143), 13-41.

Erdem, T. (2018). Turkish approaches to BEPS: where do we stand currently? In *Base Erosion and Profit Shifting in Taxation, International Tax Law Conferences Series-5* (pp. 71-97). Beta Press.

Ferhatoğlu, E. (2008). Elimination of international tax disputes: European union arbitration agreement. *Ankara University. Journal of Law Faculty, 57*(4), 191–218.

Ferhatoğlu, E. (2015). The effect of beps project on hybrid financial instrument in the law of tax agreements. *Journal of Tax Issues*, (326), 17-30.

Ferhatoğlu, E. (2018). BEPS action 1: digital economy. In *Base Erosion and Profit Shifting in Taxation, International Tax Law Conferences Series-5,* (pp. 211-229). Beta Press.

GİB. (2018). Retrieved from http://www.gib.gov.tr/fileadmin/user_upload/Tebligler/5520/7.html

Gözlüklü, B., & Biçer, R. (2018). *Turkey multilateral international tax agreement signed.* Retrieved from http://vergiport.com/duyuru/Turkiye_cok_tarafli_uluslararasi_vergi_anlasmasi_imzaladi.pdf

Gücüyener, G. (2015). Transfer pricing documentation and country based reporting within the scope of BEPS Project Action Plan. *Tax Issues*, (326), 69-76.

Kahraman, A. (2018). *Is the EU proposal tax protection in the taxation of digitalized economy?* Retrieved from https://kpmgvergi.com/Blog/Pages/FullBlog.aspx?article=884

Kara, M. C., & Öz, E. (2016). A global tax compliance project: BEPS. *Tax World, 172*(414), 172–181.

Konca & Taşkın. (2017). Common Reporting Standards (CRS). *Tax Agenda (Vergide Gündem)*, (12), 37-39.

Köprü, M. F. (2015). *What is this BEPS?* Retrieved from http://www.ekonomist.com.tr/m-fatih-kopru/nedir-bu-beps.html

Köprü, M. F. (2018). *In the tax everything will be more transparent.* Retrieved from http://www.ekonomist.com.tr/m-fatih-kopru/vergide-her-sey-daha-seffaf-olacak.html

Küçükkaya, O. (2016). BEPS 4. Interest Expenses in the Framework of Action Plan. *Tax Agenda (Vergide Gündem),* (9), 18-21.

OECD. (2012). *Hybrids Mismatch Arrangements: Tax Policy And Compliance Issues*. Retrieved from http://www.oecd.org/ctp/exchange-of-tax-information/HYBRIDS_ENG_Final_ October2012.pdf

OECD. (2015a). *Neutralising the Effects of Hybrid Mismatch Arrangements, Action 2 - 2015 Final Report. OECD/G20 Base Erosion and Profit Shifting Project*. Paris: OECD Publishing.

OECD. (2015b). *Limiting Base Erosion Involving Interest Deductions and Other Financial Payments, Action 4 - 2015 Final Report. OECD/G20 Base Erosion and Profit Shifting Project*. Paris: OECD Publishing. doi:10.1787/9789264241176-

OECD. (2015c). *Explanatory Statement*. OECD/G20 Base Erosion and Profit Shifting Project, OECD. Retrieved from www.oecd.org/tax/beps-explanatory-statement-2015.pdf

OECD. (2016). *About Base Erosion and Profit Shifting*. Retrieved from http://www.oecd.org/tax/beps/beps-about.htm

Öner, E. (2017). *Turkish Tax System*. Ankara: Seçkin Press.

Öz, S. (2018). BEPS Action 4: Interest payments. *Base Erosion and Profit Shifting in Taxation, International Tax Law Conferences Series-5*, (pp. 247-263). Beta Press.

Özgenç, S. (2018). BEPS Action 6: Prevention of tax treaty abuse. In *Base Erosion and Profit Shifting in Taxation, International Tax Law Conferences Series-5*, (pp. 279-303). Beta Press.

Tokay, U. O. (2010). *Transfer pricing in the multinational companies and its ımplementation in Turkish tax system* (Unpublished Master Thesis). Marmara Unıversity Social Sciences Institute, İstanbul, Turkey.

Tunç & Akgül. (2017). BEPS project and reflections in the world. *Tax Agenda- International Tax Agenda*, 4-11.

Yılmaz, H. G. (2015). *OECD BEPS action plan for international tax justice*. Retrieved from https://www2.deloitte.com/content/dam/Deloitte/tr/Documents/tax/hulyayilmaz_eylulkasim(1).pdf

Chapter 8
Relationship Between Tax Revenues and Globalization:
A Heterogeneous Panel Application on Advanced Nation States

İbrahim Özmen
Selcuk University, Turkey

Selçuk Balı
Selcuk University, Turkey

ABSTRACT

The aim of this chapter is to investigate the potential impacts of globalization on tax revenues with reference to theoretical explanations within the context of tax and globalization. In the study, G10 country group and the data belonging to these countries between the years of 1990 and 2015 are used. In order to determine the relationships between tax revenues and globalization, cross-sectional dependency test, slope heterogeneous tests, and bootstrap panel Granger causality tests were used to understand the direction of causality between long-term coefficient estimations and variables. While the results of the long-run coefficient obtained from the study show differences according to the countries, a bi-directional causality relationship is determined between tax revenues and foreign trade. The diminishing effect of globalization found on the tax revenues of nation states considered within the scope of the study. It can be thought that these outcomes may provide some preliminary information to policymakers.

INTRODUCTION

Although there are various opinions on exactly what is wanted to be described by the concept of globalization, it is seen that explanations are fundamentally going through two planes. The first plane is the impacts of globalization on economic processes. The second one refers to a more comprehensive characterization which refers to the change in all social life processes. This second plane contains factors such as the speed of communication and ease of travel that are brought about by technological develop-

DOI: 10.4018/978-1-5225-7564-1.ch008

ments (Tanzi, 1996). If we go back to the first plane, this process, which commenced particularly in the mid-1980s (Kazgan, 2009; Giray, 2005), refers to three changes within the economy by virtue of technological developments. These are; free market economy, free foreign trade and free capital movements (Kazgan, 2009). On the other hand, the concept of globalization comes to mean the high rate of dependency created by one country on the rest of the world, and impacts of many national policies beyond the boundaries of a country (Tanzi, 2004; 1996). However, it is useful to note that the concept of globalization is not the subject of this study due to its scope.

When we consider globalization as a phenomenon, putting conceptual debates on one side and focusing on the results of this phenomenon will at least make it more comprehensible that we want to express in this study. When the consequences of globalization are approached in the context of tax; creative destruction caused by increasing technological vigor[1] (Asher & Rajan, 1999; Tanzi, 2000) and removal of national boundaries (Razin & Slemrod, 1996) brought about many changes in economic and social fields and have also created various effects on tax and tax systems or tax policies. In this context, the tax policy of a country may affect economic activities in other countries (Razin & Slemrod, 1996). The European Union is a good example of this (Tanzi, 1996). The interaction between globalization and fiscal policies is generally stated under two headings according to Garret & Mitchell (2001) (Bretschger & Hettich, 2002, Sert, 2011). The first is named as efficiency hypothesis and the second one is named as compensation hypothesis (Bretschger & Hettich, 2002). According to the efficiency hypothesis, capital and firms, which are described as moving factors, have the possibilities to escape from tax. In order to avoid possible tax erosion to occur in tax revenues in the nation state, (Bretschger & Hettich, 2002) prefers higher taxation over relatively less mobile factors which are labor income and consumption (Garret & Mıtchell, 2001). Compensation hypothesis, on the other hand, suggests that there is a linear relationship between globalization and public expenditures, the fragility of the country's economies increase due to increased globalization and this produces effects that increase the inequalities in the economy. Against the negative effects of trade openness on citizens the approach of welfare state steps in and eliminate the potential negative effects of globalization through public expenditures. (Rodrick, 1998; Garret & Mitchell, 2001; Swank, 1998). This process can also bring about the end of the welfare state (Sert, 2011).

However, there is a slightly different approach from these two perspectives. In general, the principle of sovereignty of countries has been earlier explained by "territory principle" due to the route and process of tax policies prior to globalization, while everything has changed with globalization process (Tanzi, 1996). The globalization process reduces the taxable income sources of states and creates pressure on their financial institutions (Habermas, 2008). Habermas (2008) addresses this approach within the context of globalization and the fate of nation state. These explanations bring this question to mind: "Does globalization test the future of nation states when it reduces their tax revenues?"

With reference to above explanations, three relations between globalization and tax revenues of nation states emerge. These can be enumerated as "increasing technological momentum, increasing trade momentum" and finally "the effects of the change in the principle of sovereignty of tax on tax systems of nation states" which is called forth by the first two factors. This study consists of literature review following the introduction part, explanation of the information about the model and the data used in testing the hypotheses, explanations about the econometric methods to be used in the study, the findings and finally the conclusion.

BACKGROUND

The Effect of Globalization on Tax Revenue Composition

According to Rozin & Slemrod (1990), it can be pointed out that the economic factors underlying the modern world economic development and the factors of the international tax environment that are most directly reflected in the tax system and tax policy of any state. Moreover, economic factors act immediately in all directions of economic policy, including its tax component, while the factors of the international tax environment are focused, limited primarily to the sphere of taxation. The realization that under conditions of growing economic openness, no country in the world can no longer rely on the inviolability of national tax sovereignty, that ignoring the process of globalization and external factors that influence the formation of economic policy leads to a significant undermining of the financial base of the national government, in the 1990s.

However, Tanzi (1996) noted that after the 1990s those countries that continued to adhere to the traditional interpretation of the inviolable sovereign role of the state and public finances in their national economy, underestimating the tax consequences of the country's integration into the system of world economic relations, faced numerous financial problems (both internal and external). Among the most important global economic factors that are of greatest importance for the functioning of national tax systems and the formation of a tax policy for any country in the world, the following is attributed. The national tax system in the context of globalization should be transparent in terms of combating the global shadow business: it is the requirements for the openness of the national tax services in the information exchange of similar government departments of other states. The need for taxpayers to conduct financial and tax reporting positively affect the image of the country; prevent its involvement in international criminal operations.

Furthermore, Rodrik (1998) identified that financial globalization also affects the national tax systems and tax revenue competition as follows. It opens up new opportunities for attracting external sources of financing for the activities of the national government. Indeed, the capacity of each country to obtain external loans to cover government spending has increased significantly. At the same time, the national tax system should take into account the increase in the tax burden related to the payment of external debts, since it is the tax revenues of the budget that invariably remain the main source of financing for the economic activity of the government.

Trade Openness and Foreign Direct Investment (FDI)

As per the analysis of Grunberg (1998), the possibility of entering the commodity market of sellers from other regions (or other countries) significantly reduces market concentration, reduces the share held by local (domestic) sellers on the market. On the contrary, the weak involvement of the market in interregional (international) exchange strengthens concentration in the market and increases the share occupied by local (domestic) sellers, with all the ensuing consequences for buyers. Approximately the degree of openness of the market for participation in interregional and international trade can be estimated by the share of imported (imported) products in the total volume of sales (delivery) in a specific commodity market.

It has been evaluated by Tanzi (2000) that globalization affected many aspects of the global economy but it has a significant impact on Asia in terms of FDI because most of the Asian countries are in development phase. The challenge imposed by globalization to Asia in terms of FDI is simple, as developing countries continue to narrow the gap between them and technology leaders, they will have to rise from a growth model based on a model based on innovation, and they will have to adapt their institutions, in line with the opportunities and constraints of globalization. On the other hand, unlike short-term bank loans and portfolio investments, the FDI in Asia has demonstrated remarkable stability. During the 18 months preceding the onset of the Asian crisis in July 1997, capital flows to the most affected countries (Indonesia, Korea, the Philippines, and Thailand) reached $ 86.8 billion. Over the next 18 months, outflows accounted for $ 77.9 billion. With the advancement of globalization, restrictions on capital transactions will become increasingly difficult to manage without disrupting other forms of economic activity.

Furthermore, it would be better for developing countries to proceed quickly but cautiously with the reform of their financial system, again by opening the door to FDI to introduce the technological and managerial expertise of foreign financial institutions. This suggests the liberalization of foreign investment access from the first step of opening up the financial sector. This recommendation seems obvious except for the many governments that have failed to follow it (Houfler, 2001)

LITERATURE REVIEW

Tanzi (1996) evaluated that industrialized countries, especially Germany and France, the emerging situation are increasingly called unfair (or unfair) tax competition. The analysis shows that it is not that much in order to really counter the harmful tax competition. First, Tanzi (1996) recommends strengthening the role of international tax agreements, with special emphasis on multilateral treaties. First of all, the level of collection and exchange of relevant information between countries needs to be improved. Organization for Economic Cooperation and Development (OECD) experts consider it necessary to revise tax agreements in order to limit benefits to jurisdictions that are involved in harmful tax competition. Secondly, it is possible to toughen the national legislation of parent countries, minimizing the possibility of avoiding taxation. When transfer pricing is used, the burden of proving that economic activity has actually taken place in the performance of concluded transactions must rest on the taxpayer.

Rodrik (1998) evaluated that open economies have bigger governments because of various reasons. The first reason, which was identified by the author, was that when the country offers an open trade, it has to make different government agencies, legal bodies to implement policies and departments to implement rule and regulations. The second reason is that the when governments are focused on open trades, they also have to provide permission to trade partner countries to open their official reporting departments and offices in the country. As a result, the local government has to increase their own reporting agencies and this is the reason for increased government size in open economies.

Swenk, (1998), focused on the concept of the Welfare State and identified that collapse of the administrative and command economy in the former Soviet Union, in the countries of Central and Eastern Europe, which reduced the level of social guarantees and stability in the states that once represented the world socialist system. In addition, the financial crisis of the "welfare state" in most developed countries of the world (especially the current situation of the social market economies of Germany and France) was the result of the important expansionary role of the state in the countries of East Asia. It contributed to the transition from the period of "economic miracles" to a protracted stagnation (Japan) or triggered the monetary and financial crises of the 1990s, which had a negative impact on national development in the context of globalization. However, the researcher identified that foreign trade is the only solution because Import substitution leads to welfare growth if the corresponding products or services are competitive or become competitive in the market.

Grunberg (1998) identified that in the context of globalization, there is a certain harmonization of tax systems and tax policy. There is be a unification of tax systems of different countries, requiring harmonization of key indicators and mechanisms of tax systems, tax law of different countries, solving double taxation problems and taxation of investment activity. The next important direction of integration of tax systems in the context of globalization is the unification of direct taxation, by establishing a single mechanism of calculation, single rates, and conclusions of multilateral and bilateral agreements on the elimination of double taxation. The transfer of fiscal burden to labor (i.e. wages) makes the tax systems less fair (their redistributive function is reduced), narrow the tax base, and introduce even more distortions in the distribution of the burden on payers. Those who are not able to take advantage of the given fruits of the globalization of the economy will have to bear a double burden for themselves and for those who managed to hide from taxes in one way or another.

Brunetti & Wider (1999), noted that with the passage of time more markets are open up to FDI, it is becoming more difficult for each government to claim the license as an alternative. On the other hand, the flow of direct investment to Asia (including China, which absorbs a good half) has been steadily increasing, from $ 71.1 billion in 1996 to $ 86.9 in 1999. Certainly, there is resistance in some countries, because of the lack of a social protection system or the rigidity of the labor market. According to the researchers, FDI is the preferred form of capital inflow, but countries need to be socially prepared to deal with its side effects. Referring to mistakes made in the past in Korea or implicitly targeting Mahathir government policy in Malaysia, the researchers warned that openness cannot remain stuck at the door of the financial system. However, developing countries will have less choice in the face of multinationals that own advanced technologies and favor direct investment in future.

Tanzi (2000) highlighted that due to globalization, the entire world is facing technological developments. First, changes in information technologies become the basis for integrating the mechanisms and tools of the investment market. They presuppose more reliable information support, strict regulatory and legal regulation of investment decisions at the international and interstate levels, the introduction of common information standards for pledge mechanisms, accounting reporting, the ability to carry out transactions in the online system, etc. Accounting for this trend in the development of investment policy at the interstate and national level suggests unification of information reflection, which makes it possible to obtain operative, reliable information about every object of investment and business anywhere in the world. In addition, the final transfer of financial and banking support of business in the environment of information technology. The legislative framework of the investment market in the context of globalization is also based on information technologies, which are the result of globalization, and in the future, it will be a harmonious, balanced multi-level system.

Houfler (2001) stated that globalization has changed the taxation structure in the global economy. However, there are some positive factors experienced in taxation structure due to globalization but negative factors are along with them. In addition, tax collection and disbursement has become difficult after globalization because there are numerous ways from by which taxpayers can save their tax and the chances of corruption have been increased. From this point of view, capital is in a better position in the global economy than wage labor, because it is more mobile. In the long run, the states will eventually have to reduce the burden on mobile taxpayers, shifting it to less mobile, low-skilled workers whose factory cannot be moved to another country overnight. Now it is difficult to answer the question of whether globalization has a positive effect on taxation or not. Because there is a multibillion-dollar lobby behind MNCs and large organizations, which generally evade tax. Therefore, it can be summarized that globalization leads to a change in the fundamental parameters of the taxation process at all economic levels, from the micro level to national economies and the global economy as a whole.

Bretschger & Hettich (2002) focused on tax competition and stated that the globalization of the economy causes a natural alarm for the governments of those countries, from which the taxes swim. It is evaluated that the direct investment of the G-7 countries in the economy of tax havens of the Caribbean and the Pacific Islands for the years 1985-1994 grew more than 5 times and amounted to more than $ 2,000 billion. The growth rate of investment in offshore zones is much higher than the average growth rate of FDI. The study also showed that a panel of 14 OECD countries experienced a negative impact on corporate tax due to globalization. On the other hand, globalization has increased the tax burden on labor along with social expenditure in the name of efficiency and compensation.

Pereira (2003) studied the effects of globalization on tax systems in Brazil and identified various factors. It was revealed from the study that if the countries like Brazil with the neoliberal model of the economy are not exposed to negative consequences for public finances and taxation, for states that gravitate toward statism. The reason is that global neoconservatism has caused serious damage to national tax systems. Thus, the state should promptly react to similar actions of other countries and subjects of foreign economic relations, constantly adjusting the current tax legislation and the current national tax policy. This, to some extent, calls into question the principle of stability of tax systems, since the invariability of the national tax legislation in a rapidly changing environment can have negative financial consequences for the state. An inescapable manifestation of globalization is the erosion of national states and a decline in the economic activity of the government.

Tanzi (2004) evaluated the need for fiscal reforms in the result of globalization. This objective requires the choice of a research design that is capable of to cover as large a number of emerging and developing countries as possible and favored the choice of a predominantly quantitatively oriented design on the basis of a statistical analysis. An alternative adapted to the problem and that was a design on the basis of Interviews with decision makers of direct investments in German Company offered. From a development policy point of view, the study concluded that complementarity exists between investment determinants multinational companies and effective labor and social policy as well as financial regulation on the part of the national governments. However, these problems are present potentially in offset impact of government policies on the influx of direct investment and fiscal reforms.

Bounsgaard & Keen, (2005), discussed the historical aspects of tax revenue and collection and stated that in the middle ages, the kings received the main income from the land tax. As early as 1913 in the United States, 60% of all tax revenues were taxed on property, and nowadays it is about 10%. Today, many experts in the West believe that in the computer age the world will have to return to the tax systems of the Middle Ages. On the one hand, the study identified that developed countries try to keep their tax revenues, forbidding the rest to set lower rates of taxation. In contrast, they crush tax havens, trying to get information from them that is necessary to administer their own taxes. Finally, it was found from the study that over the past five years the US has created thousands of jobs, invested more than $ 130 million in infrastructure, and tax collection this is the largest scheme which brought the budget about $ 3.3 billion in tax revenues.

Dreher (2006) discussed and evaluated the impact of globalization taxes on the taxation system and identified different factors. It was found that now the national tax services are available as never before tax administration websites can consult on the procedure for paying taxes, and some countries massively introduce electronic systems for paying taxes using the Internet. In the US Internal Revenue Service, within the framework of the e-government project, introduced an Internet system for paying taxes, which built in the function of the automatic write-off of the tax in favor of the Internal Revenue Service. Now every American can use the address of the Internal Revenue Service to make the next tax payment, and also to check the accuracy of payment of previous taxes. On the other hand, the study revealed that the new attractive tax regimes in the respective countries are known to foreign economic agents immediately after the appearance of information in the electronic media. Moreover, new widely available mechanisms of international tax planning are being developed immediately after the adoption of the next national tax law or an instruction explaining the procedure for paying taxes.

Durinova (2006), studied taxation conditions under globalization and evaluated various aspects. It was found from the paper that economic integration has the most direct impact on national taxation systems and the national tax policy of countries that are members of the various trade and economic blocs, as well as partner countries of different integration groups. Common economic spaces formed as a result of the integration of national economies into regional trade associations, common markets, economic and monetary unions, result in close coordination of economic policies, the introduction of general principles for regulating foreign trade and investment. In the tax sphere, this is reflected in the process of coordination and harmonization of the rules for taxation of economic entities operating on a single economic space, as well as in unifying taxes (their types, amounts, collection rules) of the member countries of the integration group. Furthermore, it was argued that globalization of the economy causes a natural alarm for the governments of the globalized countries, from which taxes go away. The globalization of the economy and the growth in the volume of electronic commerce pose new challenges for the governments of industrialized countries in terms of replenishing state budgets. Modern tax systems developed after the Second World War. In those years, the movement of goods, labor, and capital across borders was low-intensity. However, today national borders are no longer barriers to production.

Crowley, Mayes, & Andt (2009) focused on the implication of integration of globalization integration and it was found that this is also one of the most difficult tasks of creating a single internal market in the space of common economic interests. However, it requires the efforts of all member states of the integration group to mutually agree on the principles of that form the basis of national tax systems. In turn, those countries that are not members of these specific regional economic unions but maintain close economic ties with them should also take into account the nature of changes in the level of direct and indirect taxes of member countries of integration groups in their national taxation. The greatest progress in harmonizing (coordinating) taxes has now been achieved in the European Union. Taxes play not only a crucial role in regulating the economic and social policies of member countries, but they also contribute to the coordination of the pan-European economic policy: the joint budget of the integration community is formed at the expense of the tax deductions of each EU member state, structural and scientific and technical programs are implemented.

Hihes & Summers (2009) discussed that effect of globalization on tax design. Results of the paper showed that the idea of introducing a tax after globalization designed to impose an international capital flow was expressed by many well-known economists, in particular J. Keynes the General Theory of Employment, Interest and Money, this tax is firmly tied to the former professor of economics at Yale University, the Nobel Prize laureate (1981) James Tobin, who in 1972 at a conference at Princeton University proposed the introduction of a similar tax on operations in the international foreign exchange market. The idea was substantiated more thoroughly in 1978 when J. Tobin proposed setting tax rates in the range from 0.2-0.5% to 1%. According to his plan, Tobin's tax could increase the stability of the global financial architecture, and could, by redistributing the amounts collected with it to the poorest countries, become a source of financing humanitarian programs to assist the development of third world countries. In addition, it was noted that one of the interesting ideas related to the possibility of preventing international monetary and financial crises is designed to have the most direct impact on the actions of national tax administrations, as well as modify the structure of existing taxation systems.

Neumann, Holman, & Aim (2009), compared globalization and tax policies and it was revealed from the study that globalization from a tax point of view is established primarily in the emergence of virtual tax jurisdiction that is the jurisdiction of the Internet, as well as in new technologies for financial transactions and tax administration (the widespread introduction of electronic tax systems). Internet technologies simultaneously and facilitated and repeatedly complicated the activities of national tax administrations, and therefore radically affected the national tax policy. Information globalization increases not only the speed of reaction of taxpayers to the actions of tax authorities but also enhances the flexibility of the tax policy of the national government.

Leviner (2011) focused on details of taxation and globalization. It was discussed and evaluated that in the tax sphere, the erosion of national states is established in two ways. Firstly, the national governments own financial base is significantly undermined by the expanded opportunities for mobility of production factors and personalized taxpayers who choose the jurisdictions of their residence and the seat of the state with the most favorable tax climate. Accordingly, those countries that for some reason lose in competition for their attractiveness to taxpayers - subjects of foreign economic activity, lose a certain part of their tax revenues. This weakens the financial potential of the state, reducing the opportunities for social and investment programs in the national economy. The second manifestation of state erosion is connected with the concept of an "effective government".

Kumar & Quinn (2012), focused on globalization and corporate taxation in their study. It was argued that a developed system of industrial taxation has been created, tax holidays have been introduced with regard to the regional rate of profit tax and corporate property tax rates, the duration of which is predetermined by the volume of investments. All of these factors are the result of globalization. Moreover, a significant part of the investment in the world is directed to the development of corporate infrastructure. Unlike FDI, portfolio investment is not made for the purpose of influencing corporate policy. They serve without exception the investment, with the aim of achieving the highest possible return. The most common types of investments include equity, corporate or investment certificates. All are the result of globalization and every activity is taxable.

Cagé & Godenne (2012), focused on the fiscal cost of liberalization. While the analysis showed that trade liberalization is one of the factors of economic growth, creating opportunities for production and exports, and also increasing welfare through specialization in industries with comparative advantages. If trade in goods involves cross-border borrowing of technology, it causes growth in the two trading countries. But the cost of liberalization of trade has taken place in terms of block trade agreements.

Ndikumana (2014), focused on tax cooperation and globalization and identified that international tax cooperation has several implications in the result of globalization. Since the main problem of assessing the current state of the national state is due to the fact that globalization contributes to neutralizing the national specifics of development, forcing governments to increasingly adapt to the neoliberal concept of an effective government. Globalization has led to the fact that the Anglo-Saxon neo-liberal concept of development, propagated with the help of the "demonstration effect" of the US achievement in the spheres of economy, politics, informatics, ideology, science, culture and the military field. While most of these areas are directly concerned with taxation system because of their role in the economy.

Cagé & Godenne (2016), discussed tax revenues and fiscal cost of trade liberalization over the period of 1792-2006. The period of analysis was quite long and the reason due to which researchers used this period was that there were many studies based on the 20th century but none of the studies focused on the aforementioned time frame. The analysis and findings showed that rich countries experience higher tax revenue because of a higher number of taxpayers while poor and small countries normally suffer from low tax income.

Seelkopf & Lierse (2017), focused on the tax competition and inequality in OECD countries. According to the findings obtained from the study; tax competition brings about equity in three ways. These can be expressed horizontally, vertically and internationally. Vertical equity in OECD countries top income tax rates have been drastically cut throughout the OECD. In Horizontal equity, OECD governments tend to apply a lower tax rate on capital income than on wage incomes. In addition to these; in international equality, the tax competition clearly undermines governments' capacity to set their tax rates independently.

Model and Data

In this study, the concepts that are frequently used in the literature in the context of topic titles are taken into consideration and dependent and independent variables referred to by the said concepts are preferred. The dependent variable of *tr* (rate of total taxes to GDP) as a reference to proportional expression of tax revenues of countries and rate of this variable to GDPs of countries are defined as an objective criterion in the denominator of the variable. On the other hand, *trade opennes* and *foreign directs investments* are preferred as independent variables as they indicate the trade dimension of globalization and capital movements dimension of globalization respectively.

In the study, the long-term relationships between the rate of total taxes of 11 developed countries which are referred to as G10, to GDP (*tr*), rate of their foreign trade to GDP (trade openness- *op*) and rate of foreign directs investments to GDP (*fdi*) are investigated with panel data analysis method but since we had fully and uninterruptedly accessed only the data of 10 countries in the context of the period of the study, the study is based on only those 10 countries. In this study trade openness and foreign direct investments are considered as projections of globalization. The impact of changes in the rate of *op* and *fdi* on total tax revenues is investigated with the help of the following logarithmic-linear model.

$$\ln tr_{it} = \alpha_0 + \alpha_1 \ln op_{it} + \alpha_2 \ln fdI_{it} + \varepsilon_{it} \qquad (1)$$

where I = 1, 2, ... 10, and t = 1, 2, ... 26. The model will be tested with the data covering the years of 1990-2015 for 10 countries (Netherlands, Canada, Sweden, Switzerland, France, Germany, United Kingdom, United States, Italy, Japan). The following hypotheses will be tested through the constituted model: i) Increased trade openness decreases tax revenues, ii) Increased capital movements reduce tax revenues.

All of the data used in the study were taken from World Bank World Development Indicators Online Database. Natural logarithmic forms of all variables included in the model are used.

ANALYSES AND FINDINGS

Cross-section independency is based on the assumption that any shock experienced in any unit included in the panel affects all countries equally and a macroeconomic shock experienced in any country does not affect other countries that compose the panel. The assumption that the imbalances that occur in the economies of one or more countries would also affect other countries in parallel to globalization process is a fairly realistic assumption. On the other hand, the assumption that the impact on countries may differ rather than the impact will be same in all countries is also realistic.If there is a cross-section dependency between the series, not considering this fact significantly affects the findings of analyses (Breush & Pagan, 1980). The status of cross-section dependency between the series that constitute the panel is investigated with LM Test developed by Berusch & Pagan (1980) or CD Test developed by Pesaran (2004).

One of the differences between the mentioned tests stems from the time (T) and cross-section (N) dimension of the panel. LM Test by Berusch and Pagan (1980) is used in the case of where T ˃ N (Equation 2) and CD Test by Paseran (2004) can be used in the case of where $N/T\rightarrow\infty$, N ˃ T (Equation 3) and CD Test (Equation 4) re-developed by Pesaran (2004) is used in both cases where $T\rightarrow\infty$ or $N\rightarrow\infty$, N ˃ T, T ˃ N. All three tests deviate from the group average is zero but individual average is different than zero (Nazlıoğlu et al., 2011). In LM_{adj} (deviation adjusted LM) test developed by Pesaran et al. (2008), the said deviation is adjusted by adding variance and mean to test statistics (Equation 5). Estimation equations related to the said test statistics are as follows:

$$CD_{lm1} = T\sum_{i=1}^{N-1}\sum_{j=i+1}^{N} p_{ij}^2 \tag{2}$$

$$CD_{lm2} = \left(\frac{1}{N(N-1)}\right)^{1/2} \sum_{i=1}^{N-1}\sum_{j=i+1}^{N} \left(Tp_{ij}^2 - 1\right) \tag{3}$$

$$CD_{lm3} = \left(\frac{2T}{N(N-1)}\right)^{1/2} \sum_{i=1}^{N-1}\sum_{j=i+1}^{N} p_{ij} \tag{4}$$

$$LM_{adj} = \sqrt{\left(\frac{2T}{N(N-1)}\right)} \sum_{i=1}^{N-1}\sum_{j=i+1}^{N} p_{ij} \frac{\left(T-k\right)p_{ij}^2 - \mu_{Tij}}{\sqrt{\nu_{Tij}^2}} \tag{5}$$

With these tests, the following hypotheses are tested:

H_0: There is no cross-section dependency.
H_1: Cross-section dependency exists.

The results obtained for these tests are separately calculated for each of the variables included in the equation in Table 1.

According to Table 1, for level values of all variables, the hypothesis of H_0 is strongly rejected (at the 1% significance). These results confirm the dependency between each series belonging to the countries composing the panel and series belonging to another country.

In the other words, the type and timing of tax policy in one country affects another country's tax system. Nation state can no longer set their tax policy independently of each other (Seelkopf &Lierse, 2017).

On the other hand, homogeneity of the coefficients of variables used in equation 1 and existence of cross-section dependency throughout the model are important for selection of following tests. For example, while cross-section dependency tests are important for selection of unit root tests to be applied on variables, it is also important to interpret the cointegration tests to be applied to the series whether the coefficients of variables are homogeneous or not. For this purpose, Slope Homogeneity Test or Delta ($\tilde{\Delta}$) test developed by Pesaran & Yagamata (2008) are used in the study. This test suggests two different methods which are valid for big and small samples. $\tilde{\Delta}$ test is valid for big samples and $\tilde{\Delta}_{adj}$ test is recommended for small samples. The equations for the said test are as follows:

$$\tilde{\Delta} = \sqrt{N}\left(\frac{N^{-1}\tilde{S} - k}{\sqrt{2k}}\right) \tag{6}$$

$$\tilde{\Delta}_{adj} = \sqrt{N}\left(\frac{N^{-1}\tilde{S} - E(\tilde{z}_{iT})}{\sqrt{Var(\tilde{z}_{iT})}}\right) \tag{7}$$

With these tests, the following hypotheses are tested:

H_0: $\beta_i = \beta$ (Slope coefficients are homogeneous)
H_1: $\beta_i \neq \beta$ (Slope coefficients are heterogeneous)

Table 2 includes the results of homogeneity and cross-section dependency tests for Equation 1.

Table 1. Results from cross-section dependence tests (for each variable)

Constant	lntr		lnop		lnfdi	
	Statistic	p-value	Statistic	p-value	Statistic	p-value
CD_{lm1} (BP,1980)	100.347***	0.000	71.823***	0.007	68.698**	0.013
CD_{lm2} (Pesaran, 2004)	5.834***	0.000	2.827***	0.002	2.498***	0.006
CD_{lm3} (Pesaran, 2004)	-2.648***	0.004	-2.922***	0.002	-2.408***	0.008
LM_{adj} (PUY, 2008)	70.083***	0.000	19.318***	0.000	2.416***	0.008

Note: Lag orders (p_i) are 1. ***,** Denotes statically significance at %1, %5.

Table 2. Results from cross-section dependence and homogeneity tests

$\ln tr_{it} = \alpha_0 + \alpha_1 \ln op_{it} + \alpha_2 \ln fdI_{it} + \varepsilon_{it}$	Statistic	p-value
Cross-section dependency tests:		
CD_{lm1} (BP,1980)	106.757	0.000
CD_{lm2} (Pesaran, 2004)	6.721	0.000
CD_{lm3} (Pesaran, 2004)	2.632	0.004
LM_{adj} (PUY, 2008)	23.615	0.000
Homogeneity tests:		
$\tilde{\Delta}$	13.922	0.000
$\tilde{\Delta}_{adj}$	14.802	0.000

Note: ***,** Denotes statically significance at %1, %5.

According to test results in Table 2, the hypothesis of "there is no cross-section dependency" is rejected for Equation 1. According to these results, the series of countries constituting the cross-section are affected from each other. According to these results, the unit root tests that consider cross-section dependency should be applied in the following stage. On the other hand, according to the results of homogeneity test, the slope coefficients of the variables are heterogeneous.

The above-mentioned tests are preliminary tests, and after this stage unit root tests, cointegration tests, long-term coefficient estimates and causality test results will be given.

Unit root test, the necessary analyses will be made to determine if the variables included in Equation 1 are affected by an external shock or if they return to their normal state. These types of tests are important in the sense that if series include unit root or not. If the examined series includes a unit root, it means that all external shocks continuously show their impact on it and it cannot go back to its previous state with market conditions. In fact, in a more comprehensible expression, the answer is sought to the question of "is the general functioning of variables prone to return to equilibrium?"

In this study, "Dicky-Fuller (Cross-Sectionally Augmented Dicky-Fuller (CADF)) test", which is proposed by Peseran (2007) and considers the cross-section dependency, is used. This test is applied to the following panel regression model.

$$\Delta y_{it} = \mu_i + \rho_i y_{it-1} + c_i \overline{y}_{t-1} + c_i \Delta \overline{y}_{t-1} + e_{it} \tag{8}$$

$$\overline{y}_{t-1} = 1 / N \sum_{i-1}^{N} y_{it-1} \tag{9}$$

$$\Delta \overline{y}_t = 1 / N \sum_{i-1}^{N} \Delta y_{it} \tag{10}$$

Since the estimation is performed separately for each section in Equation 8, this parameter also considers those belong to heterogeneous. Estimation of $\overline{y}_{t-1}$ and $\Delta\overline{y}_t$ added to the model ensures consideration of cross-section dependency depending upon a single factor (Nazlıoğlu, 2010). The CADF test is calculated separately for three different situations: Δy_{it} critical values, $\overline{y}_{t-1}$ constant, and $y_{i,t-1}$ non-constant. The CADF test, which takes into account autocorrelation and assumes that each country is differently affected by time effects, can be used in both T˃N and N˃T situations (Peseran, 2007). The CADF test can be calculated for the panel in general and separately for each cross-section. The average of the unit root test statistics for each cross-section and the CIPS (Cross-sectionally Augmented IPS) test for the panel, in general, are calculated as follows:

$$CIPS = 1 / N\sum_{i-1}^{N} CADF_i \tag{11}$$

Equation 11 is the average of Equation 9. The null and alternative hypotheses of the predicted equations are as follows:

$$H_0 : \rho_i = 0 \tag{12}$$

$$H_1 : \rho_i \langle 0\ i = 1,2,...N_1),\ \rho_i : 0\ i = N_i + 1, N_1 + 2,...N) \tag{13}$$

Equation 12 applies to all cross-sections. These hypotheses test that each series of cross-section hypothesis panels contains the unit root of the series, while the alternative hypothesis tests that a particular section of the cross-sections that form the panel does not contain unit roots. The unit root test results of the variables in Equation 1 are given in Table 3.

CADF results in Table 3 with the table values given in Pesaran (2007), it will be understood whether the series contain unit roots. The CADF and CIPS statistics developed by Pesaran (2007), the t-statistics for the ρ_i coefficients are rejected for the series belonging to each cross section if they are greater than the critical values given in Pesaran (2007), and it is decided that the series is stationary. The following critical values were used from the tables given by Pesaran (2007) with reference to the time and cross-section examined in this study (T: 26 and N: 10).

According to the results given in Table 3, the CIPS unit root test results of the variables do not include unit root at the level I (I). Therefore, it has been determined that the stationarity ratings of the variables are I (I). After this phase, cointegration analyzes will be done.

Unless tests are carried out to find out whether there is a long-term relationship between the variables in the stationary state, the estimates of their coefficients are not economically realistic and statistically correct. In this study, the "LM bootstrap cointegration" test developed by Westerlund & Ederton (2007) was preferred to determine whether the analyzed series did not move together in the long run. This test takes the cross-section dependency into consideration. Bootstrap p-value is valid when the cross-section dependency is present. The equation for this test is as follows:

Table 3. Results from panel unit root tests

	Constant		Constant and Trend	
	Lags	CADF-stat	Lags	CADF-stat
Δ*lntr*				
Netherlands	1	-3.392	1	-3.681
Canada	1	-3.709	1	-3.686
Sweden	1	-3.532	1	-3.772
Switzerland	1	-2.874	1	-3.071
France	2	-1.972	2	-2.449
Germany	2	-2.763	2	-2.849
United Kingdom	1	-3.938	1	-3.870
United States	2	-3.705	2	-3.593
Italy	1	-3.748	1	-4.129
Japan	1	-2.746	1	-3.317
CIPS		-3.240*		-3.442*
Δ*lnop*				
Netherlands	1	-2.618	3	-1.451
Canada	1	-1.912	1	-1.299
Sweden	1	-3.467	1	-5.293
Switzerland	3	-1.281	3	-0.237
France	1	-2.419	1	-2.471
Germany	2	-3.635	1	-3.122
United Kingdom	1	-3.241	1	-3.108
United States	3	-0.851	3	-0.315
Italy	1	-3.166	2	-2.575
Japan	2	-2.679	2	-2.673
CIPS		-2.527**		-2.254
Δ*lnfdi*				
Netherlands	1	-4.185	1	-4.049
Canada	1	-4.024	1	-4.027
Sweden	1	-6.522	1	-6.937
Switzerland	4	-1.677	4	-1.329
France	1	-4.745	2	-3.955
Germany	1	-5.150	1	-5.055
United Kingdom	1	-5.528	1	-5.100
United States	1	-4.724	1	-4.628
Italy	3	-1.515	3	-1.257
Japan	1	-3.792	1	-3.807
CIPS		-4.159*		-4.014*

Note: Lag orders is 4 and selected by minimizing the Swhwarz criteria. *, ** Indicate significance at the %1, % 5 level.

Table 4. Pesaran (2007) critical value

		T:30, N:10		
Table no-tests	**DT**	**%1**	**%5**	**%10**
I(a)-CADF	Intercept only	-4.11	-3.36	-2.97
I(b)-CADF	Intercept and trend	-4.67	-3.87	-3.49
II(b)-CIPS	Intercept only	-2.57	-2.33	-2.21
II(c)-CIPS	Intercept and trend	-3.10	-2.86	-2.73

$$y_{it}^{*} = \hat{a}_i + x_{it}^{*\prime}\hat{\beta}_i + z_{it}^{*},\ x_{it}^{*} = \sum_{j=1}^{t}\Delta x_{ij}^{*}, \tag{14}$$

In this equation, $\hat{a}_i$ and $\hat{\beta}_i$ are a fully adapted estimates of a_i and β_i. In this equation, y_{it}^{*} and x_{it}^{*} are calculated with the Bootstrap test statistic. The LM statistic shows a right-wing normal distribution with a critical value of 1.645 at the 5% significance level. The hypothesis for this test is as follows:

$H_0 : \sigma_i^2 = 0$; there is co integration for all cross sections.
$H_1 : \sigma_i^2 \rangle 0$; there is no cointegration for some cross sections.

The results of this test are given in Table 5.

According to the results in Table 5 (constant), the Bootstrap p-value values indicate that H_0 hypothesis can not be rejected in 1%. Accordingly, there is a long-run relationship between *tr, op,* and *fdi* .

After the existence of a long-term relationship between the series was determined by Westerlund & Ederton (2007) cointegration test, the Augmented Mean Group Estimator (AMG) method, developed by Eberhardt & Bond (2009)[2] for predicting long-run coefficients, which takes cross-section dependency into consideration was used Eberhardt & Bond (2009) developed an estimator that can calculate the panel cointegration coefficients of the countries that consist the panel and the panel in general with the AMG test. This method considers the common factors in the series and is also used in the presence of the problem of internalisability, which indicates that there is a correlation between explanatory variables and error terms (Eberhardt & Bond, 2009). Equations of the mentioned test are as follows:

$$\ldots y_{it} = \beta_i x_{it} + u_{it} \ldots u_{it} = a_i + \lambda_{i1}^{y} f_{1t} + \lambda_{i2}^{y} f_{2t} + \varepsilon_{it} \tag{15}$$

Table 5. Results from LM bootstrap panel co-integration

	Constant			Constant and Trend		
Tests	**Statistic**	**Asymptotic p-value**	**Bootstrap p-value**	**Statistic**	**Asymptotic p-value**	**Bootstrap p-value**
LM bootstrap						
LM_N^{+}	2.369	0.009	0.949*	4.573	0.000	0.494

Note: The Bootstrap test statistics are calculated using 1.000 replications. * Indicate significance at the %1 level.

$$\ldots\ x_{it} = a_i + \lambda_{i1}^{x} f_{1t} + \lambda_{i3}^{x} f_{3t} + \varepsilon_{it} \ldots \varepsilon_{it} = \rho\varepsilon_{i,t-1} + e_{it} \quad (16)$$

$$x_{it} = (1-\rho)a_i + \lambda_i^{x_1} f_{1,t} - \rho\lambda_i^{x_1} f_{1,t-1} + \lambda_i^{x_3} f_{3,t} - \rho\lambda_i^{x3} f_{3,t-1} + \rho x_{i,t-1} + e_{it} \quad (17)$$

In the Equation 17, x_{it} represents an observable common variable vector, λ_i represents the actor loads of countries. Table 6 contains the estimated long-term coefficient estimates for Equation 1, adapted to the Equation 17.

We can put together the results of cointegration coefficient estimates shown in Table 6 in two groups. We can separate each group into two subgroups. The first one these sub-groups is mainly the countries where the trade openness has a negative impact on total tax revenues. These are the Netherlands and Italy. On the other hand, trade openness has a positive impact on total tax revenues in Sweden, Switzerland, France and the United Kingdom. The effects of *fdi* on total tax revenues can be similarly evaluated in two categories. Countries, where *fdi* have a negative impact on tax revenues, are Canada, Italy, and Japan. The UK is the country in which *fdi* have a positive impact on tax revenues. On the other hand, there is no statistically significant, positive or negative impact on the tax revenues of total foreign direct investments among the other countries included in the panel. Panel-wide results show that trade openness has a positive impact on total tax revenues.

We can interpret the AMG country coefficient estimates in Table 6 as an example. For example; the impact of *op* over each country on *tr* is as follows: One unit increase in *op* increases *tr* by 0.93 in Sweden, 0.41 in Switzerland, 0.57 in France and 0.20 in the United Kingdom, while decreasing 1.19 in the Netherlands and 0.19 in Italy. On the other hand, for the *fdi* variant, the results are as follows:

Table 6. Results from AMG tests

Countries	ln*op*			ln*fdi*		
	Coef.	z-st.	Prob.	Coef.	z-st.	Prob.
Netherlands	-1.19*	-1.71	0.087	-0.01	-0.80	0.421
Canada	0.06	0.81	0.415	-0.04*	-3.77	0.000
Sweden	0.93*	6.25	0.000	-0.002	-0.15	0.880
Switzerland	0.41*	5.73	0.000	0.17	1.48	0.140
France	0.57*	11.41	0.000	0.14	1.32	0.188
Germany	0.26	0.49	0.621	-0.003	-0.34	0.736
United Kingdom	0.20*	3.01	0.003	0.28*	3.27	0.001
United States	0.12	1.01	0.311	0.005	0.18	0.854
Italy	-0.19*	-3.19	0.001	-0.01*	-2.51	0.012
Japan	0.02	0.29	0.769	-0.03*	-2.14	0.032
Panel	0.19*	1.77	0.076	-0.003	-0.57	0.569
Wald $chi^2(2)$	5.31					
Prob > chi^2	0.0703					

Note: * Indicate significance at the %5 level.

One unit increase in *fdi* causes decrease in *tr* as 0.04 in Canada, 0.1 in Italy, and 0.03 in Japan, while the mentioned coefficient has a positive impact in the UK and causes an increase of 0.28. Estimated coefficient results for other countries are not statistically significant. In addition, the *op* coefficient is significant in the general panel, and the 1-unit increase in *op* causes 0.19 increase in *tr*. The coefficient for the *fdi* variable is statistically insignificant in the panel in general.

Finally, within the scope of the study, the Bootstrap panel Granger causality test developed by Emirmahmutoğlu & Köse (2011) was used to determine the direction of causality relationship between total tax revenues, trade openness and total foreign direct capital. Emirmahmutoğlu & Köse (2011) test is a test that includes assumptions such as dependency and heterogeneity between cross-sections. The equation for this test is as follows:

$$z_{i,t} = \mu_i + A_{i1} z_{i,t-1} + \dots A_{ik} z_{i,t-k_i} + \sum_{l=k_i+1}^{k_i+d\max_i} A_{il} z_{i,t-1} + v_{i,t} \tag{18}$$

$$i = 1,2,\dots,N, t = 1,2,\dots,T$$

In this test, the H_0: $A_{12,\ ij}=0$ hypothesis is tested with the Equation 8, and k_i+d_{max} expresses the maximum number of delays, while A_{il} expresses the limits of parameters. The results obtained from the Bootstrap causality test are given in Table 7 and 8.

The results provide some clues as to the direction of the causality between total tax revenues and trade openness in Table 7. For United States, there was a unidirectional causality running from tax revenue to trade openness, supporting the capital mobility hypothesis. On the other hand in the case of Sweden and Germany there was a unidirectional causality running from trade openness to tax revenue. For Canada, there was a bi-directional causality running between trade openness and tax revenue. In

Table 7. Results from bootstrap casualty tests

Countries	k_i	Tr-Op		Op-Tr	
		Hypothesis		Hypothesis	
		W_i	P_i	W_i	P_i
Netherlands	1	0.569	0.451	0.280	0.596
Canada	2	7.694	0.021**	9.404	0.009***
Sweden	5	4.584	0.469	21.264	0.001***
Switzerland	1	0.465	0.495	0.275	0.600
France	1	0.006	0.937	2.397	0.122
Germany	1	0.014	0.907	2.931	0.087*
United Kingdom	1	0.873	0.350	0.896	0.344
United States	2	11.656	0.003***	2.900	0.235
Italy	1	0.192	0.661	1.237	0.266
Japan	2	3.422	0.181	4.335	0.114
Fisher Test St.		30.539		47.043	

Note: Lag orders k_i are selected by minimizing the Swhwarz criteria. *, **,*** Indicate significance at the %10, %5 and %1 level.

the remaining six countries of the sample there was no causality running in any direction between tax revenue and trade openness.

The results provide some clues as to the direction of the causality between tax revenues and foreign direct investments. According to the causality test results shown in Table 8. For Switzerland, there was a unidirectional causality running from tax revenue to foreign direct investments supporting the capital mobility hypothesis. In the remaining nine countries of the sample there was no causality running in any direction between tax revenue and foreign direct investments. On the other hand in the all countries of the sample there was no causality running in any from foreign direct investments to tax revenue.

CONCLUSION

In this study, the tax revenues, which make up 70-90% of the nation state revenues, are investigated by various econometric tests to find out whether and how they are affected by the globalization process. Among the tests made, the results of the CD tests are consistent with the theory: In the process of globalization, the tax policy of an individual country is affected by other countries or it affects other countries. On the other hand, the results of the homogeneity test show that this effect is at a different level in each country. The results of the unit root tests that test the stability of the series indicate that tax revenues are static, meaning that they are affected by a shock that emerges, but that they return to their previous status again. In this context, the tax revenues of the nation states, which are affected by external shocks, soon return to the balance or get rid of the crisis situation. These results show that the countries that consist cross-section are adapting to the globalization process in the context of tax revenues. Long-term coefficient results obtained from this study reveal that there may be different coefficients on the basis of countries that show a positive effect in the general panel in the "tax tension" between globalization and the nation states.

Table 8. Results from bootstrap casualty tests

Country	k_i	*tr-fdi*		*fdi-tr*	
		Hypothesis		Hypothesis	
		W_i	P_i	W_i	P_i
Netherlands	1	0.869	0.351	0.164	0.686
Canada	1	2.092	0.148	0.110	0.740
Sweden	5	6.601	0.252	1.543	0.908
Switzerland	2	5.038	0.081*	0.240	0.887
France	1	0.120	0.729	0.818	0.366
Germany	2	3.432	0.180	2.818	0.366
United Kingdom	1	0.522	0.470	2.491	0.288
United States	2	0.560	0.756	1.468	0.226
Italy	1	0.624	0.430	0.588	0.443
Japan	4	5.300	0.258	5.132	0.274
Fisher Test St.		24.240		13.884	

Note: Lag orders k_i are selected by minimizing the Swhwarz criteria. *, **,*** Indicate significance at the %10, %5 and %1 level.

Coefficient estimation results for each country provide explanatory information on tax revenues. Countries, where *op* has a negative effect on *tr*, are the Netherlands and Italy, countries, where *op* has a positive effect on *tr*, are Sweden, Switzerland, France, the United Kingdom. On the other hand, countries where *fdi* has a negative effect on *tr* are Canada, Italy, and Japan. The only country where *fdi* has a positive effect on *tr* is the United Kingdom. According to these results, UK tax revenues are increasing in the globalization process. Italy's tax revenues are declining in the globalization process. On the other hand, in Sweden, Switzerland, and France, there is a positive impact on tax revenues and the globalization process. If there are winners' club members in this process, they can be listed as; England, Sweden, Switzerland, and France. The losers' club members are mainly Italy, and the Netherlands, Canada, and Japan.

Despite the fact that the concept of globalization has not been fully defined, it is widely used in the fields of politics and economy. In addition, ambiguity in the concept of globalization brings along difficulties in understanding its causes and how. Nevertheless, an analogy can be good for the relationship between tax revenues of nation states and globalization. Globalization has not yet passed Rubicon[3] in the context of tax revenues. At least the results of this study can be read in this way. On the other hand, a different explanation may be needed in this subject. According to the results obtained from this study, the following evaluation can be made: In the context of globalization, some of the nation states may think that globalization ends in Rubicon. But who is responsible for that? Is it Caesar?

In our opinion, Caesar of globalization is the "capital". On the other hand, some states who think that Rubicon cross over the limit in globalization have taxed salaried employees, thinking that not "Caesar" but the salaried employees are responsible. At least, all nation states except Japan provide a large proportion of their total tax revenues through taxes on wages and consumption. In all of these countries, except Japan, the share of corporate tax revenues is quite low in total tax revenues. Where the "Rubicon" between tax revenues and globalization process starts and ends, where the antagonism emerges as a mystery. In this sense, globalization does not seem to have created a problem at this stage in terms of tax revenues of nation states. Because the alternative cost of indirect taxes and wages on remuneration for losses is very low.

Nation states use "compensatory tax policy" on salaried employees by using the tax mobility against the mobilization of nation states and companies. With compensatory tax policies, we would like to refer to the tax policies applied by nation states in order to make, use of the geese in the coop instead of the geese who flew away.

REFERENCES

Asher, M. G., & Rajan, R. S. (1999). *Globalization and Tax Systems: Implications for Developing Countries with Particular Reference to Southeast Asia.* Centre for International Economic Studies and Scholl of Economics University of Adelaide, Discussion Paper 99/23.

Ball, L. M. (1999). Policy Rules for Open Economies. In *Monetary policy rules* (pp. 127–156). University of Chicago Press.

Baunsgaard, T., & Keen, M. (2005). *Tax Revenue and (or?) Trade Liberalization.* International Monetary Fund, IMF Working Paper, No: WP/05/112.

Bresusch, T. S., & Pagan, A. R. (1980). A Lagrange Multiplier Test and its Applications to Model Specification in Econometrics. *The Review of Economic Studies*, *47*(1), 239–253. doi:10.2307/2297111

Bretschger, L., & Hettich, F. (2002). Globalisation, Capital Mobility and Tax Competition: Theory and Evidence for OECD Countries. *European Journal of Political Economy*, *18*(4), 695–716. doi:10.1016/S0176-2680(02)00115-5

Brunetti, A., & Weder, B. (1999). *More Open Economies Have Better Goverments*. Universität des Saarlandes, Economic Series, No. 9905.

Cagé, J., & Gadenne, L. (2012). *The fiscal cost of trade liberalization*. PSE Working Paper, 2012-27.

Cagé J., & Gadenne L. (2016). *Tax Revenues, Development, and the Fiscal Cost of Trade Liberalization, 1792-2006*. Warwick Economics Research Papers, No: 1132.

Dreher, A. (2006). The Influence of Globalization on Taxes and Social Policy: An Empirical Analysis for OECD Countries. *European Journal of Political Economy*, *22*(1), 179–201. doi:10.1016/j.ejpoleco.2005.04.006

Ďurinová, I. (2006). Taxation under Conditions of Economic Globalization. *BIATEC, 14*(10).

Eberhartd, M. (2012). Estimating Panel Time-series Models with Heterogeneous Slopes. *The Stata Journal*, *12*(1), 61–71. doi:10.1177/1536867X1201200105

Eberhartd, M., & Bond, S. (2009). *Cross-section Dependence in Nonstationary Panel Models: A Novel Estimator. MPRA paper 17870*. University Library of Munich.

Emirmahmutoglu, F., & Kose, N. (2011). Testing for Granger Causality in Heterogeneous Mixed Panels. *Economic Modelling*, *28*(3), 870–876. doi:10.1016/j.econmod.2010.10.018

Filiz, G. (2005). Küreselleşme Sürecinde Vergi Rekabeti ve Boyutları. *Akdeniz İ.İ.B.F. Dergisi*, *9*, 93–122.

Grunberg, I. (1998). Double Jeopardy: Globalization, Liberalization and the Fiscal Squeeze. *World Development*, *26*(4), 591–605. doi:10.1016/S0305-750X(97)10068-7

Habermas, J. (2003). *İnsan Doğasının Geleceği*. İstanbul: Everest Yayınları.

Hines, J. R. Jr, & Summers, L. H. (2009). How Globalization Affects Tax Design. *Tax Policy and the Economy*, *23*(1), 123–158. doi:10.1086/597056

Hiscox, M. J. (2001). *Political Integration and Disintegration in the Global Economy: The Effects of Globalization on Incentives to Alter the Structure of Governance*. In Globalization and Governance II Conference, IGCC, San Diego, CA.

Holman, N., & Thornley, A. (2015). Backlash in the London Suburbs: The Local-strategic Tension in Multilevel Governance. *Environment and Planning. C, Government & Policy*, *33*(3), 496–511. doi:10.1068/c13135

Kazgan, G. (2009). *Küreselleşme ve Ulus-Devlet, Yeni Ekonomik Düzen*. İstanbul: İstanbul Bilgi Üniversitesi Yayınları.

Kumar, M. S., & Quinn, D. P. (2012). *Globalization and Corporate Taxation.* International Monetary Fund, IMF Working Paper, WP/12/252.

Leviner, S. (2013). The Intricacies of Tax and Globalization, Columbia. *Journal of Tax Law, 5*(207), 209–227.

Nazlıoğlu, Ş. (2010). *Makro İktisat Politikalarının Tarım Sektörü Üzerindeki Etkileri: Gelişmiş ve Gelişmekte Olan Ülkeler için Bir Karşılaştırma.* Yayınlanmamış Doktora Tezi, Kayseri Üniversitesi Sosyal Bilimler Enstitüsü.

Nazlıoğlu, S., Lebe, F., & Kayhan, S. (2011). Nuclear Energy Consumption and Economic growth in OECD countries: Cross-sectionaly Dependent Heterogeneous Panel Casuality Analysis. *Energy Policy, 39*(10), 6615–6621. doi:10.1016/j.enpol.2011.08.007

Ndikumana, L. (2015). *International Tax Cooperation and Implications of Globalization, Global Governance and Rules for the Post 2015 Era: Addressing Emerging Issues in the Global Environment.* Bloomsbury Academic.

Pereira, F. M. G. (2003). *Globalization and Tax Systems. The Center of Latin American Issues and The Institute of Brazilian Business & Public Management Issues.* Washington, DC: Minevra Program.

Pesaran, H. M. (2004). *General Diagnostic Test for Cross-section Dependence in Panels.* IZA Discussion Paper 1240, Institute for the Study of Labor.

Pesaran, H. M. (2007). A Simple Panel Unit Root Test in the Presence of Cross-Section Dependence. *Journal of Applied Econometrics, 22*(2), 265–312. doi:10.1002/jae.951

Pesaran, H. M., Ullah, A., & Yamagata, T. (2008). A Bias-adjusted LM Test of Error Cross-section Independence. *The Econometrics Journal, 11*(1), 105–127. doi:10.1111/j.1368-423X.2007.00227.x

Pesaran, H. M., & Yamagata, T. (2008). Testing Slope Homogeneity in Large Panels. *Journal of Econometrics, 142*(1), 50–93. doi:10.1016/j.jeconom.2007.05.010

Rodrik, D. (1998). Why Do More Open Economies Have Bigger Governments. *Journal of Political Economy, 106*(5), 992–1032. doi:10.1086/250038

Seelkopf, L., & Lierse, H. (2017). *Taxation and Inequalty: How Tax Copmetition Has Changed the Redistributive Capacity of Nation-States in the OECD.* Welfare State Transformations and Inequality in OECD Countries, Transformations of the State, Inequality in OECD Countries, Transformations of the State. doi:10.1057/978-1-137-51184-3_5

Sert, M. (2011). Küreselleşmenin Vergi Politikalarına Etkileri: OECD'ye Üye Ülkeler Özelinde Bir İnceleme. *Vergi Dünyası, 360*, 170–178.

Swank, D. (1998). Funding the Welfare State: Globalization and the Taxation of Business in Advanced Market Economies. *Political Studies, 46*(4), 671–692. doi:10.1111/1467-9248.00161

Tanzi, V. (1996). *Globalization, Tax Competition and the Future of Tax Systems.* IMF Working Paper, WP/96/141.

Tanzi, V. (2000). *Globalization, Technological Developments, and the Work of Fiscal Termites.* IMF Working Paper, 00/181.

Tanzi, V. (2004). *Globalization and the Need for Fiscal Reform in Developing Countries.* Inter-American Development Bank, Integration and Regional Programs Department, Occasional Paper- SITI-06.

Westurlund, J., & Edgerton, D. L. (2007). A Panel Bootstrap Cointegration Test. *Economics Letters, 97*(3), 185–190. doi:10.1016/j.econlet.2007.03.003

ADDITIONAL READING

Allen, M. P., & Campbell, J. L. (1994). State Revenue Extraction from Different Income Groups: Variations in Tax Progressivity in the United States 1916-1986. *American Sociological Review, 59*(2), 169–186. doi:10.2307/2096225

Anderws, M., Pritchett, L., & Woolcock, M. (2017). *Building State Capability: Evidence, Analysis, Action.* Oxford, United Kingdom: Oxford University Press. doi:10.1093/acprof:oso/9780198747482.001.0001

Bauman, Z. (2003). *Yasa Koyucular ile Yorumcular.* İstanbul: Metis Yayınları.

Bauman, Z. (2012). *Küreselleşme Toplumsal Sonuçları.* İstanbul: Ayrıntı Yayınları.

Borgne, E. L. (2006). Economic and Political Determinants of Tax Amnesties in the U.S States. *IMF Working Paper*, WP/06/222.

Campbell, J. L. (1993). The State and Fiscal Sociology. *Annual Review of Sociology, 19*(1), 163–185. doi:10.1146/annurev.so.19.080193.001115

Elias, N. (2015). [Batılı Dünyevi Üst Tabakaların Davranışlarındaki Değişmeler İstanbul: İletişim Yayınları]. *Uygarlık Süreci, I*, II.

Gıddens, A. (2008). *Ulus Devlet ve Şiddet.* İstanbul: Kalkedon Yayınları.

Gupta, A. (2007). Determinants of Tax Revenue Efforts in Devoloping Countries. *IMF Working Paper*, WP/07/184.

Haldun, I. (2013). *Mukaddime I-II.* İstanbul: Kaynak Yayınları.

Tilly, C. (2007). *Democracy.* New York: Cambridge University Press. doi:10.1017/CBO9780511804922

KEY TERMS AND DEFINITIONS

Augmented Mean Group Estimator: This method considers the common factors in the series and is also used in the presence of the problem of internalisability, which indicates that there is a correlation between explanatory variables and error terms.

Compensation Hypothesis: Suggests that there is a linear relationship between globalization and public expenditures, the fragility of the country's economies increase due to increased globalization and this produces effects that increase the inequalities in the economy.

Cross-Section Dependency: It is based on the assumption that any shock experienced in any unit included in the panel affects all countries equally and a macroeconomic shock experienced in any country does not affect other countries that compose the panel.

Efficiency Hypothesis: Suggests that capital and firms, which are described as moving factors, have the possibilities to escape from tax.

Fiscal Termites: Effect of technology on tax systems.

Rubicon: A name of the river about 29 km North of Italy, is a border between the Roman Empire province of Cisalpine Gaul and the South of Italy. It is a boundary for military initiatives that could threaten the Roman Republic. Julius Caesar passed this river in 49 BC and was considered a threat to the Republic.

Technological Vigor: Creative destruction of technology.

ENDNOTES

1 For the effect of technology on tax systems, Tanzi (2000) used the term called "fiscal termites" for financial termites.

2 In this study, Eberhardt (2012) 's STATA codes were used for the mentioned test.

3 Rubicon, a name of the river about 29 km North of Italy, is a border between the Roman Empire province of Cisalpine Gaul and the South of Italy. It is a boundary for military initiatives that could threaten the Roman Republic. Julius Caesar passed this river in 49 BC and was considered a threat to the Republic.

Section 4
International Economic Relations in the European Union

Chapter 9
A Discussion on Fiscal Policies Implemented in EU During and After the Great Recession

Gozde Es Polat
Bilecik Seyh Edebali University, Turkey

Onur Polat
Hacettepe University, Turkey

ABSTRACT

Along with the global financial crisis that took place in 2008, the ineffectiveness of other policies used for exiting from the crisis has brought back the feasibility of fiscal policy as an alternative. It is accepted that the only way to overcome the severe shrinking of the total demand during the 2008 global financial crisis is expansionary fiscal policy applied globally. However, differences in the subjective conditions of the EU member countries in particular have not made it possible to implement an expansionary fiscal policy for all of the member countries. More developed EU countries have begun to carry out from expansionary fiscal policies, while the less developed ones have begun to conduct contractionary fiscal policies. With the awareness that the financial stability is a public good, the obstacles, challenges on the global fiscal policy implementation by the EU member states are discussed by examining fiscal policies performed during and after the 2008 global financial crisis.

INTRODUCTION

The development of financialization along with globalization has opened the way for contagious effects of financial fragility to disperse throughout the world easily. Income has been transformed from the real sector to the financial sector and consequently the importance of financial system relative to real sector has escalated in the near past. Nevertheless, the financial system has reached an unprecedented level notably after the end of the 1990s and has become vulnerable to risks and fragilities that have arisen from speculative activities in the system. Owing to the nature of the capitalist system, bubbles have become inavoidable in the financial system, and eventually they have triggered bursts and turmoils in

DOI: 10.4018/978-1-5225-7564-1.ch009

the economic system. For instance, 2008 global financial crisis (GFC) came to exist by the bubble in the US subprime mortgage market and the hazardous effects of the crisis quickly spread out to the rest of the world owing to strong financial connectedness of the countries. Similar to the rest of the world, contagious effects of the financial crisis dispersed into European Union (EU) area and EU member states have begun to perform monetary and fiscal policies in order to overcome negative effects of the crisis. Likewise, EU states have launched expansionary monetary policies along with expansionary/discreatonary, fiscal policies for exiting the global financial crisis. In the meantime, the need for carrying out coordinated and consistent policy actions has gained importance within the EU area.

EU governments have begun to benefit from fiscal policy actions since monetary policy tools were insufficient to restore financial stability from financial turmoil rapidly. However; the financialization and development level of the governments ("periphery"/"core") directly designated the type of the fiscal policy action. Primarely; more developed EU states have begun to carry out expansionary fiscal policies; while the less developed ones have begun to conduct contractionary fiscal policies on the basis of their subjective conditions.

Nonetheless, there is no fiscal authority in the EU area that has power over EU member states in contrast to European Monetary Union (EMU) that has power of sustaining common monetary policy. This impediment induced seperation of fiscal policies due to subjective conditions of the governments and made difficult to maintain contemporaneous fiscal policies within the Euro area. Hereby, each member state performs its own fiscal policy during calm and turmoil financial periods and benefits from either expansionary or contractionary fiscal policies in exiting financial turmoils.

This chapter investigates the fiscal policy actions overtaken by "core"/ "peripheral" EU member states during global financial crisis (GFC) and European Sovereign debt crisis (Eurozone crisis). In addition, challenges, impediments in exiting from financial turmoils using fiscal policy actions (expansionary/ contractionary) by governments are discussed.

The remainder of this chapter is as follows: In Section 2; Keynesian view of fiscal policy in terms of expansionary/contractionary fiscal policy actions are discussed. Section 3 reviews the studies that describe the anatomy of financial crises. It presents well-known events during the global financial crisis and policy actions applied by the US government and discusses reasons behind the "great recession". Section 4 views the fiscal developments of periphery/core EU states during the GFC and European Sovereign debt crisis (Eurozone crisis). Finally, Section 5 discusses and gives the concluding remarks.

KEYNES AND THE FISCAL POLICY

The crisis of 1929 represents an important disintegration in terms of the theory of public finance. Fiscal policy approaches differ before and after the 1929 crisis in the public finance literature. Prior to 1929 crisis classical fiscal approach ("fiscal conservatism") was dominant, while modern fiscal approach (interventionist) became dominant during post 1929 crisis era.

During pre-1929 crisis period, it was widely believed that there would not be any problems in the economy as long as the each supply create its own demand. The 1929 crisis emerged as an important event that shows that this notion is not valid. In that period, it was seen that every supply did not create its own demand and the economy would not always move in the expected direction, and subsequently the need for government intervention to the economy was come to the fore. The birth of modern fiscal approach coincides with these years.

The problem-free period of classical fiscal approach ended with the 1929 depression. After the "great depression", emergence of the high rates of unemployment in the majority of industrialized countries, especially in the Great Britain, opened the debate on the assumption that every supply creates its own demand.

The underlying demand for economic imbalance was overshadowed by the inability to use most of the resulting productive resources, which hampered the desired performance growth of the economy. The high level of unemployment that emerged during this period also changed the way of thinking about economic policy, and the ultimately equal budget understanding based on the idea of classical fiscal approach was begun to be gradually abandoned.

In that period, John M. Keynes wrote "The General Theory of Employment, Interest and Money" which stated intervention is necessary to transform the economy into the desired direction, since there is no automatic mechanism to provide exiting from the crisis for the US and other countries experiencing recession. According to Keynes, the impact that led to rise in employment is the increase in demand. The employment problem can be solved with a sufficient and constant increase in demand. Keynes points out that private consumption can be increased via public spending if the problem is the inadequacy of consumption by the private sector. As seen on Keynes, the problem is related to demand side and the recession in the economy can be avoided by policies that enhance total demand (Keynes, 1936). For that reason, fiscal policy which affect demand stronger and more predictable, has become more prominent than monetary policy.

FISCAL POLICY TOOLS

With Keynes, the preoccupation of the fiscal policy has led to a preference for fiscal policy over monetary policy, especially for demand side problems. Fiscal policy instruments are used while the fiscal policy intervenes in the economy. There are three instruments of fiscal policy: Government spending, taxes and borrowing.

Government spending, the first one of these instruments, can be defined as the government expenditure made in carrying out public activities in a narrow sense. In terms of fiscal policy, economic intervention can be achieved by changing government expenditures and components according to economic conjuncture. The most basic orientation at this point is to raise government spending to increase demand during deflationary periods and to cut government spending to reduce demand during inflationary periods. Lowering government spending can be in the form of moving through certain items in public expenditures, as well as the cancellation of planned investment expenditures and the reduction of higher-benefit spending on low-income groups (eg social transfer expenditures), even though this is not a priority choice. As we have already pointed out, what is important here is to reduce or increase demand by conjuncture.

The second tool, *taxes*, is an important source to finance government spending. However, taxes can also be used to influence economic decisions. There are two main purposes of the taxes, fiscal and extra fiscal. The fiscal purpose of the tax is to generate income. In other words, taxation for the financing of public expenditure represents the fiscal purpose of the taxes. The extra fiscal purpose of the tax is to intervene economy with socially, politically or economically except for the function of generating income. Along with the extra fiscal purpose of the tax, which is also called social purpose, it is wished to influence some decisions in the economy. For example, consumption of alcohol and tobacco, which are harmful effects on public health, is aimed to be reduced by raising the amount of tax on these products.

On the contrary, the tax on some other products can be lowered to encourage the consumption of them. For example, in order to increase both the consumption of the automobile produced in the domestic market and the competition in the domestic market, this car may be excluded from the tax, or the tax on that automobile may be lowered. In addition to the fiscal purpose of the tax, it is saught to intervene economy and by this way economic decisions are affected.

The third tool is *borrowing*. Classicals assessed the borrowing tool as an extraordinary method. Nonetheless, with the development of modern public finance, borrowing was transformed a regular method from an extraordinary method. This favorable outlook on borrowing certainly does not mean the use of borrowing in an uncontrolled way. The use of borrowing in a controlled manner is beneficial both for generating income and for interfering with economic decisions. Borrowing can be resorted to as a source of finance in periods when income and expenditure balances are not available in terms of public finance. In addition, governments may owe to private individuals in order to hamper demand during inflationary periods. Conversely, in deflationary periods, borrowings taken to increase demand can be paid together with their interest rates. Thus, borrowing creates both income and affects economic decisions in terms of fiscal policy. Nonwithstanding to these two functions of borrowing, it should be behaved very carefully due to the interest to be paid while borrowing. Since borrowing has a burden, it should be paid attention to not reduce productive capacity. Restricting budgets owing to borrowing interest payments will naturally prevent fiscal policy instruments from functioning effectively. For that reason, it is very important that the borrowing is domestic or foreign while it is performed, whether the interest rate is high or low, or whether the borrowing is spent on productive investments or borrowing cycle.

The fiscal policy instruments mentioned above are very important for the efficient use of fiscal policies. As Keynes points out, fiscal policies are very effective way to solve demand-side problems in the economy. The fiscal policies that came up with Keynes after the great depression were later reduced to financial policies such as the creation of financial space in the developing countries, the target of primary surplus, which are tight fiscal policies, and in a sense hollowed out. Budget deficits became one of the most important problems in some developing and even in developed countries. Cut in some expenditures to provide the income and expenditure balance or increase of the tax is an important option to solve these problems. However, it should not be forgotten by governments that there is a need for public support to ensure development. In that regard, for example, the establishment of factories in priority areas for development, increasing social transfer expenditures for low-income groups in order to ensure justice in income distribution, providing public education, increasing health expenditures, tax exclusion of priority areas in development, can be more preferable method.

Reduction of fiscal policy to fiscal rule instead of development of country led to decline in current expenditures on budgets or social transfers rather than education, health spending or interest payments. In order to give primary surplus in the long term, the expenditures, which can affect the economy more positively are abandoned. And, this may affect the economies more adversely in the long run.

GLOBAL FINANCIAL CRISIS AND FİSCAL POLICY ONCE AGAIN

The crisis emerged in the US real estate market and spread out to the world through financial markets and caused to the nationalization of many financial institutions. In a short span of time, crisis spilled over to the real sector from financial markets and detrimentally affected emerging countries' economies via real sector. Both the lockdown in the financial sector and the congestion in the real sector caused economic slowdowns in many countries.

One of the important differences that distinguish the 2008 global financial crisis (GFC) from other crises lays on the policies applied to overcome the crisis. The GFC, which could not be overcome by classical policy actions applied in previous crises, tried to be overcome by more interventionist, state policies.

The economic recovery option, which is seen as a way to exit from the crisis, was not possible due to economic slowdown in all over the world. The other solution, the monetary policy, did not create the expected effect owing to descending monetary transmission mechanism. In addition, in many countries, the option of monetary expansion was used at the beginning of the crisis and the areas of action in terms of policy rate cuts of central banks were narrowed. In such an environment, the fiscal policy has begun to be seen as the most important policy option to revive the total demand in the short term. For this reason, many countries, especially the industrialized countries that were the most affected by the crisis, begun to implement expansionary fiscal policies (Bocutoglu and Ekinci, 2009, p. 67).

The IMF has announced that the most effective way to exit from the crisis is implementing expansionary fiscal policies. And, countries that attended to the G-20 summit in April 2009 agreed on conducting expansionary fiscal policies for economic growth.

GLOBAL FINANCIAL CRISIS' EVENTS AND TIMELINE

Before giving timeline and events pertained to global financial crisis; the anotomy, characteristics of financial crises in a capitalist economy and the reasons behind the crises are discussed. Afterwards, the timeline and policy actions overtaken by the US government during global financial crisis are briefly given.

ANOTOMY OF FINANCIAL CRISES

Capitalist economic system is inherently unstable and subject to the erratic shocks arisen from fluctiations in financial system. The worst depression in capitalist economy took place during 1929 financial crisis and it has been hit down several times since then. Financial imbalances have been saught to be kept under control by regulalization of financial system by governments since the great depression, yet financial crises couldn`t be hindered particularly in 1970s and end of 1980s. For example, the industrialized countries met with 18 banking crises (Spain (1977), Norway (1987), Finland (1991), Sweden (1991), Japan (1992), Australia (1989), Canada (1983), Denmark (1987), France (1994), Germany (1977), Greece (1991), Iceland (1985), Italy (1990), New Zealand (1987), United Kingdom (1973, 1991,1995) and the United States (1984) in the post-war period (after World War 2) (Reinhart and Rogoff, 2008).

Along with the nature of openness to erratic shocks that come from financial imbalances there is no common agreement over the reasons, conditions and consequences of financial crises, yet some stylized facts have been described by the studies. The earlier studies describe conditions and characteristics of financial crises. For example, Minsky (1970) introduces the reasons behind financial crises as severe decline in asset prices, deflations/disinflations, deteroiration of large financial/nonfinancial firms, failure in exchange markets.

Some other studies describe characteristics of financial crises (mostly via currency crises) with "first generation models" (Krugman, 1979; Flood and Garber, 1984) or "second generation models" (Obstfeld, 1988). According to "first generation models", crises are described as consequences of budget deficits ("need for government seignorage to cover its deficit that ensures the eventual collapse of a fixed exchange rate"). And, "the second generation models" explain conditions of crises as a conflict between fixed exchange rate regime and desire to sustain a more expansionary monetary policy.

According to Eichengreen and Portes (1987); "falling asset prices and insolvency among debtors and intermediaries, which ramifies through the financial system" trigger financial crises.

1990s studies also focus on general symptoms of financial crises. For instance, Mishkin (1992) imparts the causes of financial crises as asymmetric information, adverse selection and morald hazard in financial markets. The study links main reasons behind financial crises to `increases in interest rates, stock market declines, increases in uncertainity, bank panics and unanticipated declines in aggregate price levels". Krugman (1999) explains the stylized facts of financial crises as "contagion, the transfer problem, the balance sheet problems" (pp.463-464).

Recent studies have also analyzed causes and consequences of financial crises especially after the global financial crisis. By the view of Blanchard (2009), "underestimation of risk contained in newly issued assets, the opacity of the derived securities on the balance sheets of financial institutions, the connectedness of the financial institutions, high leverage of financial system" constitute main conditions for financal crises (p. 4). According to Reinhart and Rogoff (2009), asset market failures, detorioration in output and employment and increase in government debt are observed aftermath of financial crises. Taylor (2009) states that; "loose fitting monetary policy (too easy monetary policy), complex securization, underestimation of risk on subprime, mortgage markets" induced financial crises. Fligstein and Goldstein (2010) emphasises that the global financial crisis emerged after 2003 owing to maintaining high profits and volume by performing new sources of raw mortgages in unconventional markets (B/C, Alt-A, and home equity loans).

On the other hand, the 2008 global financial crisis ("great recession") was the worst financial turmoil since the great depression of 1929 and the contagious effects of the crisis are still pursued. While the debate in terms of reasons behind the "great recession" are still persisted, some common facts have been found by the studies. Bianco (2008) states that "housing bubble" in local/global real estate market owing to low interest rates triggered financial crisis. According to the study, "risky mortgage products and lax lending standarts, securization, misratings of credit rating agencies, borrowers in mortgage market, government and federal regulatory policies" were main causes of global financial crisis. Gorton (2008) describes the global financial crisis` main causes are "asymmetric information between sellers and buyers thanks to complexity, sensitive inter linked securities to house prices, spreading risk in an opaque way".

According to another study, the reasons behind the GFC are "the behaviour of many large, complex financial institutions (LCFIs), the legitimate and worthy purpose of securization, rating agencies` role in marketing asset backed securities to investors" (Acharya and Richardson, 2009).

By the view of Crotty (2009), light financial regulatory system ("new financial architecture (NFA)") triggered financial imbalances of the US and hereby the global financial crisis emerged. Light regulation of commercial banks, excessive risks, liquidity loss as a result of innovation in financial system, weak capital requirement system, heavy reliance on complex financial tools are the main reasons behind the GFC according to the study.

Cabellero and Krishnamurthy (2009) draw attention to structural factors behind the securization process that caused the boom in real estate market in the United States. The first one is linked to large capital inflows from foreigners to the US and the second one is related to excess world savings particularly after "NASDAQ/tech bubble" (p. 584).

Claessens et al. (2010) states that the conditions of the GFC that are common to the past financial crises as "sharp asset price increases, credit booms tha led to excessive debt burdens and build-up of marginal loans and systemic risk" and the conditions that are characteristic to the GFC as "more sophisticated financial intermediaries and instruments; increased interconnectedness, both nationally and internationally, among financial markets and a prominent role of household indebtedness".

Stiglitz (2010) interprets the problems behind the 2008 financial crisis twofolds: "Incentive problems and modelling problems". Incentive problems consist of "executive compensation system, incentives for accounting firms, securitazition, rating agency incentives, new conflicts of interest and a new culture, repeal of glasss steagall, the Bernanke-Greenspan put and morald hazard, creating a credit freze, transparency and complexity". On the other hand, modelling problems constitute "failing to understand deversification, intellectual incoherence, detecting Ponzi schemes".

TIMELINE AND POLICY ACTIONS DURING GFC

Global financial crisis emerged from residential housing market in the US following decelerating house price appreciations and defaults of borrowers. Defaults on Alt-A and subprime loans began to escalate in 2006 and accordingly investment banks that are largely invested with mortgage backed securities started to have liquidity problems.

The financial crisis presented different characteristics in 2007-2009 period. In the first phase of the financial crisis (from August 2007 through August 2008), the risk level of subprime mortgage markets upsurged, while the whole financial system was relatively affected. In the second phase of the financial crisis (from September 2008 through December 2009) subprime financial crisis became global financial crisis particularly after the collapse of Lehman Brothers. And, the first deterioration in credit markets dated to August 7, 2007 when the French Bank BNP Paribas suspended redemption of its money market funds' sharess (Mıshkin, 2011).

Contagious effects of turmoil in the residential housing market rapidly dispersed into whole financial system and eventually Bear Stearns became illiquid in March 2008. Bear Stearns had weaker capital adequecy requirements since it was operated under SEC prudential supervision and accordingly it was the first financial firm that confronted to liquidity problems. The US authorities decided to assist Bear Stearns and the Federal Reserve established a fund of $30 billion ($1 billion from J.P. Morgan, $29 billion from Federal Reserve) to purchase Bear Stearns' assets (Wall, 2012).

Fannie Mae and Freddie Mac, which were created to carry out public missions (to ensure stability and liquidity in the secondary mortgage market and to provide access to mortgage credit), became to be distressed in the meantime Notwithstanding being powerful and profitable public-private partnership, the firms were exposed to systemic risk owing to their hybrid structure. Following the defaults in borrowers in residential mortgage market, Fannie Mae and Freddie Mac faced to illiquidity problems. Subsequently, federal government passed the Housing and Economic Recovery Act (HERA) on July 30, 2008 which provided the US Treasury to give unlimited inmestment authority in two firms. Consequently, taxpayers injected $187.5 bn into Fannie Mae and Freddie Mac (Frame et al., 2015).

In the midst of the financial crisis, on September 15, 2008, Lehman Brothers filed for banktruptcy protection. Lehman had been suffered large losses sourced from real estate market and consequently became illiquid. In spite of takeover wishes by authorities, the company couldn't be saved owing to lack of legal authority (Ball, 2016). Collapse of Lehman Brothers triggered failure in Reserve Money Fund as well as other money market funds. Concurrently, the systemic stress spread out to commercial paper market and American International Group (AIG). Consequently, AIG collapsed on September 16, 2008 (Acharya, 2011). Eventually, the Emergency Economic Stabilization Act was approved by the Congress which authorized Troubled Asset Relief Program (TARP) (Wall, 2012, p. 8).

EVENTS AND POLICY ACTIONS OF PERIPHERY/ CORE EU STATES DURING AND AFTER GFC

"First generation" Stability and Growth Pact (SGP) was established by passing Maastricht Treaty in 1992 which had been applied until 2005 and mainly focused on excessive deficits rather than conducting cyclical fiscal policy. On the contrary, "the second generation" SGB that took place by 2005 reform paid attention to cyclical fiscal policies (Bénétrix and Lane, 2013, p. 165). Consequently, EU member states has begun to implement contractionary or expansionary fiscal policies actively. Along with monetary policy actions, these policies have also been used by EU governments during and after THE GFC in order to exit from crisis. In this section, events and policy actions in terms of cyclical fiscal policies implemented in periphery and central EU member states are discussed.

EU member states faced to two crises. The first one is largely emerged from EU banks that are heavily invested with US subprime mortgages. European Commission launched the European Economic Recovery Plan that involves contractionary fiscal policies in order to mitigate contagious effects of global financial crisis (Riet, 2010, p.10).

The crisis in the US became highly contagious thanks to the strong connectedness of financial systems of the countries. Narrowing demand mechanisms and international capital movements have dragged peripheral countries, especially Greece, Spain, Italy and Portugal, which lacked national currency, to the debt crisis (Erdem and Dönmez Atbaşı, 2011, p. 44). Hereby, the second crisis arose from sovereign debt of peripheral EU states. With the transition to the Euro, the member states of the European Union, which abandoned their national currency, reduced their monetary policy to the inflation target and the fiscal policies to the fiscal rule and have begun to implement strict monetary and fiscal policies. These policies are shaped according to the needs of "core" countries within the European Union (Lapavitsas et al. 2011,p. 322).

One of these peripheral countries, Greece had been faced to fiscal and current account deficits prior to the GFC, yet it had been able to finance them. However, Greece's fiscal deficit and government debt increased in 2010 (government budget deficit escalated to 12.7% of GDP and government debt upsurged to 115% of GDP by May 2010). Subsequently, Greece made an agreement with International Monetary Fund (IMF) and European Commission on May 2, 2010 which involves €110 bn of funds in return for aggreeing to reform its fiscal policy (Wall, 2012, pp. 378-379). In exchange for bailout, Greece has launched contractionary fiscal policies (tax increase, government expenditure cut) to restore Greek financial sustainability. In line with that, Greece agreed to apply fiscal adjustment worth €30bn (or 12.5% of 2009 GDP) throughout the next three years (Buiter and Rahbari, 2010).

Contrary to Greece, Ireland had strong fiscal position, low foreign debt and government surpluses prior to the GFC. However, Lehman's collapse resulted to failure in Irish property market and consequently Irish banks begun to have diffuculty in funding since they had been main lenders to real estate market (Wall, 2012, p. 15). Subsequently, nationalization of banks, capital injections and asset purchases took in place by the government. Thus, Ireland faced to large amount of public debt by virtue of expansionary fiscal policies after the the GFC. Following these events, Ireland made an aggreement of €85 bn with European Financial Stability Facility (EFSF), the European Financial Stability Mechanism (EFSM), IMF and the governments of the United Kingdom (UK), Sweden and Denmark in November 2010. In the post GFC period and during European Sovereign debt crisis (Eurozone crisis) Ireland implemented contractionary fiscal policies which can be seen on Figure 1.

Prior to global financial crisis, Portugal had met with large external and budget deficits far above Maastricht limits. Unsustainable debt levels led Portugal government to seek an economic rescue program from European Central Bank (ECB), IMF and EU. On 17 May 2011, IMF and EU agreed to provide €26 bn and €52 bn funds through EFSM and EFSF mechanisms respectively (Wall, 2012, p. 16). In return, Portugal agreed to implement certain reforms in its financial and fiscal system which include contractionary fiscal policies (increase in consumption taxes (VAT taxes), reducing public expenditures) (Portugal, 2015, pp. 10-11).

Different than Greece and Portugal, Spain had low levels of government debt and budget surpluses before the GFC which can be seen on Figure 2.

Favouroble financial conditions and low interest rates ensured strong growth in corporates, household credit and debt in pre-crisis period prompted domestic imbalances in Spain. Along with consequences of global financial crisis these imbalances became more acute (Estrada et al., 2009, p. 9). Spanish government implemented expansionary fiscal situmulus packages during financial crisis (between 2008 Q1

Figure 1. Fiscal policies of Ireland in 1976-2010
Source: Bergin et al. (2011, p. R52)

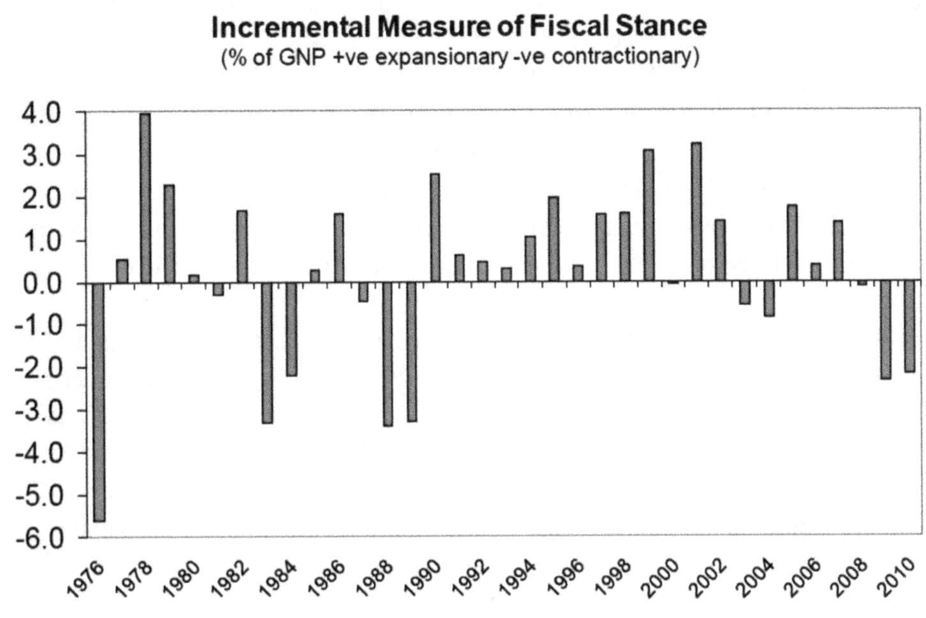

Figure 2. Dynamics of Spanish government main variables
Source: de Castro Fernández et al. (2014, p. 12)

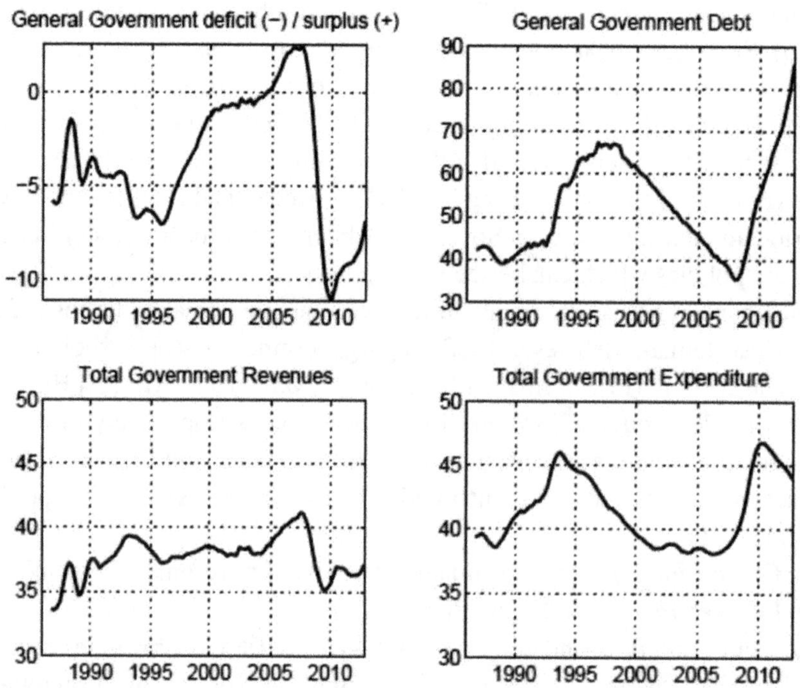

and 2010 Q3) and accordingly public consumption surged about 10% cumulatively (de Castro Fernández et al, 2014, p. 15).

At the end of 2008, Italy had public debt and government deficit 106% and 2.7% of GDP respectively. Italian government implemented both contractionary and expansionary fiscal policies in order to mitigate harmful effects of global financial crisis. In August 2008, Italy approved 3 year deficit reducing budget and subsequently Italian sitimulus package was introduced in November which involved expenditure cuts. This fiscal policy action is followed by the second and third fiscal sitimulus packages in February 2009 and in June 2009 which included contractionary/contractionary policy actions (Hamburg et al., 2009, pp. 105-106). The impacts of public finances on Italian macroeconomy can be seen on Table 1.

As it can be seen on Table 1, public expenditures net of interest payments and receipts, public deficit/ GDP soared from 2008 to 2009 owing to deterioration of financial conditions. Concurrently; GDP, private consumption, total fixed investment, exports, imports, GDP deflator, public receipts net of interest receipts dampaned.

New EU states (Bulgaria, the Czech Republic, Estonia, Hungary, Latvia, Lithuania, Poland, Romania, Slovenia and Slovakia) on the other hand, faced to adverse effects of global financial crisis particularly aftermath of the Lehman Brothers collapse. Among them; some states (Latvia, Hungary and Romania) had to turn to the IMF for help, some (Czech Republic, Poland, Slovenia and Slovakia) followed expansionary fiscal policies, some other states (Bulgaria and Estonia) sustained tight fiscal stance (Staehr, 2010).

Different than EU periphery countries, core or central countries within EU (Germany, France, Netherlands, Belgium and Luxemburg) were mostly benefited from expansionary fiscal policies during and after the GFC. In 2008, the German government revenue ratio was 43.8% along with strong expenditure

Table 1. The Impacts of public finance on ıtalian macroeconomy during GFC

	Baseline		Contractionary Policy	Contractionary Policy and Cycle	Deviations From Benchmark
	2008	2009			
GDP	-1.3	-5.1	0.6	1	1
Private consumption	-0.8	-1.8	0.5	1.1	1
Total fixed investment	-4.0	-12.2	1.3	1.4	0.7
Exports	-3.9	-19.1	0	0.3	0.4
Imports	-4.3	-14.6	0.9	1.4	1.2
GDP deflator	2.8	2.1	0	-0.6	-1.6
Public expenditures net of interest payments	3.4	4.9	1.5	1.6	2.7
Public receipts net of interest receipts	1.1	-1.9	1	-1.5	-4.5
Public deficit / GDP	2.7	5.3	0.2	1.5	3.5
Public deficit net of interest payments and receipts / GDP	-2.2	0.9	0.2	1.5	3.4
Public expenditures net of interest payments / GDP	44.2	47.8	0.4	0.6	1.6
Public receipts net of interest receipts / GDP	46.5	47	0.2	-0.9	-1.8
Public deficit net of interest payments and receipts	-2.2	0.9	0.2	1.4	3.3

Source: Produced by Table 2 in Hamburg et al. (2009, p. 114)

growth for government investment, operating expenditure and healthcare sector. The business tax reform took in place which led to reduce social contribution rates and this situation can be seen on Figure 3 (Deutsche Bundesbank, 2008, p. 51).

The French government cut tax rates in 2007-2008 period and sustained high public spending in 2008 (52.7% of GDP). In 2007, before "the great recession" France has approximately 3% of GDP public deficit and the government implemented expansionary/contractionary fiscal policies that can be seen on Table 2 (Mathieu and Sterdyniak, 2009).

As it can be seen on Table 2; public balance, output gap, cyclical component and fiscal impulse plunged from 2007 to 2008. On contrary; interest payments, cyclically-adjusted primary balance and sustainability index went up in the same period. Consequently, French government implemented expansionary fiscal policies in 2007-2008 in which fiscal imbalances were very high due to the contagious effects of the GFC.

Dutch government met with rapid deterioration of public deficit and quick decline in net government worth during the GFC. The Dutch government sustained expansionary fiscal policies during and after the GFC (government guarantees and recapitalization of financial institutions with difficulty) and limited stimulating policy measures in terms of fiscal policy were undertaken (Bos and Teulings, 2010, pp. 42-48).

In Belgium, public debt and fiscal deficit upsurged owing to financial crisis particularly in 2008-2009 and consequently it was subject to European excessive deficit procedure (EDP) at around the end of 2009. Aftermath the financial crisis, Belgian government implemented/sustained expansionary fiscal policies (rise in primary expenditure, government investment and social security benefits) (Bisciari et al., 2015).

Figure 3. German government fiscal ratios
Source: Deutsche Bundesbank (2008, p. 52)

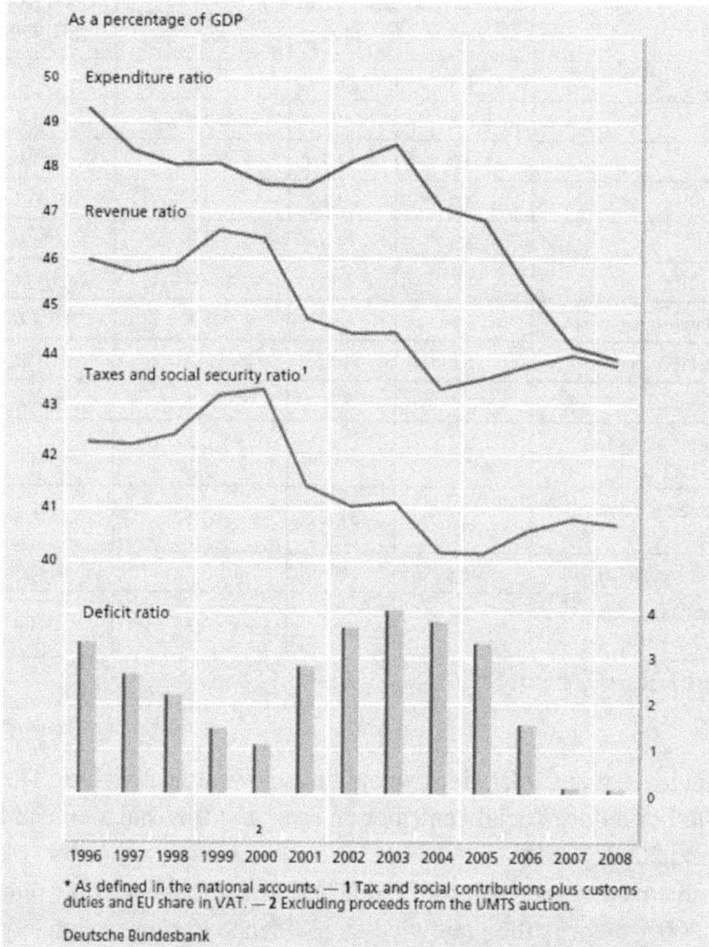

Table 2. Fiscal determinants in France

	1997	1998	1999	2000	2001	2002	2003	2004	2005	2006	2007	2008
Public balance	-3.3	-2.6	-1.8	-1.6	-1.5	-1.6	-4.1	-3.6	-3.0	-2.3	-2.7	-3.4
Output gap	-1.2	-0.1	0.7	2.4	1.8	0.6	-0.6	-0.6	-0.9	-0.7	-0.6	-2.4
Cyclical component	-0.6	-0.1	0.3	1.2	0.9	0.3	-0.3	*0.3	-0.4	-0.3	-0.3	-1.2
Interest payments	3.1	3.0	2.8	2.7	2.7	2.7	2.6	2.5	2.4	2.3	2.5	2.6
Cyclically-adjusted primary balance	0.4	0.5	0.7	0.0	0.2	-0.8	-1.2	-0.8	-0.2	0.3	0.1	0.4
Fiscal impulse		-0.2	-0.2	0.7	-0.2	1.0	0.4	-0.4	-0.6	-0.5	0.2	-0.3
Sustainability index	1.0	0.5	0.3	-1.2	-0.9	-1.1	-0.9	-0.5	0.3	0.7	0.4	1.6

Source: Mathieu and Sterdyniak (2009, p. 20)

Likewise, Austria sustained expansionary fiscal policies during and after the GFC. The Austrian government implemented bank aid programme, state subsidies for investments as well as tax reliefs for businesses and families in the midst of 2008 financial crisis (Marhold et al., 2011).

Luxemburg owned Europe's largest investment fund and the second largest second money market industries and consequently was exposed to adverse effects financial turmoil of 2008. Bank rescue programs were took in effect (Fortis and Dexia banks) to ensure financial stability (International Monetary Fund, 2009). Similar to other core EU states, Luxemburg implemented expansionary fiscal policies during the GFC (e.g., government consumption rose from 0.4% of GDP in 2008 to 4.5% of GDP in 2009 (Verduijn, 2013).

CONCLUSION

Active fiscal policies have been carried out by the governments in mitigating adverse effects of financial imbalances since the great depression. In addition, it is accepted that the only way to circumvent severe dampening in total demand is to benefit from expansionary fiscal policy implemented globally. In line with that, expansionary fiscal policies have begun to take in effect particularly in more developed countries during and after the GFC.

EU states have also begun to apply expansionary/contractionary fiscal policies in order to exit from financial tormoil during the GFC and Euro Sovereign debt crisis; while the subjective conditions of the governments determined the type of the policy action. The more developed ones have begun to benefit from expansionary fiscal policies; yet the less developed ones have begun to benefit from contractionary fiscal policies.

This chapter has analyzed fiscal policies implemented in "periphery"/"core" EU states during and after global financial crisis. The EU member countries faced to systemic stress of global financial crisis owing to EU banks and financial institutions that were largely invested with the US subprime mortgages during the GFC. In line with the policy actions held in the US, the EU countries undertook bank rescue operations, government guarantees for interbank lendings and recapitalization of financial institutions (expansionary fiscal policy actions), applied fiscal stimulus packages that involves national countercyclical fiscal policies within the EU framework.

New EU states actively undertook expansionary/contractionary fiscal policies during global financial crisis. Among them; while some (Latvia, Hungary and Romania) had to turn to IMF for help, some implemented expansionary

During the GFC, some periphery EU states (Spain, Italy) benefited from both expansionary/contractionary fiscal policy actions (fiscal stimulus packages).

Aftermath of the GFC, the EU area countries confronted to contagious effects of systemic stress spread out from periphery EU states. Bailout packages were provided to some of these periphery EU states (Greece, Ireland, Portugal) in exiting financial instability states, which in return the governments agreed to reform its fiscal policy which involves contractionary fiscal policy actions.

Core or central EU member countries (Germany, France, Netherlands, Luxembourg, Belgium) on the other hand, mostly benefited/implemented expansionary fiscal policies (increase in government expenditure, tax cut, overnment guarantees and recapitalization of financial institutions with difficulty, bank aid programme) during and after the GFC.

To sum up, governments within the EU actively benefited from expansionary/contractionary fiscal policies along with monetary policy actions in exiting the great recession and sovereign debt crisis. Nonwithstanding to the effort of the EU to act concurrently within the framework established by European Action Plan, subjective conditions of the countries directly influenced the type of the fiscal policy actions. Besides, lack of fiscal supervisory authority within the EU area that has power over member states made difficult to overtake simultaneous fiscal policies for all member states.

While the debate over the reasons behind the global financial crisis still persisted, the consequences of the crisis detrimentally affected both core/periphery EU member states. Eventually, financial firms and banks which had operated with "animal spirits" to produce more profit were rescued or recapitalized by governments or countries were funded with bailout packages provided by IMF, EU or ECB. However, the cost of government rescue programmes or government guarantees distributed to all of the citizens by fiscal stimulus packages. Therefore, more regularity supervision mechanism should be set up in order to sustain tight fiscal stance and to avoid systemic stress during financial imbalances.

REFERENCES

Acharya, V. V. (2011). *Systemic risk and macro-prudential regulation.* Unpublished working paper. Retrieved from http://pages.stern.nyu.edu/~sternfin/vacharya/public_html/ADB%20Systemic%20Risk%20and%20Macroprudential%20Regulation%20-%20Final%20-%20March%202011.pdf

Acharya, V. V., & Richardson, M. (2009). Causes of the financial crisis. *Critical Review, 21*(2-3), 195–21. doi:10.1080/08913810902952903

Ball, L. (2016). *The Fed and Lehman Brothers: Introduction and Summary*. Cambridge, MA: National Bureau of Economic Research. doi:10.3386/w22410

Bénétrix, A. S., & Lane, P. R. (2013). Fiscal cyclicality and EMU. *Journal of International Money and Finance, 34*, 164–176. doi:10.1016/j.jimonfin.2012.11.009

Bergin, A., Gerald, J. F., Kearney, I., & O'Sullivan, C. (2011). The Irish fiscal crisis. *National Institute Economic Review, 217*(1), R47-R59.

Bianco, K. M. (2008). *The subprime lending crisis: Causes and effects of the mortgage meltdown.* New York: CCH, Wolters Kluwer Law & Business.

Bisciari, P., Eugène, B., Melyn, W., Schoonackers, R., Stinglhamber, P., & Meensel Van, L. (2015). *Analysis of policies for restoring sound.* Brussels: National Bank of Belgium.

Blanchard, O. J. (2009). *The crisis: basic mechanisms and appropriate policies*. Washington, DC: International Monetary Fund.

Bocutoğlu, E., & Ekinci, A. (2009). Genel teori, küresel krizler ve yeniden maliye politikası. *Maliye Dergisi, 156*(1), 66–82.

Bos, F., & Teulings, C. (2010). *CPB and Dutch fiscal policy in view of the financial crisis and ageing*. The Hague: CPB Netherlands Bureau for Economic Policy Analysis. doi:10.2139srn.1742181

Buiter, W. H., & Rahbari, E. (2010). *Greece and the fiscal crisis in the EMU.* Centre for Policy Research Paper.

Caballero, R. J., & Krishnamurthy, A. (2009). Global imbalances and financial fragility. *The American Economic Review*, *99*(2), 584–588. doi:10.1257/aer.99.2.584

Claessens, S., Dell'Ariccia, G., Igan, D., & Laeven, L. (2010). Cross-country experiences and policy implications from the global financial crisis. *Economic Policy*, *25*(62), 267–293. doi:10.1111/j.1468-0327.2010.00244.x

Crotty, J. (2009). Structural causes of the global financial crisis: A critical assessment of the 'new financial architecture'. *Cambridge Journal of Economics*, *33*(4), 563–580. doi:10.1093/cje/bep023

de Castro Fernández, F., Martí, F., Montesinos, A., Pérez, J., & Sánchez-Fuentes, A. J. (2014). *Fiscal policies in Spain: Main stylises facts revisited.* Madrid: Banco de España.

Deutsche Bundesbank. (2008). *Annual Report 2008.* Frankfurt am Main: Deutsche Bundesbank. Retrieved 5 24, 2018, from Deutsche Bundesbank.

Eichengreen, B., & Portes, R. (1987). *The anatomy of financial crises.* Cambridge, MA: National Bureau of Economic Research. doi:10.3386/w2126

Erdem, N., & Atbaşi, F. D. (2011). Finans sermayenin kriz döngüsü: merkez-çevre "yakınsaması". *Ankara Üniversitesi SBF Dergisi, 66*(4), 033-066.

Estrada, Á., Jimeno, J. F., de Molina, M., & Luis, J. (2009). *The Spanish economy in EMU: The first ten years.* Madrid: Banco de Espana.

Fligstein, N., & Goldstein, A. (2010). The anatomy of the mortgage securitization crisis. In *Markets on Trial: The Economic Sociology of the US Financial Crisis: Part A* (s. 29-70). Içinde Emerald Group Publishing Limited.

Flood, R. P., & Garber, P. M. (1984). Collapsing exchange-rate regimes: Some linear examples. *Journal of International Economics*, *17*(1-2), 1–13. doi:10.1016/0022-1996(84)90002-3

Frame, W. S., Fuster, A., Tracy, J., & Vickery, J. (2015). *The Rescue of Fannie Mae and Freddie Mac.* New York: Federal Reserve Bank of New York.

Gorton, G. B. (2008). *Banking and the Panic of 200.* Cambridge, MA: National Bureou of Economic Research.

Hamburg, B., Momigliano, S., Manzke, B., & Siviero, S. (2010). *The reaction of fiscal policy to the crisis in Italy and Germany: Are they really polar cases in the European context?* Rome: Banca de Italia.

International Monetary Fund. (2009). *Retrieved from Luxembourg - 2009 Article IV Consultation, IMF Concluding Statement.* Retrieved from https://www.imf.org/en/News/Articles/2015/09/28/04/52/mcs033009

Keynes, J. M. (2016). *General theory of employment, interest and money.* New Delhi: Atlantic Publishers & Dist.

Krugman, P. (1979). A model of balance-of-payments crises. *Journal of Money, Credit and Banking*, *11*(3), 311–325. doi:10.2307/1991793

Krugman, P. (1999). Balance sheets, the transfer problem, and financial crises. In *International finance and financial crises* (pp. 31–55). Dordrecht: Springer. doi:10.1007/978-94-011-4004-1_2

Lapavitsas, C., Kaltenbrunner, A., Lindo, D., Michell, J., Painceira, J. P., Pires, E., ... Teles, N. (2010). Eurozone crisis: Beggar thyself and thy neighbour. *Journal of Balkan & Near Eastern Studies*, *12*(4), 321–373. doi:10.1080/19448953.2010.510012

Marhold, F., Poier, K., Aschauer, P., Kohlbacher, E., Nebauer, M., & Wewerka, L. (2011). *How has Austria overcome the economic crisis?* International Society for Labour and Social Security Law.

Mathieu, C., & Sterdyniak, H. (2009). *Global financial crisis: the french policy answer in a EU perspective.* Paris: OFCE - Centre de recherche en économie de Sciences Po.

Minsky, H. P. (1970). *Financial instability revisited: The economics of disaster*. St. Louis, MO: Board of Governors of the Federal Reserve System.

Mishkin, F. S. (1992). Anatomy of a financial crisis. *Journal of Evolutionary Economics*, *2*(2), 115–130. doi:10.1007/BF01193536

Mishkin, F. S. (2011). Over the cliff: From the subprime to the global financial crisis. *The Journal of Economic Perspectives*, *25*(1), 49–70. doi:10.1257/jep.25.1.49

Obstfeld, M. (1988). The logic of currency crises. In *Monetary and fiscal policy in an integrated Europe* (pp. 62–90). Berlin: Springer. doi:10.1007/978-3-642-79817-7_4

Portugal, P. (2015). *The Portuguese economic crisis: Policies and outcomes*. Bertelsmann Stiftung.

Reinhart, C. M., & Rogoff, K. S. (2008). Is the 2007 US sub-prime financial crisis so different? An international historical comparison. *The American Economic Review*, *98*(2), 339–344. doi:10.1257/aer.98.2.339

Reinhart, C. M., & Rogoff, K. S. (2009). The aftermath of financial crises. *The American Economic Review*, *99*(2), 466–472. doi:10.1257/aer.99.2.466

Riet, A. V. (2010). Euro area fiscal policies. In A. v. Riet (Ed.), *Euro area fiscal policies and the crisis*. Frankfurt Am Main: European Central Bank.

Staehr, K. (2010). *The global financial crisis and public finances in the new EU countries in Central and Eastern Europe: Developments and challenges*. Tallinn: Bank of Estonia.

Stiglitz, J. E. (2010). The Financial Crisis of 2007/2008 and its Macroeconomic Consequences. In Time for a visible hand: Lessons from the 2008 World Financial Crisis (pp. 19–50). Oxford University Press.

Taylor, J. B. (2009). *The financial crisis and the policy responses: An empirical analysis of what went wrong*. Cambridge, MA: National Bureau of Economic Research. doi:10.3386/w14631

Verduijn, M. (2013). *RaboResearch-Economic Research.* Retrieved from https://economics.rabobank.com/publications/2013/may/country-report-luxembourg/adresinden alındı

Wall, D. L. (2012). *Central Banking for Financial Stability: Some Lessons from the Recent Instability in the United States and Euro Area.* Tokyo: Asian Development Bank Institute.

KEY TERMS AND DEFINITIONS

Contractionary Fiscal Policy: Use of fiscal policy by decreasing government spending or raising taxes.

Contractionary Monetary Policy: Use of monetary policy (raising interest rates, selling treasury notes, or reserve requirements) in order to reduce inflation.

Eurozone Crisis: Economic downturn starting initially from Portugal, Ireland, Spain, Greece and Italy with symptoms of the collapse of financial institutions, high government debt, and raising yield spreads in government securities within the Euro area in 2008.

Expansionary Fiscal Policy: Use of fiscal policy by increasing government spending or cutting taxes.

Expansionary Monetary Policy: Expanding money supply by lowering interest rates, reducing reserve requirements for banks or buying Treasury notes.

Fiscal Policy: Implementation of tax policies, government spending, and borrowing in order to affect macroeconomic determinants including inflation, employment, economic growth, or aggregate demand.

Great Depression: The worst economic downturn starting after stock market crash of October 1929 and lasting to 1936.

Great Recession: Global economic turmoil emerging from the US residential mortgage market and spreading to global financial markets as well as real sectors in 2007-2009 period.

Monetary Policy: The action of monetary authority in identifying the size and rate of money supply.

Chapter 10
An Investigation of the Maastricht Fiscal Criteria and the European Union's Harmonization

Sami Buhur
Balikesir University, Turkey

ABSTRACT

The Maastricht Treaty brought many innovations in the process of harmonization of the EU. This treaty, which was realized in 1993, aims to harmonize the economic, financial, legal, and political aspects of the EU members. Two basic financial criteria were identified in the financial stability and harmonization process. The first is the ratio of member countries' budget deficits to GDP. The second is the ratio of the member country's public debt to the GDP. In this chapter, it will be revealed how EU member countries are adapting to financial criteria. For this purpose, reports and statistics published by international organizations such as OECD and EU will be examined. It will be seen in many of the EU member countries can not adapt to these criteria. Especially after the 2008 Global Financial Crisis, there were difficulties in adapting to these criteria. The EU Council put into effect several legal regulations in the harmonization process. Although many legal sanctions were put into effect for this purpose, success in complying with the financial criteria were not achieved.

INTRODUCTION

The Maastricht Treaty was signed in 1991 and entered into force in 1993. It is an important milestone in the process of creating a stable and stronger EU. With the Maastricht Treaty, basically two criteria have been asserted. The first criteria of these is to assure the fiscal discipline, the second one is to assure the monetary discipline. Both criteria are aimed at achieving stable growth and strengthening the economies of the member countries. Occasionally, control mechanism becomes a part of putting both these criteria into effect, in fact; sanctions can be imposed to the concerned countries.

DOI: 10.4018/978-1-5225-7564-1.ch010

Stability and Growth Pact (SGP) entered into force in 1997 in order to ensure the implementation of these criteria, which was established by the Maastricht Treaty, in a more powerful and decisive manner. The accordance of the concerned country is observed, the report is prepared, the recommendations are presented and the measures to be taken are set forth with Stability and Growth Pact.

When considered the accordance of EU member countries with the criteria that is stated by the Maastricht Treaty, it is seen that the criteria for monetary discipline has achieved a certain success. However, when considered the ratio of budget deficit and general administrative debt to GDP(in other words, in view of compliance with the criteria for achieving fiscal discipline), it seems difficult to say that it provides the same success.

In Turkey, a situation arises in contrast to EU countries. Turkey's budget deficit and the ratio of general administrative debt to GDP seem better than the EU countries. However, the inflation rate of Turkey, it is seem to be well above the EU average in terms of long-term government bond interest rate and the exchange rate. This situation is reached the result that Turkey should take certain measures for the future in terms of financial and economic stability. Otherwise, it will be left alone with bigger economic problems.

AN OUTLINE OF THE EUROPEAN UNION AND THE TREATY OF MAASTRICHT

The origin of EU is based on European Coal and Steel Community (ECSC) that is founded on Paris Agreement in 1951. The destructive effects of wars that happened between Germany and France for years and the issue of coal and steel between these countries are influential on the origins of idea of union (Falay, 2007, pp.223). Six member- community that had Belgium, Federal Republic of Germany, Luxemburg, France, Italy and Holland was constituted European Economic Community (EEC) and European Atomic Energy Community (EURATOM) established by the Treaty of Rome in 1951 (EU Ministry,2018).

The ECSC, EEC and EURATOM, which had previously organized and operated in separate communities, were named as the European Community (EC) with two treaties signed in 1957 and 1965 as a result of the idea of merger or fusion. In 1973, England, Denmark and Ireland; in 1981, Greece; in 1986, Spain and Portuguese; in 1995, Sweden, Finland and Austria have joined the community and the number of the members has reached 15. After the collapse of the Eastern Bloc and the Soviet Regime, ten countries were included in the community in 2004, following the transition of the Eastern European countries to the market economy (Hungary, Czech Republic, Poland, Estonia, Latvia, Lithuania, Slovenia, Slovakia, Malta, South Cyprus), (European Union, 2018).

After the Treaty of Rome that established the EU, the Treaty of Maastricht which included the most comprehensive amendment was signed on 9th-10th December,1991 and came into force on 1st November,1993. This treaty, which holds the qualification that is a kind of EU Constitution and establishes the European Union which is called current name, has many provisions ranging from financial-economic and monetary union, EU citizenship, foreign policy, justice mechanism and common security (Bilici, 2012, pp. 40-43).

STRUCTURE AND BASIC CHARACTERISTICS OF EU BUDGET

The foundations of the EU budget are based on the ECSC, the EEC and the EURATOM, which have the founding treaty. By the time of progress, three institutional budgets were merged into a single budget starting in 1968. Accordingly, while the budget is drawn up and implemented, the earning and charge are included in a single budget as a matter of the union principle. There are basically three organizations involved in the EU budgeting process. The European Commission, the first of these, is responsible for the budget process and its implementation. The second is the European Parliament and is involved in the ratification process of the EU budget. The third important role in budgeting belongs to the European Court of Auditors and is responsible for the control of budgetary accounts (Falay, 2007, p. 224).

As it can be seen the table below, the most important share is allocated to Sustainable Growth and Natural Resources from the annual budget. 42.5 billion Euros of this expenditure item are allocated to the European Agricultural Guarantee Fund. That is to say; the EU attaches great importance to agricultural support. Besides this, Economic, Social and Regional Integrity are ranked as the second. Within this item, the remedial expenditures for regional differences are ranked as the most important with 19.3 billion Euros. The share that is allocated to Joint Research and Innovation expenditure from the item of Growth and Employment for Competitive Capacity is approximately 10.5 billion Euros. In Global European expenditure item, pre-accession financial aids attract the attention.

By 2017, the total income of the EU budget is around 135 billion Euros. The most important source of income within the EU budget is the GNP contributions of the member countries. The share in the total union budget is around 80%. Other incomes include incomes such as agricultural taxes, customs taxes, VAT (European Commission, 2018).

THE CONCEPT OF BUDGET DEFICIT

Balanced budget which is among the basic assumptions of the Classical Economic Approach, limited public expenditure and limited government activities, have been started to be considerably discussed with the unemployment and stagnation that coexisted with the 1929 Great Depression. Since then, it

Table 1. The items of payments of European Union

Budgetary Items	Billion EURO	Rates in Total Budget (%)
Annual Budget Life-Cycle	157	100
1a Competitiveness for Growth and Jobs	21,3	14
1b Economic, Social and Territorial Cohesion	53,5	33
2. Sustainable growth: Natural resources	58,6	37
3. Security and Citizenship	4,3	3
4. Global Europe	10,2	7
5. Administration	9,4	6
6. Compensations	0	0
7. Other Special Instruments	0,6	1

Source: European Commission, Annual Budget, 2018

is defended that the government will provide the full-employment and stop the business stagnation by intervening the economy in particular points that the private sector cannot be sufficient with the Compensatory Budget Theory. In addition, it has been stated that the government shouldn't refrain from budget deficits in full employment and that the budget balance between two welfare periods of economy should be based with the Cyclical Budget Theory (Bulbul, 2017, pp. 28-34).

Industrialization, population growth, urbanization, diversification of human needs increase the significance of infrastructure investments and public services. Depending on these factors, the more the government has taken part in economy, the more public expenditure and the quantity of loan have been increased. This situation has resulted in countries being away from public fiscal discipline and increasing budget deficits (Vural, 2007, p. 97).

Tersely, the budget deficit usually represents the difference between the income and expenditure of government in a year. In other words, it stated that public expenditures are higher than public income. In addition, various budget deficit definitions are included. As follows;

- *Public Deficit (Public Sector Borrowing Requirement – PSBR or Public Sector Deficit)* represents the difference between total public expenditures and total public incomes over a period of time. Thereby, PSBR includes the sum of the deficits of the social security institutions, public economic organizations, funds, revolving fund enterprises of the local administrations beside the central state organization (Sakal, 2003, p.32). Therefore, the concept of the Government Deficit discusses the budget deficit in a comprehensive manner.
- *Conventional Deficit* is the difference between public incomes and expenditures in a certain time of period when debt is excluded from principal repayments. However, in Conventional Deficit the interest paid for the debt principal is shown in the public expenditure.
- *The Primary Deficit* is the budget deficit that arises after interest payments have been removed. The fact that this deficit continues for many years shows that the country has moved away from its fiscal discipline. The primary surplus in the Stand-By Agreements with the IMF has been set as the decisive benchmarker.
- *Operational Deficit* brings about the sum of the primary budget deficit and real interest payments. In this case, if the nominal interest rates are higher than the inflation rate, it means that the debt burden of the government increases or the budget deficits increase (Bulbul, 2017, pp. 248).

THE FINANCIAL CRITERIA DETERMINED BY THE MAASTRICHT TREATY

These criteria, shortly known as the Maastricht Criteria, are aimed at ensuring a balanced and coherent transition to the common monetary system. These criteria, which are set forth in articles 104 and 121 of the Maastricht Agreement, known as the constitutional treaty and constitution of the EU, are further elaborated in the Protocol on the Harmonization Criteria Protocol and the Procedure to be Implemented in the Extreme Open (Bilici, 2012, pp. 104-106).

These criteria, which are more strongly expressed in the Stability and Growth Pact, are basically expressed under two main headings (Sen, 2010, pp. 35). First, the financial criteria aimed at fiscal discipline; and the second is the economic criteria that tries to provide the monetary discipline. These criteria, which are consisted of five items in total, are shown below (European Commission, 2018).

Criteria for Ensuring Fiscal Discipline

- **Budget Deficit:** The budget deficits of member state should not exceed 3% of GDP.[1]
- **Public Debts:** Public debt of the member country should not exceed 60% of GDP.[2]

The Criteria for Ensuring Monetary Discipline

- **Inflation Rate:** The average annual inflation rate of any member country should not exceed the average rate of inflation of the three member states with the lowest inflation rate in the EU by 1.5 points.
- **Interest Rate:** The long-term government bond interest rate of any member state should not exceed the average interest rate of the three member states with the lowest inflation rate by more than two points.
- **Foreign Exchange Rates:** Member countries' money must be included in the European Monetary System Exchange Mechanism and the exchange rate of the national currency must be left to normal fluctuations in the last two years and the value exchange (+/-) within the exchange mechanism must not exceed 15% without devaluation.

FINANCIAL CRITERIA DATA

There are two criteria determined by the Maastricht Treaty. The first of these is the share of budget deficit in GDP and the second is the share of public debt in GDP.

Budget Deficit Data

Under the budget deficit criterion, which is the first criterion for ensuring fiscal discipline, the figure resulting in comparing the budget deficit of the member country to GDP must not exceed 3%. In following table, which is based on the OECD data, it primarily should be checked at the financial performance of the EU member states.

Looking at the average of the EU member countries, it is observed that it has stayed below 3% until 2009. With the impact of the 2008 Global Financial Crisis, this rate has started to increase since 2009. After 2014, the rate has fallen to less than 3%, which is the result of countries distinctly implementing fiscal stabilization programs. On the other hand, the same trend appears in the average of the countries including Euro. Thus, it comes into a picture that a stable monetary and fiscal structure, one of the main objectives of the common currency, cannot be achieved in times of crisis.

Estonia, Switzerland and Sweden are countries that have not passed the 3% rate for a whole period. In fact, after the 2008 Global Crisis, the budget deficits of these countries have been further reduced. It is needed to tell the countries; Greece, Norway, Portuguese, Spain, Ireland and Slovakia among the countries with high levels of budget deficits. These countries have faced high budget deficits for almost the entire period. Ireland reached the highest level in 2010 with 32.05%. Also, Norway is seen as reaching 18.67% in 2008 and Greece in 15.14% in 2009.

The budget deficit has followed an unstable course in many EU member countries. However, in general, it is observed that the budget deficits have increased after the 2008 Global Financial Crisis. It appears that a similar trend has emerged in other non-EU countries as well. However, in Chile and Korea, unlike in other countries, budget deficits are likely to decline since 2008. The country with the lowest budget deficits is Mexico. It is appeared that in countries such as Australia, Canada, China, Chile, Denmark, Finland, Luxembourg, and New Zealand, have had a surplus in the budget in many years.

Public Debt Data

The second financial criteria of the Maastricht Treaty is that the ratio of the general administrative debt of EU member countries to GDP does not exceed 60%. The table below shows the percentage of the ratio of the general administrative debt of selected countries to GDP based on OECD data. Since the financial criteria of Maastricht are the criteria that the EU member states must respect, firstly it is analyzed the data of these countries and then compared with the other countries.

Countries that did not exceed 60% during the whole period were the Czech Republic, Estonia, Latvia, Lithuania, Luxembourg, Norway, Slovakia and Switzerland. It is observed that the general administrative debt of many EU member countries has dramatically increased after the 2008 Global Financial Crises. Especially, in Greece this rate has increased to 180%. The highest increase is seen in Ireland. The ratio of general administrative debt to GDP, which was around 30% before the Global Crisis, increased to around 130% after the Global Crisis. A similar trend also occurred in Portuguese. This ratio, which was around 60-70% before the crisis, reached 150% after the crisis.

Considering the EU member-countries and the countries outside the EU, it is seen that the share of developed countries' general government debt in GDP is higher than in emerging economies. For instance, this rate has recently surpassed 230% in Japan. Japan is one of the countries with the highest debt trend in the world. The similar situation is experienced in strong countries like the USA, the UK, Germany, France. The ratio of general government debt of these countries to GDP has almost doubled in the last decade. From this point of view, it can be concluded that there is a parallelism between the level of development and general administrative debt. In other words, it is seem that the public debt of developed or economically powerful countries have a higher trend than developing countries. The question is what kind of consequences this situation will create in terms of the financial structure and financial stability of the developed countries in the future.

Chile, Mexico and Turkey are ranked among the non-EU countries that have the lowest ratio of general administrative debt to GDP. These countries are OECD member countries and are included in the classification of developing countries. Especially, financial stability programs that were implemented in Turkey after 2000, have been effective in reducing the share of public debt in GDP.

THE SCOPE OF APPLICATION OF THE FINANCIAL CRITERIA REVEALED BY THE MAASTRICHT TREATY IN EU COUNTRIES

Measures that were taken to ensure fiscal stability may be at the legal or constitutional level (Yuzbaşıoğlu, 2012, pp. 44 - 48). When it can be determined at the legal level in some Latin American countries, in the countries such as; Canada, Spain, Sweden, it can be determined at the constitutional level in the

Table 2. The rates of general administrative budget deficit to GDP in selected countries

	2000	2001	2002	2003	2004	2005	2006	2007	2008	2009	2010	2011	2012	2013	2014	2015	2016	2017
Australia	-1.23	-0.80	0.72	0.82	0.97	1.69	1.64	0.71	-3.75	-5.50	-4.38	-4.56	-2.86	-2.83	-2.36	-2.24	-1.44	
Austria	-2.40	-0.66	-1.38	-1.79	-4.80	-2.51	-2.54	-1.35	-1.50	-5.33	-4.44	-2.55	-2.19	-1.95	-2.73	-1.05	-1.59	-0.70
Belgium	-0.07	0.17	0.05	-1.76	-0.16	-2.76	0.22	0.07	-1.10	-5.38	-4.00	-4.13	-4.23	-3.14	-3.08	-2.48	-2.48	-1.03
Brazil											-2.96	-2.54	-2.32	-3.31	-5.88			
Canada	2.65	0.53	-0.23	-0.13	0.77	1.56	1.83	1.82	0.18	-3.89	-4.75	-3.32	-2.53	-1.87	0.18	-0.13	-1.10	-0.97
Chile				-0.19	2.77	5.02	7.38	7.74	4.67	-4.04	-0.17	1.29	0.54	-0.52	-1.51	-2.07	-2.68	
China (People's Republic of)	-7.80	-6.91	-4.64	-3.70	-0.91	-0.47	0.82	2.94	1.26	0.13	1.48	1.53	1.27	0.76	0.84	-0.88		
Colombia	-5.25	-4.78	-4.09	-3.04	-3.48	-3.33	-1.91	-1.58	-1.87	-1.01	-2.18	-0.97	-0.62	-2.36	-3.17	-3.21	-4.90	
Costa Rica	-0.94	-1.49	-2.25	-1.18	-1.39	-2.27	0.15	1.22	-1.50	-2.85	-5.92	-4.81	-1.76	-2.68	-1.45	-2.51	-2.99	
Czech Republic	-3.57	-5.48	-6.36	-6.88	-2.38	-2.99	-2.17	-0.65	-1.98	-5.45	-4.19	-2.72	-3.93	-1.25	-2.10	-0.61	0.73	1.60
Denmark	1.89	1.14	-0.02	-0.13	2.07	4.96	4.99	5.02	3.17	-2.80	-2.71	-2.06	-3.49	-1.24	1.14	-1.47	-0.41	1.00
Estonia	-0.07	0.20	0.42	1.80	2.39	1.12	2.91	2.72	-2.67	-2.18	0.19	1.16	-0.26	-0.17	0.68	0.07	-0.29	-0.29
Euro area	-0.27	-2.03	-2.72	-3.19	-2.96	-2.59	-1.49	-0.65	-2.16	-6.26	-6.17	-4.22	-3.64	-3.01	-2.57	-2.07	-1.55	
European Union		-1.56	-2.59	-3.18	-2.84	-2.50	-1.61	-0.87	-2.49	-6.61	-6.40	-4.56	-4.27	-3.30	-2.91	-2.34	-1.62	-0.96
Finland	6.86	4.98	4.07	2.44	2.21	2.59	3.93	5.13	4.18	-2.53	-2.61	-1.04	-2.18	-2.61	-3.21	-2.76	-1.79	-0.57
France	-1.31	-1.37	-3.15	-4.00	-3.58	-3.34	-2.44	-2.63	-3.26	-7.17	-6.88	-5.15	-4.99	-4.09	-3.91	-3.63	-3.41	-2.59
Germany	0.86	-3.11	-3.94	-4.18	-3.74	-3.42	-1.72	0.19	-0.18	-3.23	-4.22	-0.96	-0.03	-0.14	0.53	0.84	1.01	1.26
Greece	-4.06	-5.47	-6.02	-7.83	-8.83	-6.19	-5.95	-6.71	-10.18	-15.14	-11.20	-10.28	-8.87	-13.15	-3.62	-5.67	0.63	0.82
Hungary	-3.03	-4.05	-8.83	-7.12	-6.54	-7.77	-9.27	-5.02	-3.68	-4.54	-4.47	-5.41	-2.40	-2.62	-2.60	-1.91	-1.66	-1.95
Iceland	1.23	-0.98	-2.79	-3.12	-0.33	4.48	5.86	4.91	-13.03	-9.64	-9.72	-5.56	-3.72	-1.83	-0.07	-0.81	12.57	1.51
Indonesia											-0.34	-1.04	-1.34	-2.07	-1.86	-2.77	-2.40	
Ireland	4.87	0.97	-0.49	0.39	1.34	1.62	2.82	0.32	-6.96	-13.80	-32.05	-12.72	-8.03	-6.10	-3.63	-1.89	-0.52	-0.34
Israel	-3.23	-5.61	-6.78	-7.64	-5.19	-4.06	-1.73	-0.68	-2.77	-5.66	-3.68	-2.93	-4.79	-4.14	-3.35	-2.11	-2.11	
Italy	-2.44	-3.39	-3.00	-3.34	-3.50	-4.11	-3.52	-1.46	-2.63	-5.25	-4.21	-3.68	-2.92	-2.92	-2.99	-2.58	-2.48	-2.31
Japan						-4.41	-2.97	-2.76	-4.12	-9.78	-9.15	-9.09	-8.30	-7.64	-5.38	-3.55	-3.42	
Korea	4.36	2.97	3.51	-1.96	0.23	1.55	2.33	4.24	2.34	-1.32	0.97	0.98	1.01	1.34	1.27	1.28	2.37	2.82
Latvia	-2.73	-1.95	-2.28	-1.46	-0.92	-0.36	-0.49	-0.51	-4.20	-9.13	-8.69	-4.31	-1.21	-1.16	-1.49	-1.36	0.06	-0.49
Lithuania	-3.18	-3.53	-1.86	-1.26	-1.39	-0.34	-0.27	-0.82	-3.08	-9.11	-6.90	-8.94	-3.15	-2.61	-0.62	-0.24	0.27	0.53

continued on following page

Table 2. Continued

	2000	2001	2002	2003	2004	2005	2006	2007	2008	2009	2010	2011	2012	2013	2014	2015	2016	2017
Luxembourg	5.89	5.91	2.44	0.19	-1.28	0.08	1.94	4.15	3.32	-0.67	-0.66	0.51	0.34	0.98	1.33	1.36	1.61	1.52
Mexico				-1.31	-0.85	-0.72	-0.97	-0.71	-0.93	-3.08	-2.97	-5.30	-4.72	-4.55	-4.21	-5.16	-2.70	
Netherlands	1.88	-0.35	-2.08	-3.02	-1.72	-0.26	0.21	0.21	0.22	-5.43	-4.99	-4.29	-3.88	-2.37	-2.27	-2.05	0.37	1.09
New Zealand	1.69	1.37	3.32	3.44	3.89	4.53	5.08	4.24	0.46	-2.82	-7.16	-4.05	-2.18	-0.37	0.18	0.21	1.18	
Norway	15.10	13.19	9.05	7.25	10.92	14.82	18.02	17.11	18.67	10.33	10.99	13.43	13.83	10.77	8.75	6.06	3.99	4.45
Poland	-2.97	-4.78	-4.85	-6.08	-5.04	-3.96	-3.56	-1.85	-3.60	-7.25	-7.34	-4.83	-3.71	-4.11	-3.62	-2.65	-2.35	-1.66
Portugal	-3.21	-4.79	-3.34	-4.42	-6.19	-6.19	-4.33	-3.01	-3.77	-9.81	-11.17	-7.38	-5.66	-4.84	-7.17	-4.40	-1.98	-2.96
Russia												3.15	1.95	-0.19	-2.33	-1.47		
Slovak Republic	-12.02	-6.40	-8.09	-2.70	-2.31	-2.88	-3.59	-1.95	-2.43	-7.80	-7.48	-4.28	-4.34	-2.72	-2.70	-2.73	-2.21	-1.04
Slovenia	-3.64	-3.88	-2.40	-2.62	-1.96	-1.33	-1.20	-0.08	-1.41	-5.84	-5.63	-6.67	-4.04	-14.68	-5.52	-2.86	-1.93	0.03
South Africa									-1.74	-3.85	-3.14	-2.96	-3.19	-3.27	-4.06			
Spain	-1.10	-0.55	-0.41	-0.36	-0.04	1.21	2.20	1.92	-4.42	-10.95	-9.38	-9.64	-10.47	-6.99	-5.97	-5.28	-4.51	-3.11
Sweden	3.22	1.42	-1.45	-1.28	0.35	1.83	2.21	3.35	1.90	-0.72	-0.03	-0.21	-0.98	-1.36	-1.56	0.18	1.19	1.27
Switzerland	0.42	0.28	-1.78	-1.39	-1.42	-0.67	0.86	1.61	1.93	0.50	0.36	0.74	0.38	-0.43	-0.21	0.65	0.33	
Turkey										-6.17	-2.68	-0.74	-0.19	0.21	0.24	1.31		
United Kingdom	1.40	0.25	-1.86	-3.13	-3.07	-3.14	-2.76	-2.64	-5.17	-10.12	-9.42	-7.47	-8.15	-5.40	-5.45	-4.26	-2.97	-1.93
United States	0.80	-1.37	-4.73	-5.88	-5.44	-4.15	-2.97	-3.55	-7.02	-12.67	-12.01	-10.61	-8.86	-5.36	-4.78	-4.22	-4.94	

Source: OECD, 2018, General Government Deficit, https://data.oecd.org/gga/general-government-deficit.htm

Table 3. Rates of general administrative debt to GDP in selected countries

	2000	2001	2002	2003	2004	2005	2006	2007	2008	2009	2010	2011	2012	2013	2014	2015	2016	2017
Australia	41.1	40.4	38.7	35.6	32.1	30.0	29.3	28.0	30.0	38.7	41.9	46.3	59.2	55.8	61.4	64.1	68.1	64.6
Austria	71.1	72.1	74.0	72.5	71.8	76.3	72.7	69.0	74.2	86.3	90.5	91.5	97.3	94.4	101.8	100.4	102.0	
Belgium	120.4	119.0	118.1	114.6	110.2	108.1	100.1	93.9	101.1	109.5	107.8	110.4	120.4	118.3	130.6	127.3	128.4	121.8
Canada	105.4	105.2	104.0	99.7	95.7	94.2	91.4	87.2	90.0	103.1	105.2	107.9	111.5	107.5	108.5	114.7	114.1	108.9
Chile				23.9	20.6	16.3	13.1	11.3	12.4	13.3	15.3	17.9	18.4	19.0	22.4	24.4	28.1	29.6
Colombia																69.0	73.8	
Czech Republic	24.4	28.3	30.6	33.4	32.9	32.4	31.9	30.5	34.3	41.1	45.6	48.3	57.9	58.0	56.7	53.4	49.0	
Denmark	60.5	58.3	58.1	56.1	52.3	45.1	40.5	34.6	41.9	49.3	53.4	60.1	60.6	56.7	59.1	53.8	52.4	
Estonia	6.8	6.7	7.6	8.4	8.6	8.2	8.0	7.2	8.4	12.6	11.9	9.5	13.2	13.6	14.1	12.9	13.1	
Finland	51.0	48.4	48.2	49.2	49.4	46.5	43.1	39.1	38.3	49.2	55.1	57.5	64.3	64.8	71.7	75.1	75.4	73.3
France	71.9	71.0	74.6	78.5	80.0	81.7	76.9	75.6	81.5	93.2	96.8	100.7	110.4	111.0	119.9	120.5	123.4	
Germany	59.5	58.8	61.2	64.6	67.5	70.1	68.3	64.2	68.1	75.5	84.5	84.2	88.1	83.1	83.3	78.9	76.2	
Greece	111.1	114.0	114.5	106.9	111.4	115.1	115.2	112.7	117.4	134.6	126.6	108.3	164.7	178.8	180.3	183.1	187.7	
Hungary	60.5	58.5	59.5	60.2	63.6	66.7	70.3	70.9	74.5	83.4	85.3	94.2	97.3	95.3	98.6	97.4	97.3	91.7
Iceland				66.0	59.5	49.9	54.9	49.8	95.0	108.6	114.0	121.5	119.4	110.9				
Ireland	38.7	35.5	34.1	32.8	31.5	31.3	27.6	27.5	47.5	67.5	83.6	110.9	129.1	131.4	121.6	88.7	83.4	
Israel		91.2	94.9	100.1	97.9	95.4	85.2	80.1	80.6	83.9	80.1	78.2	79.0	76.6	77.9	77.9	75.6	
Italy	119.0	118.1	117.0	114.3	114.7	117.4	115.0	110.7	113.0	126.0	124.9	117.9	136.2	143.7	156.0	156.9	155.6	
Japan	142.6	148.9	159.1	168.9	175.4	176.2	176.2	177.7	181.6	202.8	207.5	222.3	230.4	233.2	238.5	237.4	234.5	
Latvia	14.5	15.9	15.9	16.8	17.7	14.6	14.6	12.8	22.9	41.6	53.2	47.5	45.7	43.4	45.8	41.1	49.3	
Lithuania	34.4	33.5	32.0	28.6	27.3	24.9	22.0	19.4	17.1	34.1	45.5	45.7	51.3	48.0	52.6	53.8	51.7	
Luxembourg	15.8	16.2	16.2	17.6	18.5	17.1	16.1	15.8	24.4	22.0	27.0	26.6	28.3	28.9	29.4	29.1	27.9	
Mexico				36.5	31.5	30.9	30.7	32.4	34.3	30.6	31.1	37.1	41.1	47.1	49.5	53.5	53.0	
Netherlands	60.4	56.4	57.2	58.2	58.2	57.3	51.2	48.5	61.3	64.1	68.0	71.9	77.7	76.6	81.2	77.5	75.3	68.8
Norway	32.2	31.3	38.7	48.0	49.9	46.9	57.8	55.5	54.2	48.0	48.4	33.8	34.9	35.2	33.0	38.6	42.5	42.4
Poland	45.0	43.7	53.3	55.5	53.1	54.7	54.4	51.1	53.4	56.7	61.1	61.2	64.4	65.0	70.1	69.5	72.1	67.8

continued on following page

Table 6. Continued

	2000	2001	2002	2003	2004	2005	2006	2007	2008	2009	2010	2011	2012	2013	2014	2015	2016	2017
Portugal	62.0	63.5	66.8	70.6	76.7	80.0	79.4	78.1	82.8	96.1	104.1	107.8	137.1	141.4	151.4	149.2	146.1	146.3
Slovak Republic	57.9	56.6	49.4	47.5	45.1	38.4	36.2	34.8	33.8	42.5	47.4	50.0	58.3	61.2	60.4	60.0	60.0	
Slovenia		37.1	37.8	36.7	37.1	35.2	35.0	30.1	29.7	43.7	47.8	51.4	61.7	78.8	98.9	102.1	96.8	
Spain	65.2	60.6	59.3	54.4	52.5	50.0	45.7	41.7	47.2	61.8	66.6	77.7	92.5	105.7	118.4	116.4	116.6	114.8
Sweden	63.1	64.7	64.8	63.8	63.3	64.2	58.1	52.6	51.4	55.3	52.6	53.3	54.5	57.2	63.5	61.7	59.4	
Switzerland	54.5	53.6	59.8	59.1	59.8	56.9	50.5	45.6	45.9	44.2	42.6	43.0	43.8	43.1	43.1	43.2	42.5	
Turkey											49.2	43.9	41.2	34.5	33.4	32.8	32.1	
United Kingdom	48.8	45.0	47.5	47.0	50.0	51.4	51.0	51.6	63.6	77.1	89.2	103.4	106.9	102.5	112.8	112.1	121.0	118.3
United States	61.7	64.1	69.8	71.5	78.8	79.0	77.0	77.3	93.1	106.4	116.9	122.4	124.6	124.6	123.9	125.2	126.9	124.3

Source: OECD, 2018, General Government Debt, https://data.oecd.org/gga/general-government-debt.htm

countries such as the USA, Poland, Germany. In the EU, financial criteria are set forth by the Maastricht Treaty and the Stability and Growth Pact based on it (Vural, 2007, p. 99).

Figure 1 shows the distribution of the rules applied to ensure fiscal stability in EU countries by type[3]. It is observed that among the rules that are ranked since 1990, the budget balance(budget deficit) rules have been applied most in number. Then debt rules and expenditure rules are applied. It is understood that the revenue rules in EU countries are the least applicable rules.

It is shown separately the numerical distribution of the financial rules applied in EU Member States at the level of general government, central government, regional government, local government and social security. It is seen that the budget balance rule is applied in the highest level in the general management and the income rule is applied in the least in terms of number. It is also seen that local governments are applied the budget balance rule the most.

Stability and Growth Pact (SGP) entered into force in 1997 in order to ensure that the financial criteria established by the Maastricht Treaty were implemented in a more powerful way. The SGP is an actualized version of the financial criteria that were asserted by the Maastricht Treaty. SGP includes preventive and remedial rules for the implementation of financial criteria in member countries (Sen, 2010, p. 35).

The most important innovation that was brought by the SGP is the Early Warning System and the Excessive Deficit Procedure (EDP). The Early Warning System foresees that it is intervened in the member state being in a position of the tendency of occurrence of excessive budget deficit. Excessive Deficit Procedure begins to process if the budget deficit of member state determined by the Maastricht Treaty exceeds 3% of GDP (Sen, 2010, p. 35).

The Early Warning System includes a package of remedial precautions or a package of precautions that must be taken to be forestalled the deficit or to prevent further increases for the countries that are able to have the budget deficit. In other words, it contains the necessary steps and financial reforms.

Figure 1. Distribution of fiscal rules implemented in EU countries by type
Source: European Commission (2018), Numerical Fiscal Rules in EU Member Countries, https://ec.europa.eu/info/sites/info/files/economy-finance/f1_nfr_type.pdf

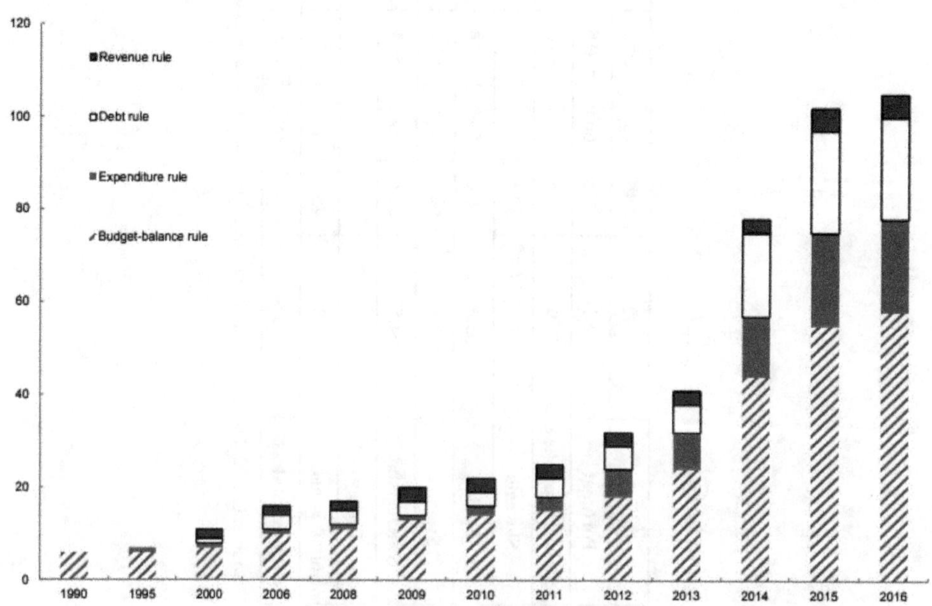

Figure 2. Distribution of fiscal rules in EU countries by public administration areas
Source: European Commission (2018), Numerical Fiscal Rules in EU Member Countries, https://ec.europa.eu/info/sites/info/files/economy-finance/fl_nfr_type.pdf

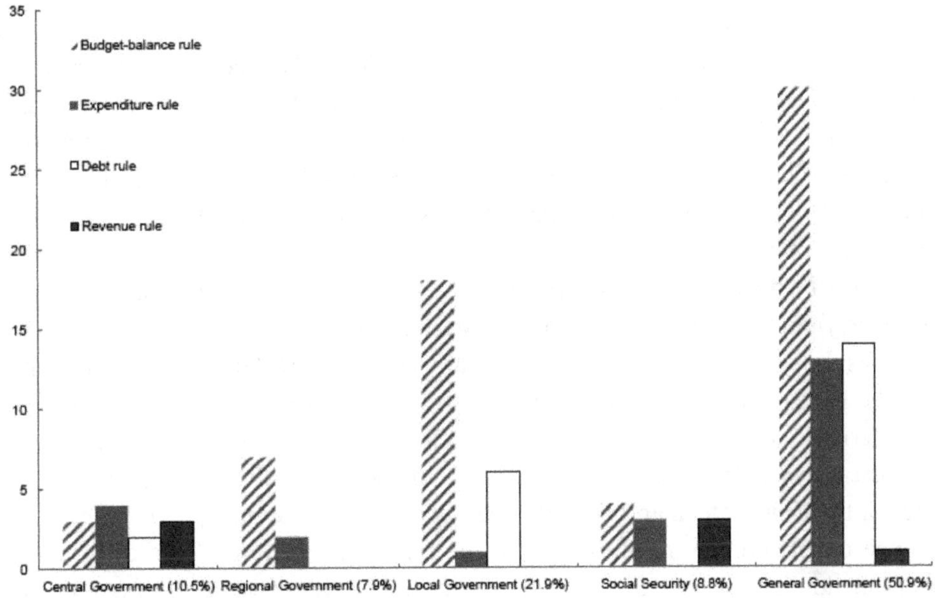

Accordingly, EU member countries were called at various periods. For example, between 2002 and 2010, countries such as Portuguese, France and Germany were called to meet their fiscal deficits. Also, countries such as Greece, Romania and France were made proposals that included a series of financial reforms (European Commission, 2018).

The European Commission monitors the countries within the scope of the Early Warning System and reports on whether the deficit is an exceptional case or not. The Excessive Deficit Procedure is abolished for the countries that meet these recommendations. The Excessive Deficit Procedure was applied to countries such as Greece, Spain, Ireland, the UK within the EU member countries (European Commission, 2018).

In order to reduce and even eliminate the 2008 Global Financial Crisis and the negative effects on the EU countries, the Six-Pack was accepted and entered into force by the Council of Europe in 2011 upon the proposal of the European Commission. The Six-Pack includes a vision of structural fiscal reforms towards strengthen fiscal structure, controlling more effectively of the budget deficits and precautions to be taken (European Commission, 2018).

THE EMERGENT PROBLEMS AND POSSIBLE RESULTS OF ACTUALIZING THE MAASTRICHT FISCAL CRITERIA

The implementation and monitoring of the fiscal and economic criteria mentioned above by all member states is important from two perspectives. The first is that the EU's financial and economic integration process can be completed wholesomely; the second is that it can be created a stronger EU.

It is a fact that there are some risks or problems at actualizing of The Maastricht Fiscal Criteria. It is ranked the main causes and the possible results as follows:

- Although the EU has taken important steps towards monetary union, it is still an important future risk for public finance to be dominated by national policies. The fact that the euro is accepted by seventeen member states and the monetary policy is carried out from a single instrument (the European Central Bank) but the fiscal policies are left to the powers of the member states and as a result failure of running these two policies together prevents the Maastricht Criteria from succeeding (Yuksel, 2014, pp. 2 -3). Member states have been able to act independently on issues such as debt, labor force, foreign trade.
- *Not required to be financed the countries that are weak in terms of financial and economic, especially Greece, from the union budget.* This has started to be discussed more strongly after the 2008 Global Crisis. Loans to Greece have been critically criticized by the public opinion within the EU. Because the Greek crisis is not simply linked to the Global Financial Crisis. The EU has been criticized seriously that Greece misrepresents consciously its financial and economic indicators.
- *The problems created by the 2008 Global Crisis.* In addition to the interdependence of the member states of the Union, the inability of the member states to take independent decisions and their dependence on EU common policies led to the further deepening of the crisis within the EU. However, due to the excessive debt of countries such as Spain, Greece, Portuguese and Italy, and structural problems of the EU, the crisis deepened and made to be taken permanent measures against crisis obligatory. (Yuksel, 2014, pp. 2 -3).
- *At certain periods, these criteria have been used to stretch.* For example, it is allowed that the limit of 3% is allowed to be exceeded on condition that it is "temporary" and "close to the limit", and each country exceeding this limit has been decided to prepare a report containing the reasons for the border crossing and the given time to decrease 3% for the countries exceeding has been increased from a year to two years. On the other hand, sanctions do not go into effect if there is a decrease of at least 2% in the GDP of the member country in extraordinary circumstances such as the economic crisis that has taken place out of its control of related member and has caused great effects in the financial situation (Aysu, 2010, pp. 472).
- These criteria, which have been mentioned above, have not been fully implemented for strong and arbiter countries within the EU, such as Germany and France. The inability of operating the penal mechanism in such countries has lifted the persuasiveness of the fiscal criteria established by the Maastricht Treaty. Indeed, it has been had a discriminatory attitude against some countries in their application of fiscal criteria.
- The fact that the Council of the EU Finance Ministers is responsible for sanctions and the fact that this council is made up of politicians is also a criticism (Aysu, 2010, pp. 393-395).
- It is not seen to be easy that the EU which has still continuing problems in tax harmonization actualized entirely these mechanisms of a fiscal nature.
- *The separation of England from EU membership.* The UK's cautious approach to EU membership from the beginning, and at result its separation with the referendum, has caused the EU's criticisms to be voiced aloud.

As a result, the existence of the problems mentioned above removes the persuasiveness of the full implementation of the Maastricht Criteria. Countries such as Germany and France need to take important steps in this regard. Although the financial and economic backgrounds of the member countries are different, more decisive steps must be taken to ensure harmonization. It is impossible to think the EU which cannot provide financial and monetary union. The foundations of the EU have been laid down in this direction and it is an obligation that financial and economic harmonization be ensured in order to strengthen the union. Otherwise, some other countries such as the UK will be able to make decisions for separation.

THE SANCTIONS TO BE APPLIED IN THE CASE OF FAILURE TO COMPLY THE MAASTRICHT FISCAL CRITERIA

The main objective of the fiscal and monetary criteria laid down by the Maastricht Treaty is to ensure financial stability and sustainable growth. However, it will not be sufficient to set only fiscal and monetary criteria. It is also important to develop control mechanisms for this and to apply certain sanctions to countries that do not comply with these criteria. In case of failure to comply with financial criteria sanctions can be changed from country to country (Aysu, 2010, pp. 468 - 469).

The basic fiscal criteria set within the EU are budget deficit (not exceeding 3% of GDP) and debt criteria (not exceeding 60% of GDP). In case of exceeding these equal values, the Excessive Deficit Procedure is introduced and monetary sanctions can be applied on the concerned country (Schuknecht, 2004, p.11). This is clearly demonstrated in Article 126 of the Treaty on the Functioning of the EU and the European Commission has been tasked with monitoring it (Bali & Celen, 2010, pp. 189-190).

If the concerned country is observed under the Excessive Deficit Procedure and it is determined that the budget deficit is not temporary and exceptional, an amount of 0,1% of the GDP of the concerned country is kept in an account in the EU as interest free for every 1% exceeding the budget criteria. In addition, the following types of sanctions may be introduced: being announced of the countries that do not comply with the criteria in the EU public opinion [4], being proclaimed of extra information about new debt securities or problems in economic situation when it is issued the bonds of the concerned country, the failure of the European Investment Bank loans to be used in countries that do not meet the criteria, etc. (Gungor, 2011, p. 85).

Due to the fact that the UK is not in a monetary union, the EU Commission has decided to recommend that these criteria are not binding for the UK but that they meet the criteria. Due to the fact that the UK is not in a monetary union, the EU Commission has recommended that these criteria are not binding for the UK but that they meet the criteria. On the other hand, the separation of the UK from the EU after the referendum has made it debatable for the credibility and validity of these criteria, which were generally established by the Maastricht Treaty and strengthened by the SGP.

HARMONIZATION OF TURKEY WITH FİSCAL CRITERIA

Looking two main fiscal criteria laid down by the Maastricht Treaty from the harmonization of Turkey aspect, it is seen that the ratio of Turkey's budget deficit and general government department to GDP is under the EU average (See Table 2 and Table 3). It is appeared that fiscal criteria of Turkey is at a better level as it is compared with the strongest economy of Europe especially, Germany, Fransa etc. This situation shows that Turkey seeks to provide a certain financial discipline.

Turkey has taken important steps towards ensuring fiscal discipline and financial stability since 2000. Many regularizations that have the characteristics of financial reform have been actualized with the Stand-By Treaties that is concluded with IMF, the Anti-Inflation Programme and Strengthening of the Economic Transition Programme. That some of the innovations that have the characteristics of financial reform have been actualized since 2000 are listed below:

- "By amending the Central Bank Act (Law no. 4651) on April 25, 2001, it has been prevented that the Central Bank gives advance payments to the Treasury and other public institutions and organizations, opens a credit and buys the debt instruments that was issued of these institutions from the primary market" (Buhur, 2016, pp. 133-148).
- "The Law on the Regulation of Public Finance and Debt Management No. 4749 published in 2002 introduced indebtment limits and open indebtment rules for the public sector"[5] (Toker, 2002, p. 32).
- The funds, whose source is uncertain, which it cannot be obtained certain information on where they are spent and which constitute a significant risk to maintain fiscal discipline, have dramatically been liquidated.
- With the Public Financial Management and Control Law No. 5018 adopted in 2003, an important step has been taken towards ensuring fiscal discipline and financial transparency. It is a crucial legislative act to establish an effective mechanism to ensure fiscal discipline and financial transparency and accountable in public financial management. In Article 16 of this Law, it is stated that the Medium Term Program and the Medium Term Fiscal Plan based on this will be prepared. The Medium Term Fiscal Plan, which includes the predictions of total income and expenditure for the next three years, target deficit and debt and the limits of supplies offer of public administrations, is one of the most important instruments to ensure fiscal discipline in public fiscal management (Buhur, 2016, pp. 133-148).

When it is checked the given the criteria for securing monetary discipline (inflation rate, interest rate and exchange rate criteria), it is difficult to say that it is successful. According to data of Turkish Statistical Institute (TSI), the Consumer Price Index (CPI) figures are seen to show a change at the ratio of 10.85% compared to the same month of the previous year in April 2018 (TSI, 2018). It is seen that the EU average is 1.3% in the same period (OECD, 2018). Being in rise such very high levels of the most important criteria for providing monetary discipline (almost ten times the EU average) is a risk factor for the economy and future of Turkey.

When it is checked long-term public bond interest rates, it is seen that public bond annual accumulated interest rate in Turkey is around % 13 – 14 (Turkey Is Bank, 2018). On the other hand, this rate is observed to be around 4% in developed countries such as Germany, France, England and the USA (OECD, 2018). It is understood that long-term interest rates in Turkey compared to developed countries are about three times more. This situation causes the crowding-out effect of private sector investment expenditures (Atac, 2006, p. 15).

Besides, being above $ 50 billion of Turkey's foreign trade deficit for the year 2018 (Ministry of Development, 2018), the depreciation of the Turkish Lira and increasing the prices of petrol products cause to increase the costs for domestic manufacturers.

Tax structure in Turkey contains certain problems. Namely; the emphasis is on indirect taxes, the exemption and the multiplicity of exceptions, the predominance of the tax burden on salary earner, frequent tax amnesties and the opinions on inability of running the tax system fairly are the problems that should be resolved.

That the ratio of Turkey's budget deficit and general government debt to GDP is close to the criteria mentioned in in the Maastricht Treaty must be assessed in a positive way. However, while setting out the Maastricht Criteria, it has been underlined that it is important to provide monetary discipline in addition to ensuring fiscal discipline. Only ensuring the fiscal discipline will not be enough. Turkey must take important future steps towards especially controlling the inflation rate and reducing the long-term public bonds interest rates, reducing the foreign trade deficit.

CONCLUSION

The first of the criteria laid down by the Maastricht Treaty is the criteria for achieving fiscal discipline. The second is the criteria for ensuring monetary discipline. It seems that a majority of EU member states have failed to achieve financial criteria. Given the ratio of the budget deficit to the GDP, it appears that many EU member states are not able to adapt the criteria of %3 that is the basic criterion. Also, it is understood that many EU member states are not able to adapt to the criteria of 60% which is the rate of general government debt to GDP.

The share of general government debt in GDP appears to be higher in developed countries. Especially a high-rate public debt trend is observed in countries like Japan, the USA, the UK. This indicates that there is a parallel between public debt and development levels. On the other hand, it is understood that emerging economies have a relatively lower level of public debt. This situation is concluded that public debt has a rising trend around the world. What kind of consequences this situation will have on public finance in the future is waited as a question mark.

Referring to the criteria for providing monetary discipline which is the second criteria laid out by the Maastricht Treaty, it appears that especially inflation rate, long-term government bond interest rates in the countries such as; Germany, France, the UK, the USA are better than in Turkey. In Turkey, these rates are much higher than the determined criteria. This situation shows the parallelism with the level of development. In other words, inflation rates and long-term interest rates in developed countries are better than those in developing countries.

It has been observed that the Fiscal Criteria have not been effective especially during periods of economic and financial crises. In many EU member countries, along with the 2008 Global Financial Crisis, both the share of general government debt in GDP and the share of budget deficits in GDP have increased considerably. In this case, the financial criteria set out in the Maastricht Treaty should clearly state what kind of operability it has in the period of economic and financial crises and what kind of mechanisms should be put in place to counteract the crises impacts.

The Maastricht Criteria, which were tried to be implemented since 1993, aimed at providing monetary and fiscal discipline and stability. In terms of harmonization with these criteria, countries such as Germany and France, which have a say in the EU, seem to be unable to comply with financial criteria at certain times. In fact, the inability of imposing sanctions on these countries has severely damaged the faith and confidence in the Maastricht Criteria.

REFERENCES

Acar, M., & Bilir, H. (2013). Türkiye'de Sivil Anayasa Arayışları, Anayasal İktisat ve Anayasada Bulunması Gereken İktisadi-Mali Hükümler. *KMÜ Sosyal ve Ekonomik Araştırmalar Dergisi*, *15*(24), 87–96.

Atac, B. (2006). *Maliye Politikası, Gelişimi, Amaçları, Araçları ve Uygulama Sorunları*. Eskişehir, Turkey: Etam Press. Retrieved from https://www.ab.gov.tr/index_en.php

Aysu, A. (2010). Gelişmiş Ülkelerde Maliye Politikası Kurallarının İhlaline İlişkin Başlıca Yaptırımlar. *Maliye Dergisi*, *158*(January-June), 468–469.

Bali, B. B., & Celen, M. (2010). Mali Kurallar, Maliye Politikası Yönetiminde Yeni Bir Eğilim: Kurallar ve Sınırlamalar Vergi, Harcama, Borçlanma vs. Üzerine Kurallar ve Sınırlamalar. In Avrupa Birliği'nde Mali Kurallar. Maliye Bakanlığı SGB (Ministry of Finance).

Bilici, N. (2012). *Avrupa Birliği ve Türkiye*. Seçkin Press.

Buhur, S. (2016). Türkiye'de 2000 Yılından Sonra Mali Disiplini Sağlamaya Yönelik Alınan Önlemler. Balıkesir Üniversitesi Sosyal Bilimler Enstitüsü Dergisi, 19(36), 133 – 148.

Bulbul, D. (2017). *Bütçe*. Ankara, Turkey: Gazi Bookstore.

European Commission. (2018a). *Annual Budget*. Retrieved from http://ec.europa.eu/budget/annual/index_en.cfm?year=2017

European Commission. (2018b). *Convergence Criteria For Joining*. Retrieved from https://ec.europa.eu/info/business-economy-euro/euro-area/enlargement-euro-area/convergence-criteria-joining_en

European Commission. (2018c). *Numerical Fiscal Rules in EU Member Countries*. Retrieved from https://ec.europa.eu/info/sites/info/files/economy-finance/f1_nfr_type.pdf

European Commission. (2018d). *EU Economic Governance "Six-Pack" Enters Into Force*. Retrieved from http://europa.eu/rapid/press-release_MEMO-11-898_en.htm

European Commission. (2018e). *The History of The European Union*. Retrieved from https://europa.eu/european-union/about-eu/history_en

Falay, N. (2007). Avrupa Birliği Bütçesi (Devlet Bütçesi İçinde). Eskişehir, Turkey: Anatolian University Press.

Gungor, K. (2011). *Küresel Kriz Mali Kural ve Türkiye*. Ankara, Turkey: Nobel Press.

OECD. (2018a). *General Government Deficit*. Retrieved from https://data.oecd.org/gga/general-government-deficit.htm

OECD. (2018b). *Data, Inflation*. Retrieved from https://data.oecd.org/price/inflation-cpi.htm#indicator-chart

OECD. (2018c). *Data, Long-Term Interest Rates*. Retrieved from https://data.oecd.org/interest/long-term-interest-rates.htm

Republic of Turkey, Ministry of Development. (2018). *Temel Ekonomik Göstergeler* [Basic Economic Indicators]. Retrieved from http://www.kalkinma.gov.tr/Pages/TemelEkonomikGostergeler.aspx

Sakal, M. (2003). *Anayasal Bütçe Reformunun Esasları*. Ankara, Turkey: Gazi Bookstore.

Schuknecht, L. (2004). *EU Fiscal Rules Issues and Lessons From Political Economy*. European Central Bank Working Paper Series, No. 421.

Sen, K. (2010). Mali Kural, Bazı Uluslararası Uygulamalar ve Türkiye İncelemesi. *Bütçe Dergisi, 34*.

Toker, M. (2002). Mali Saydamlık ve Türkiye. Sayıştay Başkanlığı (Court of Accounts).

Turkey Is Bank. (2018). *Hazine Bonosu ve Devlet Tahvilleri*. Retrieved from https://www.isbank.com.tr/TR/fiyatlar-ve-oranlar/turk-lirasi-bono-tahvil/hazine-bonosu-ve-devlet-tahvilleri/Sayfalar/hazine-bonosu-ve-devlet-tahvilleri.aspx

Turkish Statistical Institute. (2018). *Temel İstatistikler, Enflasyon ve Fiyat* [Basic Statistics, Inflation, Price]. Retrieved from http://www.tuik.gov.tr/UstMenu.do?metod=temelist

Vural, I. Y. (2007). Kurumsal Maliye Politikası – Ekonomi Politikası Yönetiminde Mali Kurallar ve Kurumlar. In Mali Disiplin ve Ekonomik İstikrarın Sağlanmasında Yeni Bir Araç: Maliye Politikası Kuralları. Ankara: Seçkin Press.

Yuksel, O. (2014). Euro Krizinin Kurumlar ve Politikalar Çerçevesinde İncelenmesi. *Politik Akademi*. Retrieved from http://www.politikakademi.org/2014/01/euro-krizinin-kurumlar-ve-politikalar-cercevesinde-incelenmesi/

Yuzbasıoglu, N. (2012). Anayasadan Mali ve Vergisel Beklentiler. In Anayasa ve Ekonomi. Levha Press.

KEY TERMS AND DEFINITIONS

Budget Deficit: Budget deficit usually represents the difference between the income and expenditure of government in a year.

Early Warning System: Foresees that it is intervened in the member state being in a position of the tendency of occurrence of excessive budget deficit.

European Union (EU): The origin of EU is based on European Coal and Steel Community (ECSC) that is founded on Paris Agreement in 1951.

Excessive Deficit Procedure: Begins to process if the budget deficit of member state determined by the Maastricht Treaty exceeds 3% of GDP.

Inflation Rate: The average annual inflation rate of any member country should not exceed the average rate of inflation of the three member states with the lowest inflation rate in the EU by 1.5 points.

Maastricht Treaty: This treaty, which holds the qualification that is a kind of EU Constitution and establishes the European Union which is called current name, has many provisions ranging from financial-economic and monetary union, EU citizenship, foreign policy, justice mechanism and common security

Primary Deficit: Is the budget deficit that arises after interest payments have been removed. The fact that this deficit continues for many years shows that the country has moved away from its fiscal discipline.

Public Deficit (Public Sector Borrowing Requirement – PSBR or Public Sector Deficit): Represents the difference between total public expenditures and total public incomes over a period of time.

Six-Pack: Includes a vision of structural fiscal reforms towards strengthen fiscal structure, controlling more effectively of the budget deficits and precautions to be taken.

Stability and Growth Pact: The accordance of the concerned country is observed, the report is prepared, the recommendations are presented and the measures to be taken are set forth with Stability and Growth Pact. Stability and Growth Pact (SGP) entered into force in 1997 in order to ensure that the financial criteria established by the Maastricht Treaty were implemented in a more powerful way.

ENDNOTES

1 Based on the historical average of public investments (Gungor, 2011, pp. 84-85).

2 The central administration, which is expressed in terms of Public Debt, occurs of the total amount of the debt of the local administrations and social security institutions.

3 The European Commission has also defined these criteria as fiscal rules (European Union (2018), Numerical Fiscal Rules in EU Member Countries, https://ec.europa.eu/info/sites/info/files/economy-finance/f1_nfr_type.pdf).

4 The announcement to the public that the concerned country does not comply with the fiscal criteria causes this country to lose its reputation.

5 In Article 5 of the Law No. 4749 on the Regulation of Public Finance and Debt Management; "The debt limit can not be changed. However, taking into account the needs and development of debt management, this limit can be increased by up to 5% during the year. Where this amount is not sufficient, an additional 5% may be increased by the decision of the Council of Ministers just on the opinion of the Undersecretariat and the proposal of the Minister. If the budget is matched, the debt can be increased up to 5% of the principal payment" are said.

Section 5
International Finance

Chapter 11
Global Corporate Governance in Financial Markets:
Need for Consensus on Standard Practices

Satya Sekhar Venkata Gudimetla
https://orcid.org/0000-0002-0320-6608
Gandhi Institute of Technology and Management, India

ABSTRACT

In the context of globalization, there is a dire need for understanding various governance practices abroad. Good corporate governance needs to address the principles of government and public enterprise relationship and create the fundamental pillars based on which the governing board can become effective. This chapter focuses on understanding the standard practices in global corporate governance issues and problems, policy implications by considering a select country-wise analysis like Australia, Canada, Scotland, New Zealand, Iceland, India, UAE, etc. Hence, the chapter makes a comparative study of present corporate governance practices in selected countries.

INTRODUCTION

The foundation for modern corporate governance is said to be laid after the issue of Watergate scandal originated in USA. The FBI investigated and discovered a connection between cash found on the burglars and a *slush fund* used by the *Committee for the Re-Election of the President* (CRP), the official organization of Nixon's campaign It was found that control failures that had allowed several major corporations to make illegal political contributions and bribe government officials.

The enactment of Foreign and Corrupt Practices Act in 1977 in US was perhaps the beginning of the concept of corporate governance. On the other hand, Japan experienced many downturns and low returns in business, which was because of failures of the corporate sector. In the same way UK experienced many frauds and scandals in the corporate sector since the introduction of globalisation in the 1980s. It was realised by corporate experts that there was something fundamentally wrong in the corporate sector. The Asian financial crisis of 1997 also put the blame on the inefficient corporate governance of the

DOI: 10.4018/978-1-5225-7564-1.ch011

East Asian economies. All these experiences put together suggested that poor corporate governance was the real culprit; hence, there started an organised movement in the business world to formulate certain principles and policies to put the corporate world on a sound footing.

Various failure incidents of corporate governance practices can be traced across the globe. In India, the Unit Trust of India (UTI), faced turbulence and the relief packages had been worked out by the government of India.

In this context, this paper is aimed to understand the various corporate governance practices across the globe and a need for consensus on standard practices.

THE WORLD BANK

The *Global Corporate Governance Forum*, co-founded by the World Bank and the Organization for Economic Co-operation and Development (OECD), is an advocate, supporter, and disseminator of high standards and practices of corporate governance in developing and transition economies. The goal of the Forum is to:

- Bring together developed and developing countries,
- Tap the private sector through its close working relationship with the International Finance Corporation and the Forum's Private Sector Advisory Group of international business leaders, investors and professionals,
- Focus on practical, targeted corporate governance initiatives at the local, regional, and global level, and
- Promote government reform and private sector self-help.

The *Corporate Governance Department's Investor and Corporate Practice* developed the *IFC Corporate Governance Methodology*, a set of *tools and practices* that IFC staff uses to assess the quality of the governance of potential investee companies and that serves as a guide for their work with clients to add value via improved client governance practices. In addition to working directly with clients, the functions of the Investor and Corporate Practice include:

- Leading IFC's role in the global policy dialogue on corporate governance,
- Providing technical assistance to regulators, stock markets, private sector associations and others, drawing from the practical investment and business experiences of IFC and its investees, and
- Supervising and supporting IFC's directorships and share voting policies and practices.

Corporate governance is a priority for the *International Finance Corporation* because it presents *opportunities to manage investment risks and add value to clients.* In addition to the value-added provided to individual client companies, working to improve the business climate for corporate governance contributes more broadly to IFC's mission to promote sustainable private sector investment and deepen capital markets.

The *Corporate Governance Policy Practice* helps client countries assess their corporate governance institutional frameworks and practices under the auspices of the joint Bank-Fund initiatives on the Reports on the Observances of Standards and Codes (ROSC). The assessments serve to:

- Increase transparency in international financial markets and assist country-level and global reform initiatives,
- Underpin policy dialogue, strategic work and programmatic operations, and
- Provide input to technical assistance and capacity building efforts, such as the establishment of institutes of directors.

The Corporate Governance Policy Unit synthesizes the knowledge drawn from the assessments in best practice papers and notes. The table 1 shows challenges faced by various countries.

Table 1. Challenges faced by global financial markets 1987-2007

Year	Challenge	Details	Country
1987	**FALL IN DJIA**	Dow Jones Industrial Average (DJIA) falls 508 points or 22.6 per cent in the steepest decline since 1929. Hence, portfolio insurance and computerized trading takes some of the blame for what ranks as the 5th largest point drop in DJIA.	USA
1988	**DEREGULATED MARKETS**	Deregulated S & Ls gets in over their heads, and more than 1000 institutions fail, in many cases as the result of malfeasance and fraud. The ensuring bailout costs the US government an estimated $125 billion in direct subsidies	USA
1990	**TROUBLE IN JAPANESE MARKET**	After the bank of Japan raises rates to cool its overheated economy, the Nikkei stock index plunges more than 30000 points. It continues to struggle for more than a decade until its post-bubble low of 7,608 in 2003, down 80% from its high.	JAPAN
1992	**UK EXITS ERM**	Britain is forced to leave European Exchange Rate Mechanism following a wave of speculative attacks on its currency.	UK
1995	**CAUSE FOR PROBLEM OF BARINGS BANK**	Leeson, a 28-year old trader based in Singapore, losses more than $1 billion on futures pegged to the Nifty 225 stock index in Japan and single-handedly brings down Barings Bank, the UKs oldest investment banks.	SINGAPORE
1997	**ASIAN FINANCIAL CRISIS**	Thailand runs out of foreign exchange reserves to support its currency and floats the baht, which falls 20 per cent to a record low. The prices spreads through much of Asia with the Philippines, Indonesia, South Korea and Thailand, the most affected. The IMF establishes a $40 billion programme to support these currencies.	THAILAND
1998	**RUSSIAN FINANCIAL CRISIS**	The Russian economy is hit by declining oil prices in the global recession of 1998 that follows the Asian financial crisis. The Rusian central bank widens the trading band for the ruble, which drops 12 per cent on the day of the announcement. The government also imposes a 90-day moratorium on foreign debt payments.	RUSSIA
1999	**RECESSION IN ARGENTINA**	As its exports are hurt by a devaluation of the Brazilian real, Argentina's GDP falls 4 per cent, marking the beginning of a recession that would last for three years the crisis boils over in to riots in December, 2001, when the government devalued the peso and freezes bank assets.	ARGENTIA
2001	**FINANCIAL CRISIS IN TURKEY**	Prime Minister Bullent Ecevit clashes openly with president Ahmed Necdet Sezer over reforms, triggering a crisis. Interest rates shoot upto 7000 per cent and stock prices fall. The Turkish lira losses more than 40 per cent of its value as the government abandons exchange controls.	TURKEY
2002	**URUGUAY BANKING CRISIS**	Uruguay suffers a massive run on its banks, causing the government to freeze banking operations. Uruguay's real GDP falls by 12 per cent in 2002 as a result of its heavy dependence on neighboring Argentina. The US treasury provides a $1.5 billion bridge loan to the Uruguayan government to tide it over to a bank-rescue fund financed by multinational organizations including the IMF.	URUGUAY
2007	**US SUBPRIME MORTGAGE CRIRIS**	Losses in the sub-prime market trigger a credit crunch. The risks are distributed widely through securitization, and worries that the crisis would spread to the broader economy disrupt global financial markets for months. The Federal Reserve cuts interest rates and floods the market with liquidity.	USA

Source: Prepared by Gordon Plant, Global Finance, December, 2007

REVIEW OF LITERATURE

Investment Company Institute published ‘Global corporate governance issues for mutual funds’ after conducting a survey of the legal, regulatory, and practical framework of corporate governance. While the survey allows a comparison of the strengths and weaknesses of corporate governance systems in different jurisdictions, the survey is not intended to suggest that a mutual fund should avoid investing in a market because of the corporate governance practices of the particular jurisdiction. Ultimately, the appropriateness of a foreign equity security as a portfolio investment is within the purview of the portfolio manager and the fund’s board of directors, taking into consideration the investment and risk policies of the fund.

The earliest work on evolving a regulatory framework in India, for the mutual fund industry was done by Barua, Varma and Venkiteswaran (1991), drawing heavily on the regulatory framework for operation of mutual funds in the U.S.A.. The authors proposed detailed guidelines that could be adopted for mutual funds operating in the Indian capital markets.

Verma (1994) study on mutual fund covers the conceptual and regularity aspect of Indian mutual fund with some information task and guidelines to the investors in selection of mutual fund. Seema Vaid (1994) study covers the regulatory frame work, review of the growth of mutual funds and primary information about mutual fund schemes.

Mohan Rao (1998) studied various issues like organization structure of mutual funds, investment procedure, accounting and reporting standards and so on. He states that a lot of structural changes and innovations have occurred both in international and national financial system, which lead to change in housing savings and investment attitude also.

Shleifer and Vishny (1997) states that “there is a broader view of corporate governance, which views the subject as the methods by which suppliers of finance control managers in order to ensure that their capital cannot be expropriated and that they earn a return on their investment. Furthermore, bureaucrats are by nature risk averse, and will therefore undertake less risk than is optimal from the taxpayers’ point of view. In order to partially mitigate such opportunism, bureaucrats may be given little autonomy”.

Bhattacharya et al (1998) paper focuses on the special nature of banking requires not only a broader view of corporate governance, but also government intervention in order to restrain the behaviour of bank management. Depositors do not know the true value of a bank’s loan portfolio as such information is incommunicable and very costly to reveal, implying that a bank’s loan portfolio is highly fungible.

Allen and Gale (2000) argue that “competition in the product or service market may act as a substitute for corporate governance mechanisms. The basic argument is that firms with inferior and expropriating management will be forced out of the market by firms possessing non-expropriating managers due to sheer competitive pressure. However the banking industry, possibly due to its information-intensive nature, may be a lot less competitive than other business sectors”.

Stephen Erlichman’s report (2000) revealed important information on the different fund governance structures in Canada, that have grown-up in the absence of a mandated fund governance regime. This piece of research gives a sense of which governance models have been embraced by the industry and which have not. It also gives some insight into what mutual fund managers *think* is important to investors when it comes to the governance of their funds.

Macey and O’Hara (2001) argue that “a broader view of corporate governance should be adopted in the case of banking institutions, arguing that because of the peculiar contractual form of banking, corporate governance mechanisms for banks should encapsulate depositors as well as shareholders”.

A further issue, which complicates the corporate governance of banks in developing economies, are the activities of 'distributional cartels' (Oman, 2001). These cartels consist of corporate insiders who have very close links with or partially constitute the governing elite. The existence of such cartels will undermine the credibility of investor legal protection and may also prevent reform of the banking system. Unsurprisingly, good political governance can be considered as a prerequisite for good corporate governance (Oman, 2001).

Capiro and Levine (2002) study reveals that the opaqueness of banks also makes it very costly for depositors to constrain managerial discretion through debt covenants. Consequently, rational depositors will require some form of guarantee before they would deposit with a bank. Government-provided guarantees in the form of implicit and explicit deposit insurance might encourage economic agents to deposit their wealth with a bank, as a substantial part of the moral hazard cost is borne by the government. Nevertheless, even if the government provides deposit insurance, bank managers still have an incentive to opportunistically increase their risk taking, but now it is mainly at the government's expense. This well-known moral hazard problem can be ameliorated through the use of economic regulations such as asset restrictions, interest rate ceilings and separation of commercial banking from insurance and investment banking, and reserve requirements. Amongst the effects of these regulations is that they limit the ability of bank managers to over-issue liabilities or divert assets into high risk ventures. The existence of deposit insurance may reduce the need for banks to raise capital from large, uninsured investors who have the incentive to exert corporate control.

Arun and Turner (2002) find interesting facts relating to corporate governance. They stated that the general principles of sound corporate governance are also beneficial to government-owned banks". The inefficiencies associated with government-owned banks, especially those emanating from a lack of adequate managerial incentives have led developing economy governments to begin divesting their ownership stakes. The divestment of government-owned banks raises several corporate governance issues. If banks are completely privatized then there must be adequate deposit insurance schemes and supervisory arrangements established in order to protect depositors and prevent a financial crash.

Khurshid et al (2009) studied the structure of the mutual fund industry in India and analyzed the state of competition among all the mutual funds in private sector and public sector. The levels of competition and their trends have been obtained for the periods March 2003 to March, 2009. This study found over-all mutual fund industry is facing a high competitive environment. An increasing trend of competition was observed within bank-institution, private sector foreign and private sector joint venture mutual funds.

Martin E. Lybecker (2005) writes on corporate governance mechanism in USA. His study narrates that Investment Company Act of 1940 ("Investment Company Act") has always required that at least forty percent of the members of the mutual fund's board of directors be independent. In July 2004, the Securities and Exchange Commission ("SEC" or "Commission"), in a three-to-two vote, amended certain existing rules (the "Corporate Governance Amendments") to require that no less than seventy-five percent of the members of a mutual fund's board of directors be independent, that the chairman of the board of directors be an independent director, and that the board of directors engage in certain specific corporate governance practices. He argue that the Commission's decision to adopt the Corporate Governance Amendments was without statutory authority and usurped the proper legislative role of Congress, was not adequately justified, and will be of questionable efficacy.

Ping Yu II (2011) study on Chinese Fund Management Companies (FMC) at the firm level also incorporates new analysis of the impact on board effectiveness from shareholding structure and the unique China governance management of the supervisory board. Using panel data of 288 firm-year observations covering more than 97% of FMC in China over the period from 2006 to 2010, this paper aims to address governance issues of FMC in China's regulatory context by investigating the key governance variables and empirically testing their impact on the effectiveness of the board. It examines what governance mechanisms enhance board effectiveness under the contractual form of China's FMC.

Jingjing Yang et al., (2011) study on internal and external corporate governance mechanisms in China. Chinese regulatory bodies have made considerable efforts to improve the corporate governance of listed firms. However, research has shown that most of the governance instruments that are effective in developed nations are less effective in China. This study attributes the ineffectiveness to the large stake of the state in listed firms, strong political connections between listed firms and the government, and the lack of a truly independent judicial system. Some suggestions for making corporate governance more effective in China are provided.

Eric Doiter (2015) study focuses on corporate governance of mutual funds. He states that there are two essential features of mutual funds that differentiate them from ordinary corporations. First, mutual funds are not only separate legal entities; they are also financial products or services, the means by which fund investors obtain professional investment management from investment advisers. To be sure, investment management is a fiduciary product, but it is a product nonetheless. Mutual funds have, therefore, a hybrid nature i.e., both entity and product. This means that fund investors, too, have a hybrid character: They are both customers of the fund's adviser and shareholders of a legal entity, the fund. This stands, of course, in marked contrast to ordinary corporations, whose shareholders and customers are two groups, distinct in law and in the marketplace. For an ordinary corporation, decision-making authority and oversight of all facets of its business rest squarely with the board of directors, and for this reason corporate director are called upon to exercise wide-ranging business judgment over the corporation's business and operations. Most notably, the Investment Company Act of 1940 leaves decision making over a fund's core business viz., investing in securities. The fund's investment adviser, who has taken the risks and borne the expenses of organizing and promoting the fund,. Second, mutual funds are fundamentally different from ordinary corporations owing to the right of redemption, a right of the investor to withdraw her capital.

ETHICAL ISSUES IN CORPORATE GOVERNANCE

Corporate governance has been a topic high on the agenda of all major economies in recent years. This started with the 'dot-com bubble' and the financial scandals of the early 2000s, which saw the spectacular bankruptcy of companies such as Enron, Tyco, and WorldCom in the US, and shocking revelations of financial irregularities across the globe. Recent attention has turned to the collapse of many banks and financial institutions in the financial crisis in 2008, where managers took major financial risks unknown to the shareholders.

Executive Accountability and Control

The difference governance frameworks globally come with important differences in how this board is structured and composed. These are basically two extremes. In the *Anglo-American model*, there is usually a single-tier board that comprises both executive and non-executive directors.

In *Continental Europe*, however a two-tier board is more common. The upper tier is composed of non-executive directors and the lower tier of executive directors. The upper tier, often called a supervisory board, effectively oversees the lower tier, which is more concerned with the day-to-day running of the company. The supervisory board commonly includes representatives of stakeholders, including banks and employees, other than just shareholders.

Regardless the structure, the central ethical issue here is clearly the independence of the supervisory, non-executive board members. They will only be able to reasonably act in the principal's interest if they have no directly conflicting interests. In order to achieve this, a number of points are important:

- Non-executive directors should be largely drawn from outside the corporation.
- They should not have a personal financial interest in the corporation other than the interests of the shareholders. This includes the fact that the remuneration for the non-executive director role must not significantly exceed a reasonable compensation for time and other expenses.
- They should be appointed for a limited period in order to prevent them from getting too close to the company.
- They should be competent to judge the business of the company. This would require, and to some degree allow, a limited number of insiders, such as former executives or even works council members.
- They should have sufficient resources to get information or commission research into the corporation.
- They should be appointed independently.

A further element of supervision comes from an independent auditor who audits the work of the executive board, normally the main aspect of their role, and also of the non-executive board.

Despite the guidelines above, the independence of non-executive directors remains a delicate issue. Often they belong to the same peer group as executive directors, or are themselves in executive role elsewhere, or have been in such role in the past. This means that a completely neutral and independent approach will always be quite difficult to achieve.

Executive Remuneration

The financial crisis of the late 2000s brought the issue of executive pay centre-stage in an unprecedented fashion, given that executives of bankrupt or failing companies continued to earn millions in salaries and billions in bonuses. 'Shameful' and 'the height of irresponsibility' were President Obama's comments in January 2009 on what continued to be common practice not only in the US, but in many other countries globally. The general trend towards million dollar salaries has been fuelled by the revitalization of the shareholder value ideology, combined with the massive privatization move in the late 1980s and early 1990s, which saw the remuneration enjoyed by bosses of formerly public companies skyrocket.

Probably the key element in continuing escalation in executive pay actually derives from an attempt to address the core of the agency problem: in order to align the interests of both parties, the perfect solution appeared to be to pay executives in the same 'currency' that matters to shareholders, namely dividends and rise in share price. The logical conclusion then is to pay executives in shares through options that allow executives to buy share at a future date. In order to make the incentive work, it would not be sufficient to pay them with jut a few shares or options but to a degree that substantially impacts on their wealth. As a consequence, the US in particular has led the way in rewarding senior managers with massive stock option deals. This approach of performance-related pay has particularly spread in the financial industry, resulting in high salaries and bonuses even for mid-level executives in financial services and banking.

According to a 2008 survey, executives such as Sir Martin Sorrell, CEO of the advertising and communications group WPP, earned 550 times more than their average employee. The same survey identified the averase rise in salary of the top earners to be 125% in the past year. However, while the financial crisis of the late 2000s has exposed the start contrast between the performance of many managers and their pay, the link between executive remuneration and stock market performance has always been somewhat tenuous.

Examples such as the above expose many of the ethical problems with executive pay in firm-shareholder relations, some of which are:

- **Performance-Related Pay:** To tackle the problem of divergent interests, most executive salaries nowadays contain a significant amount of shares and share options to align shareholder and manager's interests. However, the problem here is that by including these elements, salary levels have exploded, often leading to considerable unrest within companies. .
- **Influence of Globalization:** These shifts in remuneration show the influence of globalization on executive pay. The market for executive talent is a global one and so the standards of the highest level of pay seem to be applicable across the board. This means that in regions such as Europe, where the introduction of performance-related pay has entered recently, further significant rises in pay can still be expected. This domination of the Anglo-American shareholder value orientation has also had its influence in newly privatized companies.
- **Influence of the Board:** It is also illustrated that, influence of the board is limited, and often fails to reflect shareholder interests. Why would shareholders want to reward a CEO who had overseen a period of poor performance?

CORPORATE GOVERNANCE PRATICES: A COMPARATIVE STUDY OF DEVELOPED AND DEVELOPING ECONOMIES

USA

The seeds of modern ideas of corporate governance were probably sown by the Watergate scandal during the Nixon presidency in the United States. The need to arrest such unhealthy trends was translated into the legislation of the Foreign and Corrupt Practices Act of 1977 in America that provided for the establishment, maintenance and review of systems of internal control. In the same year, the Securities and Exchange Commission (SEC) proposed mandatory reporting on internal financial controls. In 1985, a series of high-profile business failures rocked the United States, which included the collapse of Savings and Loan. With a view to identifying the main causes of misrepresentation in financial reports and to recommend ways of reducing such incidents, the government appointed the Treadway Commission. The Treadway Report, published in 1987, highlighted the need for a proper control environment, independent audit committees and an objective internal audit system. As a result o this recommendation, the Committee of Sponsoring Organisations (COSO) came into being. Between 2000 and 2002, the exposing of corporate frauds in United States were of such magnitude and inflicted such damage on investors that company reputations were irreparably damaged and investors' confidence dipped to a new low. The fraud and self-dealing revelations resulted in investigations by the Congress, the SEC, and the State Attorney General in New York, and the emergence of the Sarbanes-Oxley Act (SOX) enacted into law in July 2002.

United Kingdom

A series of corporate frauds and collapses in the late 1980s and the early 1990s made the United Kingdom realise that the existing rules and regulations were inadequate to curb unlawful and unfair practices of corporations. It was with this view a committee under the chairmanship of Sir Adrian Cadbury was appointed by the London Stock Exchange in 1991. The Cadbury Committee, consisting of representatives drawn from the British industry, was assigned the task of drafting a code of practices to assist corporations in England in defining and applying internal controls to limit their exposure to financial loss, from whatever cause it arose. The committee submitted its report along with the 'Code of best practices' in December 1992. In this globally well-received report, the Committee elaborated the methods of governance needed to achieve a balance between the essential powers of the board of directors and their proper accountability. Though the recommendations of the committee were not mandatory in character, the companies listed on the London Stock Exchange were required to stat explicitly in their accounts, whether or not the code has been followed by them, and if not complied with, were advised to explain to explain the reason for non-compliance.

Australia

There are approximately 1500 public companies listed on the Australian Stock Exchange (ASX) and other public non-listed corporate entities. Australian listed companies generally have a unitary board structure with a balance of executive and non-executive directors and a separate chief executive and chairman. The ASX Corporate Governance Council As a central reference point for companies to understand stakeholder expectations, in order to promote and restore investor confidence, ASX convened the ASX Corporate Governance Council in August 2002. Its purpose is to develop recommendations which reflect international best practice. Australia operates under a common law system that entails courts interpreting legislation in particular factual circumstances to develop a body of precedent or common law. Judges interpret previous cases in Australia, and increasingly from overseas, in constant process of review and adaptation. The following enactments will govern the corporate governance in Australia.

- **The Corporate Law Reform Program Act 1999:** It introduced a statutory business judgement rule, rewrote many of the previsions about director's duties, revolutionized the rules on takeovers and fundraising, and clarified some issues about accounting standards and the rules generated by accounting standards setting bodies.

- **The Financial Service Reforms Act 2001:** Introduced standardized regulation for all people and companies that deal in financial products or that give investment advice.
- **The Corporate Law Simplifications Act 1995:** Amongst many other reforms, provided for a new form of company in Australia, the one person company consisting of one director and one shareholder with the aim of providing greater flexibility for small business to incorporate in Australia.

Canada

Canada is originally inhabited by various native American people, mainland Canada was explored by the English and the French. A major problem for Canada is that large segments of its economy-notably in manufacturing, petroleum and mining- are controlled by foreign, especially US interests. This deprives the nation of much of the profits of its industries and makes the economy vulnerable to development outside Canada. This situation is mitigated somewhat by the fact that Canada itself is a large foreign interest.

New Zealand

The New Zealand corporate governance system is relatively unusual by international standards in a number of respects. First, unlike the financial systems of many countries, in New Zealand the banks form a very dominant part of the financial sector. Registered banks, of which there are currently 18, represent the lion's share of the total financial system, both in terms of total financial system assets and deposit liabilities. In terms of financial system stability, registered banks are by far the most important players in the financial system. And of the 18 registered banks, only about 5 banks could be regarded as systemically important, together holding more than 80% of total registered bank assets. The New Zealand approach is an effective way of promoting a sound financial system. It reduces the moral hazard risks associated with conventional banking supervision, and strengthens the effectiveness of market discipline on banks. New Zealand's approach to financial sector regulation seeks to create an environment conducive to robust market disciplines. This is achieved through a number of measures, including the promotion of a relatively open, contestable banking sector, a competitively neutral approach to regulation - enabling banks and non-banks to compete on largely equal terms - and the absence of deposit insurance. In addition, the Reserve Bank's approach to responding to a bank failure stresses the importance of being able to manage a bank failure in ways that avoid the need for a government-funded bail-out, and seeks to ensure that shareholders, subordinated creditors and senior creditors, including depositors, bear their fair share of losses.

Scotland

The Scottish parliament has legislative authority for all other areas relating to Scotland and has limited power to vary income-tax but has never exercised this power. Scottish parliament can defer devolved matters back to westminister to be considered as part of united kingdom-wise legislation by passing a legislative by passing a legislative consent motion if UK-wide legislation is considered to be more appropriate for certain issues. The programmes of legislation enacted by the Scottish parliament have been a divergence in the provision of public services compared to the next of United Kingdom.

Iceland

Iceland is the fifth most productive country in the world based on GDP per capita at purchasing power parity. It is also ranked second on the 2006 united nations human development index. The centre-right government plans to continue its generally neo-liberal policies of reducing the budget and current account deficits, limiting foreign borrowing, containing inflation, revising agricultural and fishing policies etc. The government remains opposed to European Union membership, primarily because of Iceland's concern about losing control over their fishing resources. The president of Iceland is largely ceremonial office that serves as a diplomat, figurehead and head of state, but who can also block a law voted by the parliament and put it to a national referendum.

Germany

The German corporate governance system is different from that of the Anglo-Saxon countries because it foresees the possibility, and even the necessity, to integrate lenders and employees in the governance of large corporations. The German corporate governance system is generally regarded as the standard example of an insider-controlled and stakeholder-oriented system. Moreover, only a few years ago it was a consistent system in the sense of being composed of complementary elements which fit together well. However, the past decade has seen a wave of developments in the German corporate governance system, which makes it worthwhile and indeed necessary to investigate whether German corporate governance has recently changed in a fundamental way.

The German corporate governance system is generally regarded as the standard example of what Franks and Mayer (1994) has called an insider-controlled and stakeholder-oriented system. Moreover, only a few years ago the German corporate governance system was a consistent system in the sense of being composed of complementary elements which fit together well. The first objective of this paper is to show why and in which respect these characterizations were once appropriate. Today, however, it may no longer be appropriate to characterize German corporate governance in this way. It is worthwhile and indeed necessary to investigate whether German corporate governance has recently changed in a fundamental way. More specifically one can ask which elements and features of German corporate governance have in fact changed, why they have changed and whether those changes which did occur constitute a structural change which have transformed the old insider-controlled system into an outsider-controlled and shareholder-oriented system, or have at least deprived the system of its former consistency.

Hungary

Hungary is small, middle income economy with a remarkable degree of integration into the world economy. The country's savings, however, are not sufficient for a catching-up growth, thus, it must fiercely compete for foreign direct investment. Under these conditions it is obvious that she cannot risk the divergence with international trends. She has no choice but follow international standards in all important fields - including up-dated CG practices. Being a member of the European Union since 1 May 2004 she has to adjust to the European benchmark in the first place. Thus, new CG legal regulations and codes of conduct have been imported from the European Union extensively. Both a successfully completed transition from plan to market and the accession to the EU would have been impossible without creating a proper legal environment. Hungary's accomplishments in this field are unanimously acknowledged. There is, however, a gap between laws on the books (law extensiveness) on the one hand, and law enforcement (law effectiveness) and the real working of the economy on the other.

Hungarian civil law is German in legal origin. By the analysis of La Porta et al (1997), this fact would suggest that the chances are not very good for investors' rights being particularly strongly protected by the laws. The sample used by La Porta et al (1997) and La Porta et al (1998) contained six German legal origin countries (Germany, Switzerland, Austria, Japan, South Korea, Taiwan). (The other three groups included common law-origin, French-origin, and Scandinavian-origin countries.) The general result was that outside investors' rights are best protected in common law countries, though German origin countries perform relatively well in protecting creditors' rights. Among transition economies Pistor (2000) identifies many other German-origin countries, such as Croatia, the Czech Republic, Estonia, Latvia, Lithuania, Poland, the Slovak Republic and Slovenia.

India

In India, the real history of corporate governance dates back to the year 1992, following efforts made in many countries of the world to put in place a system suggested by the Cadbury Committee. The corporate governance movement in India began in 1997 with a voluntary code framed by the Confederation of the Indian Industry (CII). In the next three years, almost 30 large listed companies accounted for 25 per cent of India's market capitalization voluntarily adapted the CII code. This was followed by the recommendation of the Kumar Manglam Birla Committee set up in 1999 by the Securities and Exchange Board of India (SEBI), culminating in the introduction of Clause 49 of the standard listing Agreement to be complied with by all the listed companies in stipulated phases. The said committee divided its recommendations into mandatory and non-mandatory. Mandatory recommendations included such issues as, the composition of the board, appointment and structure of audit committees, remuneration of directors, board procedures, and additional information regarding management, discussion and analysis as a part of the annual report, disclosure of directors' interest, shareholders' rights, and the compliance level of corporate governance, in the annual report. From 1 April 2001, over 140 listed companies accounting for almost 80 per cent of market capitalization were to follow a mandatory code which was in line with some of the best international practices. By April 2003, every listed company followed the SEBI code.

The Reserve Bank of India (RBI) has asked all listed commercial banks to follow SEBI's committee report on corporate governance. Some of the important recommendations of the SEBI committee on corporate governance that will henceforth be applicable to listed commercial banks include, that all pecuniary relationship or transactions of the non-executive directors should be disclosed in the annual report. The committee has suggested that emphasis must be laid on the caliber of the non-executive directors, especially independent directors, since non-executive directors help bring an independent judgment to bear on the boards deliberations, especially on issues of strategy, performance, management of conflicts and standards of conduct. It has been recommended that the board of the company have an optimum combination of executive and non-executive directors with not less than 50 per cent of the board comprising the non-executive directors. The number of independent directors depends on the nature of the chairman of the board. In case a company has a non-executive chairman, at least half of the board should be independent (mandatory recommendation).

According to the RBI circular, the audit committee of the board may look into the reasons for default in payment to depositors, debenture holders, shareholders (non-payment of dividends) and creditors, wherever there are any cases of defaults in payment. Before deregulating banking systems, much attention will need to be paid to the speedy implementation of robust corporate governance mechanisms in order to protect shareholders. The introduction of sound corporate governance principles into banking has been partially hampered by poor legal protection, weak information disclosure requirements and dominant owners. Furthermore, in many developing countries, the private banking sector is not enthusiastic to introduce corporate governance principles. For example, in India, this problem can be summarised in the corporate sector as the privileging of the interests of one group over all other interests in a company.

UAE

The United Arab Emirates(UAE) is a middle eastern federation of seven states which are termed as emirates viz., Abu Dhabi, Ajman, Dubai, Fujairah, Ras Al-Khaiman, Sharjah and Ummal- quwain. UAE is rich in oil and it expects recent additional economic diversification to draw more financial and banking firms. The GDP per capita is currency third in the world, while at $168 billion in 2006. The presidency and premiership of UAE is hereditary to Al Nahyan clan of Abu dhabi and Al Makotum clan of Dubai respectively. The supreme council will be consisting of the rulers of the seven emirates. Petroleum and natural gas exports till play an important role in the economy, especially in Abu Dhabi. A massive construction boom, an expanding manufacturing base, and a thriving service sector are helping the UAE. At present $350 billion worth of active construction projects are undertaken by UAE. Third place goes to tourism industry.

France

The French government has chosen to stipulate a legal "minimum service" for corporate governance. In fact, the preparatory work for these laws (the Viénot reports in 1995 and 1999 and the Bouton report in 2002) helped to define the principles of corporate governance more precisely and completely, particularly as regards the role and structure of the Board of Directors. For example, these reports shed a great deal of new light on sensitive subjects:

- Issues relating to the balance of power within the Board of Directors, such as, for example, the presence of independent directors;
- The quality of directors and of the work of the Board: selection of directors, committees, etc.
- Evaluation of the Board of Directors;
- Communications on items not included in the balance sheet, and on the company's risks.

France passed two new laws, with a view to strengthening the legal position on corporate governance: the NRE law (on new economic regulations) dated 15 May 2001, and the LSF, dated 1 August 2003. These laws provide the basic framework, specifically targeting transparency and ethics within companies.

The French banking industry is experiencing an increasing amount of regulation, mainly deriving from the European initiative for promoting a safe and sound banking system.

Three main layers of rules and regulations apply to banking activities:

- **EU Law:** Most of this is directly applicable in France. This includes principally the CRD IV package, which transposes the global standards on bank capital (commonly known as the Basel III agreement) into the EU legal framework. This is achieved through Directive 2013/36/EU on capital requirements (CRD IV) and Regulation (EU) 575/2013 on prudential requirements for credit institutions and investment firms (CRR).
- **French Legislation (Oliver, 2018):** Most of this is codified into the Monetary and Financial Code (*Code Monétaire et Financier*). The Monetary and Financial Code has recently been amended in particular in relation to:
    - The separation of banking activities, which requires the separation of own account trading activities from other activities, and imposes bans on certain other activities;
    - The resolution and recovery of credit institutions;
    - The regulation of payment services (which are no longer part of the French banking monopoly rules), electronic currencies and FinTech.

Switzerland

Switzerland, considered the "grandfather of bank secrecy", has been one of the largest offshore financial centers and tax havens in the world since the mid-20th century. Swiss social and political forces have minimized and reverted much of proposed roll backs. Disclosing client information has been considered a serious social and criminal offence since the early 1900s. Employees working in Swiss banks "have long adhered to an unwritten code similar to that observed by doctors or priests" (Thomasson, 2013).

Switzerland is ranked in first position in the 2018 Financial Secrecy Index, based on a high secrecy score of 76 and a large global scale weight for the size of offshore financial services (approximately five percent of the global market). Its famed banking secrecy laws remain firmly in place, though with exceptions permitted for some countries to obtain necessary information.

SUGGESTED MEASURES

- In order to deal with the problems of corporate governance, it was suggested that developing economies need to adopt the following measures.
- Liberalisation policies need to be gradual, and should be dependent upon improvements in prudential regulation.
- Developing economies need to expend resources enhancing the quality of their financial reporting systems.
- Given that capital plays such an important role in prudential regulatory systems, it may be necessary to improve investor protection laws, increase financial disclosure and impose fiduciary duties upon directors so that firms can raise the equity capital required for regulatory purposes.
- A further reason as to why this policy needs implemented is the growing recognition that the corporate governance has an important role to play in assisting supervisory institutions to perform their tasks, allowing supervisors to have a working relationship with bank management, rather than adversarial one.
- It was suggested that the corporate governance in developing economies is severely affected by political considerations.

- Given the trend towards privatization of government-owned firms in developing economies, there is a need for the managers of such firms to be granted autonomy and be gradually introduced to the corporate governance practices of the private sector prior to divestment.
- Where there has only been partial divestment and governments have not relinquished any control to other shareholders, it may prove very difficult to divest further ownership stakes unless corporate governance is strengthened.
- Given that limited entry of foreign firm may lead to increased competition, which in turn encourages domestic banks to emulate the corporate governance practices of their foreign competitors

CONCLUSION

In developed economies, protection of depositors in a deregulated environment is typically provided by a system of prudential regulation, but in developing economies such protection is undermined by the lack of well-trained supervisors, inadequate disclosure requirements, the cost of raising capital and the presence of distributional cartels. Although, corporate governance reforms have been proposed in many countries, the issue of executive remuneration touches an ethical chord. This is not actually so much because the public feels sorry for shareholders, but because the pay differentials between the those at the top and those at the bottom appear to be so inequitable.

Corporate governance in banking sector is being implemented under the guidance and regulations of SEBI and RBI. Indian financial markets are is facing some problems while implementing corporate governance. Since most of corporate entities in India are protected by the government rules and regulations, the employees also somewhat negligent towards implementation of corporate governance. However, now all public sector firms are facing severe competition from private sector. In this, context, the implementation of corporate governance in a systematic and strategic manner is becoming the need of the hour.

The corporate governance of financial institutions in developing economies is important for several reasons. First, banks have an overwhelmingly dominant position in developing-economy financial systems, and are extremely important engines of economic growth. Second, as financial markets are usually underdeveloped, banks in developing economies are typically the most important source of finance for the majority of firms. Third, as well as providing a generally accepted means of payment, banks in developing countries are usually the main depository for the economy's savings. Fourth, many developing economies have recently liberalised their banking systems through privatisation/disinvestments and reducing the role of economic regulation. Consequently, managers of banks in these economies have obtained greater freedom in how they run their banks.

REFERENCES

Allen, F., & Gale, D. (2000). Corporate Governance and Competition. In X. Vives (Ed.), *Corporate Governance: Theoretical and Empirical Perspectives*. Cambridge, UK: Cambridge University Press. doi:10.1017/CBO9781139175333.003

Arun, T. G., & Turner, J. D. (2002). Financial Sector Reform in Developing Countries: The Indian Experience. *World Economy*, *25*(3), 429–445. doi:10.1111/1467-9701.00440

Barua, S.K., Varma, J.R., & Venkiteswaran, N. (1991). A Regulatory Framework for Mutual Fund. *Economic and Political Weekly, 26*(21), 55-59.

Bhattacharya, S., Boot, A. W. A., & Thakor, A. V. (1998). The Economics of Bank Regulation. *Journal of Money, Credit and Banking, 30*(4), 745–770. doi:10.2307/2601127

Capiro, G., Jr., & Levine, R. (2002). *Corporate Governance of Banks: Concepts and International Observations*. Paper presented in the Global Corporate Governance Forum research Network Meeting.

Dickinson, W. B., Cross, M., & Polsky, B. (1973). Watergate: chronology of a crisis. Washington, DC: Congressional Quarterly Inc.

Doiter, E. (2015). Disentangling Mutual Fund Governance From. *Harvard Business Law Review*, 5.

Erlichman. (2000). *Making it Mutual: Aligning the Interests of Investors and Managers: Recommendations for a Mutual Fund Governance Regime for Canada*. Prepared for the Canadian Securities Administrators.

Investment Company Institute. (2000). *Global Corporate Governance Issues for Mutual Funds*. Author.

Khurshid, S. M. Z., Rohit, & Singh, G. P. (2009). Level and trends of competition among the mutual funds in India. *Research Journal of Business Management, 3*(2), 47–67. doi:10.3923/rjbm.2009.47.67

La Porta, R., Lopez-de-Silanes, F., & Shleifer, A. (1999). Corporate Ownership Around the World. *The Journal of Finance, 54*(2), 471–517. doi:10.1111/0022-1082.00115

La Porta, R., Lopez-de-Silanes, F., Shleifer, A., & Vishny, R. W. (2000). Investor Protection and Corporate Governance. *Journal of Financial Economics, 58*(1-2), 3–27. doi:10.1016/S0304-405X(00)00065-9

Levine, R. (1999). *Foreign Bank Entry and Capital Control Liberalization: Effects on Growth and Stability*. University of Minnesota.

Lybecker. (2005). Enhanced Corporate Governance for Mutual Funds: A Flawed Concept that Deserves Serious Reconsideration. *Wash. U. L. Q., 83*, 104.

Macey, J. R., & O'Hara, M. (2001). *The Corporate Governance of Banks*. Federal Reserve Bank of New York Economic Policy Review.

Macey, J. R., & O'Hara, M. (2001). *The Corporate Governance of Banks*. Federal Reserve Bank of New York Economic Policy Review.

Mohan Rao, P. (1998). *Working of Mutual Fund Organizations in India*. New Delhi: Kanishka Publishers.

Oman, C. P. (2001). *Corporate Governance and National Development*. OECD Development Centre Technical Papers, Number 180.

Oman, C. P. (2001). *Corporate Governance and National Development*. OECD Development Centre Technical Papers, Number 180.

Partner & Pince. (2018). *Banking regulation in France: Overview*. Retrieved from: https://uk.practicallaw.thomsonreuters.com/

Peek, J., & Rosengren, E. (2000). *Implications of the Globalization of the Banking Sector: The Latin American Experience* New England Economic Review.

Satya Sekhar, G.V. (2018). *Financial Innovation- Theories, Models, Regulation*. Vernon Press.

Seema, V. (1994). *Mutual Fund Operations in India*. New Delhi: Rishi Publications.

Shleifer, A., & Vishny, R. (1997). A Survey of Corporate Governance. *The Journal of Finance*, *52*(2), 737–783. doi:10.1111/j.1540-6261.1997.tb04820.x

Shleifer, A., & Vishny, R. (1997). A Survey of Corporate Governance. *The Journal of Finance*, *52*(2), 737–783. doi:10.1111/j.1540-6261.1997.tb04820.x

Stiglitz, J. E. (1994). The Role of the State in Financial Markets. *Proceedings of the World Bank Annual Conference on Development Economics 1993*, 19-52.

Thomasson, E. (2013, April 18). *Special Report: The battle for the Swiss soul*. Reuters.

Verma, J. C. (1994). Merchant Banking and Financial Services. Taxmann Publishers Ltd.

Vives, X. (2000). Corporate Governance: Does it Matter. In X. Vives (Ed.), *Corporate Governance: Theoretical and Empirical Perspectives*. Cambridge, UK: Cambridge University. doi:10.1017/CBO9781139175333.002

Yang, J., Chi, J., & Young, M. (2011). *A review of corporate governance in China*. Crawford School of Economics and Government, The Australian National University and Blackwell Publishing Asia Pty Ltd; doi:10.1111/j.1467-8411.2011.01283.x

YuP. (August 26, 2011Corporate Governance of Chinese Fund Management Companies. Available at SSRN: http://ssrn.com/abstract=1917426

Chapter 12
Determinants and Welfare Impacts of Foreign Aids

Gülsüm Akarsu
https://orcid.org/0000-0002-4877-1969
Ondokuz Mayıs University, Turkey

ABSTRACT

Foreign aids are important for the development of poor countries. Therefore, in the literature, special attention is given to the analysis of foreign aids. This chapter investigates the factors affecting flow of foreign aids to developing and less developed countries and also welfare impacts on foreign aids. For this purpose, panel data on 71 countries receiving aids from Development Assistance Committee member countries are employed for the period between 1996 and 2013. The results show statistically significant impacts of real income per capita, trade openness, migration flows as a share of total population and governance measures. Moreover, although foreign aids are found to improve the welfare of receipt countries, for donor countries, results do not indicate any evidence of welfare effects. As a conclusion, the poverty, donor's interest represented by decline in migration flows, and governance quality are found to be significant determinants of foreign aid allocation.

INTRODUCTION

Foreign aids are important for humanitarian assistance in the case of conflict and natural disasters as well as for the development of countries which cannot have access to basic needs and financial sources for improving their social and economic infrastructure. Particularly, for inclusive growth and climate change mitigation and adaptation, it is difficult to replace foreign aids with any other financial flow especially for those countries which has limited access to many of these instruments other than aids (Addison et al., 2017). Official Development Assistance (ODA) has taken special attention as ODA is the official and concessional flow of resources to developing countries from developed countries.

The literature for aid has shown a rapid growth after the first aid programs begun in 1940's in such a way that impacts, determinants and substitutability of foreign aid has been discussed widely (Addison et al., 2017). Among developmental studies, literature has shown interest for the factors affecting aid

DOI: 10.4018/978-1-5225-7564-1.ch012

allocation since 1970s (Hoeffler and Outram, 2011). In the aid-growth literature, some studies fail to obtain a result showing the growth effect of foreign aid. Therefore, another group of studies have tried to understand the reason for this failure by investigating the determinants of aid allocation and therefore, claimed that there can be some problems in allocation (Clist, 2011). According to Hoeffler and Outram (2011), the literature before their study mostly showed that the dominant factor for aid allocation is donor's self-interest. In this context, Swiss (2017) argues that aid allocation is a complex issue and cannot be explained by one or two factors. There are many factors affecting the allocation of foreign aids, such as the recipient needs (such as, growth, poverty, infants mortality rate and age dependency ratio), donor countries' interests (for example, foreign policy and trade), global ties of recipient country (for instance, membership in international nongovernmental organizations (NGOs) and ratification of international agreements/treaties) and governance of the recipient countries (as an example, political stability, political participation, corruption control, regulatory quality) (In'airat, 2014; Swiss, 2017). There are different approaches in the literature for the determination of factors affecting the aid allocation. One of these approaches is traditional hybrid model which combines altruistic (international humanitarian) and realist motives, in other words, consider two factors only which are recipient needs and donor's interest (Clist, 2011; Swiss, 2017). Poverty (Bandyopadhyay and Wall, 2007; Opeskin, 1996) and population (Alesina and Dollar, 2000; Bandyopadhyay and Wall, 2007; Neumayer, 2003; Trumbull and Wall, 1994) are the two main factors which show the recipient need and as poverty per capita increases, the donor countries are expected to give more aids. On the other hand, donor's interest can also affect the aid allocation. The wealthier countries may provide aids based on their foreign policy as well as to strengthen their commercial relations (see for example, Alesina and Dollar (2000); Morgenthau (1962); Neumayer (2003); Woods (2008); Dreher et al. (2011)).

Some studies extend traditional hybrid models by including policy variables (Clist, 2011). Effectiveness of aid is another dimension that needs attention. Because of budgetary problems encountered in donor countries, donors may provide aid based on some other criterion in addition to recipient's need. In the literature, there are many studies examining the effect of good governance on the growth resulted from aid flows started by the pioneering study of Burnside and Dollar (2000). Besides, good governance can be desirable for ideological reasons. Furthermore, as discussed by In'airat (2014) and Winters and Martinez (2015) and shown by many empirical studies (such as, Berthélemy and Tichit (2004) and Dollar and Levin (2006)), the aid policy has shifted from conditionality to selectivity after failures experienced in 1980s and 1990s. Both multilateral (for example, World Bank International Development Association and development banks) and bilateral donors provide aid to the countries with better performance with respect to their policies and institutions (McGillivray and Pham, 2017). As an example, World Bank International Development Association has distributed aid according to Country Policy and Institutional Assessment (Epstein and Gang, 2009). Therefore, governance quality is another important factor (see for example, Bandyopadhyay and Wall (2007); Chhotray and Hulme (2009) and Hermes and Lensink (2001)) although some studies (such as, Clist (2011) found that donor countries are not much sensitive to the policy of recipient countries.

The main aim of this chapter is to analyze the determinants of bilateral ODA from DAC members to developing and less developed (LDC) countries and its welfare impacts using panel data analysis for the period between 1996 and 2013. The welfare effect of ODA is investigated for both recipient and donor countries. In the model for the determination of the factors affecting bilateral ODA, following explanatory variables are employed: aid recipient country's GDP per capita, presence of conflict, number of natural disasters in a year in the recipient country showing recipient's needs; trade openness, donor country's migration flows from recipient countries as indicators for donor's interest and governance (political stability, rule of law and regulatory quality index). A priori, one can expect negative effects of recipient countries' income, and positive impacts of governance of recipient country, presence of the conflict and natural disasters in the recipient country, trade openness and migration flows to donor country. As after the conflicts and wars in the Middle East countries beginning from 2001 and the huge levels of migration flows from these countries, the inclusion of migration flows as a factor is expected to increase the explanatory power of the model employed in the analysis. As already mentioned by Vázquez and Sobrao (2016), in the literature, there are only few studies considering the effect of immigration on foreign aid allocation, such as, Bermeo (2017), Vázquez and Sobrao (2016), Bermeo and Leblang (2015), Czaika and Mayer (2011), Czaika (2005) and Lahiri and Raimondos-Møller (2000). However, among these studies, some of them analyzed the aid commitments (Bermeo (2017), Bermeo and Leblang (2015)) and effect of migrant stock in donor country (Bermeo and Leblang (2015), Czaika (2005) and Lahiri and Raimondos-Møller (2000)). Some performed the analysis for one donor country (Germany in Czaika (2005) and Spain in Vázquez and Sobrao (2016)) or for the earlier periods (the years between 1992 and 2003 in Czaika and Mayer (2011) for 18 OECD donor countries). Different from some studies, in this study, aid disbursements are preferred to be analyzed because decisions of donor countries may be based on the projected future situations of receipt countries. Therefore, this study aims to contribute to the existing literature by considering 26 DAC countries and employing the most recent data and panel data techniques which are known to have many advantages, such as allowing for heterogeneity, improving the efficiency of estimates and decreasing the aggregation bias. For more information on the advantages of panel data, one can refer to Hsiao (2007) and Baltagi (2008).

The organization of the chapter will be as follows. After this brief introduction related to recent aid policies of donor countries and its importance for the recipients, related literature is reviewed in section 2. Empirical models and data used both for determinants and welfare impacts of ODA are presented in section 3. In section 4, empirical findings and their implications are discussed. Last section concludes.

BACKGROUND

ODA was defined by DAC first in 1969 and the definition was revised in 1972. According to OECD DAC, ODA is aid from governmental agencies (state or local) and it aims economic development and welfare improvement in developing countries. The eligibility of countries for receiving ODA is determined based on per capita income (OECD, 2018). Also, in order to achieve 2030 UN Sustainable Development Goals, ODA is used as a supportive tool. In year 1960, net total ODA disbursement was around \$36000 million US dollars. In some years, net total ODA disbursement declined which can be related to the financial status of donor countries. In year 2017, net total ODA disbursements was realized as \$159309 million US dollars with an average annual nominal growth rate of 2.94% over the period between 1960 to 2017.

Figure 1 illustrates Total Net ODA as a share of Gross National Income (GNI) for Development Assistance Committee (DAC) countries over the period between 1960 and 2017. Overall Net ODA has declined steadily since 1960s provided by these countries. However, ODA disbursements of Switzerland, Sweden, Luxembourg and Austria show increasing trend over the period. Moreover, in 1970, the donor countries agreed to have a target of 0.7% ODA/GNI and in 2005, 15 EU member countries proposed their aims to reach 0.7% ODA/GNI target by year 2015. Some of the countries have already exceeded this target beginning from 1980s such as Denmark, Luxembourg, Netherlands, Norway and Sweden. This target needs to be revised based on the current conditions as also discussed by Carter et al. (2015).

There are many issues related to foreign aid which needs attention. According to Swiss (2017), in the literature, different strands of issues related to foreign aid has been discussed, such as the effectiveness of foreign aid, the factors affecting the decision of aid allocation, the effects of foreign aid on growth, poverty and sustainable development. As the focus of this chapter is on the determinants of foreign aid, only related literature is reviewed. Detailed literature review for the effects of foreign aid on growth and poverty can be found in Glennie and Sumner (2016) and for aid-growth, one can refer also to Addison et al. (2017) in which they discussed that there has not been any consensus among the studies for the effect of aid on growth started with the very early studies on this topic. In addition, for macroeconomics effects of aid, the recent study by Carter (2017) provides a theoretical analysis. The studies analyzing the allocation of foreign aid date back to late 1960s and to beginning of 1970s (Hoeffler and Outram, 2011; Vázquez and Sobrao, 2016). Most of the studies employ econometric methods, however, the analysis of some studies are based on economic modelling. Seminal study of Dudley and Montmarquette (1976) can be shown as an example for these theoretical contributions (Vázquez and Sobrao, 2016). Moreover, as an recent example for the latter, in the context of dynamic allocation model with more than two recipient countries, Carter et al. (2015) found that recipient's welfare, aid absorption capacity, balanced growth path and the distance from this path initially are the important factors determining the aids to be distributed. Also based on economic modelling approach, Epstein and Gang (2009) showed that if the allocation of aid both depends on poverty and governance, this can worsen the situation of poor countries.

In the literature, earlier studies considered only two factors which are recipient's need and donor's interest and among them, empirical studies mostly employed cross sectional data, but as already mentioned before, the more recent studies focused on three different factors, such as recipient's need, donor's interest and governance and used more sophisticated techniques (Vázquez and Sobrao, 2016). Moreover, some studies (for example, Swiss (2017)) considered other determinants such as global ties.

Although most studies analyzed the bilateral or multilateral official aids, there are studies examining the factors affecting the aid allocation of NGOs. For example, Koch et al. (2009) focused on the deter-

Figure 1. Total net ODA (% of GNI), 1960-2017

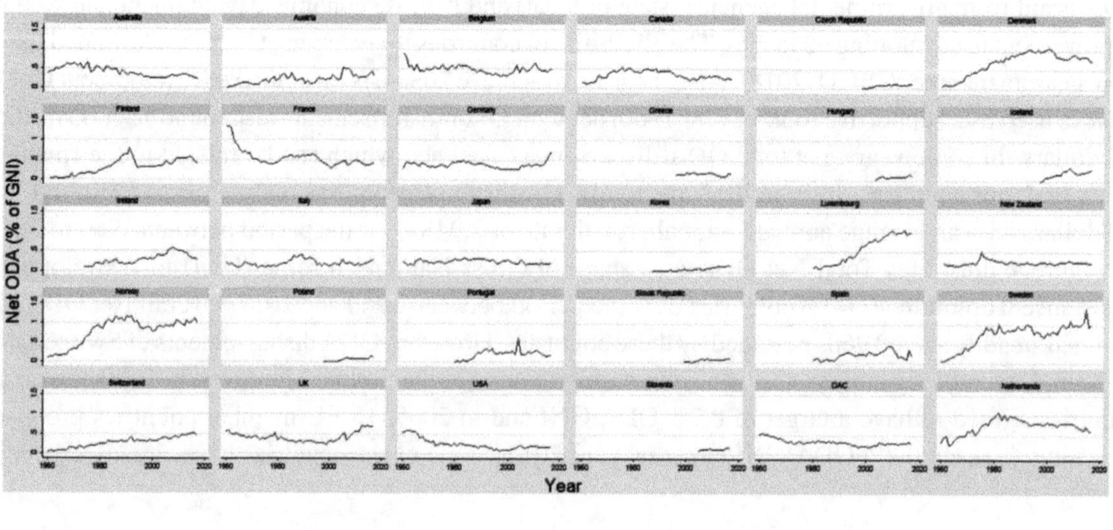

minants of aid for 61 NGOs for year 2005. Their results suggest that recipient's need, religion, colonial history and decisions of other NGOs and official donors are main determinants of aid allocation. Also Nunnenkamp and Ohler (2011) analyzed the determinants for both official and private donors separately for Germany between 2005-2007 and stressed on the need for the analysis for different aid channels as the findings showed the motivations differentiate highly among the different donor types within a country.

On the other hand, some studies performed donor by donor analysis and compared the factors affecting aid allocation of different donor countries. For example, Schraeder et al. (1998) investigated the factors affecting the aid flows from US, Japan, France and Sweden to African countries for the period between 1980-1999. Recipient's needs are measured by average life expectancy and daily diet requirements. GNP per capita, strategic importance (security related issues) and trade are employed as a sign for donor's interest. In addition, the effects of colonial relations, ideological beliefs and region were analyzed. Their results indicate that the significance of factors differ across donor countries. Another study performed by Clist (2011) also found similar result. Clist (2011) investigated the factors affecting the aid allocation from a different perspective and introduced 4P framework (Poverty, Population, Policy and Proximity). This study employed aid commitments as dependent variable and in the first stage, eligible countries are determined estimating Probit model. Poverty is measured by GDP per capita. For policy, three variables are used: Freedom Index, Political Terror Scale and Corruption Control. By proximity which is considered instead of donor interest, the relation between donors and recipient countries are included into the analysis. Proximity can be reflected by common language, religion, history, geography, commercial activity, military aid and arm exports. Employing two part model and using the data on top seven donors over the years from 1982 to 2006, he showed that traditional hybrid model (which focus on recipient need and donor interest) may not be suitable for all donors, for example, for some donors only one aim can be important for the aid allocation, while aid selectivity of others may be based on multi-purpose. However, according to Clist (2011), this heterogeneity in priorities of donors cause the aids to be ineffective for sustainable development of countries. The aid allocation analysis was performed for different types of aid also (see for example, Fink and Redaelli (2011) for emergency aid). Below, some selected studies are reviewed, briefly.

Migration flows was found to be an important factor by some studies. Vázquez and Sobrao (2016) investigated the effect of immigration flows on ODA allocation of Spain for the period from 1998 to 2009 considering also other factors such as recipient's need, donor's interest, path dependence and effectiveness of aid and found that immigration flows are important determinants of recipient country selection and foreign aid allocation. Also there are other significant factors for recipient selection and aid allocation such as, corruption control, population of recipient country, post-colonial ties and life expectancy at birth. Other studies analyzing the effect of migration on foreign aid flows found that immigrant stock has an important influence on the aid allocation of a donor country (see for example, Czaika (2005) for Germany's ODA allocation and Lahiri and Raimondos-Møller (2000)). One more study by Czaika and Mayer (2011) found the significant impact of migration flows on aid allocation of 18 OECD donors for the period between 1992 and 2003. Bermeo and Leblang (2015) also found significant impact of immigrant stock in donor country, donors' immigration policy and migrant mobilization on the foreign aid commitments of 22 OECD donors to 150 recipients over the years between 1993 and 2008. Lastly, the findings of Bermeo (2017) indicated the positive and statistically significant effects of migrant flows from receipt to donor countries for 23 OECD donor countries and the period covering the years from 2002 and 2012. This study also compared the factors affecting the foreign aid commitments for two different periods: Cold War period and post-2001 period and showed that during Cold-War, income level, strategic importance and trade relations are found to be important determinants, however, after 2001, targeted development became an important factor for foreign aid flows.

Furthermore, some studies' main findings indicate the significance of governance quality for the aid allocation. In'airat (2014) analyzed the determinants of foreign aid allocation to developing countries for the years between 2001 and 2010 focusing on the effects of governance quality. Different factors (income per capita, population and regional dummies as a proxy for donors' interest) and different governance quality indicators (composite index, voice and accountability, effectiveness of government, quality of regulation, rule of law, corruption control, political stability) are employed by this study. Result of the study shows that governance quality is an important criterion for the aid allocation of donor countries in addition to per capita GDP and population. Another study by De Matteis (2013) analyzed the relations between aid, growth, governance and poverty. The result of this study shows that effectiveness of aid is highly related with governance of recipient country and increases if the main focus of aid is to diminish the poverty in the recipient country. To deal with endogeneity problem, simultaneous equations are estimated for aid, growth, governance and poverty. For the determinants of aid per capita, in this study, GDP per capita, population, poverty and governance measured by civil and political liberties are taken as important factors. But the results indicate statistical significant negative effect of only GDP per capita and population. Alternatively, when per poor measures are employed for aid and GDP instead of per capita measures, in addition to previous finding of statistical significance of coefficient on GDP and population, poverty becomes statistically significant factor having negative influence on aid per poor. Furthermore, as a proxy for poverty, Human Development Index was used and estimation results indicate that all the variables have statistically significant effects with signs which are in line with a priori expectations. On the other hand, McGillivray and Pham (2017) evaluated the performance-based aid allocation system of multilateral aid agencies. Their findings show that the effectiveness of aid, i.e., the impact of aid on growth is not only affected by performance but also, lack of human capital and economic vulnerability (measured by using terms of trade and goods and services exports' instability).

For DAC donors, Younas (2008) and Hoeffler and Outram (2011) found similar results, such as the significant impacts of donor's interest and recipient's needs. Younas (2008) examined the determinants of bilateral aid flow from DAC members to 78 net aid recipient countries between 1991 and 2003. Bilateral real aid per capita was explained by population, income per capita, infant mortality, share of imports from donor countries disaggregated based on product out of total imports, aid per capita from multilateral donors, trade openness, political and civil rights index, distance, reserves per capita, domestic purchasing power, political and strategic concerns for Middle East, religion and colonial relations. The similar analysis was also performed for major six donors. The findings indicate the most important determinants are trade benefits (capital good imports of donor countries to recipients) and political and strategic concerns. In addition, infant mortality rate, religion and conditions related to human rights were also found to be significant factors. However, results show that poverty effect is not so influential. Hoeffler and Outram (2011) examined the determinants of aid flow from 22 DAC donors to 168 recipients over the period 1980-2004. Within DAC donors, they examined top 5 donors and compared them with average donor's allocation behavior. They considered four groups of factors: recipient's need (income per capita and bilateral aid per capita from other donors), donor's interest (trade and voting in UN in line with the donor country's interest), recipient's merit (GDP per capita growth, democracy index, human rights index) and controls (population). They found that unobserved country specific factors are significant determinants and there is little evidence for the recipient's merit as an influential factor. Moreover, although donors give importance to recipient's need and their own interests while making aid allocation decision, allocation decision of donors depend on different factors. In general, they concluded that there is not much support for the recipients to improve the situation with respect to growth, democracy and human rights.

Different from other previous studies, Swiss (2017) argued that there are three different motivations for aid allocation: recipient's need (altruistic motive-international humanitarianism), donor self-interest (realist motives) which was first mentioned by Morgenthau (1962) as an important factor in aid allocation and recipient countries' global networks (institutional motive-global ties). In this study, different from In'airat (2014), most of the attention is put on recipient countries' global networks. Taking into account international networks of aid recipients, Swiss (2017) analyzed the determinants of the number of donors for 117 aid recipient countries between the years 1975 and 2006 by using fixed effect negative binomial regression model which includes number of human right treaties ratified, number of membership in International NGOs, aid per capita, GDP per capita, population, exports as a share of GDP, democratic transition variable, polity score, dummies for showing the presence of conflict, the time in which the country becomes independent and having past colonial relation and categorical time variable measuring the growth and expansion of global aid ties over time as explanatory variables. This study found robust effect of global ties on the number of donor countries regardless of the measure for the aid ties. However, although not robust, the findings showed also effect of other variables indicating the validity of altruistic view (humanitarian approach) and realist motive in some cases. Lastly, another finding is such that as number of donor increases aid amount per capita declines. However, only focusing on human right treaties ratified, Magesan (2013) showed that this factor increases aid flows to the 83 countries from OECD donors over the period 1972-2006.

The overall analysis of recent literature shows that the studies found different results which can be result of different level of analysis, different methods, time periods, country groups for both donors and recipients and different factors included into the models. The analysis performed in this chapter includes all the factors discussed in the literature by using the most recent data for all the variables. Next section presents the analysis results.

PANEL DATA ANALYSIS FOR THE DETERMINANTS OF FOREIGN AID AND WELFARE IMPACTS

In this section, after giving information on the data employed, the author discusses the methodological issues and presents the estimation results for the analysis related to the determinants of foreign aids and welfare impacts of aids on both donors and recipients by taking GDP per capita as a proxy for welfare. Although it was widely discussed in the literature that the GDP per capita is not a suitable indicator for the welfare (see, for example van den Bergh (2011)), because of data unavailability, the analysis is restricted by considering this measure as an indication of welfare improvement.

Data

For the analysis, balanced panel data is employed on 71 aid recipient countries over the period from 1996 to 2013. These recipient countries are the developing and less developed countries[1] which receive ODA from DAC members. In order to analyze the determinants of foreign aids and welfare impacts, panel data series shown in Table 1 are used. Table 1 also presents the data sources for each series. The panel data used for the analysis of welfare effects on donor countries includes 26 DAC members [2] covering the period from 1998 to 2013. In order to calculate real aid disbursements per capita (realodapc), Aid (ODA) disbursements from DAC (net total) (Current Prices, US Dollars) is divided by Consumer price index (2010 = 100) and population. In addition, per capita values of realgdp and migflow are calculated by taking the ratio of related variable to population in order to obtain realgdppc and migflowpc, respectively. Different from Clist (2011), aid disbursements are used as they show actual realization of aid flows to the countries.

Descriptive statistics and cross-sectional dependence test results are presented in Table 2 and yearly averages of series are given in Table 3. According to Table 2, there are statistically significant cross-sectional dependency problem in all the panel data series except polstability. In the estimation of the models, this problem is taken into account by employing appropriate estimation method. Moreover, as shown in Table 2, real ODA disbursements per capita from DAC members to developing and less developed countries are on average 0.45 but with high level of variability over time and across countries. Highest level of realodapc was realized for Suriname in 1996 and lowest level for Panama in 2007. For other series, such as, conflict and disasters, variability is higher over time and across countries compared to other series. On average, Pakistan and China are the countries which experience severe and frequent displacements of people due to conflict, violence and disasters, respectively in recent years (see Table 3). Highest level of real GDP per capita was recorded by Uruguay in 2013 and migration from Albania to DAC members in 2008 as a ratio of its population is the highest among the countries and period under investigation. In addition, Table 3 shows that on average over time, Uruguay has the highest level of real GDP per capita and Albania is also the country in which larger share of its population migrate to DAC members compared to other countries.

Table 1. Data sources

Series	Code	Source	Variable
Aid (ODA) disbursements from DAC (net total) Current Prices, US Dollars, Millions		OECD.Stat Database	aidoda
GDP (constant 2010 US$)	NY.GDP.MKTP.KD	The World Bank, World Development Indicators (WDI) Database	realgdp
Population, total	SP.POP.TOTL	The World Bank, WDI Database	population
Number of cases for displacement after conflict and violence	VC.IDP.NWCV	The World Bank, WDI Database	conflict
Number of cases for displacement after disasters	VC.IDP.NWDS	The World Bank, WDI Database	disasters
Trade (% of GDP)	NE.TRD.GNFS.ZS	The World Bank, WDI Database	openness
Consumer price index (2010=100)	FP.CPI.TOTL	The World Bank, WDI Database	
Political Stability	PV.EST	The World Bank, WDI Database	polstability
Regulatory Quality	RQ.EST	The World Bank, WDI Database	regquality
Rule of Law	RL.EST	The World Bank, WDI Database	rulelaw
Migration Inflows (by nationality)		OECD.Stat Database	migflow

Table 2. Descriptive statistics and cross-sectional dependence test statistic (N=71, T=18)

	Mean	Standard Deviation	Coefficient of Variation	Minimum	Maximum	CD
realodapc	0.448073	1.228415	2.741554	-0.45883	32.22509	29.78*
realgdppc	3060.827	2793.741	0.912741	209.8617	13467.44	150.29*
conflict	8269.568	97323.1	11.76883	0	3000000	
disasters	95397.8	888483.3	9.313457	0	1.87E+07	
openness	74.19323	34.98481	0.471536	15.63556	220.4073	41.30*
polstability	-0.42309	0.767831	-1.81483	-2.81004	1.283388	0.49
regquality	-0.31063	0.508054	-1.63554	-1.72011	1.12727	7.96*
rulelaw	-0.46888	0.510623	-1.08904	-1.80231	1.07713	6.29*
migflowpc	0.001612	0.002886	1.789741	5.44E-06	0.026157	62.06*

CD is cross-sectional dependence test statistic developed by Pesaran (2004) and asymptotically distributed as N(0, 1) and is performed by using xtcd command in Stata 11. For conflict and disasters variables, as there are too many zero values, statistics cannot be computed. Statistical significance of test statistic is shown by ***, **, * at 10%, 5% and 1% levels.

Pairwise correlations given in Table 4 indicate that there is not any severe problem of collinearity among the most of explanatory variables to be included into the model in order to analyze the determinants of real ODA disbursements from DAC members to developing and less developed countries. But, as among polstability, regquality and rulelaw, cross-correlations are larger; these variables are included into the model one by one in order to avoid the possible collinearity problem.

Methodology

This study employs panel data techniques in order to investigate the determinants of ODA disbursements and examine the impact of foreign aid on welfare of both recipient and donor countries. For the analysis of ODA disbursement's determinants, the model given by equation (1) is estimated by panel data techniques. In the model, three different sets of factors are considered following In'airat (2014): recipient needs (realgdppc, conflict and disasters), donor countries' interests (openness and migflowpc) and governance of the recipient countries (governance). Different from previous studies, the population is excluded from the model as per capita values are employed for all the appropriate variables.

$$\begin{aligned} realodapc_{i,t} &= \delta_i + \varphi_t + \beta_1 rea\lg dppc_{i,t} + \beta_2 conflict_{i,t} + \beta_3 disasters_{i,t} + \beta_4 openness_{i,t} \\ &+ \beta_5 governance_{i,t} + +\beta_6 migflowpc_{i,t} + \varepsilon_{i,t} \end{aligned} \tag{1}$$

In equation (1), error terms ($\varepsilon_{i,t}$) are assumed to be identically and independently normally distributed with mean 0 and variance σ^2 for all country i=1,…,71 and year t=1996,...,2013. As the polstability, regquality and rulelaw variables are included into the model one by one, in equation (1) $governance_{i,t}$ is added to represent these variables. δ_i and φ_t show country-specific fixed effects (FEs) and time period fixed effects (TEs) which are included in order to account for heterogeneity among countries and over time. In order to test for the statistical significance of fixed effects, various Wald tests are employed.

Table 3. Yearly averages of series over the period from 1996 to 2013

Code	realodapc	realgdppc	conflict	disasters	openness	polstability	regquality	rulelaw	migflowpc
ALB	0.715	3107.452	0	34	65.494	-0.176	-0.017	-0.603	**0.01456**
DZA	0.063	4011.966	0	1547	63.378	-1.327	-0.882	-0.819	0.00101
ARM	0.596	2411.271	0	0	70.880	-0.149	0.171	-0.404	0.00260
AZE	0.187	3410.837	0	3770	87.901	-0.727	-0.534	-0.869	0.00041
BGD	0.075	621.196	783	232387	34.909	-1.239	-0.920	-0.856	0.00022
BEN	0.326	724.390	0	27264	55.817	0.435	-0.409	-0.452	0.00016
BTN	0.966	1623.069	0	1111	94.086	0.852	-0.698	0.254	0.00390
BOL	0.717	1781.412	0	6980	63.349	-0.482	-0.571	-0.799	0.00214
BWA	0.741	5636.662	0	117	96.092	**1.026**	0.585	0.635	0.00024
BRA	0.022	9795.224	0	74980	***23.832***	-0.142	0.100	-0.196	0.00039
BDI	0.307	***230.434***	0	237	35.487	-1.778	-1.133	-1.197	0.00018
KHM	0.372	601.953	0	25333	114.156	-0.427	-0.425	-1.119	0.00057
CMR	0.326	1241.239	0	2444	51.182	-0.615	-0.831	-1.117	0.00058
CHN	***0.011***	3015.221	0	**3041928**	47.585	-0.466	-0.266	-0.482	0.00029
COL	0.159	5523.756	58684	183545	35.915	-1.652	0.191	-0.496	0.00122
CRI	0.079	7127.555	0	1039	81.470	0.685	0.509	0.554	0.00060
CIV	0.313	1271.121	58708	560	83.727	-1.357	-0.700	-1.127	0.00034
DOM	0.184	4472.190	0	4633	69.301	-0.028	-0.189	-0.603	0.00471
ECU	0.360	4283.147	0	1484	54.668	-0.568	-0.881	-0.912	0.00334
EGY	0.252	2177.969	0	1111	49.269	-0.859	-0.444	-0.230	0.00029
SLV	0.391	3253.990	0	5153	68.218	0.020	0.156	-0.632	0.00397
FJI	0.630	3532.324	0	3239	123.052	0.275	-0.432	-0.376	0.00683
GAB	0.300	9820.007	0	233	89.608	0.270	-0.419	-0.501	0.00051
GMB	0.205	525.049	0	1864	64.710	0.158	-0.430	-0.407	0.00188
GEO	0.731	2203.029	0	85	76.492	-0.844	0.132	-0.420	0.00180
GHA	0.726	1142.096	0	8108	85.972	-0.035	-0.095	-0.010	0.00071
GTM	0.298	2672.696	0	15233	58.895	-0.755	-0.200	-1.035	0.00109
GNB	0.501	552.068	0	153	50.586	-0.738	-1.112	-1.369	0.00289
GUY	1.090	2662.975	0	0	172.038	-0.408	-0.453	-0.497	0.01116
HND	0.655	1790.061	0	5142	117.382	-0.398	-0.357	-0.942	0.00134
IND	0.013	1011.320	42028	1451969	38.718	-1.160	-0.372	0.068	0.00015
IDN	0.090	2632.201	3250	112398	55.745	-1.140	-0.361	-0.637	0.00012
IRN	0.051	5496.000	0	3234	44.335	-0.972	***-1.457***	-0.857	0.00048
KAZ	0.163	6868.662	0	1080	83.872	0.143	-0.349	-0.826	0.00066
KEN	0.289	897.742	12389	25140	55.229	-1.190	-0.248	-0.835	0.00023
KGZ	0.394	761.198	16667	59	109.157	-0.804	-0.356	-1.045	0.00047
LAO	0.964	883.600	244	5412	77.023	-0.108	-1.078	-0.973	0.00042
MKD	0.636	3841.884	0	91	90.720	-0.559	0.108	-0.326	0.00478

continued on following page

Table 3. Continued

Code	realodapc	realgdppc	conflict	disasters	openness	polstability	regquality	rulelaw	migflowpc
MDG	0.342	416.968	0	30783	65.637	-0.222	-0.490	-0.559	0.00012
MWI	0.603	403.208	0	4696	58.811	-0.032	-0.537	-0.239	***0.00003***
MYS	0.014	7987.951	0	8757	**186.876**	0.223	0.588	0.460	0.00060
MLI	0.360	635.530	19444	3288	56.591	-0.360	-0.445	-0.403	0.00042
MRT	0.527	1112.592	0	532	94.762	-0.379	-0.498	-0.753	0.00065
MUS	0.252	6542.174	0	0	120.592	0.912	**0.703**	**0.949**	0.00255
MEX	0.021	8714.298	8972	111113	55.353	-0.579	0.328	-0.483	0.00158
MNG	1.214	2192.857	0	1198	112.659	0.704	-0.257	-0.166	0.00302
MAR	0.173	2428.754	0	1143	66.521	-0.347	-0.156	-0.109	0.00339
MOZ	0.870	336.759	0	27679	71.218	0.076	-0.459	-0.692	0.00003
NPL	0.194	511.677	278	18214	49.225	-1.394	-0.620	-0.615	0.00050
NER	0.188	339.453	0	54686	50.331	-0.643	-0.595	-0.601	0.00007
PAK	0.092	944.843	**230111**	766528	33.180	-2.093	-0.644	-0.828	0.00041
PAN	0.096	6612.514	0	284	139.547	0.083	0.426	-0.105	0.00062
PRY	0.185	2921.964	0	1559	97.219	-0.637	-0.519	-0.878	0.00134
PER	0.151	4081.773	0	17528	43.785	-0.831	0.361	-0.598	0.00121
RWA	0.527	442.615	0	946	36.862	-0.752	-0.468	-0.589	0.00015
SEN	0.436	929.817	287	17041	67.959	-0.288	-0.204	-0.169	0.00109
SRB	1.960	4467.042	0	259	65.901	-0.548	-0.311	-0.598	0.00551
ZAF	0.156	6547.710	0	5630	55.795	-0.132	0.474	0.139	0.00058
LKA	0.326	2244.644	15556	120440	69.169	-1.023	-0.093	0.040	0.00133
SDN	0.357	1521.928	116944	29608	32.139	***-2.250***	-1.367	***-1.406***	0.00021
SUR	**4.766**	7034.205	0	17	82.993	0.231	-0.572	-0.110	0.00506
SWZ	0.253	3339.266	0	0	133.515	-0.198	-0.485	-0.579	0.00006
TZA	0.407	581.333	0	2502	44.197	-0.362	-0.420	-0.376	0.00005
THA	0.022	4279.255	2783	162907	121.178	-0.696	0.239	0.044	0.00061
TGO	0.210	501.161	0	2895	90.459	-0.337	-0.779	-0.871	0.00059
TUN	0.250	3455.728	0	0	92.505	-0.156	-0.110	-0.062	0.00173
TUR	0.035	9535.812	11	15139	47.360	-1.027	0.276	0.026	0.00115
UGA	0.340	496.466	0	2880	41.517	-1.092	-0.140	-0.451	0.00006
URY	0.089	**9966.590**	0	56	48.941	0.833	0.467	0.623	0.00155
VNM	0.226	1012.851	0	112204	129.650	0.252	-0.607	-0.460	0.00084
ZMB	1.276	1164.040	0	3637	65.024	0.261	-0.480	-0.411	0.00009
Max.	Suriname	Uruguay	Pakistan	China	Malaysia	Botswana	Mauritius	Mauritius	Albania
Min.	China	Burundi			Brazil	Sudan	Iran	Sudan	Malawi

Table 4. Pairwise correlations

realodapc	1								
realgdppc	-0.0329	1							
conflict	-0.0177	-0.0333	1						
disasters	-0.0348	0.0081	0.1006	1					
openness	0.0265	0.1386	-0.0694	-0.0637	1				
polstability	0.1166	0.2735	-0.1661	-0.0747	0.3803	1			
regquality	-0.05	0.5131	-0.0564	-0.0032	0.2219	0.4019	1		
rulelaw	0.0267	0.4502	-0.0492	0.0112	0.2245	0.578	0.6961	1	
migflowpc	0.2051	0.099	-0.0333	-0.0433	0.2227	0.1367	0.0673	0.0337	1

By assuming homogeneity of intercept term across countries and over time, estimation of pooled model shown in equation (2) is performed by OLS putting the following restrictions, $\delta_i = \delta$ and $\varphi_t = \varphi$ to the model (1).

$$realodapc_{i,t} = \beta_0 + \beta_1 rea\lg dppc_{i,t} + \beta_2 conflict_{i,t} + \beta_3 disasters_{i,t} + \beta_4 openness_{i,t} + \beta_5 governance_{i,t} + +\beta_6 migflowpc_{i,t} + \varepsilon_{i,t} \quad (2)$$

First, this pooled model is tested against model with only country-specific fixed effects given in equation (3) by imposing $\delta_i = \delta$.

$$realodapc_{i,t} = \delta_i + \beta_1 rea\lg dppc_{i,t} + \beta_2 conflict_{i,t} + \beta_3 disasters_{i,t} + \beta_4 openness_{i,t} + \beta_5 governance_{i,t} + +\beta_6 migflowpc_{i,t} + \varepsilon_{i,t} \quad (3)$$

Then, time period fixed effects and presence of both effects are tested in a similar manner. Autocorrelation, heteroscedasticity and cross-sectional dependence tests are performed for the correct specification of the model. If the tests show misspecification in the model, the models are estimated by Feasible Generalized Least Square Dummy Variable (FGLSDV) and Feasible Generalized Least Squares (FGLS) methods. Negative effect of realgdppc is expected as the real income per capita of recipient countries decline, the donor countries may provide larger amount of foreign aid for humanitarian assistance and overall economic development. On the other hand, the countries are expected to receive more aid in cases of conflicts, wars and disasters and also if there is high level of migration from these countries to donor countries in order to diminish the migration. Furthermore, good governance show that the foreign aid can be used very effectively, therefore, the donor countries may prefer to provide aid to countries with good governance structure. As countries are more integrated globally, one can expect positive impact of this on the ODA disbursements received which is measured by openness in Model (1). Trade openness can be regarded as a measure showing donor interest, more clearly, commercial motive.

To analyze the welfare impacts of foreign aids, Panel Granger Causality tests developed by Dumitrescu and Hurlin (2012) are performed for both recipient and donor countries. Real GDP per capita is used as an indicator for welfare due to data constraints. In order to test the causality, equations (4) and (5) are employed assuming country specific coefficients;

$$rea\lg dppc_{i,t} = \omega_{1,i} + \sum_{k=1}^{K} \gamma_{1k,i} rea\lg dppc_{i,t-k} + \sum_{k=1}^{K} \vartheta_{1k,i} realodapc_{i,t-k} + u_{1i,t} \tag{4}$$

$$realodapc_{i,t} = \omega_{2,i} + \sum_{k=1}^{K} \gamma_{2k,i} realodapc_{i,t-k} + \sum_{k=1}^{K} \vartheta_{2k,i} rea\lg dppc_{i,t-k} + u_{2i,t} \tag{5}$$

First, F tests are performed for every country i separately, then, average of these Wald statistics are taken to obtain Wbar. Granger causality running from realodapc to realgdppc is tested by restricting coefficients on lags of realodapc in equation (4) as shown in equation (6). On the other hand, causality test from realgdppc to realodapc is performed by testing the null hypothesis given in equation (7).

$$H_{01} : \vartheta_{11,i} = \ldots = \vartheta_{1k,i} = 0 \tag{6}$$

$$H_{02} : \vartheta_{21,i} = \ldots = \vartheta_{2k,i} = 0 \tag{7}$$

Standardized statistics (Zbar and Ztilde) are used to test the null hypotheses given in equations (6) and (7). One can find more information on the test, test statistics and their distribution in Lopez and Weber (2017). If null hypotheses are rejected, the panel causality exists in either side or both sides of the directions.

Empirical Results of Panel Data Analysis

Table 5 and 6 present the results of analysis. In Table 5, the estimation results for pooled model and model with only country-specific fixed effects are not given in order to save space but can be available upon request. In all the estimations, the tests indicate the statistical significance of both country-specific effects and time-period effects as well as that there is evidence of heteroscedasticity, autocorrelation and cross sectional dependency problems. Therefore, the conclusions are based on the estimation results obtained by performing FGLSDV estimation. As there are different variables showing the governance quality of a country, there are three different models considered. But regardless of this, robust results are obtained. In all the estimations performed by FGLSDV method, realgdppc, openness, governance and migflowpc are statistically significant. As, real per capita GDP of the recipient country decreases, ODA disbursements to this country increases. Same conclusion is valid for openness. There is an inverse relation between openness and realodapc which is contrary to the finding of Younas (2008) and a priori expectations. Trade may not be regarded as a donor's interest in this case, it can show the recipient's need. As trade openness increases, the countries can be more engaged to the international system and may not need foreign aid. Similar result is obtained by Clist (2011) and De Matteis (2013) for per capita GDP and although not robust, findings of Swiss (2017) show the negative effect of income level on aid ties.

Polstability, regquality and rule of law all affect the realodapc positively. Therefore, donor countries prefer to give ODA to countries which have better governance quality. In'airat (2014) and De Matteis (2013) also found that foreign aid allocation depends on governance quality and per capita real GDP. Furthermore, Acht et al. (2015) showed that poor governance lead to donors to deliver aids through NGOs, instead of governmental organizations. Findings show that as migration flow as a share of the population from developing and developed countries to DAC members rises, the realodapc increases. This result is consistent with the findings of Bermeo (2017), Vázquez and Sobrao (2016), Bermeo and Leblang (2015), Czaika and Mayer (2011), Czaika (2005) and Lahiri and Raimondos-Møller (2000). Donor countries may attempt to decrease the migration inflow to their countries from developing and developed countries by using ODA. However, according to the results, the occurrences of conflict and violence events and disasters may not be the main determinants of ODA as the results indicate positive but statistically insignificant effects. This result is also supported by the findings of Swiss (2017).

Table 6 shows the results of Granger Causality Tests for both ODA recipient countries and donor DAC members. For recipient countries, there is evidence of bi-directional causality between realgdppc and realodapc. Thus, real per capita GDP of a recipient country is determined by real per capita ODA disbursements that this country takes and vice versa. However, for donor countries, real per capita ODA disbursement given to these countries do not have any growth effect. The causality runs from realgdppc to realodapc. Countries with higher income per capita tend to give more real per capita ODA disbursement. For recipient countries although ODA contributes to welfare improvement, for donor countries, there is not any evidence for welfare improvement. In the literature, there is conflicting results for the growth effect of aid for recipient countries as mentioned by Addison et al. (2017).

Solutions and Recommendations

The findings show the welfare impact of ODA for recipient countries. Therefore, the donor countries should further increase ODA to these countries in order to encourage and contribute the development of developing and low developed countries. Although the donor countries may use ODA to mitigate the migration inflow to their countries from developing and low developed countries in addition to aiming development of these countries, governance structure of the recipient country is also found to be an important factor determining the ODA disbursements. The recipient countries should improve their governance structure in order to obtain more ODA disbursements for their development.

FUTURE RESEARCH DIRECTIONS

The analysis in this study is limited due to data constraints. Instead of using trade openness, bilateral trade flows can be used in order to include the bilateral trade connections between countries which can show the trade motive of donors more accurately. In addition, welfare index can be calculated as performed by Menegaki and Tugcu (2017) for the correct measurement of welfare. Moreover, nonlinearity in the model can be considered by employing nonlinear panel data models, such as threshold panel data model based on data availability. Other determinants can be included into the model (such as population density) but by considering collinearity problem. Similar analysis can be performed for other types of foreign

Table 5. Fixed effects and FGLSDV estimations for model 1

realodapc	FEs & TEs	FGLSDV	FEs & TEs	FGLSDV	FEs & TEs	FGLSDV
realgdppc	-0.0000950*** (-1.83)	-0.00017* (-6.51)	-0.000111 (-1.56)	-0.0001783* (-6.23)	-0.0001079*** (-1.77)	-0.0001711* (-6.11)
conflict	0.000000108 (1.38)	0.000000089 (0.6)	0.000000104 (1.5)	0.00000009 (1.3)	0.00000008 (1.47)	0.00000007 (1.00)
disasters	0.000000027 (1.43)	0.000000638 (1.33)	0.000000028 (1.39)	0.00000006 (0.2)	0.00000003 (1.4)	0.00000021 (0.85)
openness	-0.0063876 (-1.56)	-0.0054* (-10.67)	-0.0066815 (-1.47)	-0.0042217* (-6.31)	-0.0065902 (-1.52)	-0.0040288* (-6.06)
polstability	0.0400498 (0.62)	0.045617*** (1.69)				
regquality			0.2039769 (0.93)	0.2239182* (5.21)		
rulelaw					0.2328943 (1.46)	0.1920711* (4.49)
migflowpc	99.7881200** (2.83)	102.718* (14.85)	99.8984** (2.72)	110.9583* (20.06)	100.1367** (2.73)	112.6865* (19.11)
constant	1.712021* (4.51)	0.921803** (2.53)	0.6877301*** (1.78)	0.8627702** (2.32)	0.8049533** (2.2)	0.8390299** (2.25)
R^2	0.3097		0.3107		0.3107	
AC	9.711*		9.597*		9.604*	
HC	450000*		540000*		720000*	
CD	53.064*		51.826*		52.168*	
CFE	5.314*		5.503*		5.558*	
TFE	2.182*		2.069*		2.137*	
Joint FE	21.257*		21.607*		21.585*	

Notes: t statistic are given in parentheses which are calculated based on Driscoll and Kraay (1998) standard errors in order to correct for heteroscedasticity, cross-sectional dependence and autocorrelation. FGLSDV estimation was performed including country and time fixed effects and allowing for country specific AR(1) coefficients. AC is the Wooldridge first order autocorrelation test performed by using xtserial command in Stata 11 and based on Wald statistics which is distributed as F (1, 70) under the null hypothesis of no autocorrelation in the residuals. HC is the groupwise heteroskedasticity test based on Modified Wald statistic which has asymptotic chi-square distribution with 71 degrees of freedom under null hypothesis of homoscedasticity and is performed by using xttest3 command in Stata 11. CD is cross-sectional dependence test statistic developed by Pesaran (2004) and asymptotically distributed as N(0, 1) and is performed by using xtcsd, pesaran command in Stata 11. CFE, TFE and Joint FE are the test statistics which test for the statistical significance of country fixed effects, time fixed effects and both effects. In order to save space, the estimation results for pooled OLS and model with only country specific fixed effects are not presented but are available upon request. In all cases, country fixed effects are statistically significant when the restricted model is pooled model. Statistical significance of estimated coefficients and test statistic are shown by ***, **, * at 10%, 5% and 1% levels.

Table 6. Granger causality test for ODA recipients (developing and low developed countries) and donors (DAC members)

	ODA Recipients			ODA Donors		
	Wbar	Zbar	Ztilde	Wbar	Zbar	Ztilde
realgdppc→realodapc	3.3451	13.9723**	9.7573**	3.6205	9.4482***	6.2021***
realodapc →realgdppc	1.9713	5.7874***	3.6042***	1.3078	1.1097	0.2762

Lag length was determined according to BIC. Tests allowed for heterogeneity among countries. Bootstrapped p-values were calculated to consider the cross-sectional dependency by performing 1000 bootstrap replications. ***,**,*denote the statistical significance level at 10%, 5%, and 1%.

aid and considering different sectors as the one performed by Kilby (2011) for the investigation of the factors affecting aid project size and aid fragmentation. In addition, as in Swiss (2017), the analysis can be performed considering aid networks by using alternative measures showing aid ties between countries. Donor heterogeneity is another issue which calls for further attention (Clist, 2011), in such a way that each donor can be analyzed separately by considering other motivations for aid although there are already some studies (such as Schraeder et al. (1998) and Berthélemy and Tichit (2004)) which analyze the donors separately and found that different combinations of factors are important for each donor.

CONCLUSION

This chapter aims to analyze the main determinants of foreign aid focusing on total ODA disbursements from DAC donor countries to developing and low developed countries as well as the welfare impact of foreign aid for both donor and recipient countries. The analysis is performed employing panel data on 71 recipient countries and all DAC members over the period from 1996 to 2013 based on data availability. The panel data techniques are employed for this analysis, such as fixed effect model estimated by FGLSDV and panel Granger causality test. Results show that per capita real income, migration flows, governance structure and trade openness play an important role in determining the ODA disbursements taken by these countries. In addition, ODA contributes to the well-being of recipient countries. Therefore, donor countries should increase ODA to these countries in order to ensure their economic, infrastructural and sustainable development. However, the recipient countries should improve their governance structure for the effectiveness of aid.

REFERENCES

Acht, M., Mahmoud, T. O., & Thiele, R. (2015). Corrupt governments do not receive more state-to-state aid: Governance and the delivery of foreign aid through non-state actors. *Journal of Development Economics*, *114*, 20–33. doi:10.1016/j.jdeveco.2014.11.005

Addison, T., Morrissey, O., & Tarp, F. (2017). The Macroeconomics of Aid: Overview. *The Journal of Development Studies*, *53*(7), 987–997. doi:10.1080/00220388.2017.1303669

Alesina, A., & Dollar, D. (2000). Who gives foreign aid to whom and why? *Journal of Economic Growth*, *5*(1), 33–63. doi:10.1023/A:1009874203400

Baltagi, B. H. (2008). *Econometric Analysis of Panel Data.* West Sussex, UK: John Wiley.

Bandyopadhyay, S., & Wall, H. J. (2007). The determinants of aid in the post-cold war era. *Federal Reserve Bank of St Louis Review*, *89*(6), 533–547.

Bermeo, S. (2017). Aid Allocation and Targeted Development in an Increasingly Connected World. *International Organization*, *71*(4), 735–766. doi:10.1017/S0020818317000315

Bermeo, S., & Leblang, D. (2015). Migration and Foreign Aid. *International Organization*, *69*(3), 627–657. doi:10.1017/S0020818315000119

Berthélemy, J.-C., & Tichit, A. (2004). Bilateral donors' aid allocation decisions—A three-dimensional panel analysis. *International Review of Economics & Finance, 13*(3), 253–274. doi:10.1016/j.iref.2003.11.004

Burnside, C., & Dollar, D. (2000). Aid, Policies, and Growth. *The American Economic Review, 90*(4), 847–868. doi:10.1257/aer.90.4.847

Carter, P. (2017). Aid econometrics: Lessons from a stochastic growth model. *Journal of International Money and Finance, 77*, 216–232. doi:10.1016/j.jimonfin.2017.06.004

Carter, P., Postel-Vinay, F., & Temple, J. (2015). Dynamic aid allocation. *Journal of International Economics, 95*(2), 291–304. doi:10.1016/j.jinteco.2014.11.005

Chhotray, V., & Hulme, D. (2009). Contrasting Visions for Aid and Governance in the 21st Century: The White House Millennium Challenge Account and DFID's Drivers of Change. *World Development, 37*(1), 36–49. doi:10.1016/j.worlddev.2007.11.004

Clist, P. (2011). 25 Years of Aid Allocation Practice: Whither Selectivity? *World Development, 39*(10), 1724–1734. doi:10.1016/j.worlddev.2011.04.031

Czaika, M. (2005). Aid Allocation and Asylum Migration in the 1990s. *Applied Economics Quarterly, 51*(3), 289–303.

Czaika, M., & Mayer, A. (2011). Refugee Movements and Aid Responsiveness of Bilateral Donors. *The Journal of Development Studies, 47*(3), 455–474. doi:10.1080/00220388.2010.492855

De Matteis, A. (2013). Relevance of poverty and governance for aid allocation. *Review of Development Finance, 3*(2), 51–60. doi:10.1016/j.rdf.2013.04.001

Dollar, D., & Levin, V. (2006). The increasing selectivity of foreign aid, 1984-2003. *World Development, 34*(12), 2034–2046. doi:10.1016/j.worlddev.2006.06.002

Dreher, A., Nunnenkamp, P., & Thiele, R. (2011). Are 'New' Donors Different? Comparing the Allocation of Bilateral Aid Between nonDAC and DAC Donor Countries. *World Development, 39*(11), 1950–1968. doi:10.1016/j.worlddev.2011.07.024

Dudley, L., & Montmarquette, C. (1976). A Model of the Supply of Bilateral Foreign Aid. *The American Economic Review, 66*(1), 132–142.

Dumitrescu, E.-I., & Hurlin, C. (2012). Testing for Granger non-causality in heterogeneous panels. *Economic Modelling, 29*(4), 1450–1460. doi:10.1016/j.econmod.2012.02.014

Epstein, G. S., & Gang, I. N. (2009). Good governance and good aid allocation. *Journal of Development Economics, 89*(1), 12–18. doi:10.1016/j.jdeveco.2008.06.010

Fink, G., & Redaelli, S. (2011). Determinants of International Emergency Aid-Humanitarian Need Only? *World Development, 39*(5), 741–757. doi:10.1016/j.worlddev.2010.09.004

Glennie, J., & Sumner, A. (2016). *Aid, Growth and Poverty*. London: Palgrave Macmillan. doi:10.1057/978-1-137-57272-1

Granger, C. W. (1969). Investigating causal relations by econometric models and cross-spectral methods. *Econometrica, 37*(3), 424–438. doi:10.2307/1912791

Hermes, N., & Lensink, R. (2001). Changing the conditions for development aid: A new paradigm? *Journal of Development Studies, 37*(6), 1-+. doi:10.1080/713601080

Hoeffler, A., & Outram, V. (2011). Need, Merit, or Self-Interest-What Determines the Allocation of Aid? *Review of Development Economics, 15*(2), 237–250. doi:10.1111/j.1467-9361.2011.00605.x

Hsiao, C. (2003). *Analysis of Panel Data.* Cambridge, UK: Cambridge University. doi:10.1017/CBO9780511754203

In'airat, M. (2014). Aid allocation, selectivity, and the quality of governance. *Journal of Economics, Finance and Administrative Science, 19*(36), 63–68. doi:10.1016/j.jefas.2014.03.002

Kilby, C. (2011). What Determines the Size of Aid Projects? *World Development, 39*(11), 1981–1994. doi:10.1016/j.worlddev.2011.07.023

Koch, D. J., Dreher, A., Nunnenkamp, P., & Thiele, R. (2009). Keeping a Low Profile: What Determines the Allocation of Aid by Non-Governmental Organizations? *World Development, 37*(5), 902–918. doi:10.1016/j.worlddev.2008.09.004

Lahiri, S., & Raimondos-Møller, P. (2000). Lobbying by Ethnic Groups and Aid Allocation. *Economic Journal (London), 12*(9), 879–900.

Lopez, L., & Weber, S. (2017). *Testing for Granger causality in panel data.* IRENE Working paper 17-03. University of Neuchatel, Institute of Economic Research.

Magesan, A. (2013). Human Rights Treaty Ratification of Aid Receiving Countries. *World Development, 45*, 175–188. doi:10.1016/j.worlddev.2012.11.003

McGillivray, M., & Pham, T. K. C. (2017). Reforming Performance-Based Aid Allocation Practice. *World Development, 90*, 1–5. doi:10.1016/j.worlddev.2015.05.006

Menegaki, A. N., & Tugcu, C. T. (2017). Energy consumption and Sustainable Economic Welfare in G7 countries; A comparison with the conventional nexus. *Renewable & Sustainable Energy Reviews, 69*, 892–901. doi:10.1016/j.rser.2016.11.133

Morgenthau, H. (1962). A Political Theory of Foreign Aid. *The American Political Science Review, 56*(2), 301–309. doi:10.2307/1952366

Neumayer, E. (2003). The determinants of aid allocation by regional multilateral development banks and United Nations agencies. *International Studies Quarterly, 47*(1), 101–122. doi:10.1111/1468-2478.4701005

Nunnenkamp, P., & Ohler, H. (2011). Aid Allocation through Various Official and Private Channels: Need, Merit and Self-Interest as Motives of German Donors. *World Development, 39*(3), 308–323. doi:10.1016/j.worlddev.2010.08.001

Opeskin, B. R. (1996). The moral foundations of foreign aid. *World Development, 24*(1), 21–44. doi:10.1016/0305-750X(95)00118-V

Schraeder, P. J., Hook, S. W., & Taylor, B. (1998). Clarifying the foreign aid puzzle - A comparison of American, Japanese, French, and Swedish aid flows. *World Politics, 50*(2), 294. doi:10.1017/S0043887100008121

Swiss, L. (2017). Foreign aid allocation from a network perspective: The effect of global ties. *Social Science Research, 63*, 111–123. doi:10.1016/j.ssresearch.2016.09.011 PMID:28202136

Trumbull, W. N., & Wall, H. J. (1994). Estimating Aid-Allocation Criteria with Panel-Data. *Economic Journal (London), 104*(425), 876–882. doi:10.2307/2234981

van den Bergh, J. C. J. M. (2011). Environment versus growth— A criticism of "degrowth" and a plea for "a-growth". *Ecological Economics, 70*(5), 881–890. doi:10.1016/j.ecolecon.2010.09.035

Vázquez, S. T., & Sobrao, D. G. (2016). Reshaping geographical allocation of aid: The role of immigration in Spanish Official Development Assistance. *Journal of International Relations and Development, 19*(3), 333–364. doi:10.1057/jird.2014.19

Winters, M. S., & Martinez, G. (2015). The Role of Governance in Determining Foreign Aid Flow Composition. *World Development, 66*, 516–531. doi:10.1016/j.worlddev.2014.09.020

Woods, N. (2008). Whose aid? Whose influence? China, emerging donors and the silent revolution in development assistance. *International Affairs, 84*(6), 120. doi:10.1111/j.1468-2346.2008.00765.x

Younas, J. (2008). Motivation for bilateral aid allocation: Altruism or trade benefits. *European Journal of Political Economy, 24*(3), 661–674. doi:10.1016/j.ejpoleco.2008.05.003

ADDITIONAL READING

Adams, D. W. (1983). Disrupting Economic-Development with Foreign-Aid. *American Journal of Agricultural Economics, 65*(5), 1193–1193.

Arnold, W. (1994). Japan Foreign-Aid - Power and Policy in a New Era - Koppelk,Bm, Orr,Rm. *Journal of Developing Areas, 28*(3), 452–453.

Aroonpipat, S. (2018). Governing aid from China through embedded informality: Institutional response to Chinese development aid in Laos. *China Information, 32*(1), 46–68. doi:10.1177/0920203X17730330

Bailey, R. (1991). Foreign-Aid in Practice - Browne,S. *International Affairs, 67*(3), 590–590. doi:10.2307/2621990

Baker, A. (2015). Race, Paternalism, and Foreign Aid: Evidence from US Public Opinion. *The American Political Science Review, 109*(1), 93–109. doi:10.1017/S0003055414000549

Bakewell, R. D. (1981). Foreign-Aid - a Discussion Paper. *Australian Outlook, 35*(1), 59-77. doi:10.1080/10357718108444733

Bandow, D. (1997). Death to foreign aid. *Fortune, 136*(6), 52.

Bauer, P. T. (1975). How True Are Truisms + More on the Issue of Foreign-Aid. *Encounter, 45*(1), 90–91.

Bauer, & Yamey. (1982). The Political-Economy of Foreign-Aid - Reply. *Lloyds Bank Annual Review*(143), 60-61.

Bouakez, H., & Gouba, F. E. (2017). A Note on Foreign Aid, Human Capital, and Welfare. *Macroeconomic Dynamics, 21*(6), 1484–1507. doi:10.1017/S136510051500084X

Brautigam, D. (1992). Governance, Economy, and Foreign-Aid. *Studies in Comparative International Development, 27*(3), 3–25. doi:10.1007/BF02687132

Burnside, C., & Dollar, D. (2000). Aid, Policies, and Growth. *The American Economic Review, 90*(4), 847–868. doi:10.1257/aer.90.4.847

Caucutt, E. M., & Kumar, K. B. (2008). Africa: Is Aid an Answer? *The B.E. Journal of Macroeconomics, 8*(1). doi:10.2202/1935-1690.1761

Chung, J. S., Kim, K. S., Roemer, M., & Krueger, A. O. (1980). The Developmental Role of the Foreign Sector and Aid - Krueger,Ao. *Pacific Affairs, 53*(3), 563–565. doi:10.2307/2757337

Clawson, P. (1992). Foreign-Aid and Economic-Development in the Middle-East - Lavy,V, Sheffer,E. *Orbis-a Journal of World Affairs, 36*(1), 133–134.

El Khanji, S. (2018). An empirical exploration of relationships between official development assistance (ODA) and advances in water and sanitation subsectors. Cogent Economics & Finance, 6(1). doi. *Artn, 1437661*. doi:10.1080/23322039.2018.1437661

Ezaki, M. (1975). 2-Gap Analysis of Foreign Aid. *Journal of Southeast Asian Studies, 6*(2), 151–163. doi:10.1017/S002246340001729X

Handke, W. (1982). Foreign-Aid in Indian Domestic Politics. *Aussen Politik, 33*(4), 408–415.

Hanlon, J. (2008). Does foreign aid really work? *Development and Change, 39*(3), 491–492. doi:10.1111/j.1467-7660.2008.00490_2.x

Heltberg, R., & Nielsen, U. (2000). Foreign aid, development and the environment. *Foreign Aid and Development: Lessons Learnt and Directions for the Future*, 271-289.

Hopkins, R. F. (2000). Political economy of foreign aid. *Foreign Aid and Development: Lessons Learnt and Directions for the Future*, 423-449.

Husain, I. (1992). External Debt and Foreign-Aid to Pakistan. *Financing Pakistan's Development in the, 1990s*, 583–603.

Islam, A. (1992). Foreign-Aid and Economic-Growth - an Econometric Study of Bangladesh. *Applied Economics, 24*(5), 541–544. doi:10.1080/00036849200000067

Ji, S. U., & Lim, S. S. (2018). An empirical analysis of the determinants of agricultural official development assistance. *Agricultural Economics-Zemedelska Ekonomika, 64*(5), 206–215. doi:10.17221/275/2016-AGRICECON

Jung, C., Cho, W., & Hwang, W. (2018). Does Official Development Assistance Promote Foreign Policy Cooperation from its Recipients? The Case of South Korea. *Pacific Focus*, *33*(1), 83–110. doi:10.1111/pafo.12106

Kragh, M. K., Mortensen, J. B., Schaumburg-Muller, H., & Slente, H. P. (2000). Foreign aid and private sector development. *Foreign Aid and Development: Lessons Learnt and Directions for the Future*, 312-331.

Kul'kova, O. S. (2018). Evolution of the International Development Assistance System in the Uk (1997-2016). Mirovaya Ekonomika I Mezhdunarodnye Otnosheniya, 62(4), 35-44. doi:10.20542/0131-2227-2018-62-4-35-44

Lahiri, S., Krueger, A. O., Michalopoulos, C., Ruttan, V. W., & Browne, S. (1991). Aid and Development - Krueger,Ao, Michalopoulos,C, Ruttan,Vw. *Economic Journal (London)*, *101*(409), 1589–1591. doi:10.2307/2234911

Lewis-Workman, S. (2018). International Norms and Japanese Foreign Aid. *Asian Perspective*, *42*(1), 85–120. doi:10.1353/apr.2018.0003

Lin, T. C. (1991). Foreign-Aid - a Theoretical Framework for Analyzing Communist-China Foreign-Policy. *Issues & Studies*, *27*(5), 78–102.

Michaely, M. (1981). Foreign-Aid, Economic-Structure, and Dependence. *Journal of Development Economics*, *9*(3), 313–330. doi:10.1016/0304-3878(81)90010-9

Musah-Surugu, I. J., Ahenkan, A., Bawole, J. N., & Darkwah, S. A. (2018). Migrants' remittances A complementary source of financing adaptation to climate change at the local level in Ghana. *International Journal of Climate Change Strategies and Management*, *10*(1), 178–196. doi:10.1108/Ijccsm-03-2017-0054

North, J. (1980). The Many Uses of Foreign-Aid - Sobhuza Limos. *New Republic (New York, N.Y.)*, *183*(12), 14–17.

Rajan, R. G., & Subramanian, A. (2008). Aid and Growth: What Does the Cross-Country Evidence Really Show? *The Review of Economics and Statistics*, *90*(4), 643–665. doi:10.1162/rest.90.4.643

Ranis, G. (1980). Foreign-Aid - Euthanasia or Reform. *Worldview*, *23*(3), 25–29. doi:10.1017/S0084255900043254

Riddell, B. (1999). The global crisis in foreign aid. *Environment and Planning. C, Government & Policy*, *17*(3), 376–378.

Robinson, S., & Tarp, F. (2000). Foreign aid and development - Summary and synthesis. *Foreign Aid and Development: Lessons Learnt and Directions for the Future*, 1-14.

Seyedsayamdost, E. (2018). Millennium Development Goals: Impact on national strategies and spending. *Development Policy Review*, *36*, O59–O88. doi:10.1111/dpr.12314

Skarbek, E. C. (2016). Aid, ethics, and the Samaritan's dilemma: Strategic courage in constitutional entrepreneurship. *Journal of Institutional Economics*, *12*(2), 371–393. doi:10.1017/S1744137415000296

Solomatin, A. (2018). The World Bank and Fragile States: Dynamics of Cooperation and Aid Structure. *Vestnik Mezhdunarodnykh Organizatsii-International Organisations Research Journal, 13*(1), 114–132. doi:10.17323/1996-7845-2018-01-07

Sothan, S. (2018). Foreign aid and economic growth: Evidence from Cambodia. *The Journal of International Trade & Economic Development, 27*(2), 168–183. doi:10.1080/09638199.2017.1349167

Taormina, R. J., & Messick, D. M. (1983). Deservingness for Foreign-Aid - Effects of Need, Similarity, and Estimated Effectiveness. *Journal of Applied Social Psychology, 13*(5), 371–391. doi:10.1111/j.1559-1816.1983.tb01746.x

Tigabu, A., Berkhout, F., & van Beukering, P. (2017). Development aid and the diffusion of technology: Improved cookstoves in Kenya and Rwanda. *Energy Policy, 102*, 593–601. doi:10.1016/j.enpol.2016.12.039

Todenhofer, J. G. (1980). Position of Foreign-Aid Policy in Relation to Total Political Context. *Politische Studien, 31*(251), 273–285.

Vanarkadie, B. (1988). Foreign-Aid Reconsidered - Riddell,Rc. *The Journal of Development Studies, 24*(3), 431–433.

Verschaeve, J., & Orbie, J. (2018). Ignoring the elephant in the room? Assessing the impact of the European Union on the Development Assistance Committee's role in international development. *Development Policy Review, 36*, O44–O58. doi:10.1111/dpr.12216

Wang, L. M., & Chu, J. F. (2008). Capital Pool Company Program - Alternative funding resources when SME goes abroad. *Modern Finance and Global Trading Cooperation: Proceedings of the 5th International Annual Conference on Wto and Financial Engineering*, 229-233.

Wasserman, G. (1983). The Foreign-Aid Dilemma. *The Washington Quarterly, 6*(1), 96–106. doi:10.1080/01636608309477588

White, H. (1996a). Japan's foreign aid challenge: Policy reform and aid leadership - Rix,A. *Development and Change, 27*(3), 585–586.

White, H. (1996b). Macroeconomic evaluation of programme aid - A conceptual framework. *Ids Bulletin-Institute of Development Studies, 27*(4), 15-&. doi:10.1111/j.1759-5436.1996.mp27004002.x

Wilson, S. Y. (1996). Foreign aid, self-reliance and economic development in West Africa - Olaniyan,RO. *The Review of Black Political Economy, 25*(1), 129–131. doi:10.1007/BF02690056

Wuyts, M. (1996). Foreign aid, structural adjustment, and public management: The Mozambican experience. *Development and Change, 27*(4), 717–749. doi:10.1111/j.1467-7660.1996.tb00609.x

Yogo, T. U. (2017). Assessing the Effectiveness of Foreign Aid in the Education Sector in Africa: The Case of Primary Education. *African Development Review-Revue Africaine De Developpement, 29*(3), 389–402. doi:10.1111/1467-8268.12276

Younger, S. D. (1992). Aid and the Dutch Disease - Macroeconomic Management When Everybody Loves You. *World Development, 20*(11), 1587–1597. doi:10.1016/0305-750X(92)90016-O

Zaytsev, Y. (2017). International Multilateral Assistance for Socio-Economic Development of the Poorest Countries of South-East Asia. *Journal of International Development*, *29*(2), 249–258. doi:10.1002/jid.2999

Zhou, H. (2017). China's Foreign Aid Policy and Mechanisms. *China's Foreign Aid: 60 Years in Retrospect*, 1-47. doi:10.1007/978-981-10-2128-2_1

KEY TERMS AND DEFINITIONS

Altruistic Motive: According to this perspective, aid is provided for recipient's needs, therefore, this is also called international humanitarianism.

Bilateral Aid Flows: Aid from one single donor to a single recipient.

Development Assistance Committee: Established in 1960. It comprises member countries and became a body under OECD dealing with the issues of aid policy assessments and aid provision to developing world.

Governance: Policymaking and policy implementation monitoring.

Institutional Motive: According to this view, aid ties are closely related with the engagement to the global system through international Non-governmental organization membership and ratification of international agreements.

Migration: Flow of people from one country to another for permanent or temporary settlement based on for example, economic, political, and social reasons.

Multilateral Donors: International institutions providing aids.

Official Development Assistance: Official and concessional aid flow to developing countries for economic growth and sustainable development.

Poverty: The situation in which income level is below to the point where basic needs (for example, food and shelter) cannot be met.

Realist Motive: The provision of aid is mostly based on donor's interest.

ENDNOTES

1 Albania, Algeria, Armenia, Azerbaijan, Bangladesh, Benin, Bhutan, Bolivia, Botswana, Brazil, Burundi, Cambodia, Cameroon, China, Colombia, Costa Rica, Cote d'Ivoire, Dominican Republic, Ecuador, Egypt, Arab Rep., El Salvador, Fiji, Gabon, Gambia, The, Georgia, Ghana, Guatemala, Guinea-Bissau, Guyana, Honduras, India, Indonesia, Iran, Islamic Rep., Kazakhstan, Kenya, Kyrgyz Republic, Lao PDR, Macedonia, FYR, Madagascar, Malawi, Malaysia, Mali, Mauritania, Mauritius, Mexico, Mongolia, Morocco, Mozambique, Nepal, Niger, Pakistan, Panama, Paraguay, Peru, Rwanda, Senegal, Serbia, South Africa, Sri Lanka, Sudan, Suriname, Swaziland, Tanzania, Thailand, Togo, Tunisia, Turkey, Uganda, Uruguay, Vietnam and Zambia.

2 Australia, Austria, Belgium, Canada, Czech Rep, Denmark, Finland, France, Germany, Greece, Iceland, Ireland, Italy, Japan, Korea, Luxembourg, Netherlands, New Zealand, Norway, Poland, Portugal, Spain, Sweden, Switzerland, UK and US.

Chapter 13

Economic Development Aids as a Financial Instrument of Global Public Goods:

Performance Assessment for Donor Countries

Hayriye Atik
Erciyes University, Turkey

Fatma Ünlü
Erciyes University, Turkey

ABSTRACT

The importance of global public goods (GPGs) is increasing every day. As a result, the concept become an important part of international policymaking. There is a huge literature on the definition and classification of GPGs, as well as the financing problems of them. GPGs are generally financed through the development aids given by international organizations and some developed countries. Literature is generally concentrated on the determination of the amount of aids devoted to different categories of GPGs, such as environment, health, peace-keeping, and knowledge. Differently from the literature, a new and more general classification is also used in this chapter. The main sectors included in the analysis are social infrastructure and services, economic infrastructure and services, production sectors, multi-sector/gross cutting, and humanitarian aid. For the first time in the literature, principal components and cluster analysis methodologies were used to determine the performance of the countries providing official development aids in this study.

DOI: 10.4018/978-1-5225-7564-1.ch013

INTRODUCTION

In a globalising world, problems and their solutions reach across national borders. This leads a growing concern for international corporations and international collective action. The unfolding tragedy of the AIDS epidemic is an instance where a disease with local origins has created consequences worldwide. Likewise, the Internet, which offers instant global communication, can be exposed to tremendous harm from hackers and the spread of insidious viruses. We live in an era where global warming, ozone-shield depletion and financial instabilities place risks on an ever-integrating world. As a result of these global challenges, the concept of global public goods (GPGs) has become an important part of international policy making.

The public goods which affect the whole world are called as GPGs. In another way, GPGs are goods with benefits or costs that extend across countries and regions. These goods are global for two reasons. Firstly, they are global across space. Secondly, they affect future generations. The concept appears in the agendas of United Nations agencies, World Bank, the European Union and other non-governmental organisations. Nobody can do without GPGs. Health, knowledge, environment, peace and security are some of the examples of global GPGs. For our common future, the finance of global peace, democracy, health, and climate change is increasingly become important.

There is a large literature on the definition, classification and the financing mechanisms of GPGs. An interesting attempt to determine the expenditure on GPGs has been provided by researches done by various authors (Raffer, 1999; World Bank, 2001; teVelde, Morrissey, & Hewitt, 2006; Reisen, Soto, & Weithöner, 2003; Reisen, Soto, & Weithöner, 2004). Using data from Official Development Aid (ODA), previous studies have documented the increase in aid-financed GPGs according to sectors and donors. However, no study has so far measured the performance of the donor countries according to the sectoral aids. So, this chapter will focus on the measurement of the relative performance of the donor countries in terms of sectoral official development aids as well as the trends and distribution of aids provided as GPGs.

This chapter has three aims. The first aim is to scrutinize the concept of GPGs. Secondly, it will examine how much aid has been allocated to finance global public goods by donor countries and by multinationals. The third aim, differently from the literature, it will try to determine relative performance of donor countries in terms of development aids provided for GPGs. Principal components analysis and cluster analysis methodologies were used to determine the performance of donor countries by using data on sectoral aids. The main sectors included in the analysis are: social infrastructure and services, economic infrastructure and services, production sectors, Multi-sector/Gross Cutting, and Humanitarian Aid. The data used in empirical work is obtained from the Organisation for Economic Co-operation and Development (OECD).

This chapter is divided into five sections. After the introductory section, section one examines the literature related with the definition of GPGs. Section two concentrates on the classification of GPGs. Section three discusses the various financing mechanisms of GPGs as well as the trends and sectoral distribution of ODA for the years from 1990 to 2016 depending on the availability of data. Section three has three sub-sections. In the first sub-section, expenditure on health related GPGs will be examined. The second sub-section will show the trends of expenditure related with peace-building activities. The last sub-section will concentrate on ODA provide for knowledge generation and environment related GPGs. Section four tries to determine the relative performance of Development Assistance Committee (DAC) countries empirically. Section five concludes the chapter.

THE DEFINITION OF PUBLIC GOODS

Although the term public good is old in economic literature, the features of public goods were first used by Samuelson (1954). According to him, a pure public good should have two features which are non-rivalry in consumption and non-excludability. Non-rivalry means that the consumption of the public good by one person will not decrease its availability to the others. Non-excludability means that it is impossible to exclude anyone from the consumption of the public good. If these two features are completely satisfied, a public good is said to be pure (Kocks, 2005). Instead of defining the global public goods, Samuelson tried to define the features of public goods and also to determine the mix of private and public goods.

The term *global public good* was first defined by Kindleberger (1986). An open trading system, well defined property rights, standards of weights and measures which may include international money, and fixed exchange rates were accepted as global public goods by Kindleberger (1986, p. 8).

Herber (1990) accepted peace and science in Antarctica as global public goods. Because, Antarctica is unique among the seven continents as a continent of sustained peace. The citizens of world and especially the citizens of the nations which signed Antarctic Treaty System consume the political stability. The consumption of peace in Antarctica is non-rival, as the benefit of peace for one person will not reduce the benefit of others. Scientific research in Antarctica will also have important collective consumption benefits.

Mendez (2002) accepted oceans, seas and ozone layers as global public goods. He used the terms "international public goods", "global public goods" and, "universal public goods" in the same sense. The most important contribution of the author was that international public goods could be accepted as global public goods when they were consumed globally.

Another definition says that GPGs are public goods that do not obey national borders, and some of them are naturally global (Kaul, Conceicao, le Goulven, & Mendoza, 2003). In another way, many of the national borders have taken away in recent decades.

The wider definition of GPGs was done by United Nations Development Programme's publication *Global Public Goods* in 1999 (Kaul, Grunberg, &Stern 1999). According to this definition GPGs are the goods whose benefits spread to all countries, generations, or at least more than one country or groups. This definition also stresses that GPGs are the goods produced for any groups or produced for the next generations according to non-discrimination principles (Kaul et.al., 1999, p.16).

Another definition which based on development belongs to World Development Bank Development Committee. This Committee defines global public goods as the goods, resources, services, systems of rules, and policy regimes with cross-border externalities which are necessary for development, and that can be produced by developed and developing countries (World Bank, 2001, p.2).

THE CLASSIFICATION OF PUBLIC GOODS

Different approaches have been adopted in attempts to classify GPGs. The first approach classifies public goods into three categories according to the benefits which they provide. While the first group of public goods directly provide utility, the second group reduce the risk. The third group of public goods enhance the capacity. If the benefit provides direct utility or reduces the risk then public good is likely an international public good. If the benefit is to enhance then the spatial range of public good will be limited (Morrissey, teVelde, & Hewitt, 2002, p. 36). Table 1 classifies GPGs based on the nature of the benefits. Public good may provide benefit to a region or to the whole world. Reducing the acid rain in one country has limited benefits for only its neighbours. However, the reduction of the pollution in oceans is a global public good/service.

Public goods can also be classified as core and complementary. While core refers to the provision of the global benefit, complementary refers to helping in providing the good. For example, knowledge is a GPG. However, the generation of knowledge requires research and education. So, education is a complementary activity (complementary public good) which is necessary for the generation of knowledge.

Another approach was suggested by Speight (2002) and then also used Reisen et al. (2003) According to this approach, GPGs are classifies thematically:

- Environment (global commons)
- Health (communicable disease eradication)
- Knowledge generation and dissemination
- Governance (international financial stability, a free and open trade system)
- Peace and security (global peace, protection from crime and narcotics).

Another classification was done by Kaul (2010) as pure GPGs, Impure GPGs, De facto GPGs and GPGs with restricted access. This classification can be observed from Table 2.

Pure GPGs are non-excludable and non-rival. Peace and security is one of the most important examples of pure GPGs. It is non-excludable and non-rival as everyone can benefit from them (Bieckmann, 2010). Impure GPGs are either non-excludable or non-rival. They are non-excludable or difficult to exclude, but rival. De facto GPGs are non-rival goods which are kept or made non-exclusive on a global scale.

Kaul (2010) also distinguishes public goods in to eight categories according to their production properties (the origins of public goods). The first category is called as natural GPGs. The sunlight and the moonlight, the atmosphere, the oceans are accepted as natural GPGs. The second category is human-made GPGs. This category consists of global norms, standards, rules and policy regime. Global infrastructure and communication networks, global knowledge networks are all in this category. The third group is known as best-shot goods. Inventions and discoveries, destruction of asteroid moving towards the earth are in this group. The fourth category is summation goods. This category contains mitigation of climate change and financial stability. The fifth group is weak-link summation goods which contain civil aviation safety-airport security screening. Group six is known as club goods. Especially, security provision by NATO is included in this category. The seventh group is final GPGs. Controlled commu-

Table 1. Classification of GPGs by range and types of benefits

	Type of Benefit		
Range of Benefit	**Direct Utility**	**Risk Reduction**	**Capacity Enhancement**
Global	Conserving Biodiversity	Reduced climatic risk; reduced risk of financial instability	Global governance institutions; global knowledge generations
Regional	Protecting forests and lakes; peace keeping	Reduced acid rain; lower incidence of disease	Research on arid agriculture

Source: Morrissey, teVelde, & Hewitt, 2002.

Table 2. The consumption properties of global public goods

Pure GPGs	Impure GPGs	De Facto GPGs	GPGs with restricted access
Financial and economic stability	The atmosphere		Patented knowledge
Peace and security	The ozone layer		The World Wide Web
Moonlight	Fresh air		International markets
Communicable disease control			
The warming rays of the sun			
The Oceans			
Integrated markets			
	Non-rival but excludable	A global gene pool to promote biodiversity preservation	
	Knowledge related goods	Medical, financial and other technologies	

Source: Kaul (2010).

nicable diseases and financial stability are included in this category. The last category is intermediate GPGs which contains pharmaceutical knowledge and international agreement on banking.

The most recent classification was done by Cepparulo and Giuriato (2016).They select 52 sectors from OECD Creditor Reporting System (CRS) and grouped them into the following six GPGs categories:

- Knowledge generation and dissemination,
- Communicable disease control,
- Global governance,
- Crime control and global peace
- Global commons and sustainability,
- Communications.

Verschraegen and Schiltz (2007) argued that knowledge should be considered as a global public good and private right. They claimed because open access and information sharing facilitate the global production and dissemination of knowledge, more people can benefit from it. Also, it facilitates the access of the knowledge goods and services and thus less developed countries get involved global knowledge network. Knowledge generation and dissemination category contains the activities of research and scientific institutions, and international institutions for knowledge. (11182) Educational research, (12182) Medical research, (16062) Statistical capacity building, (43082) Scientific institutions, (31182) Agricultural research, (31282) Forestry research, (31382) Fishery research, (32182) Technological research, (41082) Environmental research and development, (23082) Energy research are CRS sectors included in the knowledge generation and dissemination GPS. The numbers in parenthesis show the CRS codes of the sectors.

Communicable disease control category is related with the control of communicable diseases and sexually-transmitted diseases. This category includes; (12250) Infection disease control, (13040) STD control including HIV/ AIDS, and (12263) Tuberculosis control.

Global governance GPG contains the building of economic and financial capacity, the fostering financial stability, the adoption of conventions and the rules of governing. (15110) Public sector policy, (24010) Financial policy, (24020) Monetary institutions, (33110) Trade policy, (33140) Multilateral trade negotiations, (33120) Trade facilitation, (24030) Formal sector financial intermediaries are sector which constitute global governance GPG.

Crime control and global peace is the fourth category of GPGs. Narcotics control, peace building, conflict prevention and resolution are the main sub-categories of this GPGs. The following sectors generate this category: (16063) Narcotics control, (31165) Agricultural alternative development, (43050) Non-agricultural alternative development, (15220) Civilian peace building, conflict prevention and resolution, (15230) Bilateral participation in international peacekeeping operations authorised by the UN.

Global commons and sustainability is the fifth category of GPGs. This category includes actions to curb pollution and to promote alternative energies. (23030) Power generation/ renewable sources, (23066) Geothermal energy, (23067) Solar power, (23068) Wind power, (23069 (Ocean), (23070)Biomass, (31210)Forestry policy, (31220) Forestry development, 831310) Fishery policy, (31320) Fishery development, (41010) Environmental policy, (41020) Biosphere protection, (41030) Bio-diversity, (41040) Site preservation, (31192) Plant and post-harvest protection and past control, (14010) Water sector policy, (14015) water resource conservation, (41081) Environmental education, (23010) Energy policy, (31281) Forestry education, (31381) Fishery education are the sectors constitute this category.

Communications is the last GPGs. (22010) Communication policy, (22020) Telecommunications, (22030) Radio/television/ print media, (22040) Information and communication technology (ICT), (15153) Media and free flow of information sectors generate the last GPGs.

FINANCING GLOBAL PUBLIC GOODS

GPGs are financed through charges levied by supranational organisations or clubs or through voluntary contributions (aids) of countries and individuals (Sandler, 2002, p.83). The measure of aid used here is aid commitments from CRS of the DAC of OECD. ODA is generally provided by DAC countries and international organisations. In 1980s, DAC countries were; the US, Germany, Australia, Austria, Belgium, Denmark, Finland, France, The UK, Ireland, Spain, Sweden, Switzerland, Italy, Japan, Canada, Luxembourg, Norway, Portugal, New Zealand and Greece. Recently, Hungary, Slovak Republic, Poland, Iceland, Czech Republic, Slovenia, and Korea were included in the DAC group.

Table 3 presents the trends in official development aids provided by all donors for the period 1990 and 2017. The following observations can be obtained from Table 3:

1. Total development aids increased from 64.661, 198 million dollars in 1990 to 177.595,02 million dollars in 2017. The increase was nearly three times during the period.
2. DAC countries had the highest share in total aids as 54.342,39 million of 64.661,98 million were given by DAC countries in 1990. Similarly, 146.600,18 million of total 177.595,02 million, nearly 82,5%, were financed by DAC countries in 2017.
3. The amount financed by multilaterals also increased between 1990 and 2017. While the share financed by multilaterals in 1990 was 4,4% in 1990, it increased to 9,2% in 2017.
4. Although the amount of aid financed by Non-DAC countries increased the period, they had the lowest share between 1990 and 2017, except 1990.

Table 3. Trends of total development aids: 1990-2017, current dollar, million

	1990	1995	2000	2005	2010	2015	2017
All Donors Total	64.661,98	65.424,46	60.019,81	120.771,28	147.643,64	162.781,66	177.595,02
DAC Countries Total	54.342,39	58.895,70	54.021,00	108.396,79	128.483,69	131.563,12	146.600,18
Multilaterals Total	2.862,94	5.397,73	4.912,25	9.389,96	12.746,70	13.669,60	16.449,56
Non-DAC Countries Total	7.456,65	1.131,03	1.086,56	2.984,53	6.413,25	17.548,94	14.545,28

Source: https://stats.oecd.org/Index.aspx?DataSetCode=CRS1#. (10.05.2018).

Table 4 presents a different classification of ODA. Differently from Table 3, sectoral distribution of ODA is given in Table 4. The distribution of ODA according to five main sectors are examined in Table 4. These sectors are: Social Infrastructure and Services, Economic Infrastructure and Services, Production Sectors, Multi-sector/Gross Cutting, and Humanitarian Aid. We have the following observations from Table 4:

1. Development aids devoted to social infrastructure and services increased from 9.498,632 million dollars to 42.183,515 between 1995 and 2016. The increase was nearly five times.
2. Aids devoted to economic infrastructure and services approximately increased two times during the period, (from 11.876,756 million dollars to 22.004, 250).
3. Amount devoted to production sectors was lower than that of the first two sectors. The amount devoted to production sectors were changed between 2.885,519 (in 2000) and 8.054,280 (in 2010).
4. ODA given to Multi-sector/Gross Cutting increased from 3.451,964 million dollars (in 1995) to 15.281,298 million dollars (in 2010). In recent years, it started to decrease and the total amount in 2016 was 12.037,110 million.
5. ODA provided as commodity aid had the lowest amount, comparatively with the aids provided to other sectors, during the period between 1995 and 2016. While the amount was 3.826,135 million dollars in 1995, it decreased to 2.351,390 in 2016.
6. Action relating to debt started to decrease after 2005. While the amount was 26.706, 418 in 2005, it decreased to 2.433,427 million in 2016.

Expenditure on Health-Related Global Public Goods

The first GPG which will be examined here is health. Although the provision of general health is generally accepted as a national public good, some expenditure such as eradicating communicable diseases are accepted as GPGs (teVelde, Morrissey, & Hewitt, 2002, p. 122). Moon et al. (2017) examined weaknesses and opportunities in the global health system in terms of global public goods. According to them, there are three steps to better govern the financing and provision of GPGs for health. Firstly, it is to improve data showed how much money is currently going to providing which types of GPGs. Second, a legal

Table 4. Sectoral distribution of Official Development Aids done By DAC countries: 1995-2016, current dollar, million

	1995	2000	2005	2010	2015	2016
Social Infrastructure & Services	9.498,632	13.867,922	29.580,888	42.758,332	40.639,166	42.183,515
Economic Infrastructure & Services	11.876,756	7.494,375	10.573,950	19.512,911	22.222,068	22.004,250
Production Sectors	3.041,192	2.885,519	5.271,178	8.054,280	7.642,662	6.119,680
Multi-sector/Gross Cutting	3.451,964	3.399,927	3.679,530	15.281,298	11.772,258	12.037,110
Commodity Aid	3.826,135	3.943,295	3.143,921	3.487,632	2.557,437	2.351,390
Action Relating to Debt	2.779,738	3.554,163	26.706,418	3.780,667	417,510	2.433,427
Humanitarian Aid	1.246,825	2.287,384	8.875,040	10.053,594	13.268,880	15.365,729
Administrative Costs of Donor	2,575	1.328,552	2.314,858	5.948,908	6.647,309	5.631,142
Total	36.721,964	41.435,155	96.124,240	111.441,934	118.343,922	124.591,337

Source: https://stats.oecd.org/Index.aspx?DataSetCode=CRS1#. (10.05.2018).

global political process is create to decide the priority of missing GPGs Finally, new financing for GPGs would need to be identified. In addition to this, they point out that strengthening global arrangements for GPGs for health today is crucial investment for improved global health in the coming years.

In a general way, GPGs for health contain the control of disease and epidemic surveillance, disease eradication, disease research, and pollution emissions. It can be enlarged to cover poverty reduction and technical assistance in health (Sandler & Arce, 2002). Development aids for infection disease control and for sexually transmitted disease control (HIV/AIDS) are excepted as health related GPGs (teVelde at al., 2002).

Table 5 presents the total amount and the percentage of health-related development aids done by all donors, DAC countries, multilaterals and Non-DAC countries. Table 5 gives the total health related expenditures. Health related expenditure increased from 354,956 million dollars to 8916,302 million dollars between 1995 and 2016, more than 25 times. From OECD Data, expenditure on infection disease control (12250) and on sexually transmitted disease control; HIV/AIDS (13040) are provided to calculate the total health related expenditure. DAC countries had the highest share comparatively with multilaterals and Non-DAC countries which only had expenditures in 2010 and 2016. While the share of DAC countries has changed between 78,5% and 68,3% during the period between 1995 and 2016, the share of multilaterals has changed between 21,4% and 31,5% (See Table 5).

Expenditure on Peace Building Related Global Public Goods

Expenditures on preventing the effects of conflict are known as GPGs as they provide regional security. Although the global benefit is limited in some cases, peace keeping operations have important benefits especially for developing countries. Regarding peace and security, Mendez (1999), denotes peace as a

Table 5. Total health expenditures related with GPGs: 1995-2016, current US dollar, million

	1995	2000	2005	2010	2016
All Donors total (Millions Dollar)	354,956	1226,955	4928,973	8051,801	8916,302
DAC Countries' total	274,592	963,624	3602,034	5505,79	6892,737
DAC Countries' share in total, (%)	77,3	78,5	73,0	68,3	77,0
Multilaterals total	80,363	263,331	1326,94	2543,573	2023,565
Multilaterals' share in total, (%)	22,6	21,4	26,9	31,5	22,0
Non-DAC Countries Total	..	..	..	2,438	22,225
Non-DAC Countries' share in total (%)	..	..	..	0,2	0,1

Source: https://stats.oecd.org/Index.aspx?DataSetCode=CRS1#. (10.05.2018).

state of relations among people and nations. He discusses the importance of UN peace-keeping forces in providing the GPG of peace. Moller (2004) concludes that there are many ways of preventing, managing and resolving conflicts. As a result, peace is promoted as GPG. Table 6 gives the total amount devoted to peace keeping operations according to donors for the period between 2004 and 2016. By using OECD statistics, we calculated the total funds for peace keeping operations by including five categories from CRS. These categories are; (16063) Narcotics control, (31165) Agricultural alternative development, (43050) Non-agricultural alternative development, (15220) Civilian peace building, conflict prevention and resolution, (15230) Bilateral participation in international peacekeeping operations authorised by the UN.

Table 6 presents the following observations:

1. All donors spent 3832.49 million dollars for peace keeping activities in 2016.
2. 3038.44 million dollars of 3832.49 million dollars was spent by DAC countries in the last year. In fact, the amount provided by DAC countries is always has the highest share.
3. The share of DAC countries in peace keeping expenditures was about 79% during the period between 2004 and 2016.
4. Multilaterals total share was at about 20,8%, except 2012. Only, in 2012 the share of multilaterals was 21,2%.

Table 6. Total expenditures on peace keeping-related activities: 2004-2016, current US dollar, million

	2004	2008	2012	2016
All Donors total (Million Dollar)	1260.94	3582.80	3109.49	3832.49
DAC Countries total (Million Dollar)	997.11	2839.59	2456.39	3038.44
Percentage in total	79	79,2	78,9	79,2
Multilaterals total (Million Dollar)	263.83	743.22	552.31	784.51
Percentage in total	20,9	20,8	21,2	20,8

Source: https://stats.oecd.org/Index.aspx?DataSetCode=CRS1#. (10.05.2018).

Expenditure on Knowledge Generation and Environment Related Global Public Goods

Knowledge is a global public good as it is the key element for innovation. By following Cepparulo and Giuriato (2016), we included six OECD categories when we were calculating knowledge related expenditures. These categories are; (11182) Educational research, (12182) Medical research, (16062) Statistical capacity building, (43082) Scientific institutions, (31182) Agricultural research, (31282) Forestry research, (31382) Fishery research, (32182) Technological research, (41082) Environmental research and development, (23082) Energy research.

Environment: As most aspects of environment have international dimensions, environment is a global public good. The reduction of emissions will reduce the pollution and this will benefit to everyone in the world. Conservation and preservation activities of forests and natural resources will provide utility to all and as a result have international dimension. This category includes actions to curb pollution and to promote alternative energies. (23030) Power generation/ renewable sources, (23066) Geothermal energy, (23067) Solar power, (23068) Wind power, (23069 (Ocean), (23070)Biomass, (31210)Forestry policy, (31220) Forestry development, 831310) Fishery policy, (31320) Fishery development, (41010) Environmental policy, (41020) Biosphere protection, (41030) Bio-diversity, (41040) Site preservation, (31192) Plant and post-harvest protection and past control, (14010) Water sector policy, (14015) water resource conservation, (41081) Environmental education, (23010) Energy policy, (31281) Forestry education, (31381) Fishery education are the sectors constitute this category in our calculation in Table 7.

The following observations can be received from Table 7:

1. Except some countries (Austria, Belgium, Greece, Ireland, Portugal, Spain Sweden, UK, and US), environment has the highest share in GPGs expenditure. Switzerland (89%), Denmark (75%), and Italy (73%) finance environment-related aids more than other GPGs. Environment had the highest share (70.50%) for the term between 1996 and 1998 in total DAC donors' aid (telve at al., 2002, p. 135) in the past. Although some donors devoted the highest amount of aid, the share of environment has declined to 31% for the term (2004-20016) which we examined in Table 7.
2. Peace building is a GPGs with the highest share (36%) in total donors' aid. Portugal (89%), Greece (88%), Austria (82%), US (57%) had the highest percentages. Comparatively with the earlier studies (teVelde, 2002; Cepparulo & Giuriato, 2016), the share of peace building operations increased.
3. The share of health -related expenditure is 25% in total DAC donors' aids. The UK (67%), Ireland (66%), Luxembourg (44%) have higher shares than that of the total donor countries.
4. The share of knowledge related expenditure is 8% for all DAC donors. The knowledge production is very important for the prevention of disease and for the explosion of innovation throughout the world. However, other GPGs such as environment, peace building and health need urgent interventions, official development aids related with these GPGs is higher than the aids for knowledge. Differently than the other donors, France and Sweden have considerable shares for knowledge.

Table 7. Aid spending on GPGs, as a percentage of total GPG spending, 2004-2016

	Environment	Peace Building	Health	Knowledge
Australia	33	33	20	14
Austria	13	82	2	3
Belgium	23	42	29	6
Canada	46	15	36	3
Denmark	75	2	12	11
Finland	65	18	8	9
France	45	2	8	45
Germany	54	13	16	17
Greece	10	88	1	1
Ireland	25	1	66	8
Italy	73	12	10	5
Japan	67	2	20	11
Luxembourg	55	1	44	0
Netherlands	59	9	18	14
New Zealand	43	18	19	20
Norway	33	21	23	23
Portugal	2	89	0	9
Spain	34	45	12	9
Sweden	30	5	20	45
Switzerland	89	7	2	2
UK	25	3	67	5
US	16	57	25	2
Turkey [a]	10	80	6	4
Total DAC Donors	31	36	25	8

Note: [a] Turkish data is only for 2016.

RELATIVE PERFORMANCE OF DAC COUNTRIES ACCORDING TO OFFICIAL DEVELOPMENT AIDS: EMPRICAL ANALYSIS

In this chapter, principal components and cluster analysis methodologies were used to determine the relative performance of DAC countries according to official development aids provided for main sectors. The section related with the finance of global public goods indicated that nearly the highest share belongs to DAC countries. So, we included DAC counties to empirical analysis.

Principal components analysis is one of the widely used multivariate statistical methods. This analysis is used to obtain a small number of meaningful variables by classifying a large number of data by appropriate categories (DeCoster, 1998; Yong & Pearce, 2013). Hence the purpose of principal components analysis is to take *n* variables X1, X2, X3…, Xn and find the combinations of these to produce uncorrelated indices like Z1, Z2, Z3…Zn. If there is not any correlation, it means that the calculated indices measure different dimensions in the data. The "Zi" values are called the principal components (Atik & Ünlü, 2017).

Principal component analysis is used to measure the economic development performance of countries or regions, which have different level of socio-economic development, from different aspects. Although there are many studies (Gidengil 1978; Jacquemin & Sapir 1995; Artis & Zang 2002; Bakaric, 2005; Sabatini, 2006; Ersungur et al., 2007; Özbek & Atik, 2013; Gençoğlu & Ünlü, 2014; Atik 2015, Bai et al., 2015; Atik & Ünlü, 2017; Zekic et al., 2017) related to this issue in the literature, no studies have been found that measure the performance of the countries providing official development aids by using this method. Therefore, it shows the original contribution of the study to the literature.

Principal components analysis in this study will used for the two purposes. Firstly, it will reduce the number of variables that will be used in cluster analysis. Secondly, it will show the relative performance of the countries providing official development aids, by ranking them according to first principal components scores of the countries.

Cluster analysis is a method that enables a researcher to classify certain groups according to the similarities between the cases and put forward general definitions about these classes by revealing the common characteristics of the units. Variables included in the cluster analysis are not separated as dependent and independent variables. The main purpose of cluster analysis is to provide the researcher with suitable and useful information by classifying ungrouped data according to similarities (Atik& Ünlü, 2017).

This methodology was used in a number studies to group the countries according to various indicators. In one of these studies, the European Union (EU) countries were classified according to macroeconomic performance indicators (Jacquemin & Sapir, 1995). In another study, relative development of the EU countries and Turkey were determined by using socio-economic indicators (Erol, 2013). The position of Turkey within the EU countries in terms of development indicators was tested by using cluster analysis more recently (Ertaş & Atik, 2016).

The data used in empirical analysis is given in Table 8. Instead of using classical categories such as environment, health, peace building and knowledge, we prefer a different classification given in OECD- CRS data. The reason of using this classification in empirical analysis is that the data for some sub-categories -used by telve at al., 2002; Cepparulo & Giuriato, 2016- is not available for some DAC countries (Slovenia, Slovak Republic and Czech Republic) which are recently included in DAC group.

The UK, the US and Germany can easily be separated from the other DAC countries as they provide more aid in all categories presented in Table 8.

Principal Components Results

In the first place of the analysis, we performed Kaiser-Meyer-Olkin (KMO) and Bartlett's tests. The reason of applying these tests is to decide whether our data is suitable for principal components analysis. KMO statistics should be greater than o,60 and Bartlett's test should be significant (e.g. $p< 0.05$). According to our findings, KMO statistics is 0,627 and Bartlett's test is ($0.000 < 0.05$) significant (See Table 9).

In the second stage of the analysis, the principal components analysis has been performed to decide the number of the principal components that should be retained for further analysis. Examination of the values suggest that the first two principal components and the resultant principal component scores should be used in the assessment of the countries (See Table 10).Because, principal components which eigenvalues are more than "1" is accepted for further analysis. The analysis suggests that the first two principal components scores for each country might act as an adequate summary of the original scores

Table 8. DAC countries' aids according to main sectors, 2017, million dollars

Countries	Social infrastructure and services	Economic infrastructure and services	Production sectors	Multi-sector/ Gross Cutting	Humanitarian aid
Australia	984,60	215,68	157,04	460,57	148,28
Austria	279,46	36,55	39,91	30,23	46,88
Belgium	361,37	83,87	75,22	137,68	238,82
Canada	1464,46	216,24	315,83	254,73	1008,87
Czech Republic	24,12	2,05	4,44	4,28	10,67
Denmark	359,00	171,03	76,01	43,04	253,70
Finland	124,59	25,05	43,31	26,20	75,29
France	3199,85	1692,69	754,69	826,61	153,35
Germany	5983,81	4941,97	945,58	2577,95	2483,28
Greece	1,28	,01	,00	2,00	7,96
Hungary	27,41	,13	3,58	,54	,39
Iceland	14,07	4,01	3,67	,20	6,37
Ireland	198,64	3,18	36,10	21,22	111,82
Italy	372,92	34,06	37,35	25,64	190,96
Japan	3597,30	10732,21	913,86	3131,28	921,43
Korea	1030,70	871,43	145,33	162,73	67,25
Luxembourg	126,91	20,43	16,67	17,15	49,00
Netherlands	1552,42	296,10	200,07	84,32	323,24
New Zealand	135,00	41,51	58,54	14,63	26,08
Norway	1069,71	250,87	79,82	515,17	487,45
Poland	58,38	1,68	73,98	,74	31,88
Portugal	98,19	2,70	1,40	4,58	8,31
Slovak republic	10,62	,23	,54	1,21	1,15
Slovenia	15,51	,82	,35	,29	2,91
Spain	256,20	4,80	36,80	198,14	51,23
Sweden	1327,65	170,27	167,52	321,76	67,25
Switzerland	621,95	184,62	170,58	208,50	366,00
UK	3363,68	597,21	236,76	1425,26	1017,38
US	15497,40	1400,54	1500,66	1519,77	7144,09

Source: https://stats.oecd.org/Index.aspx?DataSetCode=CRS1#. (10.05.2018).

Table 9. KMO and Bartlett's Test

Kaiser-Meyer-Olkin Measure of Sampling Adequacy.		,627
Bartlett's Test of Sphericity	Approx. Chi-Square	226,790
	Df	10
	Sig.	,000

Table 10. Principal components results

Component	Initial Eigenvalues			Extraction Sums of Squared Loadings		
	Total	% of Variance	Cumulative %	Total	% of Variance	Cumulative %
1	3,789	75,790	75,790	3,789	75,790	75,790
2	1,075	21,505	97,295	1,075	21,505	97,295
3	,072	1,449	98,744			
4	,054	1,085	99,829			
5	,009	,171	100,000			

Table 11. Component matrix[a]

	Component	
	1	2
Production sectors	,976	
Social infrastructure	,914	-,399
Multisector	,881	,428
Humanitarian aid	,851	-,502
Economic infrastructure	,708	,689
Extraction Method: Principal Component Analysis.		
a. 2 components extracted.		

in any further analysis of data, these two components account nearly 97,275% of the total variation of the original variables.

The first component, explaining 75,790% of the total variance, is highly correlated with the amount of official development aids provided to production sectors (0, 976), aids provided to social infrastructure (0, 914), aids for multisector (0,881), aids for humanitarian (0, 851) and aids for economic infrastructure (0, 708) (See Table 11).

The second principal component, explaining 21, 505% of total variance, is mainly determined by economic infrastructure (0,689) and humanitarian aid (-0, 502).

We show the country rankings according to the first principal components scores of the countries. Table 12 shows that the US is the first country providing aid to finance GPGs, while Slovak Republic is the last country in rankings.

Cluster Results

Cluster analysis was performed by using Ward method. To decide the number of the clusters, the agglomeration schedule and the dendrogram (the tree chart) were observed. When the number of clusters is determined through the agglomeration schedule, the increase in the coefficients should be considered. The largest increases in the coefficients are identified to decide the number of the clusters.

Table 12. Principal components' table

Countries	PCA1	County Rankings According to PCA1	PCA2
Australia	-,16964	10	-,06177
Austria	-,32285	16	-,34927
Belgium	-,23701	12	-,29782
Canada	,31568	5	-,29604
Czech Republic	-,38826	23	-,36727
Denmark	-,23391	11	-,32981
Finland	-,33051	18	-,35150
France	,33823	4	,65102
Germany	1,10845	2	2,15136
Greece	-,39492	27	-,36902
Hungary	-,39134	24	-,36872
Iceland	-,39152	25	-,36815
Ireland	-,30974	15	-,37213
Italy	-,26194	14	-,38114
Japan	-,51010	29	4,48933
Korea	-,25102	13	-,03869
Luxembourg	-,35598	21	-,36181
Netherlands	,02061	6	-,29864
New Zealand	-,33639	19	-,34141
Norway	-,10397	7	-,10206
Poland	-,32852	17	-,35379
Portugal	-,38102	22	-,37080
Slovak republic	-,39554	28	-,36857
Slovenia	-,39439	26	-,36950
Spain	-,33745	20	-,26148
Sweden	-,12536	9	-,15466
Switzerland	-,11080	8,000	-,23202
UK	,38017	3,000	,38175
US	4,89904	1,000	-,50739

The first column in the agglomeration schedule, presented in Table 13, shows at which stage the countries create single cluster. The first row in Table 13 constitutes the first stage of the analysis. The nearest two observations which are in the first cluster and in the second cluster can be shown in cluster combined. For example, in the first stage the 23rd observation (Slovak Republic) in the first cluster and the 24th observation (Slovenia) in the second cluster are the nearest two observations.

Table 13. Agglomeration schedule

Stage	Cluster Combined		Coefficients	Stage Cluster First Appears		Next Stage
	Cluster 1	Cluster 2		Cluster 1	Cluster 2	
1	23	24	14,120	0	0	2
2	12	23	42,583	0	1	4
3	5	11	110,041	0	0	5
4	10	12	240,669	0	2	5
5	5	10	571,801	3	4	14
6	7	17	1326,543	0	0	7
7	7	19	3062,072	6	0	9
8	21	22	6774,084	0	0	9
9	7	21	12121,896	7	8	14
10	2	13	18101,061	0	0	13
11	3	6	26491,686	0	0	12
12	3	14	38221,587	11	0	16
13	2	25	58915,050	10	0	16
14	5	7	90375,864	5	9	19
15	1	20	156607,076	0	0	18
16	2	3	226686,972	13	12	19
17	18	26	321348,411	0	0	20
18	1	27	487776,810	15	0	21
19	2	5	819718,604	16	14	24
20	16	18	1215984,600	0	17	21
21	1	16	1662864,755	18	20	22
22	1	4	2315720,128	21	0	24
23	8	28	3615769,051	0	0	25
24	1	2	9882493,836	22	19	27
25	8	9	28303298,164	23	0	26
26	8	15	82352464,196	25	0	27
27	1	8	209521192,283	24	26	28
28	1	29	462548627,852	27	0	0

The information about the distance between observations is in the coefficients column and called as Squared Euclidean Distance. For instance, the distance between Slovak Republic and Slovenia is 14,120.

As it was mentioned earlier, when the number of clusters is determined from the agglomeration schedule, the difference between the coefficients is considered. When the coefficients column in Table 13 is observed, there are high increases in the coefficients after stage 26. While the coefficient in stage 25 was 28303298,164, it increased to 82352464,196 in stage 26. As there are three jumps in coefficients in the following stages, it can be decided that there are three clusters. In another word, the countries can be classified under three groups according to their science indicators.

If we want a visual representation of the distance at which clusters are combined, we can look at a display called the dendrogram. The dendrogram is read from up to down. The results of the dendrogram support the results from agglomeration schedule. We can observe three groups from dendrogram.

Cluster 1 contains Canada, Korea, Sweden, Netherlands, Switzerland, Norway, Australia, Spain, Ireland, Austria, Italy, Denmark, Belgium, Portugal, Poland, New Zealand, Luxembourg, Finland, Hungary, Czech Republic, Greece, Iceland, Slovenia, Slovak Republic This is the largest cluster which contains more countries. Japan, Germany, UK, France constitute cluster two. Cluster three contains the US (See, Table 14).

FUTURE RESEARCH DIRECTIONS

The studies in the literature generally concentrate on the determination of the countries contribution for GPGs. However, new research should concentrate on the factors determining the provision of GPGs. Additionally, the performance of the international organisations in providing public goods should also be examined in the new studies. Also, the performance of the specific DAC countries should also be evaluated.

CONCLUSION

With the acceleration of globalization, the number of public goods increases and expands, creating an effect on both regional and international levels. Countries have generally been willing to spend money on national public goods but they should be equally willing to pay for GPGs that serve common interests, be they shared or not. GPGs are the public goods which effect the whole world.

ODA is given to finance GPGs. The highest share in ODA belongs to DAC countries. The relative performance of DAC countries in terms of ODA was examined in this chapter. In the literature, the distribution and changes in ODA has been examined. In this study, the distribution and the changes in ODA was also examined for a different period (1995-2016) than the literature. Our results related with the trends and sectoral distribution of ODA is similar to the literature. Our observations indicate that the sector with the highest share was peace keeping. The share of DAC countries in peace keeping expenditures was about 79% during the period between 2004 and 2016.

For the first time in the literature, we also measured the performance of ODA countries by using a different sectoral classification containing data for 2016.Principal components and cluster analysis methodologies were performed.

Table 14. Country groups according to cluster analysis

Clusters	Countries
Cluster 1	Canada, Korea, Sweden, Netherlands, Switzerland, Norway, Australia, Spain, Ireland, Austria, Italy, Denmark, Belgium, Portugal, Poland, New Zealand, Luxembourg, Finland, Hungary, Czech Republic, Greece, Iceland, Slovenia, Slovak Republic
Cluster 2	Japan, Germany, UK, France
Cluster 3	US

We show the country rankings according to the first principal components scores of the countries. The US is the first country providing aid to finance GPGs, while Slovak Republic is the last country in rankings. We can observe three clusters from dendrogram obtained at the end of the cluster results. Cluster 1 contains Canada, Korea, Sweden, Netherlands, Switzerland, Norway, Australia, Spain, Ireland, Austria, Italy, Denmark, Belgium, Portugal, Poland, New Zealand, Luxembourg, Finland, Hungary, Czech Republic, Greece, Iceland, Slovenia, Slovak Republic This is the largest cluster which contains more countries. Japan, Germany, UK, France constitute cluster two. Cluster three contains the US.

REFERENCES

Atik, H., & Ünlü, F. (2017). Science performance of Turkey in 21st century: A multivariate statistical comparison with the OECD countries. In H. Arapgirlioğlu, A. Atik, R. L. Elliott, & E. Turgeon (Eds.), *Researches on science and art in 21st century* (pp. 1030–1038). Ankara: Gece Kitaplığı.

Bai, A., Hira, S., & Deshpande, P. S. (2015). An application of factor analysis in the evaluation of country economic rank. *Procedia Computer Science*, *54*, 311–317. doi:10.1016/j.procs.2015.06.036

Bakaric, I. R. (2005). Uncovering regional disparities – the use of factor and cluster analysis. *Economic Trends and Economic Policy*, *105*, 52–77.

Bieckmann, F. (Ed.). (2010). *Collective self-interest, global public goods and responsible sovereignty. The Broker*, (20/21).

Cepprulo, A., & Giuriato, L. (2016). Responses to global challenges: Trends in aid-financed global public goods. *Development Policy Review*, *34*(4), 483–507. doi:10.1111/dpr.12163

DeCoster, J. (1998). *Overview of factor analysis*. Retrieved July 05, 2016, from http://www.stat-help.com/factor.pdf

Erol, E. D. (2013). Türkiye ve Avrupa Birliği üyesi ülkelerin sosyo-ekonomik gelişmişlik düzeylerinin karşılaştırmalı analizi. *Sosyal ve Beşeri Bilimler Dergisi*, *5*(1), 198–208.

Ertaş, S. A., & Atik, H. (2016). Kalkınma göstergeleri bakımından Türkiye'nin Avrupa Birliği ülkeleri arasındaki yeri: Istatistiksel bir analiz. *Erciyes Üniversitesi İktisadi ve İdari Bilimler Fakültesi Dergisi*, *48*, 199–218.

Gençoğlu, P., & Ünlü, F. (2014). Afrika ülkelerinin sosyo-ekonomik gelişmişlik düzeyi: istatistiksel bir analiz, In İ. G. Yumuşak (Ed.), *12. International Conference on Knowledge, Economy and Management Proceedings Book*, (pp.59-74). Antalya.

Herber, B. P. (1990). The International Public Goods of Antarctica: A New Politico Economic Regime for the World's Seventh Continent. In *Proceedings of the 44th Congress of the International Institute of Public Finance*. Detroit, MI: Wayne State University Press.

Jacquemin, A., & Sapir, A. (1995). *Is a European hard-core credible?* CEPR Discussion Paper.

Kaul, I. (2010). What is a Global Public Good. *The Broker*, (20/21). Retrieved from http://www.search-4dev.nl/document/181021

Kaul, I., Conceicao, P., Le Goulven, K., & Mendoza, R. (2003). *Providing global public goods: Managing globalization*. New York: Oxford University Press. doi:10.1093/0195157400.001.0001

Kaul, I., Grunberg, I., & Stern, M. A. (Eds.). (1999). *Global public goods: International co-operation in the 21st Century*. New York: Oxford University Press. doi:10.1093/0195130529.001.0001

Kindleberger, C. P. (1986). International public good without international government. *The American Economic Review*, *76*(1), 1–13.

Kocks, A. (2005). *The Financing of UN Peace Operations-An Analysis from A Global Public Good Perspective, INEF Report* (Vol. 77). InstitutfürEntwicklung und Frieden der Universitat Duisburg-Essen, Campus Duisburg.

Mendez, R. P. (1999). Peace as a global public good. In I. Kaul, I. Grunberg, & M. Stern (Eds.), *Global Public Goods: International Cooperation in the 21st Century* (pp. 382–416). New York: Oxford University Press. doi:10.1093/0195130529.003.0020

Moller, B. (2004). *Peace as a Global Public Good Research Center on Development and International Relations (DIR)*. Development Research Series Working Paper, No. 127, Aalborg University.

Moon, S., Rottingen, J., & Frenk, J. (2017). Global public goods for health: Weaknesses and opportunities in the global health system. *Health Economics, Policy, and Law*, *12*(02), 195–205. doi:10.1017/S1744133116000451 PMID:28332461

Morrissey, O., teVelde, D., & Hewitt, A. (2002). Defining international public goods: conceptual issues. In M. Ferroni & A. Mody (Eds.), *International public goods: Incentives, measurement and financing* (pp. 31–46). Boston: Kluwer Academic Publishers. doi:10.1007/978-1-4615-0979-0_2

Özbek, H., & Atik, H. (2013). İnovasyon göstergeleri bakımından Türkiye'nin Avrupa Birliği ülkeleri arasındaki yeri: Istatistiksel bir analiz. *Erciyes Üniversitesi İktisadi ve İdari Bilimler Fakültesi Dergisi*, *42*, 193–210.

Raffer, K. (1999). ODA and Global Public Goods: A Trends analysis of past and present spending patterns. ODS Background Papers. New York, NY: United nations Development Programme.

Reisen, H., Soto, M., & Weithöner, T. (2003). *Financing global and regional public goods through ODA: Analysis and Evidence from the OECD Creditor Reporting System*. Paper presented at the UN Wider Conference "Sharing Global Prosperity", Helsinki, Finland. Available online at: http://www.eldis.org/static/DOC14272.htm

Reisen, H., Soto, M., & Weithöner, T. (2004). *Financing global and regional public goods through ODA: Analysis and Evidence from the OECD Creditor Reporting System*. Paris: OECD.

Samuelson, P. A. (1954). The pure theory of public expenditure. *The Review of Economics and Statistics*, *36*(4), 387–389. doi:10.2307/1925895

Sandler, T. (2002). Financing international public goods. In M. Ferroni & A. Mody (Eds.), *International public goods: Incentives, measurement and financing* (pp. 81–118). Boston: Kluwer Academic Publishers. doi:10.1007/978-1-4615-0979-0_4

Sandler, T., & Arce, D. (2002). A conceptual framework for understanding global and transnational public goods for health. *Fiscal Studies*, *23*(2), 195–222. doi:10.1111/j.1475-5890.2002.tb00059.x

Speight, M. (2002). *How Much Should DFID Allocate to Global Actions and Funding?* London: Department for International Development.

teVelde, D. W., Morrissey, O., & Hewitt, A. (2002). Allocating aid to international public goods. In M. Ferroni & A. Mody (Eds.), *International public goods: Incentives, measurement and financing* (pp. 31–46). Boston: Kluwer Academic Publishers.

teVelde, D. W., Morrissey, O., & Hewitt, A. (2006). *Aid financing of international public goods- recent developments*. Vienna: UNIDO Publications.

Verschraegen, G., & Schiltz, M. (2007). Knowledge as a global public good: The role and importance of open access. *Societies Without Borders*, *2*(2), 157–174. doi:10.1163/187219107X203540

World Bank. (2001). *Global development Finance 2001: Building coalitions for effective development finance*. Washington, DC: Wold Bank.

Yong, A. G., & Pearce, S. (2013). A beginner's guide to factor analysis: Focusing on exploratory factor analysis. *Tutorials in Quantitative Methods for Psychology*, *9*(2), 79–94. doi:10.20982/tqmp.09.2.p079

Zekić, S., Kleut, Z., & Matkovski, B. (2017). An analysis of key indicators of rural development in Serbia: A comparison with EU countries. *Economic Annals*, *62*(214), 107–120. doi:10.2298/EKA1714107Z

ADDITIONAL READING

Addison, T. (2004). The Global Economy, Conflict Prevention, and Post-Conflict Recovery. World Institute for Development Economics Research (WIDER), Helsinki, (United Nations University) DESA Paper, ADDISON, First Draft (8.11.04).doc.

Atkinson, A., & Stilitz, J. (1980). *Lectures in Public Economics*. New York: McGraw Hill Publishing Co.

Bieckmann, F. (Ed.). (2010). Collective Self-interest, Global Public Goods and Responsible Sovereignty, The Broker, issue 20/21 July.

Blackden, C. M. (2009). *Gender Equality and Global Public Goods: Some Reflections onShared Priorities, OECD DAC Network on Gender Equality*. GENDERNET.

Bradley, D. (2001). The Biological and Epidemiological Basis of Global Public Goods for Health, Paper prepared for Working Group 2 of the Commission on Macroeconomics and Health.

Chen, L., Evans, T., & Cash, R. (1999). Health as a Global Public Good. In I. Kaul, I. Grunberg, & M. Stern (Eds.), *Global Public Goods: International Co-operation in the 21st Century*. New York: Oxford University Press. doi:10.1093/0195130529.003.0014

Collier, P. (2008). *The Bottom Billion: Why the Poorest Countries are Failing and What can be Done About It*. Oxford: Oxford University Press.

Conceição, P. (2003). Assessing the Provision Status of Global Public Goods. In I. Kaul, P. Conceicao, K. Le Goulven, & R. Mendoza (Eds.), *Providing Global Public Goods: Managing Globalization*. New York: Oxford University Press. doi:10.1093/0195157400.003.0007

Cook, L. D., & Sachs, J. (1999). Regional Public Goods in International Assistance. In I. Kaul, I. Grunberg, & M. Stern (Eds.), *Global Public Goods: International Co-operation in the 21st Century*. New York: Oxford University Press. doi:10.1093/0195130529.003.0022

Cornes, R., & Sandler, T. (1996). *The Theory of Externalities, Public Goods, and Club Goods. 2ndEdition*. Cambridge: Cambridge University Press. doi:10.1017/CBO9781139174312

Coyne, C. J., & Ryan, M. E. (2008). Foreign Intervention and Global Public Bads, *Mimeo*. http://econ.as.nyu.edu/docs/IO/9831/Coyne.pdf

Desai, M. (2003). Public Goods: A Historical Perspective. In I. Kaul, P. Conceicao, K. Le Goulven, & R. Mendoza (Eds.), *Providing Global Public Goods: Managing Globalization*. New York: Oxford University Press. doi:10.1093/0195157400.003.0003

Ferguson, N. (2004). *Colossus: The Price of America's Empire*. New York: The Penguin Press.

Ferguson, N., & Schularick, M. (2006). The Empire Effect: The Determinants of Country Riskin the First Age of Globalization, 1880-1913. *The Journal of Economic History*, *66*(2), 283–312. doi:10.1017/S002205070600012X

Ferroni, M. (2000). Reforming Foreign Aid: The Role of International Public Goods. *OECD Working Paper Series*, No 4. The World Bank.

Fidler, D. (1998). Legal issues associated with antimicrobial drug resistance. *Emerging Infectious Diseases*, *4*(2), 169–177. doi:10.3201/eid0402.980204 PMID:9621187

Galtung, J. (1975). Violence, Peace, and Peace Research. In *Peace: Research, Education, Action.Essays in Peace Research* (Vol. I, pp. 109–134). Copenhagen: Christian EjlersForlag.

Gardiner, R., & Le Goulven, K. (2001a). Sustaining Our Global Public Goods. Economic Briefing No.3. UNED Forum project "Towards Earth Summit 2002".

Gardiner, R., & Le Goulven, K. (2001b). *Global Public Goods, Briefing Paper, Towards EarthSummit 2002 Economic Briefing No. 3*. Germany: Heinrich Boell Foundation.

Hamburg, D. A., & Holl, J. E. (1999). Preventing Deadly Conflict from Global Housekeeping to Neighbourhood Watch (Peace and Security). In I. Kaul, I. Grunberg, & M. Stern (Eds.), *Global Public Goods: International Co-operation in the 21st Century*. New York: Oxford University Press.

Hardin, G. (1968). The Tragedy of the Commons. *Science*, *162*(3859), 1243–1248. doi:10.1126cience.162.3859.1243 PMID:5699198

Heal, G. (1999). New Strategies for the Provision of Global Public Goods: Learning From International Environmental Challenges. In I. Kaul, I. Grunberg, & M. Stern (Eds.), *Global Public Goods: International Cooperationin the 21st Century* (pp. 220–239). New York: Oxford University Press. doi:10.1093/0195130529.003.0011

Jayaraman, R., & Kanbur, R. (1999). International Public Goods and the Case for Foreign Aid. In I. Kaul, I. Grunberg, & M. Stern (Eds.), *Global Public Goods: International Co-operation in the 21st Century* (pp. 418–435). New York: Oxford University Press. doi:10.1093/0195130529.003.0021

Kammas, P., & Philippopoulos, A. (2010). The Role of International Public Goods in TaxCooperation, CESifo Economic Studies. Oxford University Press. Volume: 56.2.

Kaul, I. (2010). What is a Global Public Good, *The Broker special report*, issue 20/21 July 2010,http://www.search4dev.nl/document/181021

Kaul, I., & Conceicao, P. (2006). *The New Public Finance: Responding to Global Challenges*. New York: Oxford University Press. doi:10.1093/acprof:oso/9780195179972.001.0001

Kaul, I., Conceicao, P., Le Goulven, K., & Mendoza, R. (2003). *Providing Global Public Goods: Managing Globalization*. New York: Oxford University Press. doi:10.1093/0195157400.001.0001

Kaul, I., Grunberg, I., & Stern, M. A. (1999). *Global Public Goods: International Cooperation in the21st Century*. New York: Oxford University Press. doi:10.1093/0195130529.001.0001

Kaul, I., Grunberg, I., & Stern, M. A. (Eds.). (1999). *Global Public Goods: International Co-operation in the 21st Century* (pp. 436–449). New York: Oxford University Press. doi:10.1093/0195130529.001.0001

Kindleberger, C. P. (1986). International Public Goods without International Government. *The American Economic Review*, *76*(1), 1–13.

Kocks, A. (2005). *The Financing of UN Peace Operations – An Analysis from a Global Public Good Perspective, INEF Report* (Vol. 77). InstitutfürEntwicklung und Frieden der Universität Duisburg-Essen / Campus Duisburg.

Lal, D. (2004). *In Praise of Empires: Globalization and Order*. New York: Palgrave Macmillian.

KEY TERMS AND DEFINITIONS

Club Goods: Public goods with benefits restricted to a specific group may be considered club goods. For example, expenditures that benefit all of the children in a household but not the adults.

Common Goods: Are defined in economics as goods which are rivalrous and non-excludable.

DAC Countries: DAC countries were the US, Germany, Australia, Austria, Belgium, Denmark, Finland, France, The UK, Ireland, Spain, Sweden, Switzerland, Italy, Japan, Canada, Luxembourg, Norway, Portugal, New Zealand and Greece. Recently, Hungary, Slovak Republic, Poland, Iceland, Czech Republic, Slovenia, and Korea were included in the DAC group.

Global Public Good: GPGs are goods with benefits or costs that extend across countries and regions.

Non-Rivalrous: A good is considered non-rivalrous or non-rival if, for any level of production, the cost of providing it to a marginal (additional) individual is zero.

Public Good: A public good is a good that is non-rival and non-excludable.

Regional Public Goods: Public goods with positive effects on some countries within a geographical region.

Chapter 14
Causal Interactions Between Foreign Direct Investments, Trade, and Economic Growth:
Evidence From Middle-Income Countries

Fındık Özlem Alper
Niğde Ömer Halisdemir University, Turkey

Ali Eren Alper
Niğde Ömer Halisdemir University, Turkey

ABSTRACT

The main objective of this chapter is to detect the impacts of FDI and foreign trade on the economic growth of middle income countries. Therefore, this study aims to examine the relationship among economic growth, foreign direct investments, and trade in 27 middle-income countries according to the United Nations (UN) classification through panel data analysis method. According to the results of the Pedroni cointegration test, the null hypothesis suggesting no cointegration among the series at 1% significance level is rejected in all seven tests. According to pooled mean group estimator estimation results, the coefficients of foreign direct investment and trade which have long-term impacts on economic growth are also identified. Accordingly, the coefficients of both variables are statistically significant. A 1% increase in foreign direct investment and trade increase economic growth by 0.24% and 0.02%, respectively.

INTRODUCTION

The Geographical Explorations had provided tremendous opportunities for countries which could have benefited from them. Countries with advanced maritime and navigational capabilities had acquired new territories and their opulent resources. Besides using these resources as a provenience of labor in order to boost their production, they also utilized them as a market for the products they produced and eventually they constituted contemporary developed countries. Countries which lacked the ability to benefit from the Geographical Explorations and the Industrial Revolution have formed the group of developing countries.

DOI: 10.4018/978-1-5225-7564-1.ch014

As soon as the globalization phenomenon began with the Geographical Explorations, the free circulation of goods and services was facilitated first and then it was followed by the financial liberalization movements towards the end of the 20th century.

Developing middle-income countries had been the ones with insufficient capital accumulation and savings in particular. Most of those countries need external capital movements to overcome structural bottlenecks and finance development processes. The emergence of international financial movements due to financial liberalization is of great importance in eliminating this shortcoming of the middle-income countries. International financial institutions and other countries with surplus savings are the first resource options that the middle-income countries consider in coping with their shortcomings. Besides these two options, foreign capital inflow is the most crucial external financing resource. As a result of the wide-spreading financial liberalization practices in both developed and developing countries along with the globalization process, capital movements increased, and foreign capital inflows accelerated especially toward developing countries. Capital movements are characterized as either the short- or the long-term, depending on the length of stay in the host country. The short-term capital movements are portfolio investments by which foreign investors buy bonds and stocks in the capital market of the host country.

Since these investments are highly sensitive to the rate of return and risk factors among the countries, they may leave the country upon the occurrence of extraordinary risks as quickly as they enter. The long-term capital movements are foreign direct investments (FDIs), which are made by purchasing a company in a host country, providing foundation funds for a newly established company, or increasing the capital of an existing company. It takes time for these investments to enter the country and to exit from the country as well. Due to the physical presence of certain components belonging to foreign direct investment such as personnel, equipment, and buildings within the boundaries of the host country, the investor cannot leave the host country immediately. On the one hand, the increase in foreign capital inflows contributes to the capital accumulation of the developing countries, but on the other hand, they create significant problems. These problems, which lead to countries becoming vulnerable to crises, are mostly the result of the short-term investments. The crises that created global impacts such as the European Monetary Zone crisis, the Asian crisis, Malaysia crisis, the Russian crisis, the Argentine crisis, the Brazilian crisis and the Turkish crisis of 2001 are thought to trigger the short-term capital inflow and outflow. Foreign direct investments, by courtesy of their long-run nature, tend to be more reliable than other sources of funding in fulfilling the foreign financing needs of developing countries. These investments have other positive effects in favor of the host country, such as increasing production/export capacity, creating jobs, and providing technology and transferring of knowledge. As the foreign direct investment's contribution to the country's economy becomes undeniably crucial, developing countries have begun to take some measures to attract foreign direct investment, such as the liberalization of markets, making promotions and providing incentives.

As a necessity in developing countries, FDI has become even more important especially with the financial liberalization movements that began in the 1980s. In this process, multinational corporations preferred to maintain their production in the countries with advantageous features, while developing countries pursued the entry of FDI into the country since they also wish to boost their economic growth. An positive relationship is considered between economic growth and FDI, which has impacts on resource utilization, infrastructure investments and technological improvement, especially in developing middle-income countries. According to the Neo-classical theory, FDI may promote economic growth by boosting the volume and effectiveness of total investments. Since FDI may increase export of capital goods by leading to the capital formation and employment growth, may bring forth resources such as knowledge and experienced managers, and may contribute to technological improvement and expansion and, in turn, economic growth is backed by increased productivity.

In theories defining FDI, it is predicted that FDI would yield employment growth. For instance; according to the OLI-framework, also known as the eclectic paradigm, the advantages regarding location, internalization, and ownership are the requirements that must be concurrently met before an international corporation ventures in foreign investment. According to this framework, FDI can generate new employment opportunities in the host countries and can be even more successful in creating more employment in comparison to domestic companies.

The impacts of foreign trade on economic growth have been explicated by many researchers. Lewer (2002) referred to trade liberalization as a direct or indirect restriction and control over the flow of goods and services, and as an opportunity for developing countries to converge developed countries with the courtesy of cheap labor along with increased trade openness.

Similarly, Rodrigues and Rodrik (2000) thought that foreign trade policies, especially when dealing with developing countries, play a crucial role in ensuring economic growth and that the best way of accelerating economic growth in all countries is achieved by integrating with the world economy.

The main objective of this study is to detect the impacts of FDI, as one of the most important international financial movements, and foreign trade on the economic growth of developing countries. Therefore, this study aims to examine the relationship among economic growth, direct foreign investments, and trade in 27 middle-income countries according to the United Nations (UN) classification through panel data analysis method.

The study differs from other studies in the literature in two main features. The first one involves the impossibility of generalization about the results obtained from single-country studies (Almfraji et al., 2014; Dritsaki and Stiakakis, 2014, etc.), since those results are based on the characteristics of the examined country, and consequently the results and policy recommendations for country groups cannot be procured.

The second distinguishing feature of the study involves homogeneity of the sampling group, one of the most basic assumptions of the panel data analysis method used. Since the countries included in the analysis belong to middle-income group according to the UN classification, the problem of non-homogeneous sampling frequently encountered in multinational studies is also abolished.

THEORETICAL BACKGROUND

There are many different countries in the world in terms of their level of development. The level of income had always been an important indicator of development, notwithstanding development is measured by such factors determining civilization as education, health, safety, environment, democratic infrastructure, and culture. In this context, the World Bank divided countries into three main income groups, namely, low (income per capita <$ 825); lower-middle (between $ 826 and $ 3,255); upper-middle (between $ 3,256 and $ 10,065) and high (income per capita > $ 10,066). Many factors influence the distribution of income. One of these factors is the foreign capital, especially FDI, which allows low-income countries to increase their incomes and compensate for their lower savings. Although there have been many studies over the last 60 years that aimed to explain FDI, the existence of a commonly accepted theory cannot be mentioned in this respect. Dunning (2001) stated that the OLI paradigm constituted the most comprehensive framework in explaining the determinants of FDI, however, it also claimed that it is not possible for a theory to successfully explain all types of FDI. It is because; FDI attain highly distinctive motivations. For example, the parameters explaining FDI seeking resources and the parameters explaining FDI seeking market completely differ from each other. Ricardo's theory of comparative advantage can be considered as the first attempt to explain FDI. Nonetheless, it is not possible to explain FDI with this theory, which is based on the assumptions of two-country, two-commodity and full competition of factors at the domestic level (Denisia, 2010). The three most important theories that have made significant contributions to the literature in explaining the basic motivations of FDI are the Production Life Cycle Theory, the Internalization Theory, and the OLI Paradigm.

The Production Life Cycle Theory

The theory developed by Vernon (1966) explains the manufacturing industry investments made by the US firms in Western Europe following the Second World War. The theory examines the process from birth to death of the product in three stages: introduction, growth/maturity, and decline. The production life cycle involving these three stages is illustrated in Figure 1.

In the introduction stage, companies make inventions and produce new products to be sold in domestic markets and exported to the foreign markets. Since the production and marketing processes for the products developed with R&D activities are not clear, the operations are carried out in the main country. In the first stage, the product containing technological innovation is produced only in the main country, the foreign demand for the product is met through exports. For example, following the Second World War, demand for manufacturing industry products increased in Europe. Thus, the US companies began to export since they had the advantage of having the technology for international competition. In

Figure 1. The production life cycle

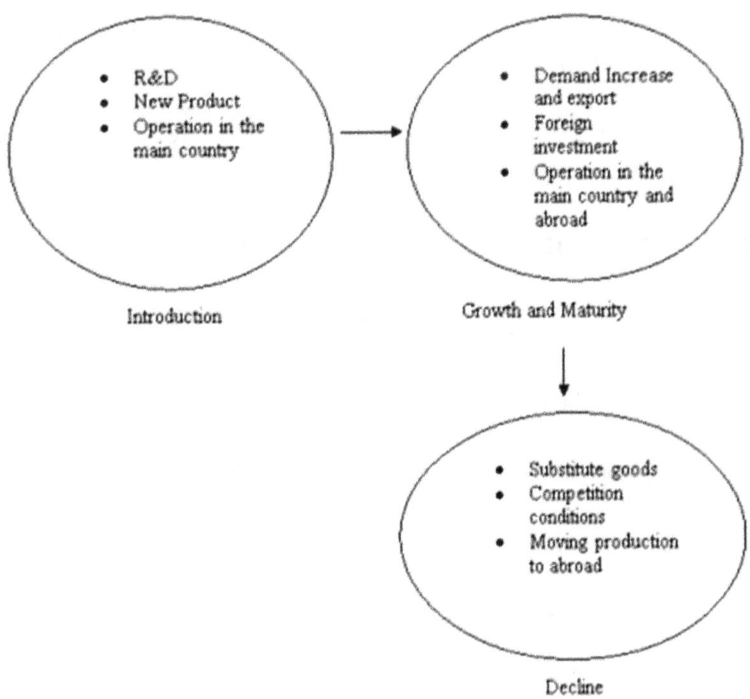

the growth/maturity stage, due to the absence of new product lines and low demand elasticity, the company can easily find a place for its product which is produced in the main country in the export markets, therefore, the exports of the product increase significantly. The increase in the foreign demand for the product inspires the company to invest in foreign countries. In the decline stage, the product manufacturing becomes a routine process. Due to the product substitutes introduced into the market, the company has to gain cost advantages in the export markets. Until this stage, production continues both in the main country and other countries. Since the product is produced by other companies in foreign countries, the main company loses its technology advantage and license superiority. Due to the cheap labor force in the foreign country, the product is produced at low cost; so it is imported by the main country hindering the domestic production of this product in the main country. The company continues to develop new products with high-profit margins and low demand flexibility, instead of producing the latest product in the main country and shifts the production preference to new products. In the final stage through which production technology becomes standard, the foreign investors shift their production facilities to emerging middle-income countries with cheaper labor costs in the form of direct investments (Vernon, 1966).

Internalization Theory

According to this theory, if foreign firms gain more proceeds from the investments made within the borders of the country than from foreign trade, then foreign direct investments are realized (Yapraklı, 2006). According to theory, the firms maximize their profits in an incomplete competition environment. At this stage;

- If transportation costs are high, and barriers to trade are plenty,
- If the risk of not obtaining information about the foreign market is high,
- If there is information asymmetry between buyer and seller,
- If there are situations that increase transaction costs in the market, the company goes into internalization and makes direct foreign investments.

As a result of internalization, firms can acquire benefits such as refraining from delays, bargaining and customer uncertainties and implementing price differentials between markets.

OLI (Ownership-Location-Internalization) Paradigm

According to Dunning (2001), a firm's production abroad depends on three conditions;

- The firm must be able to compete with the local companies in the host country of production and must possess material and non-material goods and skills.
- The FDI must become more profitable and advantageous than producing and exporting in its own country.
- The FDI made by the firm must be more profitable than selling, renting, or licensing its skills.

These are the advantages of ownership, location, and internalization that Dunning (2001) briefly explained as OLI.

ECONOMIC IMPACTS OF FDI

The impacts of FDI on the host countries' economies have caused many debates. Although there had been no consensus on the subject, FDI is considered to have many positive impacts, as well as adverse impacts, on the economies of its host countries.

Positive Impacts

It is possible to summarize the positive impacts of FDI under four main headings, namely; an economic structure in general, country standards, positive externality impacts, and positive social impacts.

Positive Impacts on Economic Structure in General

Many researchers [e.g., Borensztein et al. (1998), Barry and Bradley (1997), Almfraji et al. (2014), Ayaydın (2010), and Nistor (2014)] found that FDI is the accelerating impact of economic growth in the host countries.

- Additional capital inflows toward the host countries contribute to economic stability by leading to liquidity increase (Lairson and Skidmore, 2017). In addition, FDI can create employment (for new investments) upon implementation.
- By courtesy of the attained production advantages, FDIs can easily utilize economies of scale through their access to foreign markets.
- According to Barry and Bradley (1997), FDIs may have an export-enhancing impact on the host countries if they are considered as production bases through which foreign investors organize the sales of their products.
- According to Portelli and Narulla (2006), resources that cannot be utilized due to lack of technological improvement may be prevented from being dormant by FDI.

Positive Impacts on Country Standards

- Through technological spillover effect and know-how, the employment provided by FDI may acquire qualification which leads to higher standards of living and prosperity in this direction (Sun, 2002).
- FDIs may provide the host countries with health, safety, environmental and administrative regulations in order to increase the host country standards up to their home country standards (Sun, 2002).

Positive Externality Impacts

- As a result of the technological spillover effect, local producers would be able to benefit from innovations and technology brought by foreign investors (Alfaro et al., 2006).
- New investments can be made following the footsteps of previously implemented investments in the same industry through training provided by former employees who have already been em-

ployed and have adopted high standards in industries in which FDIs have already been implemented (Sun, 2002).

Positive Social Impacts

- Emerging opportunities to offer abundant, high-quality and affordable products for consumers would increase consumer satisfaction as well as the social welfare (Moran, 2005).
- FDIs may provide the less-developed host countries in which they are implemented with the chance to develop faster than normal and to reach the level of developed economies. Also, they may contribute positively to social indicators of the host country's community such as globalization and democratization (Sun, 2002).

Negative Impacts

The potential adverse impacts that FDIs may inflict in the host countries may be summarized under four main headlines: adverse impacts on the economic structure in general, adverse impacts on domestic producers, adverse transfer impacts, and adverse environmental and social impacts.

Negative Impacts on Economic Structure in General

- If FDIs utilize the resources needed for their new investments in the host countries, the local investors may be left with insufficient resources to make investments (Sun, 2002).
- Unemployment may increase considering the employees of the closed local businesses which cannot compete with FDIs in host countries.
- In case the employees are paid wages rate that local companies cannot afford to pay, the qualified labor force would be able to shift toward FDI firms and, as a result, local companies would have to raise wage levels to compete with FDIs. This can have a detrimental impact on the production efficiency of local companies (Lipsey, 2002).

Negative Impacts on Domestic Producers

- FDI can attain the monopoly power in those markets in the host countries by using the advantages of technology and low-cost production factors. In this case, the local companies in those markets would not be able to compete with the foreign investors and may reflect negatively on growth by being shutdown (Lairson and Skidmore, 2017).
- Even if FDIs do not gain any monopoly power, they may still mean harm to local producers. Foreign trade barriers that are imposed to protect local producers from foreign competition may be hindered by FDI and may become harmful to local producers. Local producers that cannot compete with the production advantages of FDI may be shutdown.

Negative Impacts on Transfers

- Either directly or indirectly, FDIs transfer their gained profits from the host countries toward the main investor countries. Foreign investors may resort to various means of transferring profits.

This would undoubtedly mean that a value created within the borders of the host country is being transferred abroad, which would adversely affect the balance of payments and growth.

- Perhaps the most intense criticism of FDI has targeted the supply of natural resources and raw materials for the use of foreigners. It is mainly because this situation can turn the host country into a modern colony (Poelhekke and van der Ploeg, 2010).
- Transferring a qualified labor force toward abroad by proposing attractive rates with which domestic firms cannot compete would adversely affect the human capital of the country (Lipsey, 2002).

Negative Environmental and Social Impacts

- If FDIs choose to operate by avoiding costly environmental standards of the main countries, they may mean harm to the environmental balance of the host countries which are devoid of such standards (Lairson and Skidmore, 2017).
- As amounts of FDI increase, external pressures also increase. As a result, FDIs may wish to facilitate their bureaucratic work in countries where certain conditions occur - especially in less-developed countries. In this sense, foreign investors can finance some political groups or individuals for their own interests to be favored over others. Besides, FDIs may choose to attempt bribery as a solution when they try to avoid the difficulties caused by laws and regulations of the host country. Besides being unethical, any type of corruption in which FDI may involve would be rather unfavorable since it may create an unfair competitive environment for the competitors the FDI (Egger and Winner, 2005; Sarkar, 2007; Pinto and Zhu, 2008).

LITERATURE REVIEW

Different studies have been conducted on FDI in different fields. These different studies provide us with substantial literature on the subject. The studies on FDI generally focus on the impacts of FDI in the foreign-invested countries and the determinants of FDI. Thus, this section of the research study also discusses the impacts of FDI on the foreign-invested countries. A significant part of the empirical studies indicates an positive impact of FDI on growth. Wang (2009), Li and Liu (2005) are examples of those studies which suggested such positive impacts. Wang (2009) dealt with FDI in accordance with the type of enterprise. The study utilized the data of 12 Asian countries between 1987-1997 and concluded that the contribution of FDI to economic growth in the manufacturing industry is positive. Li and Liu (2005), in their study of 84 countries for the period 1970-1999, concluded that FDI had a prominent impact on growth. Some of the empirical studies assert that FDI have no significant impact on growth.

For instance, Ericsson and Irandoust (2001) investigated the relationship between FDI and growth with the data obtained from Denmark, Finland, Norway, and Sweden. In this study, no association between direct foreign investment and growth is detected for Denmark and Finland.

Some studies concluded that FDI has an adverse impact on growth. Mencinger (2003) examined the relationship between FDI and economic growth for eight EU-candidate countries during the period of 1994-2001. The study detected a strong and negative correlation between FDI and growth. This result is explained by the type of FDI. During the observed period, FDI took place in the form of acquisitions. The proceeds from these acquisitions are spent mostly on consumption and imports. Therefore, the higher the inflow of FDI into a host country, the higher the current account deficit and foreign debt.

The productivity spillover effects of FDIs would be weakened by the host countries with smaller size and the concentration of FDI in trade and finance activities.

The differentiation of the methods used in conducted studies, the examined countries or the periods may have led to different results in this field of interest. Differences in the results of empirical studies suggest that other parameters may also be determinants on the impacts of foreign direct investment on growth. Two major factors that determine the direction and size of the impact of FDI on growth are as follows;

- The objective and the form of FDIs,
- The conditions in the foreign-invested country.

Depending on these factors, FDI can have positive impacts, as well as adverse impacts, on host countries.

Nair-Reichert and Weinhold (2001) examined the impacts of FDI on growth in 24 developing countries over a period of 25 years and concluded that the impact changes from country to country. The first issue to be considered at this point is that the objective and the form of FDI are more important than the investment volume. For instance, the impact of FDI that oriented to manufacturing industry on the growth is expected to be greater than of the investments in pursuit of natural resources. Similarly, the positive impacts of the investments aiming at establishing new production-oriented plants on growth are greater than of the investments made through acquisitions and mergers. The host country's export volume is expected to increase further as if the foreign-invested country is chosen not only as a market but rather as a production domain and as if international sales are realized from such production.

Studies that examine the role of the host country's conditions on the impact of FDI on growth indicate that the conditions of the country are generally important.

Zhang (2001), in the examination of 11 West Asian and Latin American countries, concluded that the impact of FDI on growth is based on the host country's conditions such as free-trade policy, education/ human capital conditions, and macroeconomic stability.

The competition conditions in the host country may also cause FDI to result in positive or adverse consequences. Large-scale companies making FDIs impel small-scale domestic companies to become more competitive. In such a competitive environment, some of the domestic companies may be strengthened regarding the technological level and accumulation of knowledge. Nevertheless, it is possible that the domestic industry would be compelled to compete with foreign investments and be harmed in an environment of incomplete competition. It has been observed that FDI simultaneously affect some of the domestic companies positively and some of them negatively. For example, while the profit share of the domestic firms decreases due to increased competition and the decrease of their market shares within the sectors on which FDIs are directed, the profit of the supplier companies operating in those sectors can be increased. More importantly, FDI can lead to the establishment of new supplier companies (Markusen et al., 1999). On this account, FDI contributes to the development of the industry. Another factor that causes FDIs to result in positive or adverse consequences is the policy practice in the host country.

Balasubramanyam et al. (1996) concluded that the impact of FDI on growth is stronger in the countries in pursuit of promoting exports rather than in countries adopting import-substitution policies. Infrastructure conditions of the host country also play a role in bringing forth the positive economic impacts of FDI. Because, sufficient infrastructure in the areas such as human capital, technological accumulation and financial development should be attained in order for new technologies, information, and skills to be dispersed in the host country along with FDI. According to the research studies carried out, the infrastructure elements in the host country should be sufficient for advanced technology-based investments to spread technological knowledge (Borensztein et al., 1998).

Alfaro et al. (2010) examined various relationships among FDI, financial markets, and growth. In the theoretical part of the study, a market is modeled on the assumption that there are only two alternatives for the agents in the economy. These alternatives consist of being employed by a foreign company that has made a FDI and being self-employed by one's own company to make use of externalities of FDI. Establishing one's own company creates the need for borrowing funds from financial markets. According to this scenario, it would be easier to set out on an enterprise in the presence of advanced financial markets. The empirical results of the study claim that FDIs significantly contribute to economic growth. However, in order for the positive impacts to take place, financial markets have to attain a certain level of development.

Almfraji et al. (2014) tried to examine the relationship between FDI and economic growth with the help of the vector autoregressive (VAR) model in 1990-2010 in Qatar. The results of the analysis detected a long-term positive relationship between FDI and economic growth in Qatar.

Dritsaki and Stiakakis (2014) tried to measure the FDI, export and economic growth relationship in Croatia with the help of ARDL boundary test. According to the findings of the study, FDIs have a positive impact on Croatia's economic growth, but this effect is not as large as expected.

Umoh et al. (2012) examined the relationship between FDI and economic growth using the simultaneous equilibrium estimation method for Nigeria. The existence of a bilateral relationship between the variables is detected.

Hong (2014) reviewed the impact of FDI on economic growth for China over the period 1994-2010 via the generalized momentum method (GMM). FDI is found to contribute positively to China's economic growth.

Abbes et al. (2015) investigated the relationship between FDI and economic growth in 65 countries over the 1980-2010 period using both panel cointegration and panel Granger causality analyses. The findings of the research study detected that the relationship between the variables is different for each country. Iamsiraroj (2016) investigated the relationship between FDI and economic growth for 124 countries between 1974 and 2010. The results indicated that economic growth is positively affected by FDI (*vice versa*).

Hussain and Haque (2016) examined the relationship among FDI, trade and economic growth over the period 1973-2014 for Bangladesh using the vector error correction model (VECM) method. Trade and FDI variables are detected to trigger economic growth.

Tan and Tang (2016) examined the relationship among national investment, FDI, trade, interest rates and economic growth in the ASEAN-5 countries for the period of 1970-2012 using Johansen-Juselius cointegration method. The findings of the study indicated the existence of a long-term relationship of economic growth with FDI and national investments for ASEAN-5 countries.

Abdouli and Hammami (2017) examined the relationship among FDI, environmental quality and economic growth for MENA countries. In the study using panel data analysis method for the 1990-2012 period, it is determined that an increase in FDI and capital stock have an positive impact on economic growth.

EMPIRICAL SECTION

In this section, the dataset is introduced first, then information about the model and econometric method is provided along with the empirical findings.

Sample Data, Model, and Methodology

The data used in the analysis covering the period between 1977-2016 are based on data from 27 middle-income countries (Egypt, Morocco, Tunisia, Cameroon, Chad, Kenya, South Africa, Nigeria, Senegal, Malaysia, Phillippines, Singapore, Thailand, India, Pakistan, Israel, Turkey, Mexico, Brazil, Uruguay, Colombia, South Korea, Panama, Ecuador, Argentina, Chile and Peru) mentioned in the UN's "World Economic Situation and Prospects 2014" report. Information on the data used in the study and their descriptive statistics are reported in Table 1 and Table 2, respectively.

In order to determine the effect of FDI and trade on economic growth along with the aim of this study, the model mentioned in Equation 1 is established and estimated.

$$GDPG_{it} = \beta_0 + \beta_1 FDI_{it} + \beta_2 TR_{it} + \varepsilon_{it} \quad (1)$$

Table 1. Information on the data used in the study

Variables	Definition	Source
GDP Growth (GDPG)	GDP per capita growth (annual %)	World Bank World Development Indicators
Foreign Direct Investment (FDI)	Foreign direct investment, net inflows (% of GDP)	World Bank World Development Indicators
Trade (TR)	Trade (% of GDP)	World Bank World Development Indicators

Table 2. Descrpitive statics on the related variables

Variables	Mean	Maximum	Minimum	Standard Deviation
GDPG	2.16	30.35	-22.95	4.35
FDI	2.48	46.49	-10.08	3.77
TR	69.88	52.98	9.09	65.21

The panel data can be defined as the collection of cross-sectional observations pertaining units such as individuals, countries, firms within a certain time interval. The panel is a set of data consisting of N number of units and T number of observations and, thus, having a total of N x T observations. The panel data analyses, as a combination of the cross-section and the time-series, were first introduced by Hildreth (1950), Kuh (1959), Swamy (1970), but the related practical studies in the real sense have begun as of the early 1990s.

The use of panel data analysis in econometric surveys has some advantages over the use of time-series or cross-sectional data. According to Hsiao (2007), the first one of these advantages involves more consistent determinations to be made since the higher degrees of freedom are utilized. Secondly, it is more suitable for modeling complex human behaviors than horizontal cross-sectional or time-series data sets. The third one is heterogeneity. Data sets used in the econometric analysis are usually heterogeneous. Panel data analysis can take this into account, whereas time-series and cross-sectional data cannot control this variation alone.

The cross-sectional dependence should be tested at the first stage of the panel data analysis methodology due to three basic reasons. The first reason is associated with one of the general assumptions of panel data analysis suggesting that the error terms being independent of the units, however, the errors along the cross-sectional units usually have simultaneous correlations.

The second main reason is based on the assumption that all countries are affected at the same degree by a certain shock and also that the other countries which constitute the panel are not affected by a macroeconomic shock initially emerged in any of those countries.

It is more realistic to anticipate an economic shock emerging in any country to affect other countries differently as it did in the 2008 global financial crisis, along with the rise of globalization and the increase in the level of international trade as well as the degree of financial integration in today's world. Therefore, it is necessary to test whether or not cross-sectional dependence exists between the series prior to commencing the analysis (Menyah et al., 2014), since the results obtained without consideration of cross-sectional dependence would be deviated and inconsistent.

The third and last reason involves the selection of unit root and cointegration test (referred as the second generation tests in the literature) in which such characteristics of the series should be taken into account upon the detection of cross-sectional dependence.

There are several tests in the literature to test the existence of the cross-sectional dependence. In the analysis section of the study, Breusch-Pagan Lagrange multiplier, Pesaran, Friedman and Frees cross-sectional dependence tests are used to analyze the cross-section dependence.

Breusch-Pagan Lagrange Multiplier Test

In Breusch-Pagan (1980) test, which is applied to test the hypothesis suggesting that the correlation matrix of the residuals of all cross-section units is the unit matrix, the cross-sectional dependence hypothesis is tested. In the alternative hypothesis, the cross-sectional dependence is tested. The Lagrange Multiplier (LM) test statistic is calculated by using Equation 2.

$$\lambda_{LM} = T\sum_{i=1}^{N-1}\sum_{j=i+1}^{N}\widehat{\rho_{ij}^{2}} \qquad (2)$$

Here, $\hat{\rho}_{ij}^2$ is the correlation coefficient of the residue.

Pesaran Cross-Sectional Dependence Test

The CD_{LM} test developed by Pesaran (2007) can be applied for situations where both N and T are large numbers. This test is an improved version of the Breusch-Pagan test.

$$CD_{LM} = \sqrt{\frac{1}{N(N-1)}\sum_{i=1}^{N-1}\sum_{j=i+1}^{N} T\widehat{(\rho_{ij}^2 - 1)}} \tag{3}$$

According to this test, in the case of $N \rightarrow \infty$ and $T \rightarrow \infty$, the non-existence of cross-sectional dependence is tested in the null hypothesis and the cross-sectional dependence is tested in the alternative hypothesis.

Friedman Cross-Sectional Dependence Test

Friedman (1937) proposed a nonparametric test calculated by using Spearman's rank correlation coefficient in order to test the cross-sectional dependence. The Friedman test statistic value is calculated by using Equation 4.

$$FR = \left[(T-1)(N-1)R_{AVE} + 1)\right] \tag{4}$$

The FR test statistic is asymptotically χ^2 distributed with (T-1) degrees of freedom. Here, R_{AVE} denotes the mean Spearman correlation coefficient.

Frees Cross-Sectional Dependence Test

Frees (1995) proposed a test based on the sum of the squares of the rank correlation coefficients. The test statistic for Frees is shown in Equation 5.

$$FRE = N\left(R_{AVE}^2 - (T-1)^{-1}\right) \tag{5}$$

R_{AVE}^2 denotes the squares of the rank correlation coefficients and is calculated by using the formula in Equation 6.

$$R_{AVE}^2 = \left[\frac{2}{N(N-1)}\right]^2 \sum_{i=1}^{N-1}\sum_{j=i+1}^{N} \hat{r}_{ij}^2 \doteq \frac{2}{N(N-1)}\sum_{i=1}^{N-1}\sum_{j=i+1}^{N} \hat{r}_{ij}^2 \tag{6}$$

Panel unit root tests that take information about both time and cross-sectional dimensions of the data into consideration are considered to be statistically stronger than time-series unit root tests which take only time dimension information into account (Im, Pesaran and Shin, 2003; Maddala and Wu, 1999; Taylor and Sarno, 1998; Levin, Lin and Chu, 2002; Hadri, 2000; Pesaran, 2007; Beyaert and Camacho, 2008). Because, the inclusion of cross-sectional dimension in the analysis increases variability (Charemza and Deadman, 1997). The first problem encountered in the panel unit root test is to determine whether or not the cross-sections that formed the panel are independent of each other. Panel unit root tests are divided into two categories at this point, namely, the first- and the second-generation tests. The first-generation tests are divided into two groups according to whether the cross-sections that formed the panel are homogeneous or heterogeneous. Levin, Lin and Chu (2002), Breitung (2005), and Hadri (2000) are based on the assumption of homogeneity; while Im, Pesaran and Shin (2003), Maddala and Wu (1999), and Choi (2001) are based on the assumption of heterogeneity. The first-generation unit root tests are based on the assumption that the cross-sectional units that formed the panel are independent of each other and that all other cross-sectional units are influenced at the same level by the shock initially experienced by one of the units. To eliminate this shortcoming, the second-generation unit root tests that analyze stationarity by taking the dependence among cross-sectional units into consideration have been developed. The major second-generation unit root tests include Multivariate Augmented Dickey-Fuller (MADF) developed by Taylor and Sarno (1998), Seemingly Unrelated Regression Augmented Dickey-Fuller (SURADF) developed by Breuer et al. (2002), and Cross-sectional Augmented Dickey-Fuller (CADF) developed by Pesaran (2007). In this study, Pesaran (2007) CADF unit root test is used in order to determine stationarity of the series.

Pesaran Panel Unit Root Test (CADF)

Pesaran (2007) The CADF test is the extended version of the ADF regression along with the cross-section averages of the first-differences and lagged levels of the individual series. In the test, the individual results for each cross-section are obtained by CADF statistics, while cross-sectionally augmented IPS (CIPS) statistics developed by obtaining means are used. The CADF test provides highly consistent results even if the cross-section (N) and time (T) dimensions are relatively small. Also, this test can be used when both *T*> *N* and *N*> *T* (Pesaran, 2007). Simple CADF regression is indicated in Equation 7.

$$\Delta Y_{it} = \alpha_i + \rho_i^* Y_{i,t-1} + d_0 \bar{Y}_{t-1} + d_1 \Delta \bar{Y}_t + \varepsilon_{it} \tag{7}$$

Here, $\bar{Y}_t$ is the mean of all N observations with respect to time. The lagged cross-section means and the existence of the first differences take the interunit correlation into account via a factor structure.

In Equation 7, $\alpha_i = (1 - \varnothing_i)\mu_i$, $\rho_i^* = -(1 - \varnothing_i)$ and $\Delta Y_{it} = Y_{it} - Y_{i,t-1}$. Accordingly, given $\varnothing_i = 1$, the hypotheses of the CADF unit root test are constructed as in Equation 8.

$$H_0 = \rho_i^* = 0 \left(The\, series\, is\, not\, stationary\, for\, all\, i \right) \tag{8}$$

$H_A = \rho_i^* < 0\left(The\, series\, is\, stationary\, for\, all\, i\right)$

In cases where the series of economic variables contain a unit root, the linear composition of these series may be stationary, and the series may be associated in the long-term. There are many panel cointegration tests used in the literature. These include Kao panel cointegration test, Pedroni panel cointegration test, McCoskey panel cointegration test, Hanck panel cointegration test, and Westerlund panel cointegration test. In this study, the long-run relationship between variables is tested using the Pedroni panel cointegration test.

Pedroni Panel Cointegration Test

The Pedroni panel cointegration test takes heterogeneity of the cointegration vector into consideration. This test allows dynamic and stationary effects to be different from the panel and also allows the co-integrated vector to be different among the cross-sections (Dökmen and Aysu, 2010). Pedroni (1995, 1997) used two variant models for cointegration analysis, whereas Pedroni (1999) used multivariable regression models (Pedroni, 1999).

The Pedroni cointegration test allows heterogeneity in the cointegration vector and not only allows dynamic and fixed effects to be different between the cross sections of the panel but also permits the cointegrated vector to be different between the cross-sections under the alternative hypothesis.

Pedroni cointegration tests can be divided into two categories. In the first category, the averages of the cointegration tests calculated separately for the time-series of all units are used. In the second category tests, the averages are made of fractures. The first category consists of three tests, namely, group ρ statistic, group t statistic (nonparametric), and group t statistic (parametric); whereas the second category consists of four tests, namely, panel v statistics, panel ρ statistics, panel t statistics (nonparametric), and panel t statistics (parametric).

Empirical Results

In order to explain the long-term relationships among economic growth, foreign direct investment and trade, firstly the cross-sectional dependence characteristics of the series are tried to be determined. To this end, Breusch-Pagan Lagrange multiplier, Pesaran, Friedman and Frees cross-sectional dependence tests are applied and the results are shown in Table 3.

Table 3. Cross-sectional dependence test results

Cointegration Equation	Breusch-Pagan LM	Pesaran	Friedman	Frees
GDPG = f(FDI, TR)	714.349 (0.000)	11.408 (0.000)	141.703 (0.000)	0.753 (0.000)

Note: The values in the parentheses indicate probability values.

The null hypotheses of the tests are rejected since the probability values of the four tests performed to determine the cross-sectional dependence are lower than 5%. That is to say; there is cross-sectional dependence among the series. As the cross-sectional dependence is detected among the series, CADF test as the second generation unit root test is performed. The CADF unit root test results are indicated in Table 4.

Upon the evaluation of the obtained results, the null hypothesis which expresses the stationarity at level is rejected since the CADF test values are lower than the critical table value. According to the results of CADF unit root test performed by taking the first differences, the null hypothesis is accepted since the test values are higher than the critical values at 1%, 5%, and 10% significance levels. Thus, the three variables included in the analysis are not stationary at level, and they are stationary [I (1)] when the first differences are taken.

The Pedroni panel cointegration test is applied in order to determine whether or not a long-term relationship among the series exist as the next step after determining that the series are difference stationary. The Pedroni panel cointegration test results are shown in Table 5.

As mentioned in the econometric methodology section, there are seven (four in-group and three out-group) different tests for panel cointegration. In the cointegration equation, the cointegration relationship between the dependent variable, namely, economic growth and independent variables, namely, FDI and trade is investigated. According to the results of the Pedroni cointegration test, the null hypothesis suggesting no cointegration among the series at 1% significance level is rejected in all seven tests. So, the series are cointegrated in the long-term.

The *pooled mean group estimator* (PMGE) method is used to obtain the long-run coefficients after determining that the series are cointegrated, meaning that they are related in the long-run. The most important advantage of the PMGE method is that it predicts both the short- and the long-term parameters by constructing an error-correction model. The error-correction model to be constructed is shown in Equation 8.

Table 4. CADF unit root test results

		Critical Values			Probability Value
At Level	CADF Test Value	1%	5%	10%	
GDPG	-1.204	-2.080	-2.160	-2.300	0.243
FDI	-1.747	-2.080	-2.160	-2.300	0.456
TR	-1.802	-2.080	-2.160	-2.300	0.429
		Critical Values			Probability Value
1st Differences	CADF Test Value	1%	5%	10%	
GDPG	-3.024	-2.080	-2.160	-2.300	0.000
FDI	-2.762	-2.080	-2.160	-2.300	0.000
TR	-3.287	-2.080	-2.160	-2.300	0.000

Table 5. Pedroni panel cointegration test results

Pedroni Cointegration Tests	Test Statistic	Probability Value
Panel v statistic	7.17	0.000
Panel ρ statistic	-16.28	0.000
Panel *t* statistic	-17.75	0.000
Panel *t* statistic	-15.63	0.000
Group ρ statistic	-15.08	0.000
Group *t* statistic	-21.02	0.000
Group *t* statistic	-16.85	0.000

$$\Delta Y_{it} = \varnothing_i Y_{i,t-1} + \beta_i^{'} X_{it} + \sum_{J=1}^{p-1} \lambda_{ij} \Delta Y_{i,t-j} + \sum_{j=0}^{q-1} \delta_{ij} \Delta X_{i,t-j} + \varepsilon_{it} \quad (9)$$

Here, $\varnothing_i$ denotes the error correction parameter. Given that $\varnothing_i$ is significant and negative, the existence of a long-run relationship between Y_{it} and X_{it} is confirmed. PMGE estimation results are shown in Table 6.

The error-correction parameter is statistically significant since it is negative and the probability value is lower than 5% according to the estimation results. This parameter indicates the rate at which the short-term deviations resulting from non-stationarity of the series converge toward the equilibrium level within the next period. Thus, approximately 77% of disequilibrium occurring in a period would be recovered in the next period and would be approaching to the long-term equilibrium value. In addition, the coefficients that indicate the long-term impacts of FDI and trade on economic growth are also identified. Accordingly, the coefficients of both variables are statistically significant. A 1% rise in both FDI and trade increase economic growth by 0.24% and 0.02%, respectively.

Table 6. PMGE results

Variables	Coefficients	Standart Errors	Probability Values
FDI	0.244	0.0671	0.000
TR	0.026	0.0094	0.005
Error-Correction Coefficient	-0.774	0.0498	0.000

CONCLUSION

The globalization movements that have been felt since the second half of the last century have shown a remarkable increase within the last 30 years and have brought forth a progressive FDI mobility especially throughout the last 20 years. The FDI movements that began to spread all around the world in the 1980s gained a considerable momentum following the disintegration of the East Block in the 1990s and afterward. The mutual relationship between the FDIs and globalization has led to a simultaneous increase in both concepts.

Thus, for the countries that involve in foreign investments, a new era had dawned through which those countries could have been exposed to positive and negative impacts of FDI since it took a certain place in their development strategies. Most foreign-invested countries wish to embrace FDI in order to gain the advantage of its positive effects along with the perception that FDI's positive impacts would outweigh the detrimental effects from which those countries are likely to suffer in many cases.

Middle-income countries need foreign capital inflow due to having insufficient capital and savings. FDIs for these countries are considered to be more advantageous in comparison with other external financing sources. Because FDI is a more reliable means of finance due to its long-term structure. FDIs cannot instantly leave the host country in the event of an economic crisis or other extraordinary processes. FDI also has potential to create other positive impacts such as transferring technology toward the host country and strengthening human capital.

In the econometric analysis part of the study, the cross-sectional dependence tests are applied to obtain more healthy and reliable results prior to performing unit root and cointegration tests in accordance with the panel data analysis methodology. There are several tests in the literature to test the existence of the cross-sectional dependence. The Breusch-Pagan Lagrange multiplier, Pesaran, Friedman and Frees cross-sectional dependence tests are used to analyze the cross-sectional dependence. The null hypotheses of the tests are rejected since the probability values of all four tests performed to determine the cross-sectional dependence are lower than 5%. In other words, the existence of the cross-sectional dependence among the series is determined.

The unit root and cointegration tests to be selected for the determination of the cross-sectional dependence must take this feature of the series into account. In the literature, unit root and cointegration tests that take the cross-sectional dependence into consideration are called the second generation tests. Pesaran (2007) CADF unit root test, as one of the second generation unit root tests, is utilized in order to determine the stationarity characteristics in the series. Upon evaluation of the results obtained in the CADF test, the null hypothesis expressing stationarity at level is rejected since the CADF test values at level are lower than the critical table value. According to the CADF unit root test results obtained after taking the first differences, the null hypothesis is accepted since the test values are higher than the critical values at 1%, 5%, and 10% significance levels. Thus, it is determined that all three variables included in the analysis are non-stationary at level, and they are stationary [I (1)] upon taking the first differences.

The Pedroni panel cointegration test, as one of the second-generation cointegration tests, is applied in order to determine whether or not a long-term relationship exists between the series after they are found to be difference stationary. According to the results of the Pedroni cointegration test, the null hypothesis suggesting no cointegration among the series at 1% significance level is rejected in all seven tests. So, there is a long-term cointegration among the series. The PMGE method is used to obtain the long-run coefficients after determining whether or not the series are co-integrated, in other words, they are related in the long-run.

According to PMGE estimation results, the error-correction parameter is statistically significant since it is negative and the probability value is lower than 5%. This parameter denotes the rate at which the short-term deviations stemming from non-stationarity of the series converge to the equilibrium within the next period. According to this, approximately 77% of disequilibrium occurring in a period would be recovered within the next period. Moreover, the coefficients of FDI and trade which have long-term impacts on economic growth are also identified. Accordingly, the coefficients of both variables are statistically significant. A 1% increase in FDI and trade increase economic growth by 0.24% and 0.02%, respectively.

Upon considering the contribution of FDI to growth in the middle-income countries, it is necessary to gain more advantages of FDIs. In this context, R&D studies should be carried out in order to attract FDI toward the country, the capacity of the country to create technological innovation should be increased, and a qualified labor force structure should be implemented. It is evident that FDI made toward the middle-income countries would contribute more to economic growth and employment contingent upon implementing those investments regarding creating employment, technology, and new high value-added investments.

REFERENCES

Abbes, S. M., Mostéfa, B., Seghir, G., & Zakarya, G. Y. (2015). Causal interactions between FDI, and economic growth: Evidence from dynamic panel co-integration. *Procedia Economics and Finance, 23*, 276–290. doi:10.1016/S2212-5671(15)00541-9

Abdouli, M., & Hammami, S. (2017). The impact of FDI inflows and environmental quality on economic growth: An empirical study for the MENA Countries. *Journal of the Knowledge Economy, 8*(1), 254–278. doi:10.100713132-015-0323-y

Alfaro, L., Chanda, A., Kalemli-Ozcan, S., & Sayek, S. (2006). *How does foreign direct investment promote economic growth? Exploring the effects of financial markets on linkages (No. w12522)*. National Bureau of Economic Research. doi:10.3386/w12522

Alfaro, L., Chanda, A., Kalemli-Ozcan, S., & Sayek, S. (2010). Does foreign direct investment promote growth? Exploring the role of financial markets on linkages. *Journal of Development Economics, 91*(2), 242–256. doi:10.1016/j.jdeveco.2009.09.004

Almfraji, M. A., Almsafir, M. K., & Yao, L. (2014). Economic growth and foreign direct investment inflows: The case of Qatar. *Procedia: Social and Behavioral Sciences, 109*, 1040–1045. doi:10.1016/j.sbspro.2013.12.586

Ayaydın, H. (2010). Doğrudan yabancı yatırımlar ile ekonomik büyüme arasındaki ilişkinin incelenmesi: Türkiye örneği [Evaluating relationship between foreign direct investment and economic growth: Turkey example]. *Dumlupınar Üniversitesi Sosyal Bilimler Dergisi, 26*(1), 133–145.

Balasubramanyam, V. N., Salisu, M., & Sapsford, D. (1996). Foreign direct investment and growth in EP and IS countries. *Economic Journal (London), 106*(434), 92–105. doi:10.2307/2234933

Barry, F., & Bradley, J. (1997). FDI and trade: The Irish host-country experience. *Economic Journal (London), 107*(445), 1798–1811. doi:10.1111/j.1468-0297.1997.tb00083.x

Beyaert, A., & Camacho, M. (2008). TAR panel unit root tests and real convergence. *Review of Development Economics, 12*(3), 668–681. doi:10.1111/j.1467-9361.2008.00479.x

Borensztein, E., De Gregorio, J., & Lee, J. W. (1998). How does foreign direct investment affect economic growth? 1. *Journal of International Economics, 45*(1), 115–135. doi:10.1016/S0022-1996(97)00033-0

Breitung, J. (2005). A parametric approach to the estimation of cointegration vectors in panel data. *Econometric Reviews, 24*(2), 151–173. doi:10.1081/ETC-200067895

Breuer, J. B., McNown, R., & Wallace, M. (2002). Series-Specific Unit Root Tests with Panel Data. *Oxford Bulletin of Economics and Statistics, 64*(5), 527–546. doi:10.1111/1468-0084.00276

Breusch, T. S., & Pagan, A. R. (1980). The Lagrange multiplier test and its applications to model specification in econometrics. *The Review of Economic Studies, 47*(1), 239–253. doi:10.2307/2297111

Charemza, W. W., & Deadman, D.F. (1997). New Directions in Econometric Practice: General to Specific Modelling, Cointegration and Vector Autoregression (2nd ed.). Edward Elgar Publishing.

Choi, I. (2001). Unit root tests for panel data. *Journal of International Money and Finance, 20*(2), 249–272. doi:10.1016/S0261-5606(00)00048-6

Denisia, V. (2010). Foreign Direct Investment Theories: An Overview of the Main FDI Theories. *European Journal of Interdisciplinary Studies*, 3.

Dökmen, G., & Aysu, A. (2010). Hükümet İstikrarının Doğrudan Yabancı Yatırımlar Üzerindeki Etkisi: Gelişmekte Olan Ülkelere İlişkin Ampirik Bir Çalışma. *Journal of Yaşar University, 5*(18), 3028–3037.

Dritsaki, C., & Stiakakis, E. (2014). Foreign direct investments, exports, and economic growth in Croatia: A time series analysis. *Procedia Economics and Finance, 14*, 181–190. doi:10.1016/S2212-5671(14)00701-1

Dunning, J. H. (2001). The eclectic (OLI) paradigm of international production: Past, present and future. *International Journal of the Economics of Business, 8*(2), 173–190. doi:10.1080/13571510110051441

Egger, P., & Winner, H. (2005). Evidence on corruption as an incentive for foreign direct investment. *European Journal of Political Economy, 21*(4), 932–952. doi:10.1016/j.ejpoleco.2005.01.002

Ericsson, J., & Irandoust, M. (2010). On The Causalıty Between Foreign Direct Investment and Output: A Comparative Study. *The International Trade Journal, 15*(1), 1–26. doi:10.1080/088539001300005431

Frees, E. W. (1995). Assessing cross-sectional correlation in panel data. *Journal of Econometrics, 69*(2), 393–414. doi:10.1016/0304-4076(94)01658-M

Friedman, M. (1937). The use of ranks to avoid the assumption of normality implicit in the analysis of variance. *Journal of the American Statistical Association, 32*(200), 675–701. doi:10.1080/01621459.1937.10503522

Hadri, K. (2000). Testing for stationarity in heterogeneous panel data. *The Econometrics Journal, 3*(2), 148–161. doi:10.1111/1368-423X.00043

Hildreth, C. (1950). *Combining Cross-Section Data and Time Series.* Cowles Comission Discussion Paper, No:347.

Hong, L. (2014). Does and how does FDI promote the economic growth? Evidence from dynamic panel data of prefecture city in China. *IERI Procedia, 6*, 57–62. doi:10.1016/j.ieri.2014.03.010

Hsiao, C. (2007). Panel data analysis—Advantages and challenges. *Test, 16*(1), 1–22. doi:10.100711749-007-0046-x

Hussain, M. E., & Haque, M. (2016). Foreign direct investment, trade, and economic growth: An empirical analysis of Bangladesh. *Economies, 4*(2), 7. doi:10.3390/economies4020007

Iamsiraroj, S. (2016). The foreign direct investment–economic growth nexus. *International Review of Economics & Finance, 42*, 116–133. doi:10.1016/j.iref.2015.10.044

Im, K. S., Pesaran, M. H., & Shin, Y. (2003). Testing for unit roots in heterogeneous panels. *Journal of Econometrics, 115*(1), 53–74. doi:10.1016/S0304-4076(03)00092-7

Kuh, E. (1959). The validity of cross-sectionally estimated behavior equations in time series applications. *Econometrica, 27*(2), 197–214. doi:10.2307/1909442

Lairson, T. D., & Skidmore, D. (2017). *International Political Economy: The Struggle for Power and Wealth in a Globalizing World.* Taylor & Francis.

Levin, A., Lin, C. F., & Chu, C. S. J. (2002). Unit root tests in panel data: Asymptotic and finite-sample properties. *Journal of Econometrics, 108*(1), 1–24. doi:10.1016/S0304-4076(01)00098-7

Lewer, J. (2002). International trade composition and medium-run growth: Evidence of a causal relationship. *The International Trade Journal, 16*(3), 295–317. doi:10.1080/08853900290090809

Li, X., & Liu, X. (2005). Foreign direct investment and economic growth: An increasingly endogenous relationship. *World Development, 33*(3), 393–407. doi:10.1016/j.worlddev.2004.11.001

Lipsey, R. E. (2002). *Home and Host Country Effects of FDI.* National Bureau of Economic Research Working Paper Series, No: 9293.

Maddala, G. S., & Wu, S. (1999). A comparative study of unit root tests with panel data and a new simple test. *Oxford Bulletin of Economics and Statistics, 61*(s1), 631–652. doi:10.1111/1468-0084.61.s1.13

Markusen, J. R., & Venables, A. J. (1999). Foreign direct investment as a catalyst for industrial development. *European Economic Review, 43*(2), 335–356. doi:10.1016/S0014-2921(98)00048-8

Mencinger, J. (2003). Does foreign direct investment always enhance economic growth? *Kyklos, 56*(4), 491–508. doi:10.1046/j.0023-5962.2003.00235.x

Menyah, K., Nazlioglu, S., & Wolde-Rufael, Y. (2014). Financial development, trade openness and economic growth in African countries: New insights from a panel causality approach. *Economic Modelling*, *37*, 386–394. doi:10.1016/j.econmod.2013.11.044

Moran, T. H. (2005). How Does FDI Affect Host Country Development? Using Industry Case Studies to Make Reliable Generalizations. In T. H. Moran, E.M. Graham, & M. Blomström, (Eds.), Institute for International Economics, Center for Global Development, Does Foreign Direct Investment Promote Development? Washington, DC: Automated Graphic System Inc.

Nair-Reichert, U., & Weinhold, D. (2001). Causality tests for cross-country panels: A New look at FDI and economic growth in developing countries. *Oxford Bulletin of Economics and Statistics*, *63*(2), 153–171. doi:10.1111/1468-0084.00214

Nistor, P. (2014). FDI and economic growth, the case of Romania. *Procedia Economics and Finance*, *15*, 577–582. doi:10.1016/S2212-5671(14)00514-0

Pedroni, P. (1995). *Panel Cointegration; Asymptotic and Finite Sample Properties of Pooled Time Series Tests, with an Application to the PPP Hypothesis.* Indiana University Working Papers in Economics, No. 95-013.

Pedroni, P. (1997). *Panel Cointegration; Asympt otic and Finite Sample Properties of Pooled Time Series Tests, with an Application to the PPP Hypothesis: New Results.* Working Paper Indiana University.

Pedroni, P. (1999). Critical values for cointegration tests in heterogeneous panels with multiple regressors. *Oxford Bulletin of Economics and Statistics*, *61*(s1), 653–670. doi:10.1111/1468-0084.61.s1.14

Pesaran, M. H. (2007). A simple panel unit root test in the presence of cross-section dependence. *Journal of Applied Econometrics*, *22*(2), 265–312. doi:10.1002/jae.951

Pinto, P. M., & Zhu, B. (2008). *Fortune of Evil? The Effects of Inward Foreign Direct Investment on Corruption.* Saltzman Working Paper, No: 10.

Poelhekke, S., & van der Ploeg, F. (2010). *Do Natural Resources Attract FDI? Evidence from Non-Stationary Sector Level Data.* Oxford University, Department of Economics, OxCarre (Oxford Centre for the Analysis of Resource Rich Economies) Research Paper, No:51.

Portelli, B., & Narula, R. (2006). Foreign direct investment through acquisitions and implications for technological upgrading: Case evidence from Tanzania. *European Journal of Development Research*, *18*(1), 59–85. doi:10.1080/09578810600572387

Rodriguez, F., & Rodrik, D. (2000). Trade policy and economic growth: A skeptic's guide to the cross-national evidence. *NBER Macroeconomics Annual*, *15*, 261–325. doi:10.1086/654419

Sarkar, P. (2007). *Does Foreign Direct Investment Promote Growth? Panel Data and Time Series Evidence from Less Developed Countries, 1970-2002.* MRPA Paper, No. 5176.

Sun, X. (2002). *Foreign Direct Investment and Economic Development: What Do the States Need to Do?* Prepared by the Foreign Investment Advisory Service for the Capacity Development Workshops and Global Forum on Reinventing Government on Globalization, Role of the State and Enabling Environment, Marrakech, Morocco.

Swamy, P. A. (1970). Efficient inference in a random coefficient regression model. *Econometrica*, *38*(2), 311–323. doi:10.2307/1913012

Tan, B. W., & Tang, C. F. (2016). Examining the causal linkages among domestic investment, FDI, trade, interest rate and economic growth in ASEAN-5 countries. *International Journal of Economics and Financial Issues*, *6*(1).

Taylor, M. P., & Sarno, L. (1998). The behavior of real exchange rates during the post-Bretton Woods period. *Journal of International Economics*, *46*(2), 281–312. doi:10.1016/S0022-1996(97)00054-8

Umoh, O. J., Jacob, A. O., & Chuku, C. A. (2012). Foreign direct investment and economic growth in Nigeria: An analysis of the endogenous effects. *Current Research Journal of Economic Theory*, *4*(3), 53–66.

United Nations. (2014). *World Economic Situation and Prospects 2014*. UN.

Vernon, R. (1966). International Investment and International Trade in the Product Cycle. *The Quarterly Journal of Economics*, *80*(2), 191. doi:10.2307/1880689

Wang, M. (2009). Manufacturing FDI and economic growth: Evidence from Asian economies. *Applied Economics*, *41*(8), 991–1002. doi:10.1080/00036840601019059

Yapraklı, S. (2006). Türkiye'de Doğrudan Yabanci Yatirimlarin Ekonomik Belirleyicileri Üzerine Ekonometrik Bir Analiz. *Dokuz Eylül Üniversitesi İİBF Dergisi*, *21*(2), 23–48.

Zhang, K. H. (2001). Does foreign direct investment promote economic growth? Evidence from East Asia and Latin America. *Contemporary Economic Policy*, *19*(2), 175–185. doi:10.1111/j.1465-7287.2001.tb00059.x

Compilation of References

Abbes, S. M., Mostéfa, B., Seghir, G., & Zakarya, G. Y. (2015). Causal interactions between FDI, and economic growth: Evidence from dynamic panel co-integration. *Procedia Economics and Finance*, *23*, 276–290. doi:10.1016/S2212-5671(15)00541-9

Abdouli, M., & Hammami, S. (2017). The impact of FDI inflows and environmental quality on economic growth: An empirical study for the MENA Countries. *Journal of the Knowledge Economy*, *8*(1), 254–278. doi:10.100713132-015-0323-y

Abouharb, M. R., & Cingranelli, D. (2007). *Human rights and structural adjustment*. Cambridge University Press.

Acar, M., & Bilir, H. (2013). Türkiye'de Sivil Anayasa Arayışları, Anayasal İktisat ve Anayasada Bulunması Gereken İktisadi-Mali Hükümler. *KMÜ Sosyal ve Ekonomik Araştırmalar Dergisi*, *15*(24), 87–96.

Acartürk, E. (2001). Yerel yönetimlerin hizmet sunumunda alternatif yöntemler. *Balıkesir Üniversitesi Sosyal Bilimler Dergisi*, *6*, 46–59.

Acharya, V. V. (2011). *Systemic risk and macro-prudential regulation*. Unpublished working paper. Retrieved from http://pages.stern.nyu.edu/~sternfin/vacharya/public_html/ADB%20Systemic%20Risk%20and%20Macroprudential%20Regulation%20-%20Final%20-%20March%202011.pdf

Acharya, V. V., & Richardson, M. (2009). Causes of the financial crisis. *Critical Review*, *21*(2-3), 195–21. doi:10.1080/08913810902952903

Acht, M., Mahmoud, T. O., & Thiele, R. (2015). Corrupt governments do not receive more state-to-state aid: Governance and the delivery of foreign aid through non-state actors. *Journal of Development Economics*, *114*, 20–33. doi:10.1016/j.jdeveco.2014.11.005

Addison, T., Morrissey, O., & Tarp, F. (2017). The Macroeconomics of Aid: Overview. *The Journal of Development Studies*, *53*(7), 987–997. doi:10.1080/00220388.2017.1303669

Afonso, A., & Jalles, J. T. (2013). Growth and productivity: The role of government debt. *International Review of Economics & Finance*, *25*, 384–407. doi:10.1016/j.iref.2012.07.004

Akçaoğlu, E. (2015). *Beps action 7: preventing artificial avoidance of parmanent establishment status.* Text of Speech, International Tax Law Conferences Series 5, Preventing Base Erosion and Profit Shifting in Taxation, Politcs, Law, Action, ANAMED, İstanbul, Turkey.

Akçaoğlu, E. (2018). Beps action 7: preventing artificial avoidance of parmanent establishment status. In *Base Erosion and Profit Shifting in Taxation, International Tax Law Conferences Series-5* (pp. 327-349). Beta Press.

Akdoğan, A. (2002). *Public Finance.* Ankara: Gazi Press.

Akduğan, U. (2017). Türkiye'de dış borç stokunun belirleyicileri. *Business and Economics Research Journal, 8*(2), 183–202.

Aktan, C. C., & Vural, İ. Y. (2004). *Global Terror Problem.* Retrieved June 8, 2018, from http://canaktan.org/yeni-trendler/global-sorunlar/global-teror.htm

Aktan, C. C., Dileyici, D., & Istiklal, Y. V. (2006). Contemporary Approaches in Public Finance. In C. C. Aktan & İ. Y. Vural (Eds.), *Change in Globalization and Fiscal Policy.* Ankara: Seçkin Publishing.

Alesina, A., & Dollar, D. (2000). Who gives foreign aid to whom and why? *Journal of Economic Growth, 5*(1), 33–63. doi:10.1023/A:1009874203400

Alfaro, L., Chanda, A., Kalemli-Ozcan, S., & Sayek, S. (2006). *How does foreign direct investment promote economic growth? Exploring the effects of financial markets on linkages (No. w12522).* National Bureau of Economic Research. doi:10.3386/w12522

Alfaro, L., Chanda, A., Kalemli-Ozcan, S., & Sayek, S. (2010). Does foreign direct investment promote growth? Exploring the role of financial markets on linkages. *Journal of Development Economics, 91*(2), 242–256. doi:10.1016/j.jdeveco.2009.09.004

Al-Fawwaz, T. M. (2016). Determinants of External Debt in Jordan: An Empirical Study (1990–2014). *International Business Research, 9*(7), 116–123.

Alganer, Y., & Yılmaz, Ö. (2016). OECD model tax agreement and relation between permanent establishment and transfer pricing. *Marmara University, Journal of Economics and Administrative Sciences, 38*(2), 45–61. doi:10.14780/muiibd.281307

Allen, F., & Gale, D. (2000). Corporate Governance and Competition. In X. Vives (Ed.), *Corporate Governance: Theoretical and Empirical Perspectives.* Cambridge, UK: Cambridge University Press. doi:10.1017/CBO9781139175333.003

Almfraji, M. A., Almsafir, M. K., & Yao, L. (2014). Economic growth and foreign direct investment inflows: The case of Qatar. *Procedia: Social and Behavioral Sciences, 109*, 1040–1045. doi:10.1016/j.sbspro.2013.12.586

Ar, K. N. (2016). Example of Turkey Income Inequality in the 21st Century. *Entrepreneurship and Development Journal, 10*(2), 187–202.

Arun, T. G., & Turner, J. D. (2002). Financial Sector Reform in Developing Countries: The Indian Experience. *World Economy*, *25*(3), 429–445. doi:10.1111/1467-9701.00440

Asher, M. G., & Rajan, R. S. (1999). *Globalization and Tax Systems: Implications for Developing Countries with Particular Reference to Southeast Asia.* Centre for International Economic Studies and Scholl of Economics University of Adelaide, Discussion Paper 99/23.

Assibey-Yeboah, M., & Mohsin, M. (2014). The real effects of inflation in a developing economy with external debt and sovereign risk. *The North American Journal of Economics and Finance*, *30*, 40–55. doi:10.1016/j.najef.2014.07.004

Atac, B. (2006). *Maliye Politikası, Gelişimi, Amaçları, Araçları ve Uygulama Sorunları.* Eskişehir, Turkey: Etam Press. Retrieved from https://www.ab.gov.tr/index_en.php

Ateş, L. (2018). Beps action 13: Documantation in transfer pricing. In *Base Erosion and Profit Shifting in Taxation, International Tax Law Conferences Series-5* (pp. 369-397). Beta Press.

Atik, H., & Ünlü, F. (2017). Science performance of Turkey in 21st century: A multivariate statistical comparison with the OECD countries. In H. Arapgirlioğlu, A. Atik, R. L. Elliott, & E. Turgeon (Eds.), *Researches on science and art in 21st century* (pp. 1030–1038). Ankara: Gece Kitaplığı.

Awan, R. U., Anjum, A., & Rahim, S. (2015). An Econometric Analysis of Determinants of External Debt in Pakistan. *British Journal of Economics, Management & Trade*, *5*(4), 382–391.

Ayaydın, H. (2010). Doğrudan yabancı yatırımlar ile ekonomik büyüme arasındaki ilişkinin incelenmesi: Türkiye örneği [Evaluating relationship between foreign direct investment and economic growth: Turkey example]. *Dumlupınar Üniversitesi Sosyal Bilimler Dergisi*, *26*(1), 133–145.

Aysu, A. (2010). Gelişmiş Ülkelerde Maliye Politikası Kurallarının İhlaline İlişkin Başlıca Yaptırımlar. *Maliye Dergisi*, *158*(January-June), 468–469.

Azzimonti, M., de Francisco, E., & Quadrini, V. (2012). *Financial Globalization and the Rising of Public Debt.* Retrieved March 26, 2018, from http://www-bcf.usc.edu/~quadrini/papers/PDpap.pdf

Baglan, D., & Yoldas, E. (2013). *Government debt and macroeconomic activity: a predictive analysis for advanced economies.* Board of Governors of the Federal Reserve System.

Bai, A., Hira, S., & Deshpande, P. S. (2015). An application of factor analysis in the evaluation of country economic rank. *Procedia Computer Science*, *54*, 311–317. doi:10.1016/j.procs.2015.06.036

Bailey, J. S. (1999). *Local government economics.* London: Macmillan Press Ltd. doi:10.1007/978-1-349-27415-4

Bakaric, I. R. (2005). Uncovering regional disparities – the use of factor and cluster analysis. *Economic Trends and Economic Policy*, *105*, 52–77.

Balasubramanyam, V. N., Salisu, M., & Sapsford, D. (1996). Foreign direct investment and growth in EP and IS countries. *Economic Journal (London)*, *106*(434), 92–105. doi:10.2307/2234933

Bali, B. B., & Celen, M. (2010). Mali Kurallar, Maliye Politikası Yönetiminde Yeni Bir Eğilim: Kurallar ve Sınırlamalar Vergi, Harcama, Borçlanma vs. Üzerine Kurallar ve Sınırlamalar. In Avrupa Birliği'nde Mali Kurallar. Maliye Bakanlığı SGB (Ministry of Finance).

Ball, L. (2016). *The Fed and Lehman Brothers: Introduction and Summary*. Cambridge, MA: National Bureau of Economic Research. doi:10.3386/w22410

Ball, L. M. (1999). Policy Rules for Open Economies. In *Monetary policy rules* (pp. 127–156). University of Chicago Press.

Baltagi, B. H. (2008). *Econometric Analysis of Panel Data*. West Sussex, UK: John Wiley.

Bandyopadhyay, S., & Wall, H. J. (2007). The determinants of aid in the post-cold war era. *Federal Reserve Bank of St Louis Review*, *89*(6), 533–547.

Barro, R. (1979). On the determination of public debt. *Journal of Political Economy*, *87*(5, Part 1), 240–270. doi:10.1086/260807

Barry, F., & Bradley, J. (1997). FDI and trade: The Irish host-country experience. *Economic Journal (London)*, *107*(445), 1798–1811. doi:10.1111/j.1468-0297.1997.tb00083.x

Barua, S.K., Varma, J.R., & Venkiteswaran, N. (1991). A Regulatory Framework for Mutual Fund. *Economic and Political Weekly*, *26*(21), 55-59.

Baum, A., Checherita-Westphal, C., & Rother, P. (2013). Debt and growth: New evidence for the euro area. *Journal of International Money and Finance*, *32*, 809–821. doi:10.1016/j.jimonfin.2012.07.004

Bauman, Z. (2016). *Social Results of Globalization* (6th ed.; A. Yılmaz, Trans.). İstanbul: Ayrıntı Publication.

Bauman, Z. (2018). *The Search for Politics* (4th ed.; T. Birkan, Trans.). İstanbul: Metis Publishing.

Baunsgaard, T., & Keen, M. (2005). *Tax revenue and (or?) trade liberalization*. IMF Working Paper No. 2005(112). Washington, DC: IMF.

Baunsgaard, T., & Keen, M. (2005). *Tax Revenue and (or?) Trade Liberalization*. International Monetary Fund, IMF Working Paper, No: WP/05/112.

Bayar, Y. (2014). Comparatıve Analysıs Of Eurozone Sovereıgn Debt Crısıs And European Exchange-Rate Mechanısm Crısıs. *Management and Economics Research Journal*, (22), 211-231.

Bayar, F. (2008). The concept of Globalization and the Globalization Process in Turkey. *International Economic Issues Journal*, *32*, 25–34.

Bayramoğlu, T., & Başar, E. E. (2016). *Globalization: Economic and Social Trends*. Ankara: Savaş Publication.

Bénétrix, A. S., & Lane, P. R. (2013). Fiscal cyclicality and EMU. *Journal of International Money and Finance*, *34*, 164–176. doi:10.1016/j.jimonfin.2012.11.009

Bergin, A., Gerald, J. F., Kearney, I., & O'Sullivan, C. (2011). The Irish fiscal crisis. *National Institute Economic Review, 217*(1), R47-R59.

Berke, B. (2016). Avrupa Birligi'nde Kamu Borç Stokunun Ekonomik Büyümeye Etkisi: Panel Veri Analizi. *Sosyoekonomi, 24*(27), 121. doi:10.17233e.12580

Bermeo, S. (2017). Aid Allocation and Targeted Development in an Increasingly Connected World. *International Organization, 71*(4), 735–766. doi:10.1017/S0020818317000315

Bermeo, S., & Leblang, D. (2015). Migration and Foreign Aid. *International Organization, 69*(3), 627–657. doi:10.1017/S0020818315000119

Berthélemy, J.-C., & Tichit, A. (2004). Bilateral donors' aid allocation decisions—A three-dimensional panel analysis. *International Review of Economics & Finance, 13*(3), 253–274. doi:10.1016/j.iref.2003.11.004

Beyaert, A., & Camacho, M. (2008). TAR panel unit root tests and real convergence. *Review of Development Economics, 12*(3), 668–681. doi:10.1111/j.1467-9361.2008.00479.x

Bhattacharya, S., Boot, A. W. A., & Thakor, A. V. (1998). The Economics of Bank Regulation. *Journal of Money, Credit and Banking, 30*(4), 745–770. doi:10.2307/2601127

Bianco, K. M. (2008). *The subprime lending crisis: Causes and effects of the mortgage meltdown*. New York: CCH, Wolters Kluwer Law & Business.

Biçer & Erginay. (2015, December). BEPS action plan and the effects of turkey. *Journal of Tax Issues*, 54-68.

Biçer, R. (2018). *Taxation problems continue in the digital economy*. Retrieved from https://www.dunya.com/kose-yazisi/dijital-ekonomide-vergilendirme-sorunlari-devam-ediyor/407639

Bieckmann, F. (Ed.). (2010). *Collective self-interest, global public goods and responsible sovereignty. The Broker*, (20/21).

Bilginoğlu, M. A., & Aysu, A. (2008). Dış Borçların Ekonomik Büyüme Üzerindeki Etkisi: Türkiye Örneği. *Erciyes Üniversitesi İİBF Dergisi, 31*, 1–23.

Bilici, N. (2012). *Avrupa Birliği ve Türkiye*. Seçkin Press.

Birinci, N., & Eser, L. Y. (2017, September). BEPS action plan and evaluation in preventing tax losses and leaks. *Internatıonal Journal of Economic Studies, 3*(3), 447–459.

Bisciari, P., Eugène, B., Melyn, W., Schoonackers, R., Stinglhamber, P., & Meensel Van, L. (2015). *Analysis of policies for restoring sound*. Brussels: National Bank of Belgium.

Bittencourt, M. (2015). Determinants of Government and External Debt: Evidence from the Young Democracies of South America. *Emerging Markets Finance & Trade, 51*(3), 463–472. doi:10.1080/1540496X.2015.1025667

Blanchard, O. J. (2009). *The crisis: basic mechanisms and appropriate policies*. Washington, DC: International Monetary Fund.

Blanton, R. G., Blanton, S. L., & Peksen, D. (2015). The impact of IMF and World Bank programs on labor rights. *Political Research Quarterly*, *68*(2), 324–336. doi:10.1177/1065912915578462

Bocutoğlu, E., & Ekinci, A. (2009). Genel teori, küresel krizler ve yeniden maliye politikası. *Maliye Dergisi*, *156*(1), 66–82.

Bökemeier, B., & Greiner, A. (2015). On the relation between public debt and economic growth: An empirical investigation. *Economics and Business Letters*, *4*(4), 137–150.

Bölükbaş, M. (2016). The Relationship Between Trade Openness and External Debt in Turkey: A Cointegration Analysis. *Balkan and Near Eastern Journal of Social Sciences, 2*(4).

Bölükbaş, M., & Peker, O. (2017). Ticari Dışa Açıklık ve Dış Ticaret Hadleri Dış Borçlanma Üzerinde Etkili mi? Türkiye İçin Bir Analiz. *Sosyoekonomi*, *25*(34), 213–225.

Borensztein, E., De Gregorio, J., & Lee, J. W. (1998). How does foreign direct investment affect economic growth? 1. *Journal of International Economics*, *45*(1), 115–135. doi:10.1016/S0022-1996(97)00033-0

Bos, F., & Teulings, C. (2010). *CPB and Dutch fiscal policy in view of the financial crisis and ageing*. The Hague: CPB Netherlands Bureau for Economic Policy Analysis. doi:10.2139srn.1742181

Boughton, J. M. (2001, September). Was Suez in 1956 the First Financial Crisis of the TwentyFirst Century. *Finance & Development*, 20–23.

Boyne, G. A. (1996). Competition and Local Government: A Public Choise Perspective. *Urban Studies, 33*(4-5), 703-721.

Boyne, G. A. (1998). The determinants of variations in local service contracting: Garbage in, gabage out. *Urban Affairs Review, 34*(1), 150–164. doi:10.1177/107808749803400107

Bozdoğan, D., Buyrukoğlu, S., & Bozdoğan, K. (2013). Spahn Tax as a Derivative of Tobin Tax in the Prevention of Financial Crisis. *The Journal of Customs and Trade*, (1), 90-105.

Bozkurt, V. (2000). Globalization: Concept - Development and Approaches. *The Journal of Business Power Industry Relations and Human Resources*, *2*(1), 17–26.

Brauner, Y. (2018). International approaches to BEPS: what is BEPS? In *Base Erosion and Profit Shifting in Taxation, International Tax Law Conferences Series-5* (pp. 1-37). Beta Press.

Breitung, J. (2005). A parametric approach to the estimation of cointegration vectors in panel data. *Econometric Reviews*, *24*(2), 151–173. doi:10.1081/ETC-200067895

Bresusch, T. S., & Pagan, A. R. (1980). A Lagrange Multiplier Test and its Applications to Model Specification in Econometrics. *The Review of Economic Studies*, *47*(1), 239–253. doi:10.2307/2297111

Bretschger, L., & Hettich, F. (2002). Globalisation, Capital Mobility and Tax Competition: Theory and Evidence for OECD Countries. *European Journal of Political Economy, 18*(4), 695–716. doi:10.1016/S0176-2680(02)00115-5

Breuer, J. B., McNown, R., & Wallace, M. (2002). Series-Specific Unit Root Tests with Panel Data. *Oxford Bulletin of Economics and Statistics, 64*(5), 527–546. doi:10.1111/1468-0084.00276

Brunetti, A., & Weder, B. (1999). *More Open Economies Have Better Goverments.* Universität des Saarlandes, Economic Series, No. 9905.

Bryane, M. (2003). Theorising the Politics of Globalisation: A Critique of Transformationalism. *Journal of Economic and Social Research, 4*(2), 3–17.

Buhur, S. (2016). Türkiye'de 2000 Yılından Sonra Mali Disiplini Sağlamaya Yönelik Alınan Önlemler. Balıkesir Üniversitesi Sosyal Bilimler Enstitüsü Dergisi, 19(36), 133 – 148.

Buiter, W. H., & Rahbari, E. (2010). *Greece and the fiscal crisis in the EMU.* Centre for Policy Research Paper.

Buiter, W. H., Corsetti, G. M., & Pesenti, P. A. (1998). Princeton Studies in International Finance: Vol. 84. *Interpreting the ERM Crisis: Country Specific and Systemic Issue.*

Bülbül, K. (2004). *Globalization, Culture and Politics: Globalization Approaches in Turkish Intellectual and Political Life* (Unpublished Doctoral Dissertation). Ankara University Institue of Social Sciences, Ankara, Turkey.

Bulbul, D. (2017). *Bütçe.* Ankara, Turkey: Gazi Bookstore.

Burnside, C., & Dollar, D. (2000). Aid, Policies, and Growth. *The American Economic Review, 90*(4), 847–868. doi:10.1257/aer.90.4.847

Caballero, R. J., & Krishnamurthy, A. (2009). Global imbalances and financial fragility. *The American Economic Review, 99*(2), 584–588. doi:10.1257/aer.99.2.584

Cagé J., & Gadenne L. (2016). *Tax Revenues, Development, and the Fiscal Cost of Trade Liberalization, 1792-2006.* Warwick Economics Research Papers, No: 1132.

Cagé, J., & Gadenne, L. (2012). *The fiscal cost of trade liberalization.* PSE Working Paper, 2012-27.

Calderón, C., & Fuentes, J. R. (2013). *Government debt and economic growth.* Inter-American Development Bank, IDB-WP-424.

Caliari, A. (2005). The debt-trade connection in debt management initiatives: need for paradigm change. In Debt and Trade: Time to Make the Connections. Dublin, Ireland: Veritas Publication.

Çamurcu, Z. N. (2017). Transparency as a tool for combating tax paradise: a study based on the OECD-BEPS action plan no. 5 (2015 Final Report). *International Journal of Public Finance,* (2), 226-244.

Caner, M., Grennes, T. J., & Köhler-Geib, F. F. N. (2010). Finding the tipping point-when sovereign debt turns bad. The World Bank.

Caner, M., & Hansen, B. E. (2004). Instrumental variable estimation of a threshold model. *Econometric Theory*, *20*(5), 813–843. doi:10.1017/S0266466604205011

Capiro, G., Jr., & Levine, R. (2002). *Corporate Governance of Banks: Concepts and International Observations*. Paper presented in the Global Corporate Governance Forum research Network Meeting.

Caraway, T. L., Rickard, S. J., & Anner, M. S.. (2012). International negotiations and domestic politics: The case of IMF labor market conditionality. *International Organization*, *66*(1), 27–61. doi:10.1017/S0020818311000348

Carter, P. (2017). Aid econometrics: Lessons from a stochastic growth model. *Journal of International Money and Finance*, *77*, 216–232. doi:10.1016/j.jimonfin.2017.06.004

Carter, P., Postel-Vinay, F., & Temple, J. (2015). Dynamic aid allocation. *Journal of International Economics*, *95*(2), 291–304. doi:10.1016/j.jinteco.2014.11.005

Caselli, M., & Gemelli. (2008). Measuring… What? Notes on Some Globalization Indices. In *Regionalisation and the Taming of Globalization*. West Midlands, UK: Academic Press.

Cecchetti, S. G., Mohanty, M. S., & Zampolli, F. (2011). The real effects of debt. Bank for International Settlements, 352.

Ceglowski, J. (1998, March). Has Globalization Created a Borderless World? *Business Review (Federal Reserve Bank of Philadelphia)*, 17–27.

Çelik, M. Y. (2012). Globalization with Different Perceptions and Dimensions, *Dumlupınar Üniversity. The Social Science Journal*, *32*(2), 57–73.

Cenikli, E. (2010). *Türkiye'de yerel yönetimlerin vergilendirme yetkisi, küreselleşme ve yerelleşme bağlamında bir inceleme* (Unpublished doctoral dissertation). University of Anadolu, Eskişehir.

Cepprulo, A., & Giuriato, L. (2016). Responses to global challenges: Trends in aid-financed global public goods. *Development Policy Review*, *34*(4), 483–507. doi:10.1111/dpr.12163

Chalk, N., & Tanzi, V. (2002). *Impact of large public debt on growth in the EU. The Behaviour of Fiscal Authorities*. Basingstoke, UK: Palgrave.

Chang, C.P., Berdiev, A.N. & Lee, C.C. (2013), Energy Exports, Globalization and Economic Growth: The Case of South Caucasus, *Economic Modelling*, 33, 333¬ 346.

Chang, C. P., & Lee, C. C. (2010). Globalization and Growth: A Political Economy Analysis for OECD Countries. *Global Economic Review*, *39*(2), 151–173.

Charemza, W. W., & Deadman, D.F. (1997). New Directions in Econometric Practice: General to Specific Modelling, Cointegration and Vector Autoregression (2nd ed.). Edward Elgar Publishing.

Checherita-Westphal, C., & Rother, P. (2012). The Impact of High Government Debt on Economic Growth and Its Channels: An Empirical Investigation for the Euro Area. *European Economic Review, 56*(7), 1392–1405. doi:10.1016/j.euroecorev.2012.06.007

Chhotray, V., & Hulme, D. (2009). Contrasting Visions for Aid and Governance in the 21st Century: The White House Millennium Challenge Account and DFID's Drivers of Change. *World Development, 37*(1), 36–49. doi:10.1016/j.worlddev.2007.11.004

Chiminya, A., & Nicolaidou, E. (2015). *An empirical ınvestigation into the determinants of external debt in Sub Saharan Africa*. Biennial Conference of The Economic Society of South Africa, University of Cape Town. Retrieved March 28, 2018, from http://2015.essa.org.za/fullpaper/essa_3098. pdf

Choi, I. (2001). Unit root tests for panel data. *Journal of International Money and Finance, 20*(2), 249–272. doi:10.1016/S0261-5606(00)00048-6

Chudik, A., Mohaddes, K., Pesaran, M. H., & Raissi, M. (2017). Is there a debt-threshold effect on output growth? *The Review of Economics and Statistics, 99*(1), 135–150. doi:10.1162/REST_a_00593

Çiftçi, İ. (2015). *Shaking Earth in Our Hands: Globalization*. İstanbul: Vadi Publishing.

Claessens, S., Dell'Ariccia, G., Igan, D., & Laeven, L. (2010). Cross-country experiences and policy implications from the global financial crisis. *Economic Policy, 25*(62), 267–293. doi:10.1111/j.1468-0327.2010.00244.x

Clauwaert, S., & Schömann, I. (2012). The crisis and national labour law reforms: A mapping exercise. *European Labour Law Journal, 3*(1), 54–69. doi:10.1177/201395251200300105

Clist, P. (2011). 25 Years of Aid Allocation Practice: Whither Selectivity? *World Development, 39*(10), 1724–1734. doi:10.1016/j.worlddev.2011.04.031

Cochrane, J. H. (2011). Understanding Policy in the Great Recession: Some Unpleasant Fiscal Arithmetic. *European Economic Review, 55*(1), 2–30. doi:10.1016/j.euroecorev.2010.11.002

Colombo, E., & Longoni, E. (2009). *The Politics of External Debt in Developing Countries*. Working paper series no.176. Retrieved March 13, 2018 http://dems.unimib.it/repec/pdf/mibwpaper176.pdf

Cooke, P. (1989). Locality, economic restructuring and world development. In P. Cooke (Ed.), The changing face of urban Britain: Localities. London: Unwin Hyman.

Crotty, J. (2009). Structural causes of the global financial crisis: A critical assessment of the 'new financial architecture'. *Cambridge Journal of Economics, 33*(4), 563–580. doi:10.1093/cje/bep023

Cullis, J., & Jones, P. (1998). *Public finance and public choice*. Oxford, UK: Oxford University Press.

Czaika, M. (2005). Aid Allocation and Asylum Migration in the 1990s. *Applied Economics Quarterly, 51*(3), 289–303.

Czaika, M., & Mayer, A. (2011). Refugee Movements and Aid Responsiveness of Bilateral Donors. *The Journal of Development Studies*, *47*(3), 455–474. doi:10.1080/00220388.2010.492855

Daniels, B. (2010). The Robin Hood Tax: A Rejection. *The Wilberforce Society Policy Paper*, 1-4. Retrieved from http://thewilberforcesociety.co.uk/wp-content/uploads/2011/10/The-Robin-Hood-tax-A-rejection-Ben-Daniels.pdf

Dasgupta, P. (2011). *Economy*. Ankara: Dost Publishing.

de Castro Fernández, F., Martí, F., Montesinos, A., Pérez, J., & Sánchez-Fuentes, A. J. (2014). *Fiscal policies in Spain: Main stylises facts revisited*. Madrid: Banco de España.

De Grauwe, P., & Verfaille, G. (1988. Exchange Rate Variability, Misalignment, and the European Monetary System. In R. C. Marston (Ed.), Misalignment of Exchange Rates. Chicago: University of Chicago Press.

De Matteis, A. (2013). Relevance of poverty and governance for aid allocation. *Review of Development Finance*, *3*(2), 51–60. doi:10.1016/j.rdf.2013.04.001

DeCoster, J. (1998). *Overview of factor analysis*. Retrieved July 05, 2016, from http://www.stat-help.com/factor.pdf

Denisia, V. (2010). Foreign Direct Investment Theories: An Overview of the Main FDI Theories. *European Journal of Interdisciplinary Studies*, 3.

Deutsche Bundesbank. (2008). *Annual Report 2008*. Frankfurt am Main: Deutsche Bundesbank. Retrieved 5 24, 2018, from Deutsche Bundesbank.

Diamond, P. A. (1965). National debt in a neoclassical growth model. *The American Economic Review*, 1126–1150.

Dickinson, W. B., Cross, M., & Polsky, B. (1973). Watergate: chronology of a crisis. Washington, DC: Congressional Quarterly Inc.

Diclehan, B. (2016). *Base erosion and profit shifting and Turkey experiences*. Retrieved from https://home.kpmg.com/content/dam/kpmg/pdf/2016/06/tr-sorumlu-vergicilikbasak-diclehan.pdf

Diclehan, B. (n.d.). *Part II: responsible taxation at the ınternational level*. Retrieved from https://home.kpmg.com/tr/tr/home/gorusler/2016/06/sorumlu-vergicilik.html

Dileyici, D., & Vural, T. (2006). *İdarelerarası rekabet ve mali yerinden yönetim, Kamu ekonomisi ve kamu politikası*. Ankara: Seçkin Yayıncılık.

Doiter, E. (2015). Disentangling Mutual Fund Governance From. *Harvard Business Law Review*, 5.

Dökmen, G., & Aysu, A. (2010). Hükümet İstikrarının Doğrudan Yabancı Yatırımlar Üzerindeki Etkisi: Gelişmekte Olan Ülkelere İlişkin Ampirik Bir Çalışma. *Journal of Yaşar University*, *5*(18), 3028–3037.

Dollar, D., & Levin, V. (2006). The increasing selectivity of foreign aid, 1984-2003. *World Development*, *34*(12), 2034–2046. doi:10.1016/j.worlddev.2006.06.002

DPT. (2000). *Küreselleşme Özel İhtisas Komisyon Raporu. 8. Beş Yıllık Kalkınma Planı*. Ankara: DPT Yayını.

Dreger, C., & Reimers, H. E. (2013). Does euro area membership affect the relation between GDP growth and public debt? *Journal of Macroeconomics*, *38*, 481–486. doi:10.1016/j.jmacro.2013.07.012

Dreher, A. (2006). Does Globalization Affect Growth? Evidence from a new Index of Globalization. *Applied Economics*, *38*(10), 1091–1110. doi:10.1080/00036840500392078

Dreher, A. (2006). The Influence of Globalization on Taxes and Social Policy: An Empirical Analysis for OECD Countries. *European Journal of Political Economy*, *22*(1), 179–201. doi:10.1016/j.ejpoleco.2005.04.006

Dreher, A., Gaston, N., & Martens, P. (2008). *Measuring Globalization-Gauging its Consequences*. New York: Springer.

Dreher, A., Nunnenkamp, P., & Thiele, R. (2011). Are 'New' Donors Different? Comparing the Allocation of Bilateral Aid Between nonDAC and DAC Donor Countries. *World Development*, *39*(11), 1950–1968. doi:10.1016/j.worlddev.2011.07.024

Dritsaki, C., & Stiakakis, E. (2014). Foreign direct investments, exports, and economic growth in Croatia: A time series analysis. *Procedia Economics and Finance*, *14*, 181–190. doi:10.1016/S2212-5671(14)00701-1

Dudley, L., & Montmarquette, C. (1976). A Model of the Supply of Bilateral Foreign Aid. *The American Economic Review*, *66*(1), 132–142.

Dumitrescu, E.-I., & Hurlin, C. (2012). Testing for Granger non-causality in heterogeneous panels. *Economic Modelling*, *29*(4), 1450–1460. doi:10.1016/j.econmod.2012.02.014

Dunning, J. H. (2001). The eclectic (OLI) paradigm of international production: Past, present and future. *International Journal of the Economics of Business*, *8*(2), 173–190. doi:10.1080/13571510110051441

Ďurinová, I. (2006). Taxation under Conditions of Economic Globalization. *BIATEC*, *14*(10).

Durmuş, M. (2008). *Kamu ekonomisi*. Ankara: Gazi Yayınevi.

Eberhardt, M., & Presbitero, A. F. (2015). Public debt and growth: Heterogeneity and non-linearity. *Journal of International Economics*, *97*(1), 45–58. doi:10.1016/j.jinteco.2015.04.005

Eberhartd, M. (2012). Estimating Panel Time-series Models with Heterogeneous Slopes. *The Stata Journal*, *12*(1), 61–71. doi:10.1177/1536867X1201200105

Eberhartd, M., & Bond, S. (2009). *Cross-section Dependence in Nonstationary Panel Models: A Novel Estimator. MPRA paper 17870*. University Library of Munich.

Égert, B. (2015a). The 90% public debt threshold: The rise and fall of a stylized fact. *Applied Economics*, *47*(34-35), 3756–3770. doi:10.1080/00036846.2015.1021463

Égert, B. (2015b). Public debt, economic growth and nonlinear effects: Myth or reality? *Journal of Macroeconomics*, *43*, 226–238. doi:10.1016/j.jmacro.2014.11.006

Egger, P., & Winner, H. (2005). Evidence on corruption as an incentive for foreign direct investment. *European Journal of Political Economy*, *21*(4), 932–952. doi:10.1016/j.ejpoleco.2005.01.002

Eichengreen, B., & Portes, R. (1987). *The anatomy of financial crises*. Cambridge, MA: National Bureau of Economic Research. doi:10.3386/w2126

Emirmahmutoglu, F., & Kose, N. (2011). Testing for Granger Causality in Heterogeneous Mixed Panels. *Economic Modelling*, *28*(3), 870–876. doi:10.1016/j.econmod.2010.10.018

Epstein, G. S., & Gang, I. N. (2009). Good governance and good aid allocation. *Journal of Development Economics*, *89*(1), 12–18. doi:10.1016/j.jdeveco.2008.06.010

Eraydın, A. (2001). Küreselleşme-yerelleşme ve işlevleri farklılaşan kentler. Ankara: Mülkiyeliler Birliği Yayınları.

Erdem, N., & Atbaşi, F. D. (2011). Finans sermayenin kriz döngüsü: merkez-çevre "yakınsaması". *Ankara Üniversitesi SBF Dergisi, 66*(4), 033-066.

Erdem, T. (2017). New World Order, Electronic Commerce and Tax. *Financial Solution*, (143), 13-41.

Erdem, T. (2018). Turkish approaches to BEPS: where do we stand currently? In *Base Erosion and Profit Shifting in Taxation, International Tax Law Conferences Series-5* (pp. 71-97). Beta Press.

Erdoğdu, M. (2007). Tax Policies That May Reduce Turkey's Financial Crisis Risks. *Marmara University Journal of Social Sciences Institute*, *7*(27), 259–279.

Ericsson, J., & Irandoust, M. (2010). On The Causalıty Between Foreign Direct Investment and Output: A Comparative Study. *The International Trade Journal*, *15*(1), 1–26. doi:10.1080/088539001300005431

Erlichman. (2000). *Making it Mutual: Aligning the Interests of Investors and Managers: Recommendations for a Mutual Fund Governance Regime for Canada*. Prepared for the Canadian Securities Administrators.

Erol, E. D. (2013). Türkiye ve Avrupa Birliği üyesi ülkelerin sosyo-ekonomik gelişmişlik düzeylerinin karşılaştırmalı analizi. *Sosyal ve Beşeri Bilimler Dergisi*, *5*(1), 198–208.

Ertaş, S. A., & Atik, H. (2016). Kalkınma göstergeleri bakımından Türkiye'nin Avrupa Birliği ülkeleri arasındaki yeri: Istatistiksel bir analiz. *Erciyes Üniversitesi İktisadi ve İdari Bilimler Fakültesi Dergisi*, *48*, 199–218.

Esener, Ç. S., & Biniş, B. (2012). New Solutions to Old Debates: A new Transaction Tax Proposal. *Business and Economics Research Journal*, *3*(4), 123–142.

Estrada, Á., Jimeno, J. F., de Molina, M., & Luis, J. (2009). *The Spanish economy in EMU: The first ten years*. Madrid: Banco de Espana.

European Commission. (2018a). *Annual Budget.* Retrieved from http://ec.europa.eu/budget/annual/index_en.cfm?year=2017

European Commission. (2018b). *Convergence Criteria For Joining*. Retrieved from https://ec.europa.eu/info/business-economy-euro/euro-area/enlargement-euro-area/convergence-criteria-joining_en

European Commission. (2018c). *Numerical Fiscal Rules in EU Member Countries*. Retrieved from https://ec.europa.eu/info/sites/info/files/economy-finance/f1_nfr_type.pdf

European Commission. (2018d). *EU Economic Governance "Six-Pack" Enters Into Force.* Retrieved from http://europa.eu/rapid/press-release_MEMO-11-898_en.htm

European Commission. (2018e). *The History of The European Union.* Retrieved from https://europa.eu/european-union/about-eu/history_en

Evgin, T. (2000). *Dünden Bugüne Dış Borçlarımız.* Ankara: Hazine Müsteşarlığı Matbaası.

Falay, N. (2007). Avrupa Birliği Bütçesi (Devlet Bütçesi İçinde). Eskişehir, Turkey: Anatolian University Press.

Farzin, Y. H. (1988). T*he Relationship of External Debt and Growth: Sudan's Experience, 1975-1984.* World Bank Discussion Paper. Retrieved April 16, 2018, from http://documents.worldbank.org/curated/en/534071468776091039/pdf/multi-page.pdf

Ferhatoğlu, E. (2015). The effect of beps project on hybrid financial instrument in the law of tax agreements. *Journal of Tax Issues*, (326), 17-30.

Ferhatoğlu, E. (2018). BEPS action 1: digital economy. In *Base Erosion and Profit Shifting in Taxation, International Tax Law Conferences Series-5,* (pp. 211-229). Beta Press.

Ferhatoğlu, E. (2008). Elimination of international tax disputes: European union arbitration agreement. *Ankara University. Journal of Law Faculty*, *57*(4), 191–218.

Filiz, G. (2005). Küreselleşme Sürecinde Vergi Rekabeti ve Boyutları. *Akdeniz İ.İ.B.F. Dergisi*, *9*, 93–122.

Fink, G., & Redaelli, S. (2011). Determinants of International Emergency Aid-Humanitarian Need Only? *World Development*, *39*(5), 741–757. doi:10.1016/j.worlddev.2010.09.004

Fligstein, N., & Goldstein, A. (2010). The anatomy of the mortgage securitization crisis. In *Markets on Trial: The Economic Sociology of the US Financial Crisis: Part A* (s. 29-70). Içinde Emerald Group Publishing Limited.

Flood, R. P., & Garber, P. M. (1984). Collapsing exchange-rate regimes: Some linear examples. *Journal of International Economics*, *17*(1-2), 1–13. doi:10.1016/0022-1996(84)90002-3

Frame, W. S., Fuster, A., Tracy, J., & Vickery, J. (2015). *The Rescue of Fannie Mae and Freddie Mac*. New York: Federal Reserve Bank of New York.

Fratzcher, M. (2002). On Currency Crises and Contagion. *European Central Bank Working Papers*, (139), 10-16.

Frees, E. W. (1995). Assessing cross-sectional correlation in panel data. *Journal of Econometrics*, *69*(2), 393–414. doi:10.1016/0304-4076(94)01658-M

Friedman, B. M. (1978). Crowding Out or Crowding in? The Economic Consequences of Financing Government Deficits. *NBER Working Paper*, w0284.

Friedman, M. (1937). The use of ranks to avoid the assumption of normality implicit in the analysis of variance. *Journal of the American Statistical Association*, *32*(200), 675–701. doi:10.1080/01621459.1937.10503522

Gençoğlu, P., & Ünlü, F. (2014). Afrika ülkelerinin sosyo-ekonomik gelişmişlik düzeyi: istatistiksel bir analiz, In İ. G. Yumuşak (Ed.), *12. International Conference on Knowledge, Economy and Management Proceedings Book*, (pp.59-74). Antalya.

Gençtürk, T. (2012). The Concept of Terror and Different Approaches to International Terrorism. *Başkent University Center for Strategic Studies*, 1-11. Retrieved June 8, 2018, from http://sam.baskent.edu.tr/makaleler/tgencturk/TerorUluslararasi.pdf

Ghose, A. K., Majid, N., & Ernst, C. (2010). *Global Employment Problem.* Ankara: Efil Publication.

GİB. (2018). Retrieved from http://www.gib.gov.tr/fileadmin/user_upload/Tebligler/5520/7.html

Giddens, A. (2000). *The World Fleeing from Our Hand* (O. Akınhay, Trans.). İstanbul: Alfa Publishing.

Glennie, J., & Sumner, A. (2016). *Aid, Growth and Poverty*. London: Palgrave Macmillan. doi:10.1057/978-1-137-57272-1

Gökdere, A. (2001). An Overview of Globalization, *Ankara. Journal of European Studies*, *1*(1), 71–101.

Gómez-Puig, M., & Sosvilla-Rivero, S. (2015). The causal relationship between debt and growth in EMU countries. *Journal of Policy Modeling*, *37*(6), 974–989. doi:10.1016/j.jpolmod.2015.09.004

Gorton, G. B. (2008). *Banking and the Panic of 200*. Cambridge, MA: National Bureou of Economic Research.

Gözlüklü, B., & Biçer, R. (2018). *Turkey multilateral international tax agreement signed*. Retrieved from http://vergiport.com/duyuru/Turkiye_cok_tarafli_uluslararasi_vergi_anlasmasi_imzaladi.pdf

Granger, C. W. (1969). Investigating causal relations by econometric models and cross-spectral methods. *Econometrica*, *37*(3), 424–438. doi:10.2307/1912791

Griffin, K. B., & Enos, J. L. (1970). Foreign assistance: Objectives and consequences. *Economic Development and Cultural Change*, *18*(3), 313–327. doi:10.1086/450435

Grunberg, I. (1998). Double Jeopardy: Globalization, Liberalization and the Fiscal Squeeze. *World Development*, *26*(4), 591–605. doi:10.1016/S0305-750X(97)10068-7

Gücüyener, G. (2015). Transfer pricing documentation and country based reporting within the scope of BEPS Project Action Plan. *Tax Issues*, (326), 69-76.

Güler, B. A. (1996). *Yeni sağ ve devletin değişimi, yapısal uyarlama politikaları 1980-1995*. Ankara: Todaie Yayını.

Gungor, K. (2011). *Küresel Kriz Mali Kural ve Türkiye*. Ankara, Turkey: Nobel Press.

Gurgul, H., & Lach, Ł. (2014). Globalization and economic growth: Evidence from two decades of transition in CEE. *Economic Modelling*, *36*, 99–107.

Gygli, S., Haelg, F., & Sturm, J. E. (2018). *The KOF Globalization Index–Revisited*. KOF Working Paper 439. Retrieved March 11, 2018, from https://www.ethz.ch/content/dam/ethz/special-interest/dual/kofdam/documents/Globalization/2018/KOF_Globalization%20Index _Revisited.pdf

Habermas, J. (2003). *İnsan Doğasının Geleceği*. İstanbul: Everest Yayınları.

Hablemitoğlu, Ş. (2005). *Globalization, From Dreams to Truths* (2nd ed.). İstanbul: Social Transformation Publications.

Hadri, K. (2000). Testing for stationarity in heterogeneous panel data. *The Econometrics Journal*, *3*(2), 148–161. doi:10.1111/1368-423X.00043

Hajivassiliou, V. A. (1987). The external debt repayments problems of LDC's: An econometric model based on panel data. *Journal of Econometrics*, *36*(1-2), 205–230. doi:10.1016/0304-4076(87)90050-9

Hamburg, B., Momigliano, S., Manzke, B., & Siviero, S. (2010). *The reaction of fiscal policy to the crisis in Italy and Germany: Are they really polar cases in the European context?* Rome: Banca de Italia.

Hansen, B. E. (1996). Inference when a nuisance parameter is not identified under the null hypothesis. *Econometrica*, *64*(2), 413–430. doi:10.2307/2171789

Hansen, B. E. (1999). Threshold Effects in Non-Dynamic Panels: Estimating, Testing and Inference. *Journal of Econometrics*, *93*(2), 345–368. doi:10.1016/S0304-4076(99)00025-1

Hansen, B. E. (2000). Sample splitting and threshold estimation. *Econometrica*, *68*(3), 575–603. doi:10.1111/1468-0262.00124

Harvey, D. (1989). *The condition of postmodernity: An enquiry into the origins of cultural change*. Cambridge, UK: Basil Blackwell.

Harvey, D. (2014). *The Status of Postmodernism* (7th ed.; S. Savran, Trans.). İstanbul: Metis Publishing.

Hayaloğlu, P., Kalaycı, C., & Artan, S. (2015). Küreselleşme Farklı Gelir Grubundaki Ülkelerde Ekonomik Büyümeyi Nasıl Etkilemektedir? *Eskişehir Osmangazi Üniversitesi İİBF Dergisi*, *10*(1), 119–152.

Herber, B. P. (1990). The International Public Goods of Antarctica: A New Politico Economic Regime for the World's Seventh Continent. In *Proceedings of the 44th Congress of the International Institute of Public Finance*. Detroit, MI: Wayne State University Press.

Hermes, N., & Lensink, R. (2001). Changing the conditions for development aid: A new paradigm? *Journal of Development Studies, 37*(6), 1-+. doi:10.1080/713601080

Heywood, A. (2013). *Global Politics* (N. Uslu & H. Özdemir, Trans.). Ankara: Adres Publication.

Heywood, A. (2014). *Küresel Siyaset. (Üçüncü Baskı). (Çev. N. Uslu, H. Özdemir).* Ankara: Adres Yayınları.

Hildreth, C. (1950). *Combining Cross-Section Data and Time Series.* Cowles Comission Discussion Paper, No:347.

Hines, J. R. Jr, & Summers, L. H. (2009). How Globalization Affects Tax Design. *Tax Policy and the Economy, 23*(1), 123–158. doi:10.1086/597056

Hirst, P., & Zeitlin, J. (1991). Flexible specialization versus post - fordism: Theory, evidence and policy implications. *Economy and Society, 20*, 1–51.

Hiscox, M. J. (2001). *Political Integration and Disintegration in the Global Economy: The Effects of Globalization on Incentives to Alter the Structure of Governance.* In Globalization and Governance II Conference, IGCC, San Diego, CA.

Hodge, G. (1998). Contracting public sector services: A meta-analytic perspective of the international evidence. *Australian Journal of Public Administration, Vol, 57*(4), 98–111. doi:10.1111/j.1467-8500.1998.tb01565.x

Hoeffler, A., & Outram, V. (2011). Need, Merit, or Self-Interest-What Determines the Allocation of Aid? *Review of Development Economics, 15*(2), 237–250. doi:10.1111/j.1467-9361.2011.00605.x

Holman, N., & Thornley, A. (2015). Backlash in the London Suburbs: The Local-strategic Tension in Multilevel Governance. *Environment and Planning. C, Government & Policy, 33*(3), 496–511. doi:10.1068/c13135

Hong, L. (2014). Does and how does FDI promote the economic growth? Evidence from dynamic panel data of prefecture city in China. *IERI Procedia, 6*, 57–62. doi:10.1016/j.ieri.2014.03.010

Hsiao, C. (2003). *Analysis of Panel Data.* Cambridge, UK: Cambridge University. doi:10.1017/CBO9780511754203

Hsiao, C. (2007). Panel data analysis—Advantages and challenges. *Test, 16*(1), 1–22. doi:10.100711749-007-0046-x

Hussain, M. E., & Haque, M. (2016). Foreign direct investment, trade, and economic growth: An empirical analysis of Bangladesh. *Economies, 4*(2), 7. doi:10.3390/economies4020007

Iamsiraroj, S. (2016). The foreign direct investment–economic growth nexus. *International Review of Economics & Finance, 42*, 116–133. doi:10.1016/j.iref.2015.10.044

IDS. (2018). *International Debt Statistics 2018.* The World Bank.

ILO. (2013). *Informal economy and decent work, A policy guide supporting transitions to formality*. International Labor Organization.

IMF. (2005). *IMF Survey, 34*(18).

IMF. (2008). *Globalization: A Brief Overview*. Retrieved February 02, 2018, from https://www.imf.org/external/np/exr/ib/2008/pdf/053008.pdf

Imimole, B., Imoughele, L. E., & Okhuese, M. A. (2014). Determinants and sustainability of external debt in a deregulated economy: A cointegration analysis form Nigeria (1986-2010). *American International Journal of Contemporary Research, 4*(6), 201–214.

Im, K. S., Pesaran, M. H., & Shin, Y. (2003). Testing for unit roots in heterogeneous panels. *Journal of Econometrics, 115*(1), 53–74. doi:10.1016/S0304-4076(03)00092-7

In'airat, M. (2014). Aid allocation, selectivity, and the quality of governance. *Journal of Economics, Finance and Administrative Science, 19*(36), 63–68. doi:10.1016/j.jefas.2014.03.002

International Monetary Fund. (2009). *Retrieved from Luxembourg - 2009 Article IV Consultation, IMF Concluding Statement*. Retrieved from https://www.imf.org/en/News/Articles/2015/09/28/04/52/mcs033009

Investment Company Institute. (2000). *Global Corporate Governance Issues for Mutual Funds*. Author.

Jacquemin, A., & Sapir, A. (1995). *Is a European hard-core credible?* CEPR Discussion Paper.

Jessop, B. (1990). *State theory: putting the capitalist state in its place*. University Park, PA: Pennsylvania University.

Kahraman, A. (2018). *Is the EU proposal tax protection in the taxation of digitalized economy?* Retrieved from https://kpmgvergi.com/Blog/Pages/FullBlog.aspx?article=884

Kanberoğlu, Z., & Kara, O. (2013). The Impact of the Global Crisis on Social Life: The Case of Van. Mugla Sıtkı Kocman University Institute of Social Sciences Journal, (31), 35-48.

Karabacak, B. N. (2012). *Mali yerelleşme alanında ortaya çıkan yeni yaklaşımlar: kuşaklar arası çatışma mı? Maliye dergisi, 163*. Temmuz-Aralık.

Kara, M. (2008). *Bölgesel rekabet edebilirlik kavramı ve bölgesel kalkınma politikalarına yansıması*. DPT Uzmanlık Tezi.

Kara, M. C., & Öz, E. (2016). A global tax compliance project: BEPS. *Tax World, 172*(414), 172–181.

Karaman, S., & Gökalp, Z. (2010). Impacts of Global Warming and Climate Change Over Water Resources. *Journal of Agriculture and Social Research, 3*(1), 59–66.

Karluk, R. (2009). *Cumhuriyetin İlanından Günümüze Türkiye Ekonomisinde Yapısal Dönüşüm, Tıpkı 12. Baskı*. İstanbul: Beta Yayınları.

Kaul, I. (2010). What is a Global Public Good. *The Broker*, (20/21). Retrieved from http://www.search-4dev.nl/document/181021

Kaul, I., Conceicao, P., Le Goulven, K., & Mendoza, R. (2003). *Providing global public goods: Managing globalization*. New York: Oxford University Press. doi:10.1093/0195157400.001.0001

Kaul, I., Grunberg, I., & Stern, M. A. (Eds.). (1999). *Global public goods: International co-operation in the 21st Century*. New York: Oxford University Press. doi:10.1093/0195130529.001.0001

Kaya, M. (2009). Globalization Approaches. *Journal of Dicle University. Ziya Gökalp Faculty of Education, 13*, 1–16.

Kaya, M., Doğan, B. B., & Kaya, S. B. (2017). An Assessment upon the Factors Providing a Basis for the Generation of Globalism. *Social Sciences Studies Journal, 3*(12), 2041–2060. doi:10.26449ssj.276

Kazgan, G. (1985). *Ekonomide Dışa Açık Büyüme*. İstanbul: Altın Kitaplar Yayınevi.

Kazgan, G. (2005). *Küreselleşme ve ulus devlet: yeni ekonomik düzen*. İstanbul: İstanbul Bilgi Üniversitesi Yayınları.

Kazgan, G. (2009). *Küreselleşme ve Ulus-Devlet, Yeni Ekonomik Düzen*. İstanbul: İstanbul Bilgi Üniversitesi Yayınları.

Keleş, R. (2001). Küreselleşme ve yerel yönetimler. Ankara: Mülkiyeliler Birliği Yayınları.

Keynes, J. M. (2016). *General theory of employment, interest and money*. New Delhi: Atlantic Publishers & Dist.

Khattry, B., & Rao, J. M. (2002). Fiscal Faux Pas? An Analysis of the Revenue Implications of Trade Liberalization. *World Development, 30*, 1431–1444.

Khurshid, S. M. Z., Rohit, & Singh, G. P. (2009). Level and trends of competition among the mutual funds in India. *Research Journal of Business Management, 3*(2), 47–67. doi:10.3923/rjbm.2009.47.67

Kilby, C. (2011). What Determines the Size of Aid Projects? *World Development, 39*(11), 1981–1994. doi:10.1016/j.worlddev.2011.07.023

Kindleberger, C. P. (1986). International public good without international government. *The American Economic Review, 76*(1), 1–13.

Kitapçı, İ. (2017). An Assessment of Today's Major Global Problems, *PESA Internatıonal. The Journal of Social Studies, 3*(14), 241–257.

Kizilgol, O. A., & Ipek, E. (2014). An Empirical Evaluation of the Relationship between Trade Openness and External Debt: Turkish Case. *International Econometric Review (IER)*, 42-58.

Koch, D. J., Dreher, A., Nunnenkamp, P., & Thiele, R. (2009). Keeping a Low Profile: What Determines the Allocation of Aid by Non-Governmental Organizations? *World Development, 37*(5), 902–918. doi:10.1016/j.worlddev.2008.09.004

Kocks, A. (2005). *The Financing of UN Peace Operations-An Analysis from A Global Public Good Perspective, INEF Report* (Vol. 77). InstitutfürEntwicklung und Frieden der Universitat Duisburg-Essen, Campus Duisburg.

KOF. (2018a). *KOF Globalization Index*. Retrieved May 19, 2018, from https://www.kof.ethz.ch/en/forecasts-and-indicators/indicators/kof-globalization-index.html

KOF. (2018b). *KOF Globalization Index: Globalization Down Worldwide in 2015*. Retrieved May 17, 2018, from https://www.kof.ethz.ch/en/news-and-events/media/press-releases/2018/01/kof-globalization-index-globalization-down-worldwide-in-2015.html

KOF. (2018c). *KOF Globalization Index*. Retrieved May 16, 2018, from https://www.kof.ethz.ch/en/forecasts-and-indicators/indicators/kof-globalization-index.html

Konca & Taşkın. (2017). Common Reporting Standards (CRS). *Tax Agenda (Vergide Gündem)*, (12), 37-39.

Kontbay, S. (2013). *Growth beyond the debt threshold* (Doctoral dissertation). Clemson University.

Köprü, M. F. (2015). *What is this BEPS?* Retrieved from http://www.ekonomist.com.tr/m-fatih-kopru/nedir-bu-beps.html

Köprü, M. F. (2018). *In the tax everything will be more transparent*. Retrieved from http://www.ekonomist.com.tr/m-fatih-kopru/vergide-her-sey-daha-seffaf-olacak.html

Kourtellos, A., Stengos, T., & Tan, C. M. (2013). The effect of public debt on growth in multiple regimes. *Journal of Macroeconomics*, *38*, 35–43. doi:10.1016/j.jmacro.2013.08.023

Kovancılar, B., Miynat, M., & Bursalıoğlu, S. (2007). *Kamu maliyesinde küresel değişmeler*. Ankara: Gazi Kitabevi.

Koyuncu, F. T. & Tekeli, S. (2010). 1990 Sonrası Dönemde Türkiye'de Dış Borç Stoku Üzerinde Etkili Olan Ekonomik Faktörlerin Analizi. *Ekonomi Bilimleri Dergisi*, *2*(1).

Koyuncu, C. (2016). *Principles of Constitutional Taxation*. Bursa: Ekin Publishing.

Krugman, P. (1979). A model of balance-of-payments crises. *Journal of Money, Credit and Banking*, *11*(3), 311–325. doi:10.2307/1991793

Krugman, P. (1999). Balance sheets, the transfer problem, and financial crises. In *International finance and financial crises* (pp. 31–55). Dordrecht: Springer. doi:10.1007/978-94-011-4004-1_2

Küçükkaya, O. (2016). BEPS 4. Interest Expenses in the Framework of Action Plan. *Tax Agenda (Vergide Gündem)*, (9), 18-21.

Kuh, E. (1959). The validity of cross-sectionally estimated behavior equations in time series applications. *Econometrica*, *27*(2), 197–214. doi:10.2307/1909442

Kumar, M. S., & Quinn, D. P. (2012). *Globalization and Corporate Taxation.* International Monetary Fund, IMF Working Paper, WP/12/252.

Kumar, M., & Woo, J. (2010). Public debt and growth. *IMF Working Paper*, 10/174.

Kurtoğlu, R. (2017). *Global Economic Crisis and the New World Order*. İstanbul: Destek Publication.

Kurtulmuş, N. (2001). *Trans-Industrial Transformation, Globalization and Human Resources Dimension*. İstanbul: İz Publishing.

La Porta, R., Lopez-de-Silanes, F., & Shleifer, A. (1999). Corporate Ownership Around the World. *The Journal of Finance*, *54*(2), 471–517. doi:10.1111/0022-1082.00115

La Porta, R., Lopez-de-Silanes, F., Shleifer, A., & Vishny, R. W. (2000). Investor Protection and Corporate Governance. *Journal of Financial Economics*, *58*(1-2), 3–27. doi:10.1016/S0304-405X(00)00065-9

Lahiri, S., & Raimondos-Møller, P. (2000). Lobbying by Ethnic Groups and Aid Allocation. *Economic Journal (London)*, *12*(9), 879–900.

Lairson, T. D., & Skidmore, D. (2017). *International Political Economy: The Struggle for Power and Wealth in a Globalizing World.* Taylor & Francis.

Lane, P. R. (2000). *Empirical perspectives on long-term external debt.* Retrieved March 19, 2018, from http://qed.econ.queensu.ca/pub/students/dunbar/826/4/lane.pdf

Lapavitsas, C., Kaltenbrunner, A., Lindo, D., Michell, J., Painceira, J. P., Pires, E., ... Teles, N. (2010). Eurozone crisis: Beggar thyself and thy neighbour. *Journal of Balkan & Near Eastern Studies*, *12*(4), 321–373. doi:10.1080/19448953.2010.510012

Lawton, S. J. (2011). *Demographic Change and the Environment Twenty-ninth Report*. Retrieved June 8, 2018, from https://assets.publishing.service.gov.uk/government/ uploads/system/uploads/attachment_data/file/228980/8001.pdf

Lever, W. F. (1999). Competitive cities in Europe. *Urban Studies (Edinburgh, Scotland)*, *36*(5-6), 1029–1044. doi:10.1080/0042098993349

Levin, A., Lin, C. F., & Chu, C. S. J. (2002). Unit root tests in panel data: Asymptotic and finite-sample properties. *Journal of Econometrics*, *108*(1), 1–24. doi:10.1016/S0304-4076(01)00098-7

Levine, R. (1999). *Foreign Bank Entry and Capital Control Liberalization: Effects on Growth and Stability*. University of Minnesota.

Leviner, S. (2013). The Intricacies of Tax and Globalization, Columbia. *Journal of Tax Law*, *5*(207), 209–227.

Lewer, J. (2002). International trade composition and medium-run growth: Evidence of a causal relationship. *The International Trade Journal*, *16*(3), 295–317. doi:10.1080/08853900290090809

Lipietz, A. (1986). New tendencies in international division of labour: Regimes of accumulation and nodes of regulation. In A. J. Scott & M. Storper (Eds.), Production, work and territory. London: Allen Unwin.

Lipsey, R. E. (2002). *Home and Host Country Effects of FDI.* National Bureau of Economic Research Working Paper Series, No: 9293.

Li, X., & Liu, X. (2005). Foreign direct investment and economic growth: An increasingly endogenous relationship. *World Development, 33*(3), 393–407. doi:10.1016/j.worlddev.2004.11.001

Lopez, L., & Weber, S. (2017). *Testing for Granger causality in panel data.* IRENE Working paper 17-03. University of Neuchatel, Institute of Economic Research.

Lybecker. (2005). Enhanced Corporate Governance for Mutual Funds: A Flawed Concept that Deserves Serious Reconsideration. *Wash. U. L. Q., 83*, 104.

Macey, J. R., & O'Hara, M. (2001). *The Corporate Governance of Banks.* Federal Reserve Bank of New York Economic Policy Review.

Maddala, G. S., & Wu, S. (1999). A comparative study of unit root tests with panel data and a new simple test. *Oxford Bulletin of Economics and Statistics, 61*(s1), 631–652. doi:10.1111/1468-0084.61.s1.13

Magesan, A. (2013). Human Rights Treaty Ratification of Aid Receiving Countries. *World Development, 45*, 175–188. doi:10.1016/j.worlddev.2012.11.003

Makoba, J. W. (2010). Globalization and Marginalization of Labor: Focus on Sub-Saharan Africa. In Globalization in the 21st Century (pp. 87-112). Palgrave Macmillan US.

Malik, S., Hayat, M. K., & Hayat, M. U. (2010). External debt and economic growth: Empirical evidence from Pakistan. *International Research Journal of Finance and Economics, 44*(44), 1450–2887.

Marhold, F., Poier, K., Aschauer, P., Kohlbacher, E., Nebauer, M., & Wewerka, L. (2011). *How has Austria overcome the economic crisis?* International Society for Labour and Social Security Law.

Markusen, J. R., & Venables, A. J. (1999). Foreign direct investment as a catalyst for industrial development. *European Economic Review, 43*(2), 335–356. doi:10.1016/S0014-2921(98)00048-8

Mathieu, C., & Sterdyniak, H. (2009). *Global financial crisis: the french policy answer in a EU perspective.* Paris: OFCE - Centre de recherche en économie de Sciences Po.

McGillivray, M., & Pham, T. K. C. (2017). Reforming Performance-Based Aid Allocation Practice. *World Development, 90*, 1–5. doi:10.1016/j.worlddev.2015.05.006

Mcgrew, A. (2010). Globalization and global politics. In J. Baylis, S. Smith, & P. Owens (Eds.), *The Globalization of World Politics: An Introduction to International Relations* (5th ed.; pp. 14-31). Oxford. Retrieved May 13, 2018, from http://www.good-governance-debates.de/wp-content/uploads/2015/03/Globalization-and-global-politics-by-Anthony-McGrew_2010.pdf

McLuhan, M. (2014). *The Gutenberg Galaxy; Formation of Typographic Man* (G. Ç. Güven, Trans.). İstanbul: Yapı Kredi Publishing.

Mencinger, J. (2003). Does foreign direct investment always enhance economic growth? *Kyklos, 56*(4), 491–508. doi:10.1046/j.0023-5962.2003.00235.x

Mendez, R. P. (1999). Peace as a global public good. In I. Kaul, I. Grunberg, & M. Stern (Eds.), *Global Public Goods: International Cooperation in the 21st Century* (pp. 382–416). New York: Oxford University Press. doi:10.1093/0195130529.003.0020

Menegaki, A. N., & Tugcu, C. T. (2017). Energy consumption and Sustainable Economic Welfare in G7 countries; A comparison with the conventional nexus. *Renewable & Sustainable Energy Reviews*, *69*, 892–901. doi:10.1016/j.rser.2016.11.133

Menyah, K., Nazlioglu, S., & Wolde-Rufael, Y. (2014). Financial development, trade openness and economic growth in African countries: New insights from a panel causality approach. *Economic Modelling*, *37*, 386–394. doi:10.1016/j.econmod.2013.11.044

Milanovic, B. (2002). *Can We Discern the Effect of Globalization on Income Distribution? Evidence from Household Budget Surveys*. Policy Research Working Paper; No. 2876. World Bank. Retrieved May 17, 2018, from https://openknowledge.worldbank.org/handle/10986/19276

Minea, A., & Parent, A. (2012). Is high public debt always harmful to economic growth? Reinhart and Rogoff and some complex nonlinearities. *CERDI, Etudes et Documents*, E 2012.18.

Minsky, H. P. (1970). *Financial instability revisited: The economics of disaster*. St. Louis, MO: Board of Governors of the Federal Reserve System.

Mishkin, F. S. (1992). Anatomy of a financial crisis. *Journal of Evolutionary Economics*, *2*(2), 115–130. doi:10.1007/BF01193536

Mishkin, F. S. (2011). Over the cliff: From the subprime to the global financial crisis. *The Journal of Economic Perspectives*, *25*(1), 49–70. doi:10.1257/jep.25.1.49

Mohan Rao, P. (1998). *Working of Mutual Fund Organizations in India*. New Delhi: Kanishka Publishers.

Moller, B. (2004). *Peace as a Global Public Good Research Center on Development and International Relations (DIR)*. Development Research Series Working Paper, No. 127, Aalborg University.

Montgomery, S.L. (2014). *Global Energy Powers, 21st Century and After* (E. G. Şenol, Trans.). Ankara: Salmat Printing and Publishing.

Moon, S., Rottingen, J., & Frenk, J. (2017). Global public goods for health: Weaknesses and opportunities in the global health system. *Health Economics, Policy, and Law*, *12*(02), 195–205. doi:10.1017/S1744133116000451 PMID:28332461

Moran, T. H. (2005). How Does FDI Affect Host Country Development? Using Industry Case Studies to Make Reliable Generalizations. In T. H. Moran, E.M. Graham, & M. Blomström, (Eds.), Institute for International Economics, Center for Global Development, Does Foreign Direct Investment Promote Development? Washington, DC: Automated Graphic System Inc.

Morgenthau, H. (1962). A Political Theory of Foreign Aid. *The American Political Science Review*, *56*(2), 301–309. doi:10.2307/1952366

Morrissey, O., teVelde, D., & Hewitt, A. (2002). Defining international public goods: conceptual issues. In M. Ferroni & A. Mody (Eds.), *International public goods: Incentives, measurement and financing* (pp. 31–46). Boston: Kluwer Academic Publishers. doi:10.1007/978-1-4615-0979-0_2

Mutlu, A. (2006). Health Services and Environmental Pollution in the Context Global Public Goods: Production, Finance and Management Problems. *The Journal of Finance*, *150*, 53–78.

Nair-Reichert, U., & Weinhold, D. (2001). Causality tests for cross-country panels: A New look at FDI and economic growth in developing countries. *Oxford Bulletin of Economics and Statistics*, *63*(2), 153–171. doi:10.1111/1468-0084.00214

Nakhoul, T. E. (2014). *International Labor Migration and Turkey*. Ankara: T.C. Ministry of Labor and Social Security, General Directorate of Foreign Relations and Overseas Worker Services.

Nazlıoğlu, Ş. (2010). *Makro İktisat Politikalarının Tarım Sektörü Üzerindeki Etkileri: Gelişmiş ve Gelişmekte Olan Ülkeler için Bir Karşılaştırma*. Yayınlanmamış Doktora Tezi, Kayseri Üniversitesi Sosyal Bilimler Enstitüsü.

Nazlıoğlu, S., Lebe, F., & Kayhan, S. (2011). Nuclear Energy Consumption and Economic growth in OECD countries: Cross-sectionaly Dependent Heterogeneous Panel Casuality Analysis. *Energy Policy*, *39*(10), 6615–6621. doi:10.1016/j.enpol.2011.08.007

Ndikumana, L. (2015). *International Tax Cooperation and Implications of Globalization, Global Governance and Rules for the Post 2015 Era: Addressing Emerging Issues in the Global Environment*. Bloomsbury Academic.

Neumayer, E. (2003). The determinants of aid allocation by regional multilateral development banks and United Nations agencies. *International Studies Quarterly*, *47*(1), 101–122. doi:10.1111/1468-2478.4701005

Nistor, P. (2014). FDI and economic growth, the case of Romania. *Procedia Economics and Finance*, *15*, 577–582. doi:10.1016/S2212-5671(14)00514-0

Nunnenkamp, P., & Ohler, H. (2011). Aid Allocation through Various Official and Private Channels: Need, Merit and Self-Interest as Motives of German Donors. *World Development*, *39*(3), 308–323. doi:10.1016/j.worlddev.2010.08.001

Oates, W. E. (1985). Searching for leviathan: An ampirical study. *The American Economic Review*, *75*, 4.

Oates, W. E. (1999). An essay on fiscal federalism. *Journal of Economic Literature*, *37*(3), 1120–1149. doi:10.1257/jel.37.3.1120

Oates, W. E. (2006). The many faces of tiebout model, The tiebout model at fifty: essays in public economics in honor of Wallace Oates. Cambridge, MA: Lincoln Institute of Land Policy.

Oberdabernig, D. A. (2013). Revisiting the effects of IMF programs on poverty and inequality. *World Development*, *46*, 113–142. doi:10.1016/j.worlddev.2013.01.033

Obstfeld, M. (1988). The logic of currency crises. In *Monetary and fiscal policy in an integrated Europe* (pp. 62–90). Berlin: Springer. doi:10.1007/978-3-642-79817-7_4

OECD. (2012). *Hybrids Mismatch Arrangements: Tax Policy And Compliance Issues*. Retrieved from http://www.oecd.org/ctp/exchange-of-tax-information/HYBRIDS_ENG_Final_ October2012.pdf

OECD. (2015a). *Neutralising the Effects of Hybrid Mismatch Arrangements, Action 2 - 2015 Final Report. OECD/G20 Base Erosion and Profit Shifting Project*. Paris: OECD Publishing.

OECD. (2015b). *Limiting Base Erosion Involving Interest Deductions and Other Financial Payments, Action 4 - 2015 Final Report. OECD/G20 Base Erosion and Profit Shifting Project*. Paris: OECD Publishing. doi:10.1787/9789264241176-

OECD. (2015c). *Explanatory Statement.* OECD/G20 Base Erosion and Profit Shifting Project, OECD. Retrieved from www.oecd.org/tax/beps-explanatory-statement-2015.pdf

OECD. (2016). *About Base Erosion and Profit Shifting*. Retrieved from http://www.oecd.org/tax/beps/beps-about.htm

OECD. (2018a). *General Government Deficit.* Retrieved from https://data.oecd.org/gga/general-government-deficit.htm

OECD. (2018b). *Data, Inflation.* Retrieved from https://data.oecd.org/price/inflation-cpi.htm#indicator-chart

OECD. (2018c). *Data, Long-Term Interest Rates*. Retrieved from https://data.oecd.org/interest/long-term-interest-rates.htm

Ohmae, K. (1990). *The borderless world.* New York: Harper Business.

Oman, C. P. (2001). *Corporate Governance and National Development.* OECD Development Centre Technical Papers, Number 180.

Öner, E. (2017). *Turkish Tax System.* Ankara: Seçkin Press.

Opeskin, B. R. (1996). The moral foundations of foreign aid. *World Development, 24*(1), 21–44. doi:10.1016/0305-750X(95)00118-V

Osuji, L. O., & Olowolayemo, S. O. (1998). The impact of trade liberalization policy on Sub-Saharan African countries' debt burden. *African Economic and Business Review, 1*(2), 59–73.

Öz, S. (2018). BEPS Action 4: Interest payments. *Base Erosion and Profit Shifting in Taxation, International Tax Law Conferences Series-5*, (pp. 247-263). Beta Press.

Özbek, H., & Atik, H. (2013). İnovasyon göstergeleri bakımından Türkiye'nin Avrupa Birliği ülkeleri arasındaki yeri: Istatistiksel bir analiz. *Erciyes Üniversitesi İktisadi ve İdari Bilimler Fakültesi Dergisi, 42*, 193–210.

Özdemir, S. (2007). *Welfare State in the Process of Globalization*. İstanbul: Istanbul Chamber of Commerce Publication.

Özgenç, S. (2018). BEPS Action 6: Prevention of tax treaty abuse. In *Base Erosion and Profit Shifting in Taxation, International Tax Law Conferences Series-5*, (pp. 279-303). Beta Press.

Özgür, G., & Yetkiner, H. (2011). Economics in Difficult Times. In E. Aslanoglu (Ed.), *Global Economic Crisis and Economic Policy*. Ankara: Efil Publishing.

Öztürk, S., & Özyakışır, D. (2005). Türkiye Ekonomisinde 1980 Sonrası Yaşanan Yapısal Dönüşümlerin GSMH, Dış Ticaret ve Dış Borçlar Bağlamında Teorik Bir Değerlendirmesi. *Mevzuat Dergisi*, *94*, 1–20.

Panizza, U., & Presbitero, A. F. (2013). Public debt and economic growth in advanced economies: A survey. *Schweizerische Zeitschrift für Volkswirtschaft und Statistik*, *149*(2), 175–204.

Partner & Pince. (2018). *Banking regulation in France: Overview*. Retrieved from: https://uk.practicallaw.thomsonreuters.com/

Pattillo, C., Poirson, H., & Ricci, L. (2004). External debt and growth: Implications for HIPCs. In *Debt relief for poor countries* (pp. 123–133). London: Palgrave Macmillan. doi:10.1057/9780230522329_6

Pattillo, C., & Ricci, L. A. (2011). External debt and growth. *Review of Economics and Institutions*, *2*(3), 30. doi:10.5202/rei.v2i3.45

Pedroni, P. (1995). *Panel Cointegration; Asymptotic and Finite Sample Properties of Pooled Time Series Tests, with an Application to the PPP Hypothesis.* Indiana University Working Papers in Economics, No. 95-013.

Pedroni, P. (1997). *Panel Cointegration; Asympt otic and Finite Sample Properties of Pooled Time Series Tests, with an Application to the PPP Hypothesis: New Results.* Working Paper Indiana University.

Pedroni, P. (1999). Critical values for cointegration tests in heterogeneous panels with multiple regressors. *Oxford Bulletin of Economics and Statistics*, *61*(s1), 653–670. doi:10.1111/1468-0084.61.s1.14

Peek, J., & Rosengren, E. (2000). *Implications of the Globalization of the Banking Sector: The Latin American Experience* New England Economic Review.

Pereima, J. B., Merki, M., & Correia, F. M. (2015). *Economic growth and public debt: Addressing unobserved heterogeneity*. Retrieved from https://www.anpec.org.br/encontro/2015/submissao/files_I/i6-4a0181c0d6c126116a0d2a88269dca48.pdf

Pereira, F. M. G. (2003). *Globalization and Tax Systems. The Center of Latin American Issues and The Institute of Brazilian Business & Public Management Issues.* Washington, DC: Minevra Program.

Perry, J. L. (2006). *Democracy and the new public service*. Retrieved May 13, 2018 from https://soc.kuleuven.be/io/egpa/HRM/milan/Perry2006.PDF

Pesaran, H. (2004). General Diagnostic Tests for Cross Section Dependence in Panels, University of Cambridge, *Working Paper*, 0435.

Pesaran, H. M. (2004). *General Diagnostic Test for Cross-section Dependence in Panels.* IZA Discussion Paper 1240, Institute for the Study of Labor.

Pesaran, H. M. (2007). A Simple Panel Unit Root Test in the Presence of Cross-Section Dependence. *Journal of Applied Econometrics*, *22*(2), 265–312. doi:10.1002/jae.951

Pesaran, H. M., Ullah, A., & Yamagata, T. (2008). A Bias-adjusted LM Test of Error Cross-section Independence. *The Econometrics Journal*, *11*(1), 105–127. doi:10.1111/j.1368-423X.2007.00227.x

Pesaran, H. M., & Yamagata, T. (2008). Testing Slope Homogeneity in Large Panels. *Journal of Econometrics*, *142*(1), 50–93. doi:10.1016/j.jeconom.2007.05.010

Pescatori, A., Sandri, D., & Simon, J. (2014). Debt and growth: Is there a magic threshold? *IMF Working Paper*, 14/34.

Pinto, P. M., & Zhu, B. (2008). *Fortune of Evil? The Effects of Inward Foreign Direct Investment on Corruption.* Saltzman Working Paper, No: 10.

Poelhekke, S., & van der Ploeg, F. (2010). *Do Natural Resources Attract FDI? Evidence from Non-Stationary Sector Level Data.* Oxford University, Department of Economics, OxCarre (Oxford Centre for the Analysis of Resource Rich Economies) Research Paper, No:51.

Portelli, B., & Narula, R. (2006). Foreign direct investment through acquisitions and implications for technological upgrading: Case evidence from Tanzania. *European Journal of Development Research*, *18*(1), 59–85. doi:10.1080/09578810600572387

Portugal, P. (2015). *The Portuguese economic crisis: Policies and outcomes.* Bertelsmann Stiftung.

Potrafke, N. (2015). The Evidence on Globalization. *World Economy*, *38*(3), 509–552.

Presbitero, A. F. (2006). The debt-growth nexus: A dynamic panel data estimation. *Rivista İtaliana Degli Economisti*, *11*(3), 417–462.

Proud'homme, R. (1994). *On the dangers of decentralization. Transportation, water and urban development department.* Policy research working paper, 1252.

Raffer, K. (1999). ODA and Global Public Goods: A Trends analysis of past and present spending patterns. ODS Background Papers. New York, NY: United nations Development Programme.

Reinhart, C. M., & Rogoff, K. S. (2008). Is the 2007 US sub-prime financial crisis so different? An international historical comparison. *The American Economic Review*, *98*(2), 339–344. doi:10.1257/aer.98.2.339

Reinhart, C. M., & Rogoff, K. S. (2009). The aftermath of financial crises. *The American Economic Review*, *99*(2), 466–472. doi:10.1257/aer.99.2.466

Reinhart, C. M., & Rogoff, K. S. (2010). Growth in a Time of Debt. *The American Economic Review*, *100*(2), 573–578. doi:10.1257/aer.100.2.573

Reisen, H., Soto, M., & Weithöner, T. (2003). *Financing global and regional public goods through ODA: Analysis and Evidence from the OECD Creditor Reporting System*. Paper presented at the UN Wider Conference "Sharing Global Prosperity", Helsinki, Finland. Available online at: http://www.eldis.org/static/DOC14272.htm

Reisen, H., Soto, M., & Weithöner, T. (2004). *Financing global and regional public goods through ODA: Analysis and Evidence from the OECD Creditor Reporting System*. Paris: OECD.

Republic of Turkey, Ministry of Development. (2018). *Temel Ekonomik Göstergeler* [Basic Economic Indicators]. Retrieved from http://www.kalkinma.gov.tr/Pages/TemelEkonomikGostergeler.aspx

Riet, A. V. (2010). Euro area fiscal policies. In A. v. Riet (Ed.), *Euro area fiscal policies and the crisis*. Frankfurt Am Main: European Central Bank.

Robertson, R. (1999). *Globalization - Social Theory and Global Culture* (Ü. H. Yolsal, Trans.). Ankara: Science and Art Publications.

Robin Hood Tax. (2011a). *Robin Hood Tax Campaigner Kit*. Retrieved from www.robinhoodtax.ca

Robin Hood Tax. (2011b). *There Is an Alternative (Time For a Robin Hood Tax)*. Policy Brief. Retrieved from http://robinhoodtax.org/sites/default/files/There_is_an_Alternative.pdf

Rodriguez, F., & Rodrik, D. (2000). Trade policy and economic growth: A skeptic's guide to the cross-national evidence. *NBER Macroeconomics Annual*, *15*, 261–325. doi:10.1086/654419

Rodrik, D. (1998). Why Do More Open Economies Have Bigger Governments. *Journal of Political Economy*, *106*(5), 992–1032. doi:10.1086/250038

Sakal, M. (2003). *Anayasal Bütçe Reformunun Esasları*. Ankara, Turkey: Gazi Bookstore.

Samuelson, P. A. (1954). The pure theory of public expenditure. *The Review of Economics and Statistics*, *36*(4), 387–389. doi:10.2307/1925895

Sandler, T. (2002). Financing international public goods. In M. Ferroni & A. Mody (Eds.), *International public goods: Incentives, measurement and financing* (pp. 81–118). Boston: Kluwer Academic Publishers. doi:10.1007/978-1-4615-0979-0_4

Sandler, T., & Arce, D. (2002). A conceptual framework for understanding global and transnational public goods for health. *Fiscal Studies*, *23*(2), 195–222. doi:10.1111/j.1475-5890.2002.tb00059.x

Saraç, Ö. (2006). *Global Tax Competition and National Tax Policies*. Ankara: Finance and Law Publications.

Sarkar, P. (2007). *Does Foreign Direct Investment Promote Growth? Panel Data and Time Series Evidence from Less Developed Countries, 1970-2002*. MRPA Paper, No. 5176.

Satya Sekhar, G.V. (2018). *Financial Innovation- Theories, Models, Regulation*. Vernon Press.

Savaş, V. F. (2012). *Global Finance and Macroeconomics*. Ankara: Efil Publication.

Schclarek, A. (2004). Debt and economic growth in developing and industrial countries. *Lund University Department of Economics Working Paper, 2005*, 34.

Schraeder, P. J., Hook, S. W., & Taylor, B. (1998). Clarifying the foreign aid puzzle - A comparison of American, Japanese, French, and Swedish aid flows. *World Politics, 50*(2), 294. doi:10.1017/S0043887100008121

Schuknecht, L. (2004). *EU Fiscal Rules Issues and Lessons From Political Economy*. European Central Bank Working Paper Series, No. 421.

Seelkopf, L., & Lierse, H. (2017). *Taxation and Inequalty: How Tax Copmetition Has Changed the Redistributive Capacity of Nation-States in the OECD*. Welfare State Transformations and Inequality in OECD Countries, Transformations of the State, Inequality in OECD Countries, Transformations of the State. doi:10.1057/978-1-137-51184-3_5

Seely, A. (2010). The Tobin Tax. *Business & Transport Section*. Retrieved from http://www.parliament.uk/documents/commons/lib/research/briefings/snbt-01346.pdf

Seema, V. (1994). *Mutual Fund Operations in India*. New Delhi: Rishi Publications.

Şen, H., Keskin, A., & Öz, E. (2004). Can Tobin Tax Be a Solution to Prevent Speculative Foreign Exchange Movements? *Journal of Tax Problems*, (190), 92-108.

Sen, K. (2010). Mali Kural, Bazı Uluslararası Uygulamalar ve Türkiye İncelemesi. *Bütçe Dergisi, 34*.

Sert, M. (2011). Küreselleşmenin Vergi Politikalarına Etkileri: OECD'ye Üye Ülkeler Özelinde Bir İnceleme. *Vergi Dünyası*, *360*, 170–178.

Seyidoğlu, H. (2015). Uluslararası İktisat Teori, Politika ve Uygulama. İstanbul: Güzem Can Yayınları.

Seyidoğlu, H. (2017). *International Economics, Theory and Practice*. İstanbul: Güzem Can Publishing.

Sezgin, Z. (2012). Second Episode of the Global Crisis: 2011European Debt Crisis. *Journal of Business Research*, *4*(2), 141–150.

Shafaeddin, M. S. (2005). Trade liberalization and economic reform in developing countries. *The IMF. World Bank and Policy Reform*, *155*, 2–20.

Shleifer, A., & Vishny, R. (1997). A Survey of Corporate Governance. *The Journal of Finance*, *52*(2), 737–783. doi:10.1111/j.1540-6261.1997.tb04820.x

Spahn, P. B. (1995). *International Financial Flows and Transactions Taxes: Survey and Options*. University of Frankfurt/International Monetary Fund (IMF). Working Paper WP/95/60.

Speight, M. (2002). *How Much Should DFID Allocate to Global Actions and Funding?* London: Department for International Development.

Staehr, K. (2010). *The global financial crisis and public finances in the new EU countries in Central and Eastern Europe: Developments and challenges*. Tallinn: Bank of Estonia.

Stein, H. (1992). Deindustrialization, adjustment, the World Bank and the IMF in Africa. *World Development*, *20*(1), 83–95. doi:10.1016/0305-750X(92)90138-L

Stiglitz, J. E. (1999). Promoting competition and regulatory policy: with examples from network industries. Speech. The World Bank, Beijing, China.

Stiglitz, J. E. (2010). The Financial Crisis of 2007/2008 and its Macroeconomic Consequences. In Time for a visible hand: Lessons from the 2008 World Financial Crisis (pp. 19–50). Oxford University Press.

Stiglitz, J. E. (1994). The Role of the State in Financial Markets. *Proceedings of the World Bank Annual Conference on Development Economics 1993*, 19-52.

Stiglitz, J. E. (2000). *Economics of the public sector*. New York: W.W. Norton Company.

Stiglitz, J. E. (2002). Employment, social justice and societal well-being. *International Labour Review*, *141*(1-2), 9–29. doi:10.1111/j.1564-913X.2002.tb00229.x

Stiglitz, J. E. (2002). *Küreselleşme büyük hayal kırıklığı*. İstanbul: Plan B Yayınları.

Stiglitz, J. E. (2004). Globalization and Growth in Emerging Countries. *Journal of Policy Modeling*, *26*(4), 465–484. doi:10.1016/j.jpolmod.2004.04.010

Stiglitz, J. E. (2015). *Globalization and Its Discontents*. Penguin.

Stöhr, W. B. (1990). *Global challenge and local response: ınitiative for economic regeneration in contemporary europe*. London: Mansell.

Sun, X. (2002). *Foreign Direct Investment and Economic Development: What Do the States Need to Do?* Prepared by the Foreign Investment Advisory Service for the Capacity Development Workshops and Global Forum on Reinventing Government on Globalization, Role of the State and Enabling Environment, Marrakech, Morocco.

Swamy, P. A. (1970). Efficient inference in a random coefficient regression model. *Econometrica*, *38*(2), 311–323. doi:10.2307/1913012

Swank, D. (1998). Funding the Welfare State: Globalization and the Taxation of Business in Advanced Market Economies. *Political Studies*, *46*(4), 671–692. doi:10.1111/1467-9248.00161

Swiss, L. (2017). Foreign aid allocation from a network perspective: The effect of global ties. *Social Science Research*, *63*, 111–123. doi:10.1016/j.ssresearch.2016.09.011 PMID:28202136

Tan, B. W., & Tang, C. F. (2016). Examining the causal linkages among domestic investment, FDI, trade, interest rate and economic growth in ASEAN-5 countries. *International Journal of Economics and Financial Issues*, *6*(1).

Tanör, B., & Yüzbaşıoğlu, N. (2013). *Turkish Constitutional Law According to the 1982 Constitution*. İstanbul: Beta Publications.

Tanzi, V. (1996). *Globalization, Tax Competition and the Future of Tax Systems*. IMF Working Paper, WP/96/141.

Tanzi, V. (2000). *Globalization, Technological Developments, and the Work of Fiscal Termites*. IMF Working Paper, 00/181.

Tanzi, V. (2004). *Globalization and the Need for Fiscal Reform in Developing Countries*. Inter-American Development Bank, Integration and Regional Programs Department, Occasional Paper- SITI-06.

TASAM. (2018). *Dimensions and Effects of Globalization*. Retrieved June 8, 2018, from http://tasam.org/tr-TR/Icerik/211/kuresellesmenin_boyutlari_ve_etkileri

Tatoğlu, F. (2016). *Panel Veri Ekonometrisi Stata Uygulamalı*. İstanbul: Beta Yayınevi.

Taylor, J. B. (2009). *The financial crisis and the policy responses: An empirical analysis of what went wrong*. Cambridge, MA: National Bureau of Economic Research. doi:10.3386/w14631

Taylor, M. P., & Sarno, L. (1998). The behavior of real exchange rates during the post-Bretton Woods period. *Journal of International Economics*, *46*(2), 281–312. doi:10.1016/S0022-1996(97)00054-8

Taylor, P., & Flınt, C. (2000). *Political Geography World Economy, Nation-State and Locality* (4th ed.). New York: Routledge.

Teles, V. K., & Mussolini, C. C. (2014). Public debt and the limits of fiscal policy to increase economic growth. *European Economic Review*, *66*, 1–15. doi:10.1016/j.euroecorev.2013.11.003

teVelde, D. W., Morrissey, O., & Hewitt, A. (2002). Allocating aid to international public goods. In M. Ferroni & A. Mody (Eds.), *International public goods: Incentives, measurement and financing* (pp. 31–46). Boston: Kluwer Academic Publishers.

teVelde, D. W., Morrissey, O., & Hewitt, A. (2006). *Aid financing of international public goods- recent developments*. Vienna: UNIDO Publications.

The World Bank. (1999). *World Development Report 1999/2000 Overview*. Author.

Thomasson, E. (2013, April 18). *Special Report: The battle for the Swiss soul*. Reuters.

Tiebout, C. M. (1956). A pure theory of local expenditures. *Journal of Political Economy*, *64*(5), 416–424. doi:10.1086/257839

Tiruneh, M. W. (2004). An empirical investigation into the determinants of external indebtedness. *Prague Economic Papers*, *3*(3), 261–277. doi:10.18267/j.pep.242

Tokay, U. O. (2010). *Transfer pricing in the multinational companies and its ımplementation in Turkish tax system* (Unpublished Master Thesis). Marmara Unıversity Social Sciences Institute, İstanbul, Turkey.

Toker, M. (2002). Mali Saydamlık ve Türkiye. Sayıştay Başkanlığı (Court of Accounts).

Treisman, D. (2002). *Decentralization and the quality of government. Department of Political Science,* University of California.

Trumbull, W. N., & Wall, H. J. (1994). Estimating Aid-Allocation Criteria with Panel-Data. *Economic Journal (London)*, *104*(425), 876–882. doi:10.2307/2234981

Tunç & Akgül. (2017). BEPS project and reflections in the world. *Tax Agenda- International Tax Agenda*, 4-11.

Türedi, S. (2016). *Küreselleşmenin Ekonomik Büyüme Üzerindeki Etkisi: Gelişmekte Olan Ülkeler İçin Panel Veri Analizi. International Osmaneli Social Sciences Congress, Korkuteli.*

Turkey Is Bank. (2018). *Hazine Bonosu ve Devlet Tahvilleri.* Retrieved from https://www.isbank.com.tr/TR/fiyatlar-ve-oranlar/turk-lirasi-bono-tahvil/hazine-bonosu-ve-devlet-tahvilleri/Sayfalar/hazine-bonosu-ve-devlet-tahvilleri.aspx

Turkish Statistical Institute. (2018). *Temel İstatistikler, Enflasyon ve Fiyat* [Basic Statistics, Inflation, Price]. Retrieved from http://www.tuik.gov.tr/UstMenu.do?metod=temelist

Ulucan, H. (2017). Destructive Effects of the Globalism on the Labor Market: Some Observations on the World and Turkey. Lambert Academic Publishing.

Ulusoy, V. (2016). *Devlet Borçlanması, 9. Baskı*. Trabzon: Umuttepe Yayınları.

Umoh, O. J., Jacob, A. O., & Chuku, C. A. (2012). Foreign direct investment and economic growth in Nigeria: An analysis of the endogenous effects. *Current Research Journal of Economic Theory*, *4*(3), 53–66.

United Nations Development Programme (UNDP). (2015). *World Population Prospect the 2015 Revisions, Volume II: Demographic Profiles*. Department of Economic and Social Affairs Population Division. Retrieved June 8, 2018, from http://esa.un.org/unpd/wpp/publications/Files/WPP2015_Volume-II-Demographic-Profiles.pdf

United Nations. (2014). *World Economic Situation and Prospects 2014*. UN.

Vaidya, A. K. (2006). *Globalization: encyclopedia of trade, labor, and politics* (Vol. 1). Abc-clio.

van den Bergh, J. C. J. M. (2011). Environment versus growth— A criticism of "degrowth" and a plea for "a-growth". *Ecological Economics*, *70*(5), 881–890. doi:10.1016/j.ecolecon.2010.09.035

Vázquez, S. T., & Sobrao, D. G. (2016). Reshaping geographical allocation of aid: The role of immigration in Spanish Official Development Assistance. *Journal of International Relations and Development*, *19*(3), 333–364. doi:10.1057/jird.2014.19

Verduijn, M. (2013). *RaboResearch-Economic Research.* Retrieved from https://economics.rabobank.com/publications/2013/may/country-report-luxembourg/adresinden alındı

Verma, J. C. (1994). Merchant Banking and Financial Services. Taxmann Publishers Ltd.

Vernon, R. (1966). International Investment and International Trade in the Product Cycle. *The Quarterly Journal of Economics, 80*(2), 191. doi:10.2307/1880689

Verschraegen, G., & Schiltz, M. (2007). Knowledge as a global public good: The role and importance of open access. *Societies Without Borders, 2*(2), 157–174. doi:10.1163/187219107X203540

Villaverde, J., & Maza, A. (2011). Globalization, Growth and Convergence. *World Economy, 34*(6), 952–997.

Vives, X. (2000). Corporate Governance: Does it Matter. In X. Vives (Ed.), *Corporate Governance: Theoretical and Empirical Perspectives.* Cambridge, UK: Cambridge University. doi:10.1017/CBO9781139175333.002

Vreeland, J. R. (2002). The effect of IMF programs on labor. *World Development, 30*(1), 121–139. doi:10.1016/S0305-750X(01)00101-2

Vural, I. Y. (2007). Kurumsal Maliye Politikası – Ekonomi Politikası Yönetiminde Mali Kurallar ve Kurumlar. In Mali Disiplin ve Ekonomik İstikrarın Sağlanmasında Yeni Bir Araç: Maliye Politikası Kuralları. Ankara: Seçkin Press.

Vural, T. (2015). Özelleştirme kavramının yerel yönetimler açısından değerlendirilmesi. *Maliye Araştırmaları Dergisi, 1*, 17–28.

Waheed, A. (2017). Determinants of External Debt: A Panel Data Analysis for Oil and Gas Exporting and Importing Countries. *International Journal of Economics and Financial Issues, 7*(1), 234–240.

Wall, D. L. (2012). *Central Banking for Financial Stability: Some Lessons from the Recent Instability in the United States and Euro Area.* Tokyo: Asian Development Bank Institute.

Wallerstein, I. (1993). *Geopolitics and Geoculture* (M. Özel, Trans.). İstanbul: İz Publishing.

Wang, M. (2009). Manufacturing FDI and economic growth: Evidence from Asian economies. *Applied Economics, 41*(8), 991–1002. doi:10.1080/00036840601019059

Ward, H. P., Ricci, L., & Pattillo, C. A. (2002). *External Debt and Growth.* IMF Working Papers 02/69. International Monetary Fund. Retrieved May 11, 2018, from http://www.imf.org/en/Publications/WP/Issues/2016/12/30/External-Debt-and-Growth-15714

Waters, M. (2001). *Globalization* (2nd ed.). London: Routledge.

Weingast, B. R. (1995). The economic role of political ınstitutions: Market-preserving federalism and economic development. *Journal of Law Economics and Organization, 15*(1).

Were, M. (2001). The Impact of External Debt on Economic Growth and Private Investment in Kenya: An Emprical Assessment. *Wider Development Conference on Debt Relief*, Helsinki, Finland.

Westurlund, J., & Edgerton, D. L. (2007). A Panel Bootstrap Cointegration Test. *Economics Letters*, *97*(3), 185–190. doi:10.1016/j.econlet.2007.03.003

Williamson, J. G. (2005). Winners and losers over two centuries of globalization. In *Wider perspectives on global development. Palgrave Macmillan UK.*

Winters, M. S., & Martinez, G. (2015). The Role of Governance in Determining Foreign Aid Flow Composition. *World Development*, *66*, 516–531. doi:10.1016/j.worlddev.2014.09.020

Woods, N. (2008). Whose aid? Whose influence? China, emerging donors and the silent revolution in development assistance. *International Affairs*, *84*(6), 120. doi:10.1111/j.1468-2346.2008.00765.x

Woo, J. (2003). Economic, Political, and Institutional Determinants of Public Deficits. *Journal of Public Economics*, *87*(3-4), 387–426. doi:10.1016/S0047-2727(01)00143-8

World Bank. (2000). *Beyond Economic Growth: Meeting the Challenges of Global Development*. Author.

World Bank. (2001). *Global development Finance 2001: Building coalitions for effective development finance*. Washington, DC: Wold Bank.

World Bank. (2018). *World Development Indicators*. Retrieved from http://databank.worldbank.org/data/source/world-development-indicators

WTO. (2003). *Liberalizing Trade and Safeguarding Public Revenues*. Communication from the International Monetary Fund, WT/TF/COH/16.

Yang, J., Chi, J., & Young, M. (2011). *A review of corporate governance in China*. Crawford School of Economics and Government, The Australian National University and Blackwell Publishing Asia Pty Ltd; doi:10.1111/j.1467-8411.2011.01283.x

Yapraklı, S. (2006). Türkiye'de Doğrudan Yabanci Yatirimlarin Ekonomik Belirleyicileri Üzerine Ekonometrik Bir Analiz. *Dokuz Eylül Üniversitesi İİBF Dergisi*, *21*(2), 23–48.

Yeldan, E. (2002). *Neoliberal Küreselleşme İdeolojisinin Kalkınma Söylemi Üzerine Değerlendirmeler*. Praksis.

Yılmaz, H. G. (2015). *OECD BEPS action plan for international tax justice*. Retrieved from https://www2.deloitte.com/content/dam/Deloitte/tr/Documents/tax/hulyayilmaz_eylulkasim(1).pdf

Yılmaztürk, A., & Buhur, S. (2017). Fıscal Consolidation Practices In Turkey After 1980. *Journal of Tax Issues*, *350*, 85–100.

Yong, A. G., & Pearce, S. (2013). A beginner's guide to factor analysis: Focusing on exploratory factor analysis. *Tutorials in Quantitative Methods for Psychology*, *9*(2), 79–94. doi:10.20982/tqmp.09.2.p079

Younas, J. (2008). Motivation for bilateral aid allocation: Altruism or trade benefits. *European Journal of Political Economy*, *24*(3), 661–674. doi:10.1016/j.ejpoleco.2008.05.003

Yuksel, O. (2014). Euro Krizinin Kurumlar ve Politikalar Çerçevesinde İncelenmesi. *Politik Akademi*. Retrieved from http://www.politikakademi.org/2014/01/euro-krizinin-kurumlar-ve-politikalar-cercevesinde-incelenmesi/

YuP. (August 26, 2011Corporate Governance of Chinese Fund Management Companies. Available at SSRN: http://ssrn.com/abstract=1917426

Yusufoğlu, Y. (2005). *Global Imperialism*. İstanbul: Belge Publishing.

Yuzbasıoglu, N. (2012). Anayasadan Mali ve Vergisel Beklentiler. In Anayasa ve Ekonomi. Levha Press.

Zafar, S., & Butt, M. S. (2008). *Impact of Trade Liberalization on External Debt Burden: Econometric Evidence from Pakistan*. MPRA Papers No. 9548, 1-17.

Zakaria, M. (2012). Interlinkages Between Openness and Foreign Debt in Pakistan. *Doğuş Üniversitesi Dergisi*, *13*(1), 161–170. doi:10.31671/dogus.2018.122

Zekić, S., Kleut, Z., & Matkovski, B. (2017). An analysis of key indicators of rural development in Serbia: A comparison with EU countries. *Economic Annals*, *62*(214), 107–120. doi:10.2298/EKA1714107Z

Zhang, K. H. (2001). Does foreign direct investment promote economic growth? Evidence from East Asia and Latin America. *Contemporary Economic Policy*, *19*(2), 175–185. doi:10.1111/j.1465-7287.2001.tb00059.x

About the Contributors

Gülsüm Akarsu works as a research assistant in Ondokuz Mayis Univeristy, Samsun, Turkey. She completed her PhD in Economics in Middle East Technical University in 2013. Main research interests are Energy Economics, Financial Economics and Applied Econometrics.

Fındık Özlem Alper was born in 1980. She has completed her master's degree and doctorate education in the department of Economics at Çukurova University. She is currently working as an assistant professor at Niğde Ömer Halisdemir University. Her interests cover monetary economics and economic development.

Ali Eren Alper was born in 1981. He has completed his master's degree and doctorate education in the department of Economics at Çukurova University He is currently working as an associate professor at Niğde Ömer Halisdemir University. His interests cover economic development and empirical studies.

Hayriye Atik received bachelor, master and PhD degrees from Erciyes University. Then, she received a MPhil degree from the Coventry University in the United Kingdom. She worked as research assistant from 1989 to 1998 in Erciyes University, Faculty of Economics and Administrative Sciences. She was an assistant professor until the year 2000. She worked as associate professor from 2000 to 2006. Between 2001 and 2004 she was vice-dean in the same faculty. She became professor in 2006. Between 2008-2016 she was also the head of the Economics Department. She is the author of some most widely read Turkish books. These are: European Union, Customs Union and Turkey (with co-author Prof. Dr. Cihan Dura), Information Society, Information Economy and Turkey (with co-author Prof. Dr. Cihan Dura), Modern Foreign Trade Theories (with co-author Oğuzhan Türker). She teaches International economics, Economic Integration and the European Union, Energy Economics, Information Economy.

Selçuk Balı holds MA degree in the Department of Public Finance from Ankara University- SBF Mülkiye in Ankara, Turkey and his Ph.D. degree in the business administration from Atatürk University in Erzurum, Turkey. He worked in Ministry of Customs and Trade from 2002 to 2009. He has been a professor in the Public Finance department at Akşehir Faculty of Economic and Administrative Sciences at Selçuk University since 2017. He has published studies include financial crisis, exotic options and behavior finance.

Serap Barış received his BA in Economics from the Erciyes University, Faculty of Economics and Administrative Sciences. She received his master's degree in 2007 from Gaziosmanpaşa University, Department of Economics and in 2014 his Ph.D degree from Erciyes University. Currently, she works as an assistant professor in the Department of Economics, Faculty of Economics and Administrative Sciences, Gaziosmanpaşa University. She continues her studies in fields of international economics, economic growth, technological development and innovation economy.

Gozde Es Polat currently works at the Department of Public Finance, Bilecik Üniversitesi. Gözde's bachelor and master degrees are from Public Finance Department of Gazi University, Ankara, Turkey. Her master thesis's about "The Relationship of Taxation in the Context of Theory and Practice with Economic Development and Growth". Now, she is writing her Ph.D. dissertation. She does research in Development Economics, Public Economics, Public Debt and Public Finance.

Satya Sekhar Gudimetla, M.Com, MBA, M.Phil, Ph.D, Associate Professor, Centre for Distance Learning, GITAM University, Visakhapatnam, has 18 years of teaching and research experience at Post Graduate level. He has published five books viz. 1) Management Information Systems, 2) Managerial Economics. 3) Business Policy and Strategic Management, 4) Performance Appraisal of Indian Mutual Funds and 5) Strategic Financial Management. He has contributed lessons to the study material of 'Executive MBA Programme' of Andhra University, Visakhapatnam and also study material published by Centre for Distance Learning, GITAM University. Besides this, he has participated and presented papers in various national and international seminars. So far he has published 32 articles in various national and international reputed journals.

Eglantina Hysa is a Lecturer of Economics at the Epoka University where she teaches International Economy, Development and Growth, and Microeconomics courses. Eglantina Hysa's research focuses on International Trade, Development and Econometric Models. She has been part of some training programs related to the Public Interior Auditing and International/National Standards of Accounting. Her recent papers examine characteristics that cover the economical aspects such as the pension system, demographic change, corruption, inequality, human development and the foreign direct investment in Western Balkans and with a particular focus in Albania. She is part of national networks by being either the founder or active member in associations related to economics and sociology. Actually she is head of Economics Department at Epoka University. At the same time, she is engaged as an External Expert on behalf of Public Accreditation Agency for Higher Education, Republic of Albania.

Berkan Karagöz was born on 25 May 1983 in Balıkesir. He completed primary, secondary and high school education in Balikesir. He studied undergraduate and graduate education at Marmara University. His Ph.D. degree was completed in 2014 at Ankara University on Public Economics. He has been serving as a doctoral lecturer at the Yozgat Bozok University since 2017.

İbrahim Özmen holds MA degree in the Department of Economics from Selcuk University in Konya, Turkey and his Ph.D. degree in the same program from Necmettin Erbakan University in Konya, Turkey. He worked in Revenue Administration from Ministry of Finance from 2009 to 2017. He has been an assistant professor in the Public Finance department at Aksehir Faculty of Economic and Administrative Sciences at Selcuk University since 2017. He has published studies include public finance, tax law and macroeconomic issues. His research interests include tax law, public finance, fiscal sociology and economic anthropology.

Dorina Plaku is graduated from Master of Sciences in Banking and Finance. She is interested in taxation, taxation policies and market studies. She has completed her studies with very good results. During her studies she has been part of several scientific conferences related to the economy, management and businesses. Dorina Plaku has worked as a "Brand Manager" of some of the most well-known brands which operates in Albania.

Seher Topuz was born in Ankara in 1987. She has completed her elementary, middle and high school education in Ankara. Then, she obtained her BSc in Mathematics from Faculty of Science, Anadolu University (Turkey) and MSc in Economics from Eskisehir Osmangazi University in 2011 and 2013 respectively. She obtained her PhD in Economics Department of Anadolu University. Her research interests include income inequality, economic growth and development.

Hakan Ulucan is assistant professor at department of economics in Pamukkale University, Denizli-Turkey. His research interests are labor economics, game theory, and microeconometrics.

Fatma Ünlü was born in Kayseri in 1987. After completion of her elementary, middle and high school education in Kayseri. Then, she obtained her BSc and MSc in Economics from Erciyes University (Turkey) in 2009 and 2012 respectively. She obtained her PhD in Economics from same University in 2017. She has been working in Erciyes University, Department of Economics since 2010. She published six scientific publications, six presentations at scientific conferences, one book and three book sections. Her research interests include innovation economy, European Union, international economics.

Aysun Yilmaztürk was born in Istanbul in 1981. She completed her undergraduate studies at Anadolu University Faculty of Economics and Administrative Sciences Finance Department between 1998-2001. Then, she completed her master's degree in Anadolu University SBE Public Finance Department and her doctorate education in Marmara University Public Finance Department, Department Theory of Public Finance. She is currently serving as assistant professor at Balıkesir University.

Index

S

T

W

www.ingramcontent.com/pod-product-compliance
Lightning Source LLC
LaVergne TN
LVHW062144300926
849161LV00010B/2623
* 9 7 8 1 5 2 2 5 7 5 6 4 1 *